The Business Privacy Law Handbook

For a listing of recent titles in the *Artech House Telecommunications Series*, please turn to the back of this book.

The Business Privacy Law Handbook

Charles H. Kennedy

ARTECH HOUSE
BOSTON | LONDON
artechhouse.com

Library of Congress Cataloging-in-Publication Data
A catalog record for this book is available from the U.S. Library of Congress.

British Library Cataloguing in Publication Data
A catalogue record for this book is available from the British Library.

ISBN-13: 978-1-59693-176-3

Cover design by Igor Valdman

685 Canton Street
Norwood, MA 02062

10 9 8 7 6 5 4 3 2 1

To the memory of Charles H. Kennedy IV and to his daughter,
Sarah Clare Kennedy

Contents

Preface

This book surveys, from the perspective of business managers and their advisers, the shifting landscape of privacy law in the United States. If it does so with any success, many people must share the credit.

My benefactors in this project include the clients and colleagues who have involved me in their efforts to understand and comply with the law of privacy. They also include my students at the Columbus School of Law, Catholic University of America, who keep my legal knowledge current by expecting me to know what I'm talking about, and who repay my efforts with their insight and enthusiasm.

Thanks are due to the editorial and production teams at Artech House, who now have shepherded me through a fourth book project. Mark Walsh, Artech's senior acquisitions editor, called me when my first manuscript arrived unannounced on his desk in 1993 and began a collaboration that has become a friendship. Barbara Lovenvirth has once again helped me to meet my deadlines, and Rebecca Allendorf and Mark Bergeron (from Publishers' Design and Production Services) have generated and edited the page proofs with Artech's usual dispatch.

More personally, I want to express my gratitude to some friends and family members who will be surprised to learn that they were helping to write a book. In fact, little good of any kind would have come of these last several years without the help of: Brendan, Cassie, Kori, Julie, and Sarah Kennedy; Bob and Lisa McGary; Margo and Lincoln Weed; the Vitek family; Richard Russell and his loyal readers; Jared Taylor and Evelyn Rich; George Petit and his family; and Valerie and Andy Bernat.

Finally, and always, my greatest debt is to my indispensable wife and companion, Marney.

Introduction: A Systematic Approach to U.S. Privacy Law Compliance

Until fairly recently, American businesses could decide without legal interference how to collect, use, and share information about their customers, employees, and other third parties, and could choose how to market their products and services to consumers. Businesses also could decide for themselves how to secure, or not secure, personal information in their keeping from access by unauthorized persons. A business that failed to protect privacy might suffer many consequences, but legal liability would not normally be among them.

In today's environment, business managers and their lawyers are learning to take privacy as seriously as securities law, labor law, antidiscrimination law, environmental law, and all the other staples of legal risk management. Their task is complicated, not just by the speed with which privacy law is developing, but by the fragmented and inconsistent approaches that legislators and regulators are taking to privacy issues.

Some of the confusion is caused by the decisions of legislators and regulators, both state and federal, *not* to treat all industries and lines of business the same. Many U.S. privacy obligations apply only to particular industries, such as health care insurance, credit reporting, and financial services, that handle especially sensitive kinds of personal information. Other initiatives such as the data security enforcement activities of the Federal Trade Commission, are aimed at all U.S. businesses but are complicated by the limited jurisdiction and shifting enforcement policies of the agencies involved.

Confusion also is inherent in our federal system. With limited exceptions, the states are empowered to enact laws that address the full range of privacy issues discussed in this book. Accordingly, businesses wishing to comply with all applicable privacy laws must consult the laws of every state in which they have offices, employ people, have customers, or otherwise do things that might subject them to state jurisdiction.

The confusion is compounded by the sheer volume and complexity of privacy law. The range of business activities that present privacy issues—from data collection to information security to telemarketing—is now so great that few companies can claim to be aware of them all. Even fewer companies can say with confidence that they are in compliance with the ever-expanding body of law that is associated with those activities.

This is no time, however, to be paralyzed by indecision. As executives (and former executives) at scores of U.S. companies can attest, breaches of privacy and losses of data are no longer routine business mishaps: in the present environment, they tend to escalate into public scandals that drain resources, erode customer confidence, and end careers.

This book describes the privacy law environment in what is intended to be a systematic way. Some chapters focus on specific industries (for example, financial services or health care) and describe statutes and regulations that affect only those industries. Others focus on business activities (for example, data security or telemarketing) and describe the range of laws that apply to those activities regardless of industry. To supplement these chapters, appendices to the book list many of the applicable statutes and regulations, including representative privacy laws of all 50 states. The goal is to help business managers and their lawyers acquire a basic understanding of the privacy law environment for their particular businesses.

No introductory book, however, can provide all of the information needed to create a fully compliant privacy and data security program. For one thing, the volume of applicable law is simply too great and evolving too quickly. For another, designing a compliance program is ultimately a matter of sound legal advice based on an expert's review of the facts of your business. This book is intended to be one, but not the only, guide and resource for such a compliance program.

Even so, it is possible to describe a systematic approach to privacy compliance that takes some of the mystery out of the process. In the discussion that follows, we identify the activities that are covered by privacy law; set out a method for identifying all of the associated laws, regulations, and standards *that affect your business*; and provide a method for assessing your company's privacy compliance and correcting shortfalls that might expose your company to litigation, adverse publicity, and loss of shareholder value.

The Approach to Privacy Compliance

Given the high stakes involved, how do you ensure that this job of developing a privacy compliance plan is done right? Like any compliance effort, this one involves three main stages. First, *identify* the compliance obligations to which your company is subject. Second, *assess* your company's current policies and practices against the standard set by those obligations. Third, work with responsible organizations in your company to *correct* any shortfall between your company's obligations and its performance.

If anything distinguishes privacy compliance from other compliance efforts, it's the challenge presented by the first of these three steps. Privacy includes such a wide range of rights and obligations, and privacy laws have appeared so rapidly at both the state and federal levels, that defining any company's privacy law obligations is an immense challenge. Faced with this challenge, many compliance managers fudge the first step, simply focusing on a few well-known privacy laws or borrowing a one-size-fits-all set of best practices from a standards body or other outside source.

But this quick-and-dirty approach is a major mistake. Failure to identify the precise universe of privacy-related statutes, regulations, and binding standards (for convenience, we sometimes refer to all three categories collectively as "laws") to which your company is subject means that you will work through the assessment and correction steps of the compliance process with one hand tied behind your back. When you are done and your new, improved policies and practices are in place, you still will not know if you missed any privacy obligations that *do* apply, or mistakenly took on the burden of complying with obligations that *do not* apply. The result is likely to be a combination of under-compliance, which leaves you legally exposed, or overcompliance, which is a gift to your competitors.

Our program begins with Step I, called "Narrowing the Legal Field—the First Cut." In this initial step, we identify the three sets of compliance issues that come under the broad heading of "privacy," and find that over 700 state and federal laws, regulations, and standards address those privacy issues in one way or another. Then we show how, by answering some simple questions about your business, you can eliminate most of those laws and get ready to concentrate on those that might actually affect your company.

Step II of the program is called "Narrowing the Legal Field 2—Sharpening the Focus." In this step, we look more closely at the list of laws, regulations, and standards generated by the "first cut." This stage helps you to eliminate still more laws as irrelevant to your organization and leaves you with a manageable set of requirements to guide the assessment and correction stages of the process.

Step III in the program is called "Identifying Compliance Requirements." This is where you distill, from the final list of laws, regulations, and standards generated in Step II, the actions your business must take, or avoid taking, in order to comply with those laws, regulations, and standards. The resulting compliance checklist is the yardstick against which you will measure your company's performance and identify areas that require improvement.

Step IV is called "Assessing Your Compliance." This is where you get to do some detective work. By interviewing responsible personnel and collecting samples of all existing, privacy-related policies and procedures in use at your company, you will produce a compliance profile to measure against the checklist you created in the course of Step III.

Finally, Step V calls for you to develop and supplement policies and practices that address any shortfalls identified in the course of Step IV.

Have we missed anything? Yes, we have. As a manager responsible for privacy issues, whether in IT, Human Resources, Marketing, the legal department, or any other functional organization, your work does not end when Step V is complete. Unless the universe of obligations and the associated compliance efforts are revisited and refreshed on an appropriate schedule—and unless responsible personnel are trained and retrained in their privacy compliance roles—your company will drift out of compliance and the risk of privacy incidents will grow. Accordingly, you should think of the process described here as resembling the painting of the Golden Gate Bridge. It is said that the painting crews start at one end of the bridge and work to the other end, after which they return immediately to the starting point and keep on painting. Otherwise, the bridge would rust and fall into San Francisco Bay.

Step I. Narrowing the Legal Field—the First Cut

Before deciding which privacy laws apply to your company, you need an understanding of what "privacy" means for our purposes. Once you decide on a privacy-related set of issues and business activities, you can identify the laws that address those issues and begin to figure out which of those laws apply to your company.

"Privacy," of course, is notorious for meaning different things to different people. For your purposes, most of these meanings can be ignored: there is no need for you to study the constitutional right to privacy or the rules law enforcement officers must follow when executing warrants. You want to focus on the privacy-related concerns that have been causing lawsuits, Federal Trade Commission enforcement actions, career losses, and the other kinds of unpleasantness that keep you—or your boss—awake at nights. Looked at in this way, companies have three kinds of privacy issues and three sets of associated laws, regulations, and standards with which they must comply.

Privacy Issues, Set 1: Collecting, Using, and Sharing Personal Information and Communications

Companies need to know when and how they can collect, use, and share personal information and communications of their customers, employees, and other individuals. In an age when information is perhaps the most valuable business asset, the ability to engage in such activities legally is critical to success. Unless you can collect and use consumer information, your marketing and customer relationship management efforts are crippled. Unless you can monitor communications involving your employees and customers, you have no meaningful quality control and reduced ability to detect harmful activity.

The legal questions raised by these activities are complex and growing. Is your company required to obtain a customer's permission before using personal information to market to that customer? If so, how must that permission be obtained? Is your company allowed to collect information online? May your company lawfully monitor calls between Customer Service personnel and customers? Does the answer to the last question vary from state to state? Is your company allowed to monitor employees' e-mail and Internet usage?

For examples of what happens when companies get the answers to these questions wrong, just visit www.ftc.gov and read the long list of Federal Trade Commission actions against companies that have mishandled the collection and use of personal information.

Privacy Issues, Set 2: Protecting Personal Information from Unauthorized Access and Disclosure

In today's environment, it is not enough to collect, use, and share personal information and communications in legally permitted ways. It is also necessary to protect that information from hackers, thieves, and accidental losses of all kinds. Some of the most spectacular and harmful privacy incidents of recent years—from lost laptops at government agencies to hacked credit card records at major retailers—involve these "data security" issues.

As with the first set of privacy issues, data security presents businesses with a number of hard questions. For example, is my company required to shred paper documents when they are no longer needed? If so, which documents are subject to that requirement? Similarly, must personal information in my company's possession be encrypted during transmission within my network? Must that information be encrypted in storage? Is my company required to report lost laptops to the authorities? Am I required to report those incidents to affected consumers? Is my business responsible for the errors of my vendors, including data processing contractors and records storage and disposal vendors? Is my business required to maintain written data security plans? Is it required to audit compliance with those plans? What is the applicable standard, if any, for disaster recovery?

The answers to these questions are very much a moving target, as data security becomes a growing focus of concern in the Congress, at the state legislatures, and at regulatory agencies at all levels of government.

Privacy Issues, Set 3: Electronic Marketing

A third set of privacy issues has generated a great deal of law in recent years. Specifically, both the Congress and the state legislatures have responded to public complaints about telemarketing, fax advertising, and "spam" messages with laws intended to control all three of these forms of electronic marketing. The result is a huge body of law, much of it new, much of it redundant, and much of it contradictory.

As with our first two sets of issues, the electronic marketing laws pose a long list of questions. Simply to take a few: When is my company allowed to call an existing customer to solicit a new purchase? Is my company ever allowed to call a number that appears on the national do-not-call list? Are there state do-not-call lists, and is my company required to comply with those lists, as well? When can my marketing personnel send a business customer a fax containing an updated price list? When is an e-mail considered "spam" and under what circumstances may a marketer use e-mail to advertise its products and services? Are state antispam laws preempted by federal law, or is my company required to comply with all such laws? How do we respond when those laws contradict one another?

Electronic marketing, like collection of consumer information, is critical to business success in today's environment. Electronic marketing also is under aggressive, ongoing scrutiny by prosecutors, regulators, and plaintiffs' lawyers. This is an area in which under-compliance is dangerous, overcompliance gives an immediate advantage to your less-timid competitors, and the line between the two can only be found with difficulty.

Now that we have identified the three broad areas that we will look at under the heading of "privacy," here's the bad news: in the United States today, over 700 statutes, regulations, and binding standards tell businesses how to collect and share information, protect sensitive data, and market to their customers using telephones, faxes, and e-mails. Those 700-plus laws, regulations, and standards come from all levels of government and various private entities (such as the credit card industry), and they will keep coming. The pace of new laws addressing privacy concerns will only accelerate in the years ahead.

U.S. privacy law has rightly been called a patchwork, which is actually *good* news. Fortunately, not all of the 700-odd U.S. privacy laws apply to your company. As noted earlier, many privacy laws apply to particular industries and lines of business, rather than to all businesses equally, and many privacy laws are state rather than federal laws, affecting only organizations that do business or have customers in those states.

So, a first cut at narrowing the field of applicable laws requires answers to the following questions: what business am I in, and in what states do I do business?

Let's take each of these questions in turn.

A. What Business(es) Is My Company In?

Consumer advocates, including the consumer protection enforcers in the Federal Trade Commission, have argued for years that the United States should have a single privacy and data protection law for every organization that collects, maintains, uses, or discloses personal information. Instead, what we have is a patchwork of laws that varies extensively from one industry to another. Some enterprises, such as banks and health care providers, must comply with pervasive privacy regulations enforced by government agencies that exercise close oversight of those industries. Other enterprises, such as video rental stores, are not pervasively regulated but are subject to targeted privacy laws specifically aimed at those businesses. Finally, all businesses in the United States, whether or not subject to industry-specific privacy laws, must comply with a long list of state and federal requirements based on the kinds of information they handle and the means by which they collect and use it.

Identifying your company's lines of business, therefore, is not a way of deciding if your business is subject to privacy laws *at all* (it is), but the process helps to identify any industry-specific laws to which you might be subject, and to eliminate those that do not apply to you.

You should identify every line of business in which your company—including any parent, affiliate, or subsidiary—is engaged. And if your company stores or processes information for other organizations, you should identify the lines of business in which *those* organizations are engaged.

Also, unless you are a privacy law specialist, you should think at this stage in business terms rather than legal terms. For example, you might have a subsidiary that processes data for a wide range of customers, some of which are health insurance companies. Depending on the data involved and the type and extent of your subsidiary's involvement with the data, your subsidiary might be classified as a health care clearinghouse, business associate, or hybrid entity under the privacy provisions of the Health Insurance Portability and Accountability Act (HIPAA). Your job at this stage is not to decide if your subsidiary satisfies the complex definitions of one or more of these entities. You should simply identify the nature of the business and its activities in common-sense business terms. When that information is collected, an attorney can match those activities with industry-specific privacy laws that should be included in your compliance assessment. (*See* Step II.)

With that in mind, here is a list (not necessarily complete) of some product and service lines you should be watching for:

- Banking and financial services;
- Insurance;
- Health care;

- Telephone service;
- Internet access;
- Cable television service;
- Telemarketing;
- Car rental;
- Video rental;
- Education and training.

If your business does not fall within one or more of these categories, it still is subject to state and federal privacy laws. In fact, you can be certain that many such laws apply, and you should work through the whole process described here, in order to determine which laws those are.

B. Where Does My Company Do Business?

Our federal system subjects businesses to statutes passed by the U.S. Congress, the regulations of federal agencies, and the statutes and regulations of the states that have jurisdiction over those businesses. This question of state jurisdiction is complex, and state jurisdiction to enforce privacy law is especially complex.

Licensing is one way in which states assert jurisdiction over businesses. For example, insurance companies are state-licensed and must comply with the insurance regulations, including privacy regulations, of the states in which they are licensed to write policies. Similarly, telemarketers and telecommunications companies are subject to registration and reporting requirements that effectively make those businesses licensees of the states in which they operate.

More broadly, states assert jurisdiction over companies that *do business* in their jurisdictions, even if those businesses are not state-licensed. Any systematic commercial contact between a business and a state might form a basis for such jurisdiction, whether or not the business is incorporated or maintains permanent facilities in the state.

In the case of privacy laws, states assert jurisdiction in a number of ways. For example, states enforce their telemarketing and wiretapping laws against companies that place calls to the states' residents, even where those calls are placed from out of state. Similarly, state laws that require businesses to notify the states' residents of security breaches involving personal data are asserted against companies that did not store the compromised data within the borders of the enforcing state, on the grounds that the breach of its residents' privacy rights gives the states jurisdiction.

In identifying the states where your company does business, therefore, you should cast a broad net. States in which your business is licensed, incorporated, or registered with a regulatory agency certainly belong on the list, as do states in which your business has offices or employees. Any state in which your business's customers reside also should be counted, even if you have no offices or employees there. Not all of the privacy laws of all of those states will necessarily apply to your company, but you should work from the widest possible list when you come to identifying the laws that do apply.

C. Generating Your "First Cut" Privacy Law Profile

Once you know the nature of your business and the jurisdictions in which it operates, you are ready to create an initial list of the laws, regulations, and standards to which your company's privacy compliance effort should be directed. At this point, you might wish to seek the advice of a privacy expert who already is familiar with the 700-plus laws and other requirements from which the initial list will be taken, and who can use the information you have developed to create that list.

Assume, for example, that you have identified your organization as an insurance company that offers services to policyholders in eight states. Your initial list will include both state and federal laws and regulations, some of which apply to businesses generally and some of which are specific to the business of insurance.

The *federal* list will include a number of laws that apply to all (or nearly all) businesses, such as the federal wiretapping law, the Fair and Accurate Credit Transactions Act, and perhaps the Federal Trade Commission Act. Because your company is in the business of insurance, your list also should include the federal Gramm-Leach-Bliley Act and the Health Insurance Portability and Accountability Act, which are the principal privacy laws applicable to financial institutions and health insurance companies, respectively. Other items on the list should include federal laws that apply to specific activities, such as the Telemarketing Act, the CAN SPAM Act, and the Payment Card Industry Data Security Standard. Your company will comply with those requirements to the extent it makes telemarketing calls, sends commercial e-mails, or accepts credit cards, respectively. A number of other laws also will appear on the federal portion of the initial list, but this inventory should give some idea of the list's likely scope.

The initial list for the eight *states* in which you offer services, like the federal list, will include many requirements that are not specific to the business of insurance. Those will include state "must shred" laws, data security breach notification laws, state wiretapping laws, state telemarketing laws, and laws related to employee privacy. The provisions of those laws may be different from the federal laws that address the same activities and from the counterpart laws of the other states in which your company does business, so it is important that they all be included. The list also will include the regulations of those eight states related to the business of insurance, which will contain extensive privacy provisions. Some states will impose additional restrictions, such as online privacy requirements, that are not found in all states' laws but that might be rigorously enforced.

Step II. Narrowing the Legal Field 2—Sharpening the Focus

Your first-cut list is a big step forward, but it's still only a start. The initial list includes obligations that *might* apply to a company in your line of business that operates in the states you have identified. The list still might be too narrow or too wide.

Now is the time to sharpen the focus, by taking a closer look at the company's operations and then: (1) eliminating laws on the initial list that do not apply, (2) considering whether other laws should have been included, and (3) considering any changes to the company's operations that might eliminate certain laws from the compliance list.

This is where the help of a lawyer with knowledge of privacy law will certainly be needed. A nonspecialist, no matter how diligent, might not be aware of all of the hundreds of privacy statutes and regulations that must be taken into account at this stage, and could have difficulty deciding which of those statutes and regulations apply.

A lawyer, for example, can decide whether your business really is subject to the Federal Trade Commission Act, which has proved to be an enormous source of privacy law enforcement. Insurance companies, for example, are not subject to the FTC Act to the extent they actually are engaged in the business of insurance. If your company is an insurer, a lawyer will scrutinize your operations more closely to determine whether they offer an opportunity for the FTC to take jurisdiction. If not, the FTC Act goes off the list.

A lawyer also will want to know more about the kinds of insurance you write. If your company is involved in health insurance, it will be necessary to consider whether the Health Insurance Portability and Accountability Act should be added to the compliance list.

The state portion of the list will present jurisdictional issues that a lawyer can address. For example, does your company have employees in all of the eight states in which it writes policies? In states where the company has no employees, the state employee protection laws come off the list, subject to change if persons later are hired in those states. Similarly, does the company have policyholders in states where it is not licensed to write insurance? (Policyholders move, taking their insurance coverage with them.) If so, then the must-shred and data security breach notification laws of those policyholders' states of residence must be *added* to the list.

This is also the time to inquire about *activities* that might subject the company to privacy laws. Does the company engage in telemarketing, fax advertising, or e-mail promotions? If your marketing people are certain that they do not and will not use those marketing channels, you can cross several state and federal laws off the list. Similarly, does the company accept credit cards? If not, then the Payment Card Industry Data Security Standard, with its rigorous security requirements and stiff penalties, can be taken off the list.

Finally, this "sharp focus" stage is a good time to think about changes to the company's structure or operations that might reduce the privacy law compliance burden. For example, although insurance companies generally are not subject to the FTC Act, the FTC will enforce its stringent telemarketing rules against telemarketing vendors that conduct calling campaigns on behalf of insurance companies. If the company conducts telemarketing campaigns and uses vendors for that purpose, it might consider taking that activity "in house" or eliminating it altogether. Decisions of this kind are a combination of legal and business considerations, and both lawyers and responsible managers should be involved in those discussions.

Step III. Identifying Compliance Requirements

Now that you have a list of the privacy-related laws that apply to your company, you are in a position to identify and list all of the business actions that those laws require, or forbid, your company to do. The checklist that results from this process will form the basis for your compliance assessment.

Two words of advice are especially important at this stage.

First, the job of identifying your company's compliance obligations, like the job of finding the applicable laws on which those obligations are based, is a job for an expert. The language of the privacy laws, regulations, and standards can be quite opaque, and translating those laws into required compliance actions takes knowledge of legislative history, judicial interpretation, and other context that will not be apparent on the face of the laws themselves.

Second, generating the list of compliance items will require you to make some difficult decisions, especially where different laws impose different obligations concerning the same or similar conduct.

This second point requires some explanation. Assume that your company is a retailer that collects personal information about customers, offers its own charge account, and also accepts major credit cards. To simplify the analysis, we assume that all of your business locations and customers are in California.

Your list of applicable laws will include, among many other items, two federal regulations, one state statute and one industry standard (for convenience, we'll refer to all four simply as "laws") affecting the security of information associated with these activities.

The first law is the Federal Trade Commission Safeguards Rule, which applies to data security of financial institutions and also serves as the FTC's "template" for data security enforcement actions against companies of all kinds under the Federal Trade Commission Act. The Safeguards Rule applies to the secure handling of all nonpublic personal information of a covered entity's customers.

The second applicable law is the FTC's rule implementing the records disposal provisions of the Fair and Accurate Credit Transactions Act (FACTA Disposal Rule). That rule governs the secure disposal of personal consumer information derived from credit reports.

The third law is California's "must-shred" statute, which requires secure disposal of records containing personal information of California residents.

Finally, the fourth law is the Payment Card Industry Data Security Standard (PCI Standard), which governs the secure handling of cardholder identification and authentication data.

Each of these regulations affects the handling of information maintained by your company. Information derived from credit reports, which includes data your company collects on persons who wish to open charge accounts, is covered by the FACTA regulation and also qualifies as nonpublic personal information for purposes of the Safeguards Rule. Similarly, cardholder information your company collects at point of sale and transmits for cardholder approval is covered by the PCI Standard and also is nonpublic personal information for purposes of the Safeguards Rule. Finally, to the extent these categories of information concern California residents, records containing that information are covered by California's must-shred statute.

At this point, if you review the provisions of the four laws, you will find that the obligations they impose on your company's handling of personal information are somewhat different.

You will find that the Safeguards Rule requirements are the most general and least specific. That regulation requires each covered entity to "develop, implement, and maintain a comprehensive information security program that is written in one or more readily accessible parts and contains administrative, technical, and physical safeguards that are appropriate to [the entity's] size and complexity, the nature and scope of [its] activities, and the sensitivity of any customer information at issue."[1] The Safeguards Rule also requires covered entities to designate responsible employees to conduct the security program, perform risk assessments, implement appropriate data security safeguards, oversee the security practices of contractors, and conduct periodic reassessments and modifications of the practices adopted.[2]

These highly general obligations of the Safeguards Rule leave a great deal to your company's discretion. For example, they do not expressly require your company to arrange for secure disposal of paper records that contain nonpublic personal information. They also do not impose specific security obligations for digital information, such as encryption, monitoring of network access, and use of firewalls and antivirus software.

The other applicable regulations, however, are more specific.

For example, the FACTA Disposal Rule expressly requires that all paper records containing information derived from credit reports be burned, pulverized, or shredded, and that electronic media concerning such information be destroyed or erased.[3] The California must-shred law, which applies to all personal information of California residents (not just information derived from credit reports), effectively requires that all paper records containing such information be shredded.[4]

Similarly, the PCI Standard goes well beyond the vague prescriptions of the Safeguards Rule and imposes 12 specific data protection requirements for cardholder data, including encryption of such data sent over public networks, tracking and monitoring of all access to networks containing cardholder data, and assignment of unique IDs to all persons with access to such data.[5]

Faced with these varying obligations for handling of overlapping categories of information, what should your compliance checklist say? Should there be one set of compliance items for cardholder data, another set for records containing personal information of California residents, still another for information derived from credit reports concerning non-Californians, and yet another (reflecting the more general Safeguards Rule standards) for everything else? Or, should the most rigorous applicable standard for *any* category of personal information be made the compliance standard for *all* personal information maintained by your company?

Questions of this kind will arise many times as your compliance checklist is compiled. For example, some states have telemarketing laws that are more restrictive than federal law or the laws of other states. Accordingly, telemarketers have to decide whether to avoid calling those states, use a different compliance checklist when calling those states, or simply make the laws of those states the compliance standard for calls to all states.

These decisions involve a balancing act that should be taken very seriously. Setting up different, parallel compliance practices for the same activities or types of information can be costly and inefficient. On the other hand, it can be a mistake to follow restrictive laws in cases in which those laws are legally avoidable. Overcompliance, when it causes you to forego profitable activities in which your less-cautious competitors are engaging, can be a bad business decision. At this stage of assembling the compliance checklist, all relevant interests—including lawyers and managers of the affected lines of business—should be heard from.

Step IV. Assessing Your Compliance

Now that your compliance checklist is complete, you are ready to determine whether your company is doing the things it should be doing and avoiding the things it should not be doing. At this stage of the process, nothing is more important than management support. You simply cannot assess compliance without complete, accurate information, not only about the company's privacy policies but about the actual practices in which rank-and-file employees are engaging. Unless management expresses its complete support for your efforts, you will find the needed information very hard to obtain.

As we have seen, privacy law covers a wide range of activities. Functions within your organization that handle personal information or engage in electronic marketing will include Payroll, Human Resources, Information Technologies, Marketing, Legal, Security, and Accounting. Outside vendors also likely are involved in some or all of these activities. You will need the cooperation of all of these groups, for at least two purposes.

First, you must collect all of the written materials that declare or reflect your company's current practices in each of the areas covered by the compliance checklist. This includes any privacy and information security instructions in the Employee Handbook, security guidance from Information Technologies, company training materials, records classification and retention plans, and any other materials that might be relevant. To obtain management buy-in for this stage of the project, you should emphasize that if the Federal Trade Commission or another consumer protection agency investigates the company's privacy practices, its first demand will be for copies of all privacy-related policies and procedures. The absence of those materials, or the failure of those materials to reflect actual practice, might itself be a violation of law.

Second, you must interview, as far as possible, all personnel with privacy-related responsibilities. If face-to-face interviews are not feasible, probing questionnaires should be prepared and distributed. Those interviews and questionnaires should be directed at two principal areas: the practices in which employees engage, and the level of personnel awareness of company policies affecting privacy.

This stage of the process is serious detective work. One aspect of the compliance assessment, for example, will be to determine whether personal information maintained by the company is secured and disposed of properly. To know that, you must ferret out every place and situation in the company in which personal information is collected, stored, transmitted, and discarded.

You can start with the obvious. If your company has employees, it has personnel files and payroll data. If your company sells a product or service directly to consumers, it maintains customer lists. Those records should be obtained, and interviews should be used to determine where that information originates, where and how it is stored, how it is transmitted within and outside the company, and how long (and where) it is retained before disposal.

This is no time to ask perfunctory questions or accept perfunctory answers. The company's official policy, for example, might be to store all customer lists in a secure server behind a firewall. That's fine, but you need to find the inevitable employee who prints out the lists and keeps a personal, paper copy in an unlocked cabinet. (One ironclad rule: There are always more paper records than management thinks there are!) You also need to ask how hard it is for employees to download the lists to laptops and memory sticks, and take them home. These are the questions that will give you a real-world assessment of your company's privacy compliance.

When you have obtained all of the information you need, write a report to management that summarizes the results of your assessment and recommends changes. Mark it "confidential." If a lawyer wrote or assisted with the report, mark it "confidential and privileged." Then, offer to give your management any assistance it needs to implement your recommendations.

Step V. Developing and Implementing Compliant Policies and Practices

Developing and implementing compliant policies and practices involves at least three steps.

First, you must document your new privacy compliance program. Because regulators investigating privacy incidents will demand to see your company's written policies and practices, and because those policies and practices are required by applicable laws including the FTC Safeguards Rule, you must ensure that those materials are complete and correspond precisely with your company's actual practice. Don't be satisfied with a few aspirational paragraphs in the Employee Handbook. Detailed, focused practices must be developed and put in the hands of HR, IT, Marketing, and all other functional organizations with privacy responsibility. Marketers must know how to use telephones and e-mail lawfully, IT personnel must know how to protect digitized data, and all employees must know where the shredding containers are located.

Second, you must follow through with the impressive things you say in the written policies and practices. If your written policy calls for shredding of documents and use of antivirus software, retain a shredding vendor and buy an antivirus product. Most important, train your personnel in their privacy responsibilities, and update that training as appropriate.

Third, and finally, reassess your privacy program at least once a year. New laws will be enacted and your company will acquire new lines of business and activities that gradually will make your finely-crafted program obsolete. Only periodic reassessments will keep you ahead of the game.

If you follow the program we have set out, completely and without skipping any steps, you might not be a hero at your company (although you should be!), but you most certainly will sleep better.

Notes

[1]16 CFR pt. 314, sec. 314.2(a).

[2]*Id.* sec. 314.4(a)–(e).

[3]16 CFR sec. 682.3.

[4]Cal. Civ. Code sec. 1798.80.

[5]The PCI Standard can be found at https://www/pcisecuritystandards.org/index.html.

PART I
Information About Consumers and Customers

Few resources are more valuable to a business than its customer lists and associated marketing data. Customer profiles, contact information, and purchasing histories are essential if companies are to sell to existing customers in the future or identify the kinds of customers to which their products and services might be attractive. Sale of customer lists and associated data also can be an independent revenue stream. For some companies, in fact, customer lists are the most important assets on their balance sheets.

Legal requirements aside, therefore, businesses have every incentive to protect customer information and maximize its value. Businesses maximize the value of their customer databases by collecting as much useful information as they can—not just contact information and sales histories but, where possible, household size, age, income, and other data that can be used to focus the company's marketing efforts. Businesses also protect the value of these assets by keeping them complete, current, and secure from theft, alteration, and destruction.

Privacy laws may reinforce or conflict with these business interests. Those laws reinforce business interests when they require companies to keep their customer information current and accurate, and when they require companies to take measures to protect customer data from hackers and identity thieves. Privacy laws conflict with business interests, however, when they limit the acquisition of information from customers and prevent companies from using and disclosing that information in profitable ways.

The challenge for business managers and counsel is to maximize the profitable collection and use of customer data while complying with the growing web of laws that protect consumer privacy. The materials in this part of this book attempt to explain how this can be done. We start, in Chapter 1, with the laws that affect Internet-based activities, then move on in Chapter 2 to the increasingly serious and topical issue of data security. Chapters 3, 4, and 5 review the special obligations of financial institutions, electronic communication service providers, and health care insurers and providers. We conclude this part with a chapter on the impact of the Data Protection Directive of the European Union.

CHAPTER 1

Collection and Use of Personal Information on the Internet

For most businesses, use of the Internet is no longer optional. Consumers seeking information about vendors of goods and services consult search engines as readily as they use print directories. They expect to find Web sites that describe vendors' product lines and locations and offer a Web-based method for forwarding questions and complaints. Increasingly, they also want the option of buying the vendors' goods or services online.

Like other marketing channels, the Internet offers opportunities to collect information about the people who buy, or request information about, the vendors' products. This capability has attracted the ongoing attention of legislators and regulators, who worry that online businesses will collect and use personal information in ways that consumers may not expect or approve. Those concerns have produced a growth industry of efforts to control the collection, disclosure, and use of personal information by means of the Internet.

Despite all of this official concern, and with exceptions that are specific to certain industries, jurisdictions, and activities, online businesses in the United States are free to collect, use, and disclose personal information in any way they choose, so long as those practices do not violate commitments they have made to the parties providing that information.[1] Put another way, American businesses generally are subject only to the online personal information rules they impose on themselves.[2]

For this reason, an online business's most important privacy decision is to make, or not to make, privacy commitments to customers and other users. Such commitments usually are made in posted privacy policies. Accordingly, the content of privacy policies and the consequences of violating those policies are the focus of the discussion that follows.

1.1 Should You Have a Privacy Policy? If So, What Should It Say?

There is no law of nationwide application, in the United States, that requires every Web site or online service to have a privacy policy. California requires Web sites that collect personal information to post such policies, however, and other states can be expected to follow suit. Also, privacy policies have become the kind of "best practice" that consumers expect reputable online companies to provide.[3] These pressures make it increasingly difficult for online businesses to avoid posting privacy policies.

Once a company posts a privacy policy, however, both customers and regulators may treat that policy as a set of enforceable commitments. Specifically, if the company discloses customer information in violation of the policy, customers may claim that the company has breached a contract, committed a privacy-related tort, or deceived consumers in violation of state consumer protection laws that permit private lawsuits by aggrieved consumers. Similarly, the Federal Trade Commission (FTC) and state consumer protection authorities may allege that the company's violation of the policy constitutes an unfair or deceptive act or practice subject to administrative or judicial enforcement action.

Not all of these enforcement actions are guaranteed to succeed. Consumers have had difficulty convincing courts that privacy policies are enforceable contracts, and privacy torts, such as trespass and intrusion on seclusion, have proved to be a poor fit with privacy policy violations.[4] Similarly, deceptive practice claims by the states or the FTC may be based on strained readings of a privacy policy's terms and may be successfully resisted on those grounds.[5] But all litigation, successful or otherwise, is costly and potentially damaging to a company's reputation, especially where legal action is backed by the public credibility of the FTC or a state attorney general. Privacy policies, and the practices subject to those policies, should be undertaken with a view to avoiding such complaints.

For these reasons, a privacy policy should be written in plain English, posted prominently, and crafted in a way that is consistent with the company's actual business practices. The following considerations, at least, should be kept in mind when writing a privacy policy. (An example of a privacy policy is set out in Figure 1.1.)

What Should the Scope of Your Privacy Policy Be?

A privacy policy's terms may be limited to the company's treatment of data collected *online*, or may encompass offline activities as well. For example, if a merchant takes orders by means of postal mail and toll-free telephone calls as well as through its Web site, it might wish to post a document that describes its privacy practices for all three marketing channels. If a posted privacy policy addresses offline activities, however, any differences in the treatment of customer data provided through different channels should be clearly described. (As courts and regulators see it, any confusion customers experience as the result of poor drafting is your fault.)

Privacy policies also should clearly identify the business entities and lines of business to which they apply. This is especially important for companies that sell a range of products and services, do business through subsidiaries or affiliates, or use more than one marketing channel. For example, an equipment leasing company might rent new equipment to the public and sell used equipment that is nearing the end of its useful life. The company also might operate both lines of business through a combination of wholly-owned outlets and independent franchisees. The rental and sales businesses may be subject to different privacy regulations, and the company may have little or no control over the privacy practices of its franchisees. Accordingly, the company will want to have separate privacy policies for its sales and rental operations, and will want both of those policies to disclaim responsibility for the privacy practices of independent franchisees. If the company's privacy policies do not state plainly the entities and lines of business to which they apply, in language that an ordinary consumer will understand, the company may be held responsible for any harm that results from customer confusion.

Make Sure Your Customer Has an Adequate Opportunity to Review the Privacy Policy

Privacy policies should be easy for customers to find. If privacy policies are buried deep in a Web site, and are not at least linked from appropriate text or icons on the site's opening page, the FTC or a state attorney general may find that the online business intended to deceive the public as to its treatment of personal information. (One FTC enforcement action already has been based on revisions to a privacy policy.) This result is likely if the policy permits broad disclosures of personal information, and especially likely if those disclosures exceed the usual practice for the industry in question.

Businesses also must be careful when they make substantial changes to their privacy policies. For example, a company might post a policy in January that disclaims any intention to share customer information with any third parties. In July, that company might enter into a lucrative arrangement to sell its customer lists to an independent marketing company, and might post an amended privacy policy that permits those disclosures to be made. Does a post-July sale of the lists violate the rights of a customer that submitted information in March, after reading the privacy policy that was posted in January?

In an enforcement action brought against Gateway Learning Corporation, the FTC alleged that it was, in fact, a deceptive practice to disclose personal information that was submitted to a Web site before a change to the site's privacy policy, permitting such disclosures, was posted.[6] Although the action was settled by a consent agreement without admission of liability, the Gateway Learning case shows that changes to privacy policies may be closely scrutinized by the FTC.

To avoid possible deception claims, online businesses should make clear, in all versions of their privacy policies, that customers are responsible for reviewing the posted policy from time to time. Companies also should post notices of changes on their Web sites with reasonable prominence, and should consider making especially important changes applicable only on a prospective basis—for example, by disclosing information submitted before the change was made only on the terms set out in the policy that was posted at the time the information was submitted.

Finally, if changes to a privacy policy will be made from time to time, the posted policy should include a "last revised" date to help the customer determine whether revisions have been made since the customer's last visit to the site.

Describe the Kinds of Information You Collect

Information collected from consumers varies in sensitivity, and a well-drafted privacy policy will describe the kinds of information collected and the business's privacy practices with respect to each.

Consumers will be most concerned about disclosures of personally identifiable information, including their names, postal addresses, telephone numbers, e-mail addresses, Social Security numbers, financial account numbers, and credit card numbers. Consumers also may regard their history of purchases, Web pages visited, and similar data as sensitive if that information will be associated by the collecting company with the consumers' personally identifiable information.

Consumers likely will be less concerned with disclosure of so-called aggregate information, which is derived from customer data but not identified with individual customers. For example, a Web site that carries advertising might want to tell potential advertisers that 80 percent of its customers live in zip codes with affluent populations, or have purchased products similar to those offered by the potential advertisers. As long as this information is released in a form that does not permit the advertisers to identify or contact the Web site's customers, it is classified as aggregate rather than personally identifiable information.

Other information is collected by automated processes that present minimal privacy concerns in ordinary use. For example, each time a visitor or customer accesses a Web site, the site will receive "clickstream data" that includes the Internet Protocol (IP) address of the requesting computer, the type of browser and operating system the customer is using, and other data the Web site's server will need in order to exchange information with the visitor or customer. Many online services also transmit cookies and Web beacons that remember passwords and perform other functions that facilitate online communication. With increased publicity about viruses, spyware, and other harmful code, a privacy policy that describes the service's automated online data collection functions may reassure consumers and make them more willing to engage in online transactions.

Describe How Information Collected May Be Used

Online businesses use customer data in a variety of ways. Some businesses use such information only to fill customer orders and respond to inquiries. Others collect and use customer information for internal business purposes, such as identifying those products and services that are most popular with customers. Still other businesses use customers' postal and e-mail addresses to contact those customers and encourage further purchases, or disclose customer information—in personally identifiable or aggregate form—to third parties for commercial purposes.

A privacy policy should describe all of the uses that might be made of customer information, including uses that are not part of the business's present practices but might be implemented during the effective life of the privacy policy. Most important, the business must adopt implementation policies, including personnel training, to ensure that customer information is used only in the ways described in the policy.

Describe Categories of Persons or Businesses to Which Data May Be Disclosed

Businesses are not required or expected to identify, by name, each individual entity to which various kinds of customer information will be disclosed. A privacy policy should, however, list the *categories* of entities to which customer data may be provided.[7] For example, some companies contract with "fulfillment entities" that handle the mechanics of filling customer orders or requests. Businesses also might have joint marketing arrangements with third-party vendors, and might share customer information with those joint marketing partners. And some businesses disclose customer information to any third party that will pay for it, regardless of the third party's line of business or affiliation—or lack of affiliation—with the company that collected the information from the consumer. These and other categories of recipients of customer data should be disclosed with reasonable specificity.

Privacy policies also should make clear that customer information will be disclosed as required by subpoena or other process, or as needed to protect the interests of the business, its customers, or the public.

Finally, the states are taking an increased interest in privacy disclosures. California, for example, now requires online services to disclose when they provide personal information to direct marketing organizations.[8] Accordingly, companies that collect information online should follow developments in the state legislatures as well as the Congress.

Decide Whether You Will Give Consumers a Right to Review and Change Data

Some privacy policies give customers and visitors an opportunity to review personal information about them that is maintained by the Web site or online service.[9] If you give your users such an opportunity, you should provide a single point of contact for those requests and establish a review procedure that can be promptly implemented after such requests are made. Also, you should demand proof of the requesting person's identity before complying with any such request. It will hardly serve the privacy interests of your customers if the right of review became a means for identity thieves or other unauthorized persons to acquire your customers' information.

Disclose Data Security Measures

Most privacy policies refer to data security—that is, the measures the service provider takes to prevent loss, corruption, or unauthorized disclosure of personal information submitted to the service provider. However, any assurances a privacy policy gives about data security should be cautious, qualified, and accurate. Information security is never under a service provider's complete control. It can be compromised by unforeseen technical failure and the whims and ingenuity of any hacker, rogue employee, or thief who decides to compromise your system. In this environment, strong assurances about the safety of customer information are not prudent or realistic.

The need for caution in describing data security measures is heightened by the scrutiny the FTC and state consumer protection authorities give to this subject. In a series of enforcement proceedings over the last several years, the FTC and the states have obtained consent decrees and fines from companies that promised to protect customer information and either failed to implement the practices described or experienced inadvertent compromise of customer information. The complaints in these proceedings show that even vague data security commitments can be read by regulators as implying promises of highly specific practices, and that companies can be sued even when they have suffered no breach of personal data entrusted to their care.

In order to avoid such enforcement action, companies should make only factual statements about their information security measures, accompanied always by appropriate *caveats*. For example, a company that uses Secure Sockets Layer (SSL) encryption for customers' credit card information can state that fact, but should not characterize its data protection measures as "state of the art," "strong," or even "reasonable." Statements about data security should emphasize that the Internet, like other communications channels, can never be entirely secure and that the service provider will not be responsible for losses resulting from security failures.

Protect Your Right to Sell Customer Data as an Asset in Bankruptcy or Other Transfer of Your Business

In a well-known FTC proceeding, an online toy sales company was alleged to have violated its privacy policy when it proposed to sell its customer list as an asset in bankruptcy.[10] The company settled that case with the FTC, but that experience underscores the importance of stating, in any privacy policy, that the customer's personal information may be transferred to a buyer or successor entity in connection with bankruptcy proceedings, or as part of a sale of all or substantially all of the business or its assets.

Include Disclosures Required by Privacy Regulations to Which You Are Subject

You may be subject to regulations that require disclosures in addition to, and perhaps different from, those suggested here. For example, if your Web site is directed to children under the age of 13, you must post a privacy policy and notice to parents that includes "verifiable parental consent" mechanisms and other information.[11] If you are a financial institution, your privacy policy may be required to include disclosures mandated by the Gramm-Leach-Bliley Act (GLBA).[12] You should seek expert advice on the applicability of specific statutes and regulations before drafting your privacy policy in final form.

1.2 What Happens If You Violate Your Privacy Policy?

If you violate your privacy policy, you may face legal liability from one or more of three sources: (1) enforcement action by the FTC or other federal agencies, (2) enforcement actions by state authorities, and (3) lawsuits brought by private plaintiffs. The following discusses your exposure from each of these sources.

1.2.1 Federal Regulatory Enforcement

The principal federal agency with responsibility for privacy policy violations is the FTC, but other agencies have concurrent responsibility for the privacy practices of specific industries.

The FTC derives its authority to enforce privacy commitments from Section 5 of the Federal Trade Commission Act, which broadly prohibits unfair or deceptive acts or practices.[13] When the FTC suspects that a business has committed such practices, it has a number of enforcement options. Often, the Commission first serves the business with a civil investigative demand (CID), which may request documents, written testimony, or answers to written questions.[14] The business may file a petition to quash the demand, and the FTC may respond by seeking a court order compelling compliance. Failure to comply with a CID may result in penalties of $110 a day for each day of noncompliance.

If the Commission concludes from the CID process that a violation has occurred, it may proceed against the company with an administrative action or may seek relief directly in federal court. Under either approach, the Commission must have the aid of a court in order to obtain penalties against the company for violation of its orders.

In cases involving privacy violations, including the specific enforcement actions we discuss below, the typical resolution has been the signing of a consent agreement between the company and the FTC. The company in these cases agrees to the settlement without admitting liability, but may agree to pay a penalty and almost certainly will consent to implement changes to its business practices and accept Commission oversight for several years after the agreement is entered.

If the targeted company does not settle the case and elects to contest the Commission's claims, the matter will be heard before an Administrative Law Judge (in the case of an administrative proceeding) or a federal district court (in the case of a judicial proceeding). An adverse decision of the district court may be appealed to a U.S. Court of Appeals. An adverse administrative decision also may be reviewed by a U.S. Court of Appeals, but will be heard pursuant to a different process known as judicial review. Judicial review of an administrative decision is advantageous to the Commission because its decisions are given considerable deference by appellate courts. In an appeal from a judicial decision, the reviewing court will treat the Commission as an ordinary government plaintiff, giving the FTC's position no special deference.

The FTC has brought a number of actions alleging violations of privacy policies. An early example is the Commission's case against Geocities, which collected various items of personal information from persons applying for membership in its online "community."[15] According to the FTC, Geocities's online privacy statements represented, expressly or by implication, that certain personal information it collected would be used only to provide e-mail advertising and other requested products or services, and would not be disclosed to third parties without the consumer's permission. In fact, according to the FTC's complaint, personal information collected by Geocities was "sold, rented, or otherwise marketed or disclosed . . ." to third parties for marketing purposes unrelated to the purposes for which the information was collected. As to information collected from children, in particular, the Commission alleged that children's personal information was collected by third-party operators of the child-oriented Web pages, rather than by Geocities as represented in Geocities's privacy statements. The FTC alleged that these disparities between Geocities's representations and its practices constituted unfair or deceptive acts or practices under Section 5(a) of the FTC Act. The action against Geocities was resolved by entry of a consent order in which Geocities agreed, among other things, to obtain express parental consent before obtaining personal information from children and to post a privacy policy that accurately described its handling of personal information.[16]

The year following the Geocities proceeding, the FTC brought a similar action against Liberty Financial Companies, Inc. (Liberty).[17] Liberty maintained a Web site for "young investors," and encouraged completion of an online survey that collected such information as amount of allowance and financial gifts received, along with family financial data. Liberty represented that personal information submitted to its service would be used for quarterly drawings and an e-mail newsletter, and that all online survey answers would be "totally anonymous."[18] In fact, Liberty did not maintain submitted data in anonymous form, and associated the survey responses with personal information of the persons responding. Also, no prize drawings were ever made and no e-mail surveys were sent. Like the Geocities proceeding, the Liberty case was settled by entry of a consent order that required Liberty to post a truthful privacy policy and obtain parental consent before collecting information from children.[19]

More recently, the FTC has taken a strong interest in data security representations, and has undertaken a campaign to bring all of American business in line with the approach to data security mandated by the Safeguards Rule enacted under the GLBA.[20] As these enforcement actions suggest, rather than extend data protection obligations by rulemaking, the FTC is using a case-by-case "sue and settle" approach. The mechanism is simple. When a company experiences a security breach or makes public statements about its data protection practices that the FTC suspects to be false or misleading, enforcement proceedings are brought against the company for engaging in unfair or deceptive practices. The proceedings typically end, not merely with correction of the misleading statement or security flaw that triggered the investigation in the first place, but with the company's agreement to accept the full range of GLBA-like data protection obligations. As consent orders containing these terms are entered and made public, businesses that maintain personal information can be expected to conclude that implementation of GLBA-type protections is the best way to avoid adverse regulatory action. The result is a set of "de facto security standards for companies that handle consumer information."[21]

The first step in the FTC's data security campaign began after Eli Lilly & Company inadvertently disclosed the e-mail addresses of users of its Prozac antidepressant medication. The disclosure resulted from the kind of human error that no network security safeguards can entirely prevent.[22] Nonetheless, the FTC made the incident the basis for a claim that Eli Lilly's privacy statement, which promised generally to protect the confidentiality of customer information, was false and misleading. To settle the matter, the FTC and Eli Lilly entered into a consent order that imposed a number of GLBA-type data protection requirements, only some of which directly addressed the employee training and software testing deficiencies that the FTC had identified as responsible for the security breach.[23] The consent order imposed a general obligation to identify and control all "reasonably foreseeable internal and external risks" to data security, including risks such as "attacks, intrusions, [and] unauthorized access," that were not involved in the release of the Prozac users' e-mail addresses.[24] The consent order also imposed other requirements, including designation of personnel to coordinate and oversee Eli Lilly's data security program, annual written reviews of program compliance, and adjustment of the program in light of information acquired from reviews or ongoing monitoring.[25] The Eli Lilly order will remain in effect for 20 years from the date of its entry.[26]

The FTC's next data protection enforcement action was brought against a company that had not even experienced a security breach. In October 1999, Microsoft launched its .NET Passport and Passport Wallet services, which facilitated sign-on and purchasing processes at participating Web sites. In its advertising, privacy policy, and published Q & As, Microsoft represented that information provided by Passport and Passport Wallet customers was protected by powerful online security technology. The FTC launched an investigation of the security features for these services and found them so deficient as to make Microsoft's assurances false and misleading. Specifically, the FTC alleged that Microsoft failed to implement and document procedures that were reasonable and appropriate to prevent possible unauthorized access to the system, detect such unauthorized access, monitor the system for vulnerabilities, and record and retain system information sufficient to perform security audits and investigations. Following the FTC's investigation, Microsoft and the FTC entered into a consent order that not only required Microsoft to avoid false and misleading statements about security, but also required Microsoft to implement a comprehensive security program similar to that described in the Eli Lilly order.[27]

In 2002, the FTC brought an action against Guess?, Inc. and Guess.com, Inc. (Guess) for violation of security commitments made on the Guess Web site.[28] According to the FTC's complaint, Guess represented that it had "security measures in place," and that all orders placed to its Web site were "transmitted over secure Internet connections using SSL encryption technology."[29] Guess also represented that customers' credit card information and sign-in passwords would be "stored in an unreadable, encrypted format at all times," and that the Web site and all user information were "protected by a multi-layer firewall based security system."[30]

The FTC alleged that these representations were false and that, in fact, intruders could gain access to customers' credit card and other information stored on the site in clear, unencrypted text. In fact, the FTC alleged that in February 2002, a visitor to the site used an "SQL injection attack" to read credit card numbers stored in Guess's database.[31]

Although there was no claim that the vulnerability of Guess's Web site resulted in identity theft or any other actual harm to consumers, Guess agreed to a consent order containing the usual range of GLBA-type measures. The consent order will be in place for 20 years from the date it took effect.

On April 21, 2004, the FTC brought a data protection action against Tower Records (more specifically, MTS, Incorporated, a California corporation, doing business as Tower Records/Books/Video and Tower Direct, LLC, doing business as TowerRecords.com).[32]

According to the FTC's complaint, Tower sold products through a Web site that collected certain information from visitors and purchasers, including names, billing addresses, shipping addresses, e-mail addresses, telephone numbers, and all of the Tower products the users had purchased online since 1996. An application maintained on the Web site, called the "order status application," permitted consumers to access their Tower online purchase histories by supplying a unique order number assigned by Tower. By demanding input of the unique order number,

Tower was able to authenticate the identity of persons seeking access to their purchase history information.

Apparently, Tower redesigned the "check-out" portion of its site in late 2002 but failed to transfer all of the code associated with its authentication procedures to the redesigned check-out pages. The resulting vulnerability lasted for only eight days, but during that time "personal information relating to approximately 5,225 customers was accessed by unauthorized users, and at least two Internet chat rooms contained postings about the vulnerability as well, as well as comments about some consumers' purchases."[33]

In its complaint against Tower, the FTC alleged that the 8-day security lapse in late 2002 violated Tower's posted privacy policy, which stated that "TowerRecords.com takes steps to ensure that your information is treated securely . . . [and] [o]nce we receive your transmission, we make our best effort to ensure its security on our systems." Among other alleged lapses, the FTC claimed that Tower had failed to "implement appropriate checks and controls on the process of writing and revising Web applications; adopt and implement policies and procedures regarding security tests for its Web applications; and provide appropriate training and oversight for their employees regarding Web application vulnerabilities and security testing." According to the Commission, the alleged disparity between the assurances given in Tower's privacy policy, and the security failure experienced in late 2002, constituted "unfair or deceptive acts or practices" in violation of the Federal Trade Commission Act.

In order to settle the complaint, Tower entered into a long-term consent order. Among other things, Tower agreed to adopt and implement a comprehensive information security program, including an assessment of risks and appropriate corrective measures in the areas of employee training, employee management, information systems, and prevention, detection, and response to attacks, intrusions, or other system failures. Tower also must obtain an information security report from "a qualified, objective, independent third-party professional . . . within [180 days] after service of the [FTC's] order, and biannually thereafter for ten (10) years . . ." Like other orders of its kind entered into by the FTC in recent years, the Tower Records order will remain in effect for 20 years.

The enforcement actions we have described underscore the importance of making privacy commitments generally, and data protection commitments in particular, sparingly and with a view to your company's actual practices.

More recently, the FTC has adopted new theories under which it challenges alleged data protection deficiencies of companies that have made no commitments to protect information at all, in their privacy policies or elsewhere. Because those enforcement actions are not based on alleged violations of privacy policies, we defer our discussion of those cases to Chapter 2.

1.2.2 State Actions

The states also have brought enforcement actions for alleged failure to respect privacy commitments and protect the security of customer information. One of these actions was settled in August 2002, when New York State Attorney General Spitzer announced a multistate Assurance of Discontinuance (Assurance) with Ziff-Davis

Media, Inc., which had suffered a security breach in connection with an online promotional offer for free subscriptions to one of its magazines. The breach resulted in disclosure of a subscription data file and some customers' credit card information. Ziff-Davis notified customers of the problem and acted within an hour to take the insecure promotion page offline. Those actions, and an internal review of its data control practices, were undertaken by Ziff-Davis before commencement of the state investigation. Nonetheless, the states alleged that Ziff-Davis had breached its privacy policy, which pledged that the company "use[d] reasonable precautions to keep . . . personal information [disclosed to the Ziff-Davis magazines and Web site] secure."[34]

As in the FTC's actions against Eli Lilly, Microsoft, Guess, and Tower, the terms of the Ziff-Davis settlement went well beyond retraction of false privacy assurances, or even correction of the cause of the breach that gave rise to the investigation. The settlement required Ziff-Davis to undertake a wide range of substantive security practices and measures, including encryption of sensitive consumer data and implementation of "standard practices relating to the privacy, security, and integrity of Consumer Data, where such standards have gained sufficient industry acceptance and adoption such that Ziff-Davis' adherence to the standards would not unreasonably place Ziff-Davis at a competitive disadvantage."[35] In addition, the settlement required Ziff-Davis to pay $500 to each subscriber who had provided credit card information during the promotion.

Another notable enforcement action from the New York Attorney General involved Netscape Communications, a subsidiary of America Online, and that company's SmartDownload browser function. According to the Attorney General, Netscape had saved the URLs of files downloaded by users, in violation of the company's representations that "none of this information is saved." In order to settle the case, Netscape agreed to delete all of the data in question, undergo a series of privacy audits, and pay $100,000 to the state.[36]

Not all state enforcement actions come from New York. For example, in 2002, the State of New Jersey announced an agreement with Toys Я Us.com in which that company paid $50,000 to the state and agreed, among other commitments, to correct "potentially confusing wording" in its privacy policy.[37]

As subsequent chapters of this book make clear, the states are often leaders in the creation and enforcement of privacy rights, sometimes imposing protections that go beyond those provided by federal law, and sometimes doing so in the face of strong claims that their initiatives are preempted by acts of Congress. No company's privacy program can assume that compliance with federal law alone is sufficient.

1.2.3 Private Actions—The Airlines Litigation and Other Lawsuits

Persons aggrieved by violations of privacy policies may, of course, seek redress by complaining to the FTC or state consumer protection agencies, which are empowered to bring enforcement actions of the kinds we have described. If consumers hope to collect monetary damages for such violations, however, they must bring private lawsuits on their own account, or join in class action lawsuits.

A consumer bringing an individual lawsuit might allege violations of a consumer protection statute that permits a private right of action, or might allege that a privacy policy violation constitutes a breach of contract or satisfies the elements of one of the various privacy torts.

Few private lawsuits have been based on alleged privacy policy violations, but the most significant of those few are the airline privacy cases. In those actions, consumers who had purchased airline tickets online learned that the airlines had disclosed personal information to government agencies or contractors as part of Homeland Security programs. In the Northwest Airlines litigation, the airline had supplied passenger name records (PNRs) to the National Aeronautics and Space Administration. In similar litigation involving JetBlue Airways, the airline had disclosed PNRs to a contractor retained by the Department of Defense.[38]

The decisions in the airline cases underscore the difficulty of proving that publicly-posted privacy policies are enforceable contracts. In the Northwest Airlines cases, U.S. district courts in Minnesota and North Dakota found that the privacy policies, as "broad statements of company policy," were not contractual, and that even if those policies could form the basis of contractual obligations, there was no allegation that the plaintiffs had accessed and read those policies.[39] Similarly, in both the Northwest Airlines cases and the JetBlue litigation, the courts held that loss of privacy could not support a claim of damages for breach of contract.[40]

1.3 Collecting Information from Children: The Children's Online Privacy Protection Act

If your company has a Web site that is directed to children under 13, or if your company has actual knowledge that it is collecting personal information from children under 13, you must ensure that the company is in compliance with the Children's Online Privacy Protection Act (COPPA).[41] This statute is enforced by the FTC, so you also need to understand the COPPA regulations of that agency.[42]

1.3.1 Is My Web Site Subject to COPPA?

If you are the operator of a Web site or online service, you must comply with COPPA if the Web site or online service is *operated for commercial purposes* and *is directed to children under the age of 13*, or *if you have knowledge that the Web site is collecting information from children under the age of 13*.

Deciding whether a Web site meets these criteria is not always easy (see Figure 1.1). A few sources of possible confusion should be kept in mind:

1. Who Is an "Operator?" If your company is an Internet access provider or Web site hosting company that acts as a mere "conduit" for its customers' Web sites or online services, then your company is not an "operator" of customers' Web sites for purposes of COPPA. However, if your company "owns and/or controls the information" collected by a Web site, "pays for [the information's] collection and maintenance," or "participates in collection" of the information beyond acting as a "mere conduit," your company likely will be classified as an "operator" within the meaning of COPPA.[43]

2. "Commercial Purposes." The Web site or online service is not subject to COPPA unless it is operated for commercial purposes, but that phrase is not defined in the statute or the FTC's regulations. In general, if your Web site is run by a charitable, governmental or educational entity and does not promote or sell any product or service, it should not be subject to COPPA, even if it includes hyptertext links to commercial sites. If your site is maintained to advertise or promote a commercial enterprise, however, the fact the site does not offer products or services for online sale will not remove it from the coverage of COPPA.
3. "Directed to Children." There is no clear rule that determines whether a Web site or online service is directed to children for purposes of COPPA. The FTC has announced that it will classify a Web site as directed to children based on the site's "subject matter, audio or visual content, age of models, language or other characteristics of the Web site or online service, as well as whether advertising promoted or appearing on the Web site or online service is directed to children."[44] The Commission also will consider "competent and reliable empirical evidence regarding audience composition; evidence regarding the intended audience; and whether a site uses animated characters and/or child-oriented activities and incentives."[45]
4. "Actual Knowledge." Companies that operate Web sites often ask for an explanation of the circumstances under which the Commission will find that a Web site operator had actual knowledge that it was collecting personal information from a child under 13. This question is especially important because collection-with-actual-knowledge brings even an adult-oriented Web site within COPPA.

The Commission was asked to clarify the actual knowledge standard during its COPPA rulemaking proceeding, and specifically was asked whether Web site

Privacy Policy Practice Tips

The best practice is to post a privacy policy, but your policy must not promise more than your business's actual privacy practices can deliver.

Post your privacy policy conspicuously and ensure that it is accessible from every page on your Web site.

State clearly the entities and lines of business to which your privacy policy applies and does not apply.

Describe the categories of data you collect, the purposes for which the data are collected, and the types of entities, if any, to which data are disclosed.

Reserve the right to disclose collected information as required by warrants, subpoenas, and other legal process.

Reserve the right to sell or transfer collected information as part of the sale of your business or its assets.

Make only factual statements about your data security measures, and emphasize that the Internet is inherently insecure.

An Example of a Privacy Policy: The Web Site Privacy Policy of Icarus Hang Gliders, Inc.

This Privacy Policy (Policy) describes the information collection, use and disclosure practices of the Internet Web site of Icarus Hang Gliders, Inc. ("Icarus," "we" or "us") located on the World Wide Web at icarushanggliders.com. This Policy does not describe the privacy practices of any other company or entity, and does not govern the collection, use and disclosure of personal information provided to Icarus's retail stores or in connection with mail or telephone orders submitted to Icarus.

As an Icarus customer or visitor to our Web site, you are entitled to full disclosure of the uses we will make of information that you provide to us online. Those disclosures are set out in this Policy and in no other document, and your use of our Web site constitutes your acceptance of the terms of this Policy. This Policy may be changed from time to time, and you should visit our Web site for notice of those changes, which will be prominently posted on the dates they become effective. Your continued use of our Web site after such changes are made constitutes your acceptance of those changes.

What Personal Information Do We Collect and Why Do We Collect It?

We collect four categories of information from visitors and other users and of our Web site: personal information, aggregate information, clickstream data, and cookie transmissions. The kinds of information contained within these categories, and the purposes for which we collect that information, are described below.

Personal information we collect may include your name, postal address, e-mail address, and telephone number. We collect such items of personal information in order to respond to your requests for product information and to fill online product orders. We also collect credit card information when you order our products through our Web site.

Aggregate information is data derived from personal information submitted to our Web site but not identifiable to individual persons. We may, for example, create a profile of our customer base according to zip codes, number of purchases made, and other factors that will help us to target our future marketing efforts. (That aggregate information also might be made available to advertisers and potential advertisers, as we explain below.)

Clickstream data is nonpersonal information transmitted to us automatically from your computer when you interact with our Web site. Clickstream data may include your computer's IP address, the type of Internet browser and operating system you are using, the pages and information you accessed on our Web site, the time spent on our Web site, and the domain name of the Web site from you which linked to our Web site. Information of this kind permits your computer to establish a working connection with our Web site and navigate the Web site more effectively. Clickstream data will not be used to identify you personally and will not be associated or correlated with any Web site visitor or customer in a personally-identifiable manner.

Cookies are small strings of digitized text that our Web site transmits to your computer, and that will send certain information to our Web site when you are connected with our service. Cookies are used to "remember" user names and passwords, so that you are not required to reenter that information each time you visit our Web site. We also use cookies to understand which parts of our Web site are most popular, where our visitors are going on our service and how much time they spend there. Cookies are read only by the server that placed them, and are unable to execute any code or virus.

If you do not wish to have cookies stored on your computer, you may instruct your browser to block them, erase them or warn you before a cookie is stored. Please refer to your browser instructions or help screen to learn more about these functions. However, blocking or erasing cookies may prevent you from using some of the functionalities of our Web site.

Figure 1.1 A sample privacy policy. This is the online privacy policy for the Web site of Icarus Hang Gliders, Inc. ("We Fly You to the Sun"™), a fictional company we shall visit from time to time in this handbook. The Icarus privacy policy is included here only as an illustration of the commitments a company might choose to make. Your privacy policy should reflect your own business practices and legal environment.

Some uses of cookies in connection with our Web site may be under the control of unaffiliated entities that we retain to process inquiries or orders, as further described below. We cannot be responsible for the uses of cookies by unaffiliated third parties.

When and to Whom Do We Disclose Information Collected on Our Web Site?

Personal information collected from customers and visitors to our Web site is used to respond to your inquiries and process your orders for our products. We do not sell that information to others. In some cases, we may refer your inquiries and product orders to independent companies that assist with the processing and fulfillment of those orders and inquiries. We require those independent companies to use your personal information only for the intended purpose, and we prohibit those companies from selling or otherwise disclosing your personal information to third parties. We cannot, however, be responsible for any failure of those companies to honor their privacy commitments to us. Similarly, we are not responsible for the privacy policies and practices of unaffiliated entity Web sites that are linked to our Web site.

We may compile aggregate information, as defined above, into reports that we provide to advertisers and potential advertisers. Those reports contain no information that permits their recipients to identify or contact individual persons.

We will disclose personal information concerning visitors and customers when required by legal process, or as necessary to protect the rights and safety of ourselves, our customers or the public.

We may transfer personal information to a purchaser or successor entity in connection with the sale of Icarus, a subsidiary or line of business associated with Icarus, or substantially all of the assets of Icarus or one of its subsidiaries, affiliates, or lines of business.

How Do We Protect Information Submitted to Our Web Site?

You should be aware that the Internet, like other media of communication, is subject to unauthorized intrusion and compromise. No Web site or computer network can guarantee that it will not be penetrated by hackers or suffer a security breach through technical or human failure. We take technical and administrative measures to protect your information, including Secure Sockets Layer (SSL) encryption of your credit card information. We cannot be responsible, however, for loss, corruption or unauthorized disclosure of personal information submitted to us.

Note to Parents

Our Web site is not directed to children and does not knowingly collect personal information from children under the age of 13. When we acquire actual knowledge that a visitor to our Web site is under the age of 13, we will take appropriate measures to avoid collection of personal information from that visitor or to collect and use such information only in compliance with the Children's Online Privacy Protection Act and other applicable law.

How Can You Ask Questions About Our Privacy Policy and Access Your Personal Information?

If you have questions about this Privacy Policy, wish to access your personal information, or request that we not use your personal information for a particular purpose, please follow the instructions posted at http://icarushanggliders.com.

This Privacy Policy was last modified on [date].

Figure 1.1 (Continued)

operators have a duty to investigate the ages of persons who submit personal information. The Commission gave the following response:[46]

> Actual knowledge will be present, for example, where an operator learns of a child's age or grade from the child's registration at the site or from a concerned parent who has learned that his child is participating at the site. In addition, although the COPPA does not require operators of general audience sites to investigate the ages of their site's visitors, the Commission . . . will examine closely sites that do not directly ask age or grade, but instead ask 'age-identifying' questions such as 'what type of school do you go to: (a) elementary; (b) middle; (c) high school; (d) college?' Through such questions, operators may acquire actual knowledge that they are dealing with children under 13.

1.3.2 How Do Web Sites Comply with COPPA?

If your Web site is subject to COPPA, you must take a number of compliance measures defined in the statute and the implementing regulations of the FTC. The statute includes the following requirements:

- All children's Web site operators must provide notice on the Web site of what information is collected from children, how the Web site operator uses the information and the operator's disclosure practices for such information.
- All children's Web site operators must obtain verifiable parental consent for the collection, use or disclosure of personal information from children. "Verifiable parental consent" is defined as "any reasonable effort (taking into consideration available technology) . . . to ensure that a parent of a child receives notice of the operator's personal information collection, use, and disclosure practices, and authorizes the collection, use, and disclosure . . . personal information and the subsequent use of that information before that information is collected from that child."[47]
- Children's Web site operators must provide parents, on request, a description of the types of personal information collected from a child of the requesting parent. Children's Web site operators also must, on a parent's request, give the parent the opportunity to refuse to permit the operator's further collection from, or maintenance or use of, personal information of that parent's child.
- Children's Web site operators may not condition a child's participation on a game or prize offering on the child's disclosure of more information that is reasonably necessary to participate in the activity.
- Children's Web site providers must establish and maintain reasonable procedures to protect the confidentiality, security, and integrity of personal information collected from children.

COPPA also offers Web site operators some safe harbors and exceptions. Notably, Web site operators need not obtain verifiable parental consent for information that is obtained from a child to respond on a one-time basis to a specific request, and that is not maintained in retrievable form by the operator or used to make a subsequent contact with the child.[48] More generally, children's Web site operators may comply with the statute by observing industry self-regulatory guidelines approved by the FTC.[49] The FTC must approve or reject such self-regulatory guidelines within 180 days of the filing of a request for approval of those guidelines.[50]

In November 1999, the FTC adopted rules under which it administers and enforces COPPA.[51] The rules add important detail to the general obligations established in COPPA. Notably, the FTC rules:

(a) identify factors the FTC will consider when deciding whether a Web site or online service is directed to children;
(b) establish requirements for the placement and content of notices concerning an operator's privacy policy;
(c) announce that the Commission will assess operators' methods of obtaining verifiable parental consent according to a "sliding scale," under which more or less rigorous methods of consent will be required depending on how information obtained from children will be used;[52]
(d) clarify the circumstances under which operators may acquire information from a child without a parent's advance consent.[53]

1.3.3 COPPA Enforcement Proceedings

By February 2007, the FTC had brought 12 COPPA enforcement actions, some of which resulted in payment of substantial penalties.

An early action was brought in 2002 against American Pop Corn Company.[54] American Pop Corn maintained a Web site, part of which was directed to children. The "Kids Club" portion of the site included a membership application that called for children to provide various items of personal information. The Web site instructed children completing the application to "check with your parents first," but the Commission alleged that American Pop Corn did not obtain verifiable parental consent before collecting the requested information. The FTC also alleged that the "personal information required to join the club was more than was reasonably necessary to allow children to participate in Kids Club activities." American Pop Corn also failed to disclose its data collection practices concerning children accurately in its privacy policy, and "did not provide direct notice to parents of its practices regarding the collection, use, and/or disclosure of children's personal information and other disclosures required by the Rule." The action against American Pop Corn was settled by entry of a consent decree and payment of a $10,000 civil penalty.

More recently, the Commission has brought COPPA enforcement actions against UMG Recordings and Bonzi Software that resulted in financial penalties of $400,000 and $75,000, respectively.[55] In 2006, the Commission entered into a settlement with Xanga.com, a social networking site, pursuant to which the company agreed to pay a $1 million civil penalty.[56]

Because regulators and law enforcement agencies always have the moral high ground when they act in defense of children, companies should expect COPPA to remain a high enforcement priority.

Notes

[1]This distinguishes U.S. privacy law from European privacy law, which requires all automated collectors of personal information to give notice of their privacy practices. *See* Chapter 6.

[2]The exceptions to this situation include the Gramm-Leach-Bliley Act, the Children's Online Privacy Protection Act and the California online privacy statute. In a series of reports, the Federal Trade Commission has strongly urged online U.S. businesses to adopt privacy policies and has asked Congress to pass legislation to that effect. Federal Trade Commission, *Privacy Online: A Report to Congress*, http://www.ftc.gov/reports/privacy3/toc/htm; *Self-Regulation and Privacy Online: A Report to Congress* (1999), http://www.ftc.gov/os/1999/9907/privacy99.pdf; *Privacy Online: Fair Information Practices in the Electronic Marketplace: A Report to Congress* (2000).

[3]Notably, if California residents will visit your commercial Web site *and* the site will collect personal information from those persons, then the Web site must have a privacy policy that explains the information you collect and the circumstances under which that information may be used and disclosed. Cal. Bus. & Prof. Code § 22575 (2004).

[4]For decisions rejecting attempts to enforce privacy policies as contracts, *see Dyer v. Northwest Airlines Corporations*, 334 F.Supp.2d 1196 (D.N.D. 2004); *In re Northwest Airlines Privacy Litigation*, 2004 U.S. Dist. LEXIS 10580 (D. Minn. 2004): *see also In re JetBlue Airways Corp. Privacy Litigation,* 379 F.Supp.2d 299 (E.D.N.Y. 2005). As the court in the *JetBlue* case pointed out, a plaintiff that actually read a privacy policy and relied on its contents might have a cause of action. In fact, there is no reason to believe that a privacy policy can never be enforceable as a contract, if the customer had notice of its terms and engaged in conduct that the parties agreed would demonstrate assent to those terms.

[5]So far, however, it appears that no target of an FTC or state investigation into alleged privacy policy violations has resisted those enforcement actions in the courts.

[6]*In the Matter of Gateway Learning Corp.*, Complaint available at http://www.ftc.gov/os/caselist/0423047/040707cmp0423047.pdf.

[7]For example, California's statute concerning online privacy policies only requires those policies to identify "the categories of third-party persons or entities with whom the operator may share . . . personally identifiable information." Cal. Bus. & Prof. Code § 22575(b)(1).

[8]*See* Cal. Civ. Code § 1798.83.

[9]If you collect personal information from California consumers, you may be required to offer those consumers an opportunity to review that information. Cal. Bus. & Prof. Code § 22575(b)(2).

[10]*Federal Trade Commission v. Toysmart.com, LLC*, Civ. No. 00-11341-RGS (D. Mass. 2000), First Amended Complaint for Permanent Injunction and Other Equitable Relief at http://www.ftc.gov/os/2000/07/toysmartcomplaint.htm, Stipulated Consent Agreement and Final Order at http://www.ftc.gov/os/2000/07/toysmartconsent.htm (last visited Aug. 10, 2007).

[11]*See* discussion of Children's Online Privacy Protection Act at 1.3, below.

[12]*See* discussion of Gramm-Leach-Bliley Act at Chapter 3, below.

[13]15 U.S.C. § 45(a).

[14]15 U.S.C. §§ 57b-1. For a complete description of the FTC's enforcement authority and procedures, see Appendix C.

[15]*In the Matter of Geocities, a Corporation*, File No. 9823015 (1999).

[16]*Id.*, Agreement Containing Consent and Order, http://www.ftc.gov/os/1998/08/geo-ord.htm. The FTC's complaint against Geocities was brought before the enactment of the Children's Online Privacy Protection Act, which is discussed at 1.3, below.

[17]*In the Matter of Liberty Financial Companies, Inc.*, Docket No. C-3891 (1999).

[18]*Id.*, Complaint at http://www.ftc.gov/os/1999/05/lbrtycmp.htm.

[19]Like the Geocities complaint, the action against Liberty was filed before enactment of the Children's Online Privacy Protection Act.

[20]The Safeguards Rule can be found at 16 CFR pt. 314.

[21]Testimony of Michael A. Vatis, Director, Institute for Security Technology Studies at Dartmouth College before the Technology, Information Policy, Intergovernmental Relations, and Census Subcommittee of the House Committee on Government Reform (April 8, 2003) (Federal Document Clearing House Congressional Testimony, FDCH e-Media, Inc.).

[22]Eli Lilly had initiated a program that reminded Prozac users, by e-mail, when it was time to take their medication. When Eli Lilly decided to discontinue the program, an employee accidentally sent the discontinuance announcement to individual Prozac users with the e-mail addresses of all recipients shown on the "to" line. Another company—BankWest Corporations Bank of the West (BancWest)—experienced a similar incident when it sent an e-mail to over 3,000 customers that contained the e-mail addresses of all recipients. Thomas P. Vartanian and Mark Fajfar, "Thread in Data-Safety Lapses Was Failure to Follow Policy," *The American Banker* (Jan. 17, 2003) p. 7.

[23]Eli Lilly and Co., Docket No. C-4047 (May 8, 2002); *see* http://www.ftc.gov/opa/2002/01/elililly.htm (Eli Lilly Consent Order).

[24]*Id.*

[25]*Id.*

[26]*Id.*

[27]In the Matter of Microsoft Corp., File No. 012-3240; *see* http://www.ftc.gov/spa/2002/08/microsoft.htm (Microsoft Consent Order).

[28]In the Matter of GUESS?, INC., a corporation, and GUESS.COM, INC., a corporation, File No. 022-3260, Complaint and Agreement Containing Consent Order; *see* http://www.ftc.gov/os/2003/06/guesscmphtm; http://www.ftc.gocv/os/2003/06/guessagree.htm.

[29]*Id.*

[30]*Id.*

[31]*Id.* An SQL (Structured Query Language) attack is a sophisticated, but not uncommon, method for retrieving data from a database associated with a Web site.

[32]In the Matter of MTS, Inc. doing business as Tower Records/Books/Video, a corporation and Tower Direct, LLC doing business as Tower Records.com, a corporation, File No. 032-3209, Complaint and Agreement Containing Consent Order; *see* http://www.ftc.gov/os/caselist/0323209/0323209.htm.

[33]*Id.*, Complaint at p. 3.

[34]In the Matter of Ziff-Davis Media Inc., Assurance of Discontinuance effective Aug. 28, 2002 (Office of New York State Attorney General, www.oag.ny/us) (Ziff-Davis Assurance of Discontinuance).

[35]*Id. See also* In re: InfoBeat LLC, Assurance of Discontinuance (Jan. 2000), at http://www.oag.state.ny.us/internet/litigation/infobeat.pdf.

[36]Office of the New York State Attorney General, Press Release, "Settlement with Netscape Reached in 'Spyware' Case" (June 13, 2003).

[37]New Jersey Department of Law and Public Safety, Press Release, "ToysRUs.com Enters Into Agreement with State" (Jan. 3, 2003).

[38]Cases cited at n. 4, *supra.*

[39]*Dyer v. Northwest Airlines Corporations*, 334 F.Supp.2d 1196 (D.N.D. 2004); *In re Northwest Airlines Privacy Litigation*, 2004 U.S. Dist. LEXIS 10580 (D. Minn. 2004).

[40]*In re JetBlue Airways Corp. Privacy Litigation*, 379 F.Supp.2d 299 (E.D.N.Y. 2005). Also, the District Court for the District of Minnesota found, in the Northwest Airlines litigation, that

violation of Northwest's privacy policy was insufficient to establish the tort of intrusion on seclusion. *In re Northwest Airlines Privacy Litigation, supra*, 2004 U.S. Dist. LEXIS 10580 at *14.

[41]Pub. L. No. 105-227, 112 Stat. 2681-728 (codified as amended at 15 U.S.C. secs. 6501–06).

[42]The FTC's regulations implementing COPPA are set out in the Code of Federal Regulations at 16 CFR Part 312.

[43]64 Fed. Reg. 212 at p. 59891 (Nov. 3, 1999).

[44]16 C.F.R. 312.2.

[45]*Id.*

[46]64 Fed. Reg. 212 p. 59892 (Nov. 3, 1999).

[47]COPPA, § 1302(9).

[48]*Id.* § 1301(b)(2).

[49]*Id.* § 1304.

[50]*Id.* § 1304(b)(3).

[51]The FTC's rules are codified at 16 C.F.R. Part 312.

[52]The "sliding scale" initially was effective only until April 2002, but has been extended beyond that date.

[53]16 C.F.R. Part 312.

[54]*United States of America v. American Pop Corn Company*, Complaint for Civil Penalties, Injunctive, and Other Relief (N.D. Iowa 2002).

[55]Roy Mark, "FTC Fines COPPA Violators," *Internetnews.com* (Feb. 19, 2004).

[56]Lisa Thomas, "Responsible Interactive Advertising and Children: Understanding and Complying with COPPA and the CARU Guidelines," *Metropolitan Corporate Counsel* (Jan. 2007).

CHAPTER 2

Data Protection: The Evolving Obligation of Business to Protect Personal Information

Most of the statutes and regulations discussed in this book are directed at deliberate behavior—specifically, the decisions businesses make about collecting, using, and disclosing personal information. However, as a growing list of incidents in recent years demonstrates, unintended compromises of information can be just as devastating as losses that result from intentional misconduct.

How does the law respond when personal information entrusted to a business is disclosed or misused because of an accident or third-party misconduct, rather than the deliberate choice of the business?

The law has made piecemeal responses to this problem for many years. Beginning at least as early as 1970, when the Fair Credit Reporting Act (FCRA) became law, the drafters of U.S. privacy laws have recognized that data privacy and data security go hand in hand.[1] The FCRA requires credit reporting agencies to "maintain reasonable procedures" to ensure the accuracy of consumer report information and avoid disclosure of that information to unauthorized persons,[2] and recent privacy laws impose similar obligations concerning other kinds of personal information. Notably, the Children's Online Privacy Protection Act of 1998 (COPPA) requires commercial Web site operators that collect personal information from children to "establish and maintain reasonable procedures to protect the confidentiality, security, and integrity" of that information.[3] The Gramm-Leach-Bliley Act of 1999 (GLBA) requires regulators of financial institutions to adopt standards that will: "(1) ensure the security and confidentiality of customer records and information; (2) protect against any anticipated threats or hazards to the security or integrity of such records; and (3) protect against unauthorized access to or use of such records or information which could result in substantial harm or inconvenience to any customer."[4] Finally, the standards adopted pursuant to the Health Insurance Portability and Accountability Act (HIPAA) contain some of the most extensive information security regulations in place today.[5] All of these statutes and implementing regulations require businesses in specific industries, or engaged in specific activities, to identify and control internal and external threats that place the security of personal information at risk.

As important as these industry-specific statutes and regulations are (and we discuss them in detail in subsequent chapters), they leave many players in the U.S economy without clear information security guidelines, and leave consumers with no assurances that those companies are safeguarding their information.

This gap in data security protection and regulation has been filled, in recent years, by three types of legal initiatives. First, the Federal Trade Commission (FTC) has undertaken to create a data protection regime that applies to all U.S. businesses, regardless of industry (an effort that is mirrored by enforcement actions of the states under their various consumer protection statutes). Second, several states have adopted laws that require businesses to protect the security of customer information, including information contained in records that are in the process of disposal. Finally, the states have moved to require companies doing business in their jurisdictions to give notice to affected consumers whenever the security of personal information maintained by those companies is compromised.

This chapter describes each of these initiatives in turn, and also includes a brief discussion of efforts to obtain redress for data security losses under ordinary negligence principles. Finally, a section at the end of the chapter consists of a data security assessment proposal for our fictional company, Icarus Hang Gliders; and Appendix B of this book sets out key provisions of the data security, secure records disposal, and data security breach notification laws discussed in this chapter.

2.1 The FTC's Data Security Standard

The FTC's information security campaign is an exercise of that agency's broad consumer protection authority. As discussed in Chapter 1, the FTC Act empowers the FTC to bring enforcement actions against "unfair or deceptive acts or practices in or affecting commerce . . ."[6] When it wrote the FTC Act, Congress did not create a complete list of the schemes, scams, and frauds that might run afoul of this broad prohibition. Instead, it created an expert agency and empowered that agency to scrutinize business practices, write regulations, and bring individual enforcement actions in its discretion, subject to judicial review and congressional oversight.

The FTC has exercised this authority in a number of ways. Where the questionable practices of particular industries seemed systemic, or where the Congress specifically directed the Commission to write new rules, the Commission adopted regulations. As a result of this process, we now have FTC rules aimed at a number of industries and activities, including funeral services, labeling of textiles and clothing, debt collection, and telemarketing. The FTC also has brought individual enforcement actions aimed at a wide variety of questionable business practices, based either on alleged violations of the FTC's regulations or on violations of the FTC Act's broad prohibition against unfair or deceptive acts or practices.

Where information security is concerned, the FTC has so far chosen to bring individual enforcement actions rather than enact regulations. As described in the previous chapter, most of those actions have been based on alleged deception—specifically, failures to live up to security assurances contained in privacy policies and other public statements.[7] The FTC announced a new approach, however, when it alleged that the handling of personal information by BJ's Wholesale Club was defective to the point of unfairness, even in the absence of any public statements by the company on the subject.[8] By declaring that businesses with lax security could no longer hide behind silence, the Commission in BJ's case removed the last obstacle to its ambition to protect Americans' information security rights.[9]

2.1.1 The Content of the FTC's Data Security Standard

Against this background, and in the absence of an FTC regulation that sets out clear, comprehensive rules for U.S. businesses, what are the elements of the FTC's emerging data security standard?

We can try to ferret out the standard by reviewing all of the Commission's enforcement proceedings and asking: What were the targeted companies in these cases alleged to have done wrong, and what did they promise to do in order to avoid enforcement proceedings in the future? Whatever the elusive FTC standard is, it must at least require avoidance of the particular mistakes the FTC already has challenged, and implementation of safeguards of the kind the FTC already has required.

This approach, in turn, takes us to two sets of documents: (1) the FTC's complaints against Eli Lilly, Microsoft, and the other targets of its enforcement proceedings; and (2) the consent agreements entered into between the FTC and those companies.

If we first review the *complaints*, we come up with the following unsystematic list of data security violations and obligations:

- It is a violation of the FTC Act to send e-mail messages to customers that reveal, in the "From" line, the e-mail addresses of all recipients. Companies must prevent such incidents by training and overseeing employees who send e-mail messages to customers, specifically with reference to protection of customers' e-mail addresses from disclosure to other customers (*Eli Lilly*).
- It is a violation of the Act to fail to review and protect computer programs that control transmission of e-mails to customers (*Eli Lilly*).
- It is a violation of the Act to fail to use reasonable and appropriate procedures to prevent unauthorized access to computer systems that contain consumer information (*Microsoft*).
- It is a violation of the Act to fail to monitor computer systems that contain consumer information for possible vulnerabilities (*Microsoft*).
- Companies must record and retain system information sufficient to perform security audits and investigations of computer systems that contain consumer information (*Microsoft*).
- Companies must adopt policies and procedures that are adequate to protect sensitive consumer information collected through a Web site (*Guess?, Inc., Tower, Petco*).
- Companies must test or otherwise assess a Web site's vulnerability to attacks that might disclose sensitive consumer information (*Guess?, Inc., Tower*).
- Companies must implement reasonable measures to prevent Web site visitors from gaining access to databases containing sensitive personal information about other consumers (*Tower, Petco*).
- Companies must provide appropriate oversight and training for employees regarding Web application vulnerabilities and security testing (*Tower*).

- Companies must take appropriate measures, specifically, to prevent broken account and session management (*Tower*).[10]
- A company that promises to maintain consumer's information in an encrypted format may not encrypt that information only during transmission, but also must encrypt that information while stored in the company's server (*Petco*).
- Companies must encrypt payment card information while in transit or when stored on in-store computer networks (*BJ's Wholesale Club*).
- It is a violation of the Act to permit files containing payment card information to be accessed with default user IDs and passwords (*BJ's Wholesale Club*).
- Companies must use readily available security measures to limit access to computer networks containing payment card data through wireless access points (*BJ's Wholesale Club*).
- It is a violation of the Act to store payment card data after there is no business need to retain that information (*BJ's Wholesale Club*).

This list of do's and don'ts tells us which practices the FTC has challenged in the past, but does not provide a way of identifying those practices that *might* be challenged in the future. For example, BJ's Wholesale Club apparently should have encrypted its stored payment card transaction data—but what if a store maintains personal information other than card data? Does the FTC Act also require encryption of noncard personal information? Similarly, what are "reasonable and appropriate procedures to prevent unauthorized access to computer systems" or to secure Web sites from attacks on associated databases? What "system information" must be retained in order to perform security audits and investigations? What form should security audits and investigations take, and how should those be performed? Compliance with these requirements might call for any of a wide range of measures, varying significantly in their effectiveness and cost to the organization. In order to choose among the alternatives, we need a standard that helps us make real-world choices in the present and future—not just a random list of choices that have been found wanting in the past.

In search of such guidance, we turn from the FTC's *complaints* to its *consent agreements*. These various agreements are almost identical in their principal terms, and require the consenting companies to implement security programs that do much more than correct the vulnerabilities that gave rise to the associated complaints.[11] Because the consent agreements are both comprehensive and consistent, they look an awfully lot like real standards intended to guide the future conduct, not just of the companies that signed the agreements, but of all businesses that handle personal information. A prudent business will assume that this is exactly how the FTC intends them to be read.

With some variations, the consent agreements include the following parts.

Promises Not to Deceive

In cases in which the respondent company was accused of misrepresenting its data security practices, the consent agreements require that the companies not make similar deceptive statements in the future. The Eli Lilly consent agreement, for example, includes the following language:[12]

> IT IS ORDERED that respondent shall not misrepresent in any manner, expressly or by implication, the extent to which it maintains and protects the privacy or confidentiality of any personally identifiable information collected from or about consumers, in connection with the advertising, marketing, offering for sale or sale, in or affecting commerce, of any pharmaceutical, medical or other health-related product or service by respondent's Lilly USA division, directly or through any corporation, subsidiary, division, or other entity.

In the *Microsoft* case, that company agreed to refrain from making several types of representations concerning its data security:[13]

> IT IS ORDERED that respondent, directly or through any corporation, subsidiary, division, or other device, in connection with the online advertising, marketing, promotion, offering for sale, or sale of a covered online service, in or affecting commerce, shall not misrepresent in any manner, expressly or by implication, its information practices, including:
>
> A. what personal information is collected from or about consumers;
> B. the extent to which respondent's product or service will maintain, protect or enhance the privacy, confidentiality, or security of any personally identifiable information collected from or about consumers;
> C. the steps respondent will take with respect to personal information it has collected in the event that it changes the terms of the privacy policy in effect at the time the information was collected;
> D. the extent to which the service allows parents to control what information their children can provide to participating sites or the use of that information by such sites; and
> E. any other matter regarding the collection, use or disclosure of personally identifiable information.

These commitments to refrain from misleading statements do not appear in all of the consent agreements—only those that settled claims of alleged deception—but they underscore a point that the FTC expects all businesses to heed. Specifically, an information security program should be strong enough to back up the company's privacy policy and other public statements, or those statements will be challenged as deceptive.

Promises to Adopt a Written Security Program (and Put Someone in Charge)

In each of the FTC's data security consent agreements, respondents agreed to establish and maintain an information security program. Beginning with the *Microsoft* settlement, the consent agreements have required those programs to be in writing and to contain certain common elements. The *Guess?, Inc.* settlement, for example, includes the following commitment:[14]

> IT IS FURTHER ORDERED that Respondent, directly or through any corporation, subsidiary, division, or other device, in connection with the online advertising, marketing, promotion, offering for sale, or sale of any product or service, in or affecting commerce, shall establish and maintain a comprehensive information security program, in writing that is reasonably designed to protect the security, confidentiality, and integrity of personal information collected from or about

> consumers. Such program shall contain administrative, technical, and physical safeguards appropriate to Respondent's size and complexity, the nature and scope of Respondent's activities, and the sensitivity of the personal information collected from or about consumers . . .

Several features of this standard commitment are worth noting.

First, the respondent's plan will not satisfy the FTC unless it is written down. As anyone who has been the target of an FTC data security investigation can attest, this requirement is critical. Early in any such investigation, the Commission will ask to see your company's written security program, and the FTC will be very skeptical of any claim that your company follows procedures for which no documentation can be produced.

Second, the program must include *administrative*, *technical*, and *physical* safeguards against unauthorized acquisition of personal information or other security breaches. This is the FTC's way of saying that the plan must take all of the aspects of information security into account. For example, a firewall is a fine technical means of protecting your server from outside attacks, but you must also have a schedule and process for updating the firewall (an administrative measure), and you should put a lock on the server room door to protect that server against flesh-and-blood intruders (a physical measure). To be adequate, the safeguards for securing any item of valuable personal information will combine administrative, technical, and physical measures.

Third, the standard consent agreement acknowledges, in language that many companies might find deceptively soothing, that not all organizations must have equally complex and expensive information security programs. If your company is small, if the amount of personal information you maintain is small, or if that information you maintain is not highly sensitive, your program may reasonably reflect those facts. Companies must be very cautious, however, in deciding that their size or the type of information they maintain gives them a license to cut corners on data security. In the event of an investigation, the burden will be on you to prove that more extensive security measures were not warranted.

Finally, each of the consent agreements entered into so far requires the targeted company to put someone in charge of its information security program. In the case of a very large company, this might be a Chief Privacy Officer. In other companies, the Chief Financial Officer, General Counsel, Chief Information Officer, or Compliance Officer might add this function to his or her other duties. Regardless of how the responsibility is assigned, companies should ensure that the person who runs the information security program has the knowledge, authority, and resources to do the job properly.

Promises to Conduct a Risk Assessment

A critical element of the required information security program is the *risk assessment*. In each of the FTC consent agreements, the targeted companies agreed that the administrative, technical, and physical safeguards they adopted would be appropriate based on an assessment of the real-world risks of unauthorized acquisition or other compromise of the personal information those companies maintain. For example, the commitments made by Tower in its consent agreement include:[15]

> The identification of material internal and external risks to the security, confidentiality, and integrity of personal information that could result in the unauthorized disclosure, misuse, loss, alteration, destruction, or other compromise of such information, and assessment of the sufficiency of any safeguards in place to control these risks. At a minimum, the risk assessment should include consideration of risks in each area of relevant operation, including, but not limited to: (1) employee training and management; (2) information systems, including network and software design, information processing, storage, transmission, and disposal; and (3) prevention, detection, and response to attacks, intrusions, or other systems failures.

The risk assessment is a critical part of the information security process. Until your company has identified the ways in which personal information can be compromised at each stage of its life cycle, from creation to disposal, and whether recorded in paper or electronic form, you can never be assured that your information security program is complete.

Promises to Review and Modify the Program

Changed circumstances, including new laws and the addition or elimination of lines of business, can make an information security program obsolete. In order to detect and accommodate these changes, the FTC requires companies to reassess and update their programs regularly. For example, the Eli Lilly consent agreement includes the following language:[16]

- Conducting an annual written review by qualified persons, within ninety (90) days after the date of service of this order and yearly thereafter, which review shall monitor and document compliance with the program, evaluate the program's effectiveness, and recommend changes to it; and
- Adjusting the program in light of any findings and recommendations resulting from reviews or ongoing monitoring, and in light of any material changes to its operations that affect the program.

In some settlement agreements, the FTC requires the reviews to be conducted by outside experts, and requires the expert reviewer to certify the sufficiency of the respondents' programs.[17]

2.1.2 How to Comply with the FTC Standard

Many elements of the FTC standard, as reflected in the complaints and consent agreements, remain frustratingly vague no matter how closely they are examined. Notably, the FTC refers to "reasonable" and "appropriate" measures, without offering much guidance as to which practices it will find to be "reasonable" and "appropriate" (although, as we have noted, the facts alleged in specific FTC complaints give us examples of practices that apparently *failed* those tests). The Commission also implies that reasonable and appropriate measures will address each of the vulnerabilities discovered in the course of a risk assessment, but gives no specific guidance as to how a risk assessment should be performed.

In the absence of a clear yardstick in the FTC documents themselves, affected companies must look outside those sources for guidance as to the types of safeguards and practices, including risk assessment procedures, that a regulator might find to be sufficient. In this connection, companies should keep in mind that the FTC and its personnel are not experts in the various disciplines that combine to make an information security program. In judging the adequacy of your program, the FTC may rely heavily on "best practice" templates and guidelines that have been developed by private industry, standards-making bodies, and expert governmental organizations.[18] The FTC also will expect companies to guard against threats that have become widely known among information security or information technology experts.[19] Accordingly, you should be aware of the practices of other companies in your industry, if that information can be obtained, and the recommendations of authorities that command respect in your industry or among experts in the data security field. No matter how carefully your information security program is constructed, your company's failure to meet standards that have become accepted for organizations of comparable size and scope, dealing with similarly sensitive information, will be hard to justify.

Accepted standards and procedures for conducting risk assessments are available from a number of sources, including the National Institute of Standards and Technology (NIST) Special Publication 800-30,[20] The Carnegie-Mellon Software Engineering Institute OCTAVE system,[21] and the Facilitated Risk Analysis Process (FRAP) developed by Tom Peltier.[22] Whichever method is used, a true risk assessment will include substantial fact-gathering; valuation of the company's information assets; identification of threats, threat agents, and vulnerabilities that might result in loss-causing events; measures of the potential magnitude of losses that threats might cause; and examination of the sufficiency of existing safeguards to address those threats and vulnerabilities. Expert assistance with this process will greatly enhance the assessment's credibility and value.

To give some flavor of the data security risk assessment process, a sample proposal for such an assessment, made to our fictional company, Icarus Hang Gliders, appears in Section 2.7 of this chapter.

Similarly, a number of standards and best practices have evolved for all the elements of information security that your program will address. Documents that can be helpful include NIST Special Publications 800-12 and 800-53,[23] the Director of Central Intelligence Directive 6/3 Manual,[24] Control Objectives for Information and Related Technology (COBIT),[25] Generally Accepted Information Security Practices (GAISP),[26] and ISO 17799.[27] These sources, although they differ in their details and levels of specificity, all attempt to define a set of core information security practices that organizations maintaining sensitive information should implement to the extent consistent with the size and scope of their operations.

2.2 State Enforcement Actions

The states also have brought enforcement actions for alleged failure to respect privacy commitments and protect the security of customer information. These actions generally are based on state consumer protection statutes, many of which permit injured consumers to bring private lawsuits and at least two of which authorize class action suits.[28]

One of these actions was settled in August 2002, when New York State Attorney General (now Governor) Spitzer announced a multistate Assurance of Discontinuance (Assurance) with Ziff-Davis Media, Inc., which had suffered a security breach in connection with an online promotional offer for free subscriptions to one of its magazines. (California and Vermont also were parties to the settlement.) The breach resulted in disclosure of a subscription data file and some customers' credit card information. Ziff-Davis notified customers of the problem and acted within an hour to take the insecure promotion page offline. Those actions, and an internal review of its data control practices, were undertaken by Ziff-Davis before commencement of the state investigation. Nonetheless, the states alleged that Ziff-Davis had breached its privacy policy, which pledged that the company "use[d] reasonable precautions to keep . . . personal information [disclosed to the Ziff-Davis magazines and Web site] secure."[29]

As in the FTC's actions against Eli Lilly, Microsoft, Guess?, Tower, and BJ's, the terms of the Ziff-Davis settlement went well beyond retraction of false privacy assurances, or even correction of the cause of the breach that gave rise to the investigation. The settlement required Ziff-Davis to undertake a wide range of substantive security practices and measures, including encryption of sensitive consumer data and implementation of "standard practices relating to the privacy, security, and integrity of Consumer Data, where such standards have gained sufficient industry acceptance and adoption such that Ziff-Davis' adherence to the standards would not unreasonably place Ziff-Davis at a competitive disadvantage."[30] In addition, the settlement required Ziff-Davis to pay $500 to each subscriber who had provided credit card information during the promotion.

The states also have begun to invoke "unfairness" theories of the kind relied on by the FTC in the *BJ's Wholesale Club* case. On June 6, 2005, the Ohio Attorney General announced that DSW, Inc. (DSW), a retailer of shoes, had committed an "unfair or deceptive act or practice" under Ohio law when it failed to notify all affected customers of a theft of personal information concerning transactions made by means of checking accounts, credit cards, and debit cards.[31] Although the complaint alleged that DSW's conduct was both deceptive and unfair, there is no allegation that DSW had made any commitments to consumers concerning disclosure of data security incidents. Accordingly, the complaint is effectively an unfairness action and signals the willingness of at least one state to act, as the FTC acted in the BJ's case, against companies that have given no assurances as to their data security practices.

2.3 State Secure Disposal Laws

At the time of this writing, at least 26 states require companies doing business in those states, or maintaining records that include personal information of residents of those states, to take reasonable measures to prevent the unauthorized disclosure of personal information contained in such records when they are undergoing disposal.[32] California's statutory language is typical:[33]

> A business shall take all reasonable steps to destroy, or arrange for the destruction of a customer's records within its custody or control containing personal information which is no longer to be retained by the business by (1) shredding, (2) erasing, or (3) otherwise modifying the personal information in those records to make it unreadable or undecipherable through any means.

These state secure disposal laws impose obligations similar to those of the FTC's Disposal Rule adopted pursuant to the Fair and Accurate Credit Transactions Act (FACTA), discussed later in this book. The principal difference between the FACTA Disposal Rule and the state secure disposal statutes, however, is that the state statutes are not confined to disposal of information derived from consumer reports. The state disposal laws apply to a wide variety of categories of personal information, and are intended to give consumers the broadest scope of protection.

A number of state enforcement proceedings already have been brought under these secure disposal laws, with most of those actions involving discovery by law enforcement agencies of paper records discarded in dumpsters and other insecure disposal locations.

Key provisions of the state secure disposal statutes are set out in Appendix B.

2.4 Comprehensive State Data Security Protection Laws

In May 2007, Maryland enacted its new Personal Information Protection Act. Effective January 1, 2008, the new Maryland law combined secure records disposal obligations and a data security breach notification requirement. Tucked in among those familiar obligations, however, and with no separate heading or other means of calling attention to itself, there appeared the following language:

> To protect personal information from unauthorized access, use, notification, or disclosure, a business that owns or licenses personal information of an individual residing in the state shall implement and maintain reasonable security procedures and practices that are appropriate to the nature of the personal information owned or licensed and the nature and size of the business and its operations.[34]
>
> A business that uses a nonaffiliated third party as a service provider to perform services for the business and discloses personal information about an individual residing in the state under a written contract with the third party shall require by contract that the third implement and maintain reasonable security procedures and practices that:
>
> (1) are appropriate to the nature of the personal information disclosed to the nonaffiliated third party; and
>
> (2) are reasonably designed to help protect the personal information from unauthorized access, use, modification, disclosure, or destruction.[35]

With these provisions, Maryland quietly joined at least six other states (as of this writing) whose laws go well beyond the security disposal and security breach notification obligations that have been the focus of most state data security legislation in recent years. Like Maryland, the seven other states—Arkansas, California, Nevada, Oregon, Rhode Island, Texas, and Utah—include these provisions as part of their secure disposal or breach notification statutes.[36] In view of their importance, however, these provisions deserve to be highlighted and discussed separately as comprehensive state "information security" laws. Taken together, these laws create a data security regime that: (1) covers a broad range of personal information, regardless of its origins or medium of storage; (2) requires that personal information be protected at all stages of its life cycle; and (3) in the case of three of the statutes, provides that companies that disclose personal information to vendors must require those vendors to take reasonable measures to protect that information.

Key provisions of the comprehensive state data protection laws are set out in Appendix B.

2.4.1 The State Information Security Laws Apply to a Wide Range of Information and Media

The state information security laws define the types of personal information to which they apply very broadly. California, for example, defines "personal information" to include "an individual's first name or first initial and his or her last name in combination with" a Social Security number, a driver's license or California identification card number, an account number, credit or debit card number (in combination with an access code), or medical information.[37] The other statutes' definitions of the information they protect are similarly broad.

These definitions go beyond the data categories covered by many other state and federal laws. Many of the state data security breach notification statutes, for example, apply only to computerized data; the data protection obligations of the Gramm-Leach-Bliley Act (GLBA) and the Health Insurance Portability and Accountability Act (HIPPA) reach only financial and health care information, respectively; and the Disposal Rule adopted by the FTC under FACTA applies specifically to information derived from credit reports. The state information security laws have no comparable limitations. They effectively reach all important categories of personal information, regardless of the sources from which they are collected or the media in which they are stored.

2.4.2 The State Laws Protect Information at All Stages of Its Life Cycle

As discussed in Section 2.3, a majority of states now have enacted laws that require businesses to protect the security of records when they are discarded or destroyed. The information security laws enacted by Maryland and seven other states, however, require businesses to protect the security of personal information whenever that information is collected or maintained, as well as when it is discarded.

With this expanded coverage, the eight states effectively mandate all of the technical, administrative, and physical "best practice" measures by which responsible companies protect information from unauthorized access, disposal, and use. Those measures might range from antivirus software and firewalls, to employee security training, to secure records storage and control of physical access to premises where personal information is maintained. In fact, the states may even look to the terms of the FTC's data security consent agreements, discussed earlier, in deciding how to interpret and apply the obligations set out in these laws.

2.5 The States' Data Security Breach Notification Laws

When a company experiences a security incident that has not come to the attention of the public, the temptation is to fix the problem, keep quiet, and move on. With California's enactment in 2003 of the first data security breach notification law, however, the states began to foreclose this option. Since California's law was enacted, at least 39 additional states have written similar laws, creating what is effectively an obligation to notify consumers nationwide when a security breach is discovered.[38]

The state breach notification laws already on the books create a crazy-quilt of obligations for U.S. business. All of those statutes require business and/or public organizations to report certain occurrences involving defined categories of unencrypted personal information, and all of those statutes impose penalties for failure to comply. The laws vary widely, however, in significant ways, including the entities to which they apply, the types of information they are intended to protect, and the level of the security breaches that give rise to a duty to report.

For example, some of the state laws apply to all persons or businesses within the state that own or license personal information (although they may exempt financial and health care organizations already subject to federal data security regulations).[39] Other states limit their breach notification requirements to specially-defined entities, such as "information brokers"[40] and "data collectors."[41] Still other laws apply to state agencies and political subdivisions.[42]

Equally confusing is the range of "personal information" categories to which the breach notification laws apply. For example, most of the statutes apply to "computerized" personal data; but North Carolina's law requires notification of breaches of the security of "personal information in any form (whether computerized, paper, or otherwise)."[43] Similarly, most of the statutes define the "personal information" to which they apply as including a person's name combined with one or more standard items, such as a Social Security number, driver's license number, or financial account numbers and access codes.[44] Some laws, however, cover additional categories of data, such as date of birth, mother's maiden name, medical history, and digital signatures.[45]

Even more confusing are the states' different definitions of the circumstances that constitute reportable security breaches. This element of the statutes is especially important to both businesses and consumers. At one extreme, consumers will not benefit from (and will learn to ignore) repeated notices of trivial system incidents that create no real risk of identity theft or other harm. At the other extreme, notifications that are withheld until harm to consumers is confirmed may be "too little, too late" to prevent losses. Ideally, breach notification laws will strike a balance between these extremes, by only requiring companies to give notice of breaches that create a significant, if less than certain, risk that personal information has fallen into the wrong hands and will be misused.

Many of the notification laws now on the books resolve this dilemma by erring on the side of more notice rather than less. The template for this type of statute is the California law, which requires disclosure of "any breach of the security of the system following discovery or notification of the breach in the security of the data to any resident of California whose unencrypted personal information was, or is reasonably believed to have been, acquired by an unauthorized person."[46] "Breach of the security of the system," in turn, is defined by California and many other states as "unauthorized acquisition of computerized data that compromises the security, confidentiality, or integrity of personal information maintained by the person or business."[47]

Under this "California" standard, the duty to notify is triggered whenever there is a risk that an unauthorized person has *acquired* personal data, even if there are no specific facts to suggest that the information will be used to harm consumers. For example, a company might discover the theft of a laptop computer that contains unencrypted personal information. The company might have no reason to believe that the thief was interested in the stored information. Nevertheless, if the laptop contains personal information of residents of California, or of any of the other states that have adopted the California approach, notification of the incident likely would be required simply because an unauthorized person—knowingly or not—now has access to the information stored in the laptop's hard drive.

Some states, however, let businesses decide *not* to disclose certain breaches that might have resulted in unauthorized acquisition of personal information. Specifically, some states have adopted "risk of harm" statutes that require notice only if the breach is reasonably likely to result in criminal activity or other harm to consumers. A company in such a "risk of harm" state might, for example, choose not to disclose the theft of a laptop that was promptly recovered from a local pawnshop, on the assumption that the thief was simply looking for quick cash and had neither the time nor the motivation to acquire and misuse the personal data stored on the machine. (Of course, if the thief later turns out to have downloaded the data and turned it over to an identity theft ring before pawning the laptop, the company's decision will be liberally second-guessed by affected consumers and state authorities.)

In order to resolve the confusion created by the conflicting provisions of the state data security breach notification statutes, a number of Senators and Representatives have introduced federal laws that potentially would create a uniform federal obligation.

For an idea of the wide range of approaches that proposed federal legislation can take, it is useful to examine the two bills that were serious contenders for enactment in 2007. Senate Bill 239, introduced by Senator Diane Feinstein (D-California) and known as the Notification of Risk to Personal Data Act of 2007, was similar to legislation she introduced in 2006 that cleared the Senate Judiciary Committee but did not proceed further. Senate Bill 495, known as the Personal Data Privacy and Security Act of 2007, cosponsored by Senator Patrick Leahy (D-Vermont) and Senator Bernie Sanders (I-Vermont), was similar to a bill Senator Leahy introduced in 2006 with Senator Arlen Specter (R-Pennsylvania).

The breach notification provisions of the Feinstein and Leahy bills were nearly identical. Both would apply only to computerized records, and both would exempt companies from notification obligations if a risk assessment gave no reason to believe that individuals were harmed by the breach (although the Secret Service would have to be notified of intent to rely on this exemption).

Specifically, under both bills, any agency or business entity that engaged in interstate commerce "that use[d], access[ed], transmit[ted], store[d], dispose[d] of or collect[ed] sensitive personally identifiable information [would be required], following the discovery of a security breach . . . [to] notify any resident of the United States whose sensitive personally identifiable information ha[d] been, or [was] reasonably believed to have been, accessed, or acquired." S 239 sec. 2(a); S 495 sec. 311(a). The bills defined "security breach" as "compromise of the security, confidentiality, or integrity of computerized data through misrepresentation or actions that result in, or there is a reasonable basis to conclude has resulted in, acquisition of or access to sensitive personally identifiable information that is unauthorized or in excess of authorization." S 239 sec. 13(5)(A); S 495 sec. 10(A). However, notice would not be required if "a risk assessment conclude[d] that there [was] no significant risk that the security breach ha[d] resulted in, or [would] result in, harm to the individuals whose sensitive personally identifiable information was subject to the security breach." S 239 sec. 3(b)(1); S 495 sec. 312(b). A company that intended to invoke the "risk assessment" exemption, however, would be required to notify the Secret Service in writing of its intent to do so. S 239 sec. 3(b)(2); S 495 sec. 312(b)(2)–(3).

Although the breach notification provisions of both bills were similar, the Leahy bill contained other provisions that went well beyond the Feinstein bill. Besides its security breach notification requirements, the Leahy bill required certain businesses that maintain sensitive personally identifiable information to establish data privacy and security programs similar to those mandated by the Federal Trade Commission Safeguards Rule. Senator Leahy also wanted criminal penalties for intentional failure to report a breach, and would have given individuals the right to review and obtain correction of personal information held in databases for third parties.

Also, the Leahy bill expressly would have required businesses to ensure that sensitive personally identifiable information was properly destroyed and disposed of, including during the destruction of computers, diskettes, and other electronic media that contain sensitive personally identifiable information.

Table 2.1 gives a side-by-side comparison of the Feinstein and Leahy bills.

Table 2.1 Key Provisions of the State Data Security Breach Notification Statutes Are Set Out in Appendix B

Feinstein Bill S 239	*Leahy Bill S 495*
Breach notification required unless risk assessment shows no reason to believe that individuals have been harmed. Notice must be given to Secret Service of intent to rely on "risk assessment" exemption.	Breach notification required unless risk assessment shows no reason to believe that individuals have been harmed. Notice must be given to Secret Service of intent to rely on "risk assessment" exemption (same as Feinstein bill).
Notification must be made to affected individuals and, if persons affected or size of database exceeds certain thresholds, or certain other conditions are met, to the Secret Service.	Notification must be made to affected individuals and, if persons affected or size of database exceeds certain thresholds, or certain other conditions are met, to the Secret Service (same as Feinstein bill).

Table 2.1 (Continued)

Feinstein Bill S 239	*Leahy Bill S 495*
Reasonable delay allowed for law enforcement reasons or as needed to investigate breach.	Reasonable delay allowed for law enforcement reasons or as needed to investigate breach (same as Feinstein bill).
No right of individuals to disclosure and correction of personal electronic records.	Individuals *have* right to disclosure and correction of personal electronic records maintained by data brokers on behalf of third parties.
Breach notification obligations apply only to computerized records.	Breach notification obligations apply only to computerized records (same as Feinstein bill).
No criminal liability for intentional concealment of data security breach.	Criminal liability for intentional concealment of data security breach.
Enforcement and Penalties:	Enforcement and Penalties:
Private lawsuits by affected individuals not authorized.	Private lawsuits by affected individuals not authorized.
For violations of breach notification requirements, the U.S. Attorney General may obtain an injunction or civil penalties of not more than $1,000 per day per individual whose sensitive personally identifiable information was, or is reasonably believed to have been, accessed or acquired by an unauthorized person, up to a maximum of $50,000 per person. State attorneys general may obtain similar relief.	For violation of breach notification requirements, civil penalties of not more than $1,000 per day per individual whose information has been or is believed to have been accessed by an unauthorized person, up to a maximum of $1,000,000 per violation, unless the conduct is found to be willful or intentional. Enforcement by U.S. Attorney General or state attorneys general.
	For intentional concealment of security breach, fines, imprisonment for up to five years, or both (no counterpart provision in Feinstein bill). For failure of data broker to permit inspection and correction of records, or for certain other violations, injunction, civil penalties of up to $1,000 per violation per day up to a maximum of $250,000 per day. If violations are willful, additional penalties of $1,000 per day to a maximum of $250,000 per violation. These data broker provisions are enforceable by the Federal Trade Commission. State and local authorities also may bring enforcement actions. (No counterpart provisions in the Feinstein bill.) For failure to implement the required data security plan, civil penalties of not more $5,000 per violation per day, to a maximum of $500,000 per violation. If violations are willful, additional penalties of $5,000 per violation per day, with a maximum of $500,000 per violation. These provisions are enforceable by Federal Trade Commission and state authorities. (No counterpart provisions in Feinstein bill.)
State breach notification laws are preempted, except that states may provide for victim protection assistance notices.	State breach notification laws are preempted, except that states may provide for victim protection assistance notices (same as Feinstein bill).

2.6 Private Negligence Actions

Most of the legal actions against companies that allegedly failed to protect personal data have been brought by public consumer protection and law enforcement agencies, and have alleged violations of consumer protection laws and other statutes. Fewer actions have been brought by private parties under common-law theories such as negligence, breach of contract, or breach of fiduciary duty.

The obstacles to private actions against companies that suffer data breaches are substantial. Contract actions are available only to plaintiffs that had a contractual relationship with the defendant, and the damages that can be awarded in contract cases are limited. Similarly, claims that a defendant breached a fiduciary duty by failing to protect personal information generally are available only against physicians, lawyers, accountants, and other professionals that owe their clients and patients more than an ordinary duty of care.

Because of these limitations of the remedies available for breach of contract and breach of fiduciary duty claims, potential plaintiffs and their lawyers will explore the potential of negligence and other torts. Tort actions may be brought against nonprofessionals and persons with whom the plaintiff did not have a contract, and also have the potential for higher awards of damages than those available in contract law.

Unfortunately for plaintiffs and their attorneys, there is no settled body of law that recognizes a cause of action in tort for failure to protect personal information of others. In the absence of controlling precedent, tort plaintiffs in data security cases have the pioneers' task of: (1) proving that such a duty exists, and (2) defining the standard of care that the duty imposes. When a court is convinced on those points, the plaintiff then must prove that the defendant failed to meet the standard of care, and that the defendant's failure caused an injury to the plaintiff for which damages may be awarded.

Although the law is developing slowly, some courts have found that persons who maintain personal information of others must exercise reasonable care to protect that information. Notably, in *Remsburg v. Docusearch, Inc.*, a state court found that an information broker could be liable in tort for damages resulting from the murder of a woman whose personal information was wrongfully obtained, in part, by a "pretexting" call to the victim by an agent of the broker.[48] Among other findings, the court held that increasing awareness of stalking and identity theft made "the risk of criminal misconduct . . . sufficiently foreseeable so that an investigator has a duty to exercise reasonable care in disclosing a third party's personal information to a client."[49] Accordingly, the court found that negligence in disclosing such personal information could, if other elements of the tort were proved, expose the broker or detective to liability for intrusion on the decedent's seclusion.[50]

Even if the plaintiff in a data security tort action can establish a duty of care and the defendant's violation of that duty, proof of causation and injury may be insuperable obstacles to relief. Notably, many courts refuse to award damages for economic losses, unaccompanied by physical injury, in tort actions.[51] Similarly, even where the harm alleged by a plaintiff is sufficient to form a basis for damages, it may be hard to prove a causal link between a defendant's negligent handling of information and an instance of identity theft or other injurious conduct.[52]

Although private tort actions based on insecure handling of information face many obstacles, the increasing public attention to identity theft, and the proliferation of regulations that might be cited as creating a clear standard of care for persons maintaining personal information, mean that efforts to obtain relief in tort will continue to be made when personal information is compromised.

2.7 A Data Security Assessment Proposal for Icarus Hang Gliders, Inc.

The risk assessment process described here will help Icarus decide whether its data security measures are appropriate to the risks those measures are meant to address, and reprioritize its use of data security resources as necessary. The process will also create a record that can be used, in the event of a data security incident or investigation, to show that the data security measures Icarus adopted were the product of a risk assessment study of the kind required by regulators and sound business practice.

Risk assessments often are highly complex, but the one described here takes a straightforward approach that can be implemented without excessive cost in time or money. An assessment of this kind can be conducted in-house if qualified personnel are available, or can be outsourced to a data security contractor. A contractor likely will follow its own risk assessment template, but Icarus should ensure that the contractor's process includes the essential elements set out here.[53]

A risk assessment can usefully be divided into four stages. In the *asset valuation and classification* stage, the company identifies its principal information assets and categorizes them according to their value, defined as the impact on the company if those assets are destroyed, altered, or disclosed without authorization. (We sometimes refer to unauthorized destruction, alteration, and disclosure collectively as *adverse events.*) Depending on their classifications in this process, Icarus's information assets will receive different levels of protection in Icarus's data security plan. In the *risk identification* stage, the company identifies the personnel-based, facilities-based, and information system–based vulnerabilities that might increase the likelihood of adverse events. In the *data security evaluation* stage, the company compares its present data security measures to the best-practice measures that U.S. corporations generally use to control vulnerabilities of the kinds identified in the risk identification stage, and identifies any data security shortfalls that must be corrected. Finally, in the *risk management* stage, the company adopts and implements a data security plan, including the written policies, training programs, and technical measures that are needed to carry out that plan.

Finally, the company should conduct a follow-up risk assessment after the data security plan is in place, and should conduct periodic data security audits thereafter.

The following describes how each stage of the risk assessment process works.

2.7.1 Asset Valuation and Classification

The asset valuation and classification stage is an opportunity for Icarus to inventory its information assets and assess the kinds and extent of harm the company will incur if those assets are destroyed, altered, or disclosed. Based on that assessment, Icarus can classify its information assets according to the level of protection it should receive under Icarus's Data Security Plan and Document Classification and Protection Plan.

What Are Icarus's Information Assets?

An information asset is any item of information, regardless of the form in which it is stored, distributed, or transmitted, that has value to the company. Such assets include Icarus's trade secrets, business plans, customer data, internal and external correspondence, records of clinical studies, payroll information, accounting records, and any other information that is retained and used by the company for business purposes.

Because information is retained in many forms, a useful inventory of information assets will note each type of print or electronic record in which an asset is stored. For example, Icarus's company directory might be kept in print form in the company's paper files; it also might be found in electronic form on Icarus's server, and on CD-ROMs and diskettes at various locations on Icarus's premises. Because the vulnerability of an item of information varies according to the places and formats in which it is maintained, our asset inventory should note the different forms and places in which that asset is kept.

Although the information asset inventory should strive for completeness, the process also should be streamlined where appropriate. Notably, documents with common characteristics should be grouped into common categories whenever possible.

What Is the Value of Each Information Asset?

After Icarus's information assets have been inventoried, Icarus must determine the *value* of each of those assets and *classify* those assets accordingly.

For data security specialists, the value of an asset is not the benefit it provides to the company while the asset is secure; instead, the value of the asset is the loss that the company will suffer if the asset is compromised. (This also might be called the asset's "data security value" or "impairment value.")

Viewed in this way, the higher an asset's data security value, the greater the resources that can reasonably be devoted to protecting the asset. Accordingly, most companies rank their assets in some scheme of classification, from lowest value to highest value, and prescribe different storage, transmission, and distribution requirements for documents in each classification. For Icarus, we suggest four valuation categories: public, internal-use only, restricted, and highly restricted.

The *public* category includes materials that ordinarily are disclosed to the public, such as SEC filings and advertising copy. This is the least sensitive category: the company is not harmed, for example, if hackers obtain copies of Icarus's SEC filings from its server, or if employees take copies of Icarus's promotional materials off the premises and give them to third parties. Accordingly, costly security measures should not be implemented for the specific purpose of protecting public assets.

The *internal-use only* category includes routine information that Icarus has no reason to disseminate outside the company, but that will not cause appreciable harm to Icarus if it is disclosed. This category includes policies and newsletters distributed to employees, internal telephone directories, lists of employees' e-mail addresses, and organization charts. Adverse events affecting these assets might impose some costs: for example, if all copies of an internal directory are destroyed, it will cost Icarus something to rewrite it; and if employee telephone numbers and e-mail addresses are released to the public, company personnel may find themselves the targets of telemarketing calls and e-mail spam they would not otherwise receive, with resulting loss of productivity. Such adverse events, however, will not appreciably harm the company, and data security measures undertaken to prevent them should not be costlier than the impact of the potential events themselves.

The *restricted* category includes documents that will cause substantial harm to the company if compromised. As discussed further below, such harm may include economic loss, legal liability, gains to competitors and loss of reputation. Information of this kind includes current financial performance records and strategic business plans. Icarus's data security plan will closely restrict the handling of these assets, and will permit access based on job function and/or prior approval of the asset owner.

The *highly restricted* category includes all information assets, the compromise of which will directly and substantially harm the company's market position or shareholder value. This category includes trade secret information or other intellectual property, merger and acquisition plans, and other high-value business planning information. It also may include sensitive personal information of customers and employees. Icarus's data security plan will impose the most restrictive storage, transmission, and distribution requirements on this group of assets.

In classifying individual assets or groups of assets under this scheme, Icarus should not simply make an intuitive comparison of those assets to the verbal definitions of the four asset categories. In order to ensure that the data security value of each asset has been properly assessed before it is classified, Icarus should attempt, as to each asset, to quantify the harm that would result from each type of adverse event.

The first step in such a valuation process is to identify the *kinds of adverse events* that could reduce the value of each asset to the enterprise. As noted earlier, the most important such adverse events are unauthorized *destruction*, unauthorized *alteration*, and unauthorized *disclosure*. The Asset Valuation Worksheet shown in Table 2.2 lists each of these adverse events in the first column.

Next, for each of these adverse events, Icarus should determine the type and magnitude of loss that the event will cause. The most important kinds of loss are *economic loss*, *legal liability*, *gain to competitors*, and *loss of reputation*. Table 2.2 lists these types of losses as column headings.

Table 2.2 Asset Valuation Worksheet

Asset: *Adverse Event*	*Economic Loss*	*Legal Liability*	*Gain to Competitors*	*Loss of Reputation*
Unauthorized Destruction				
Unauthorized Alteration				
Unauthorized Disclosure				

Finally, we must quantify, for each asset, the *magnitude of loss* that would result from each adverse event. For this purpose, Tables 2.3, 2.4, 2.5, and 2.6 give possible magnitudes of economic loss, legal liability, gain to competitors, and loss of reputation that each adverse event might cause. For each such event, we should select the number corresponding to the range of dollar losses we can anticipate, and place that number under the appropriate heading on the Asset Valuation Worksheet.

A review of Tables 2.2 to 2.6 yields some useful rules of thumb for classification of information assets. Notably, no asset should be placed in the public or internal-use categories if the destruction, alteration, or disclosure of that asset would produce any level of reputational loss, legal liability, or gain to competitors. Also, no asset that would cost the company an appreciable amount of money to replace (say, more than $40,000, corresponding to an economic loss score of more than 3)

Table 2.3 Economic Loss Valuation

Economic Loss (Column 1)	*Valuation Score*
Less than $2,000	1
$2,000 to $15,000	2
$15,000 to $40,000	3
$40,000 to $100,000	4
$100,000 to $300,000	5
$300,000 to $1 million	6
$1 million to $3 million	7
$3 million to $10 million	8
$10 million to $30 million	9
$30 million or more	10

Table 2.4 Legal Liability Valuation

Legal Liability (Column 2)	*Valuation Score*
Under $5,000	1
$5,000 to $10,000	2
$10,000 to $50,000	3
$50,000 to $1 million	4
Over $1 million	5

Table 2.5 Valuation of Gain to Competitors

Gain to Competitors (Column 3)	*Valuation Score*
Less than $50,000	1
$50,000 to $100,000	2
$100,000 to $1 million	3
$1 million to $10 million	4
Over $10 million	5

Table 2.6 Loss of Reputation Valuation

Loss of Reputation (Column 4)	*Valuation Score*
Loss of Reputation with Existing Customers	1
Adverse press coverage: local, limited	2
Adverse press coverage: national or international	7
Adverse impact on shareholder value	10

should be classified as public or internal use. If an asset's destruction, alteration, or disclosure will cause no loss of reputation, no legal liability, no gain to competitors, and will not cost more than $40,000 to replace, then: (1) if it has been publicly disclosed, it should be placed in the public category; and (2) if it has not been publicly disclosed, it should be placed in the internal-use category.

Harder questions are presented when we try to distinguish restricted assets from highly restricted assets. By definition, both categories include only assets that, if compromised, will cause substantial harm—or worse—to the company. Although sound judgment always will be required, a few rules for drawing the line between these categories seem reasonable. Specifically, any asset that, if compromised, would yield a score of 10 for loss of reputation belongs in the highly restricted category. Similarly, any asset that rates over $3 million (a score of 8 to 10) for economic loss, over $1 million (a score of 4 or 5) for gain to competitors, or over $1 million (a score of 5) for legal liability belongs in the highly restricted category. Assets that would, if compromised, result in lower levels of financial loss or reputational harm, but that still would present some risk of adverse impact on market share or market value, should be assessed on a case-by-case basis and classified as highly restricted in doubtful cases. All other assets that fall below the "highly restricted" thresholds in each category of harm, but exceed the thresholds for public and internal-use assets, should be classified as restricted.

To summarize, the following guidelines seem reasonable for conversion of asset valuation scores to document classifications:

- A *public* document is one the destruction, alteration, or disclosure of which would not exceed an economic loss score of 3, a legal liability score of 0, a gain to competitors score of 0, or a loss of reputation score of 0.
- An *internal-use only* document is one the destruction, alteration, or disclosure of which would not exceed the loss thresholds defined for public documents.
- A *restricted* document is one the destruction, alteration, or disclosure of which would yield an economic loss score between 4 and 7, a legal liability score between 1 and 4, a gain to competitors score between 1 and 3, or a loss of reputation score between 1 and 7.
- A *highly restricted* document is one the destruction, alteration, or disclosure of which would yield an economic loss score between an 8 and 10, a legal liability score of 5, a gain to competitors score of 4 or 5, or a loss to reputation score of 10.

A Sample Asset Valuation

To show how an asset valuation works, we might apply the process to a hypothetical Icarus business plan. For purposes of this example, we assume that the business plan contains no "market-moving" information, such as a report on pending merger discussions, that would immediately require a highly restricted classification, but that it does discuss the advisability of moving into various markets or developing particular products during the next several years. Using the Asset Valuation Worksheet (Table 2.2) and Tables 2.3 to 2.6, what kinds and magnitudes of loss to the enterprise would result if this business plan were destroyed, altered, or disclosed?

The chief impact of *destruction* of the business plan document—unaccompanied by alteration or disclosure of the information contained therein—would be the need to create a new plan from the notes and research materials of the team that wrote the original. This kind of impact is best classified as an economic loss, measured by the salaries and benefits paid to the team while they are engaged in rewriting the plan and are unavailable for other projects. (If the plan was prepared by an outside consultant that must be hired to reconstitute it, then the consultants' fees are the principal measure of economic loss from this event.) If we decide that these costs will total between $40,000 and $100,000, then a number 4 goes under the "Economic Loss" heading on the "Unauthorized Destruction" line. Because mere destruction of the plan should not result in legal liability, gains to competitors, or loss to reputation, we should place a 0 under each of those headings on the "Unauthorized Destruction" line.

We go next to the impact of unauthorized *alteration* of the business plan. To assess the impact of this event, we must choose among some possible assumptions. For example, we might assume that the alterations will go undetected and will have no effect on Icarus's business decisions. In another scenario, the changes go undetected and are so critical that they cause Icarus to make bad business decisions because of reliance on false information or recommendations inserted in the document. In yet another scenario, Icarus discovers the alterations but concludes that they are trivial and takes no corrective action. In a final scenario, important alterations are detected that call the integrity of the entire document into question, forcing Icarus to undertake the same rewrite that destruction of the plan would have required.

If we reasonably can assume that unauthorized alterations will be readily detected and fixed, without the need to rewrite the whole plan and without anyone at Icarus relying on bad information to the company's detriment, then we might assign a score of 1 for economic loss (i.e., the cost of correcting the document), and scores of 0 for legal liability, gain to competitors, and loss to reputation.

Finally, and what is most serious, we must assess the impact of unauthorized disclosure of the business plan. Given our assumptions about the plan's contents, disclosure of such a document could cause significant economic loss to Icarus and corresponding gain to competitors, but not in magnitudes that will affect market share or shareholder value. We likely should place a 6 under the economic loss column and a 3 under the gains to competitors column. Legal liability and loss of reputation are less likely to result from disclosure of the business plan, so we might place a 0 under the legal liability column and another 0 in the loss to reputation column.

These scores place the business plan in the "restricted" category.

For another example of an asset valuation, we might consider a database of customer information. Assume, for purposes of this example, that the customer database is vital to Icarus's marketing efforts and a valuable business asset in itself. Deletion of customers' information from this database, or loss of access to the database, even without disclosure of that information to the outside world, could cause significant economic loss. At the same time, destruction of, or inability to access the customer database without disclosure of its contents likely would not give rise to legal liability, and would not directly benefit competitors or harm Icarus's reputation. Given these facts, it might be reasonable to assign a value of 10 to the economic loss resulting from deletion or destruction of the database, and a value of 0 for each of the loss categories of legal liability, gain to competitors, and loss of reputation.

Alteration of the customer database presents a similar range of possible assumptions to those presented by alteration of the business plan. For the sake of this example, we might assume that alteration of the database would make it far too risky to use as a basis for contacting customers and would seriously erode the price that could be charged to a potential purchaser of the database. Accordingly, the database would have to be abandoned or reconstituted at great cost to the company. Under these circumstances, we might assign alteration of the database a value of 9 for economic loss. Again, this unfortunate incident will not give rise to legal liability, will not confer any direct benefit on competitors, and will not harm Icarus's reputation, so a score of 0 in each of those categories of harm is appropriate.

Finally, disclosure of the customer database will be a serious matter, but so long as Icarus retains an intact copy of the database in its server, the value of the asset is not destroyed and the resulting economic loss might be only in the range of 1. (This is in contrast to the business plan, as to which disclosure was the most harmful form of compromise.) However, disclosure of customer data might result in a costly FTC or other investigation, private lawsuits, some loss of reputation, and (if competitors acquire the data) benefit to competitors. Accordingly, disclosure might only cause an economic loss of 1, but a gain to competitors of 3, loss of reputation of 7, and legal liability of 4.

These scores place the customer database in the "highly restricted" category.

As a third example, we might conduct a loss valuation of a set of Icarus's publicity brochures. Because this asset is intended to be disclosed to the public, has little intrinsic value, and can be readily reconstituted, neither destruction, alteration, nor disclosure of the contents of the brochures will cause substantial harm to Icarus in any category of loss. In fact, the most that will be required is that Icarus replace the brochures if they are destroyed or altered. If the cost of replacement wil bel \$2,000 to \$15,000, then an economic loss score of 2 is appropriate for both the destruction and alteration categories, and scores of 0 will be appropriate for all other events and categories of harm.

These scores, combined with the fact that the brochures are intended for distribution to the public, place the publicity brochures in the "public" category.

2.7.2 Risk Identification

The next step in the risk assessment process is to identify specific vulnerabilities—that is, security weaknesses—that might cause the adverse events of unauthorized destruction, unauthorized alteration, or unauthorized disclosure. This analysis should be performed for each of the assets covered by our asset inventory and asset valuation and classification processes.

In order to identify risks efficiently, it is useful to identify the areas of the business in which vulnerabilities are likely to be found. For most companies, unauthorized destruction, alteration, and disclosure of information assets can be traced to vulnerabilities in the areas of *personnel*, *facilities*, or *information systems*. Within each of these three categories, in turn, we can identify a number of specific vulnerabilities that must be assessed.

A. Personnel Vulnerabilities

Employees might cause unauthorized destruction, alteration, or disclosure of data in a number of ways. They may accidentally or deliberately destroy documents by violating document retention and destruction policies, or by compromising or misusing paper and electronic storage systems. They may alter documents, either deliberately or inadvertently. They may disclose documents to which they have been granted access; or may disclose data stored in documents and systems to which they have not been granted access, but that they have acquired by exceeding their authorized access. Finally, they may cause unauthorized destruction, alteration, or disclosure themselves, or may enable others to do so.

B. Facilities Vulnerabilities

These primarily involve the ability of unauthorized persons to enter and leave the premises, or the ability of employees and other authorized persons to enter sensitive areas or to remove information assets, stored in physical media, from the premises.

C. Information System Vulnerabilities

Information systems have a number of vulnerabilities. Some are the result of technical flaws in hardware and software that can be exploited by attackers. Others are the result of human exploitation of systems that are working correctly. In the first category, for example, are "back doors" in programs, left deliberately or inadvertently by programmers, that are discovered by hackers and may be exploited before a "patch" can be deployed. Examples of the second category are acquisitions of passwords by unauthorized persons, "spoofing" of domain names, and other vulnerabilities that are discussed in more detail below.

Not all vulnerabilities, if exploited, will lead to the same kinds of harm. For example, denial of service attacks may cripple a system or cause loss of data, but are less likely to permit the attacker to gain access to information stored in the system. Accordingly, a list of information system vulnerabilities leading to possible disclosure of a document might not include denial of service attacks, but a list of vulnerabilities leading to possible destruction of a document would include denial of service attacks.

There is no single, most logical way of classifying all of the vulnerabilities an information system might face, and no single list of those vulnerabilities is likely to be exhaustive. The following list, however, describes some of the information system vulnerabilities that might lead to unauthorized destruction, alteration, or disclosure of information maintained on a company's network. This list assumes that the document is stored on a server in a typical office environment, i.e., that it is accessible from employee workstations; that those workstations are protected by individual passwords assigned to those employees; and that all employees have e-mail accounts and access to the Internet.

1. Acquisition and Use of Passwords by Unauthorized Persons

Shoulder Surfing

Shoulder surfing, as the phrase implies, is accomplished by persons walking through an office and watching employees enter their passwords. The shoulder surfers may be outsiders or fellow employees.

Physical Scavenging

Intruders or employees might find passwords or other valuable information on post-it notes, employee desk calendars, and other unsecured materials.

Misrepresentation and Social Engineering

Intruders and employees sometimes persuade personnel to disclose their passwords voluntarily. This can be accomplished by pretending to be an authorized person (misrepresentation) or simply taking advantage of an employee's cooperativeness (social engineering).

Password Attacks

Programs and techniques exist that permit intruders to capture passwords while those passwords are in storage or in the process of transmission, or to generate or guess at valid passwords.

Capture of passwords that are stored in the company's server can be accomplished by means of the same hacking and other techniques that are used to acquire other kinds of stored data, as described below.

Capture of passwords while in transit is easiest if passwords are not encrypted. If passwords are transmitted "in the clear," they may be acquired by placing interception devices between the employee's desktop computer and the company's server, or by acquiring transmissions made while the employee is working from home or at other remote locations.

Guessing or randomly generating passwords requires other techniques. Attackers can guess employees' passwords by using common derivations, such as dates of birth, that personnel often use as a basis for their choice of passwords. Hackers also may use random password-generation programs to make what are sometimes called "brute force" attacks on the network's password verification system.

2. Physical Removal of Hardware and Storage Media

No matter how secure a company's server and networked computers are, the system is compromised if the devices in which sensitive data are stored are physically removed from the premises. Such acts of physical removal range from relatively difficult acts, such as stealing a server or desktop computer, to such relatively simple acts as walking out the door with a printout, diskette, or CD-ROM to which sensitive information has been transferred.

Companies also must be concerned about the ongoing miniaturization of data storage and processing devices. Laptops and personal digital assistants (PDAs) are much smaller and more portable than servers and desktop computers, but can hold as much information as mainframes held a generation ago. Even if the person who takes such devices off the company's premises is authorized to use the data contained in those devices, the removal of those devices to a less-secure environment creates new and unpredictable risks for the security of the data.

3. Internet-Based and Internet Protocol-Based Attacks

Most companies' networks are connected to the Internet or communicate by means of Internet protocols, and intruders often use those connections and properties as a means of entering and compromising companies' networks. These intrusions use a variety of techniques, including:

IP Address Spoofing

Some networks use IP addresses to identify the users, hosts, or processes by means of which applications running on the system communicate. If the company's network uses IP addresses to route communications internally, a hacker trying to access the network from outside might show a false internal IP address as the source address. IP address spoofing is difficult to use as a means of retrieving information from the company's network, because the packets in any response transmission will go to the source address rather than the hacker's actual IP address. However, a message using a spoofed address that penetrates the company's firewall can alert a Trojan horse, previously installed on the network by the hacker, that may facilitate unauthorized access to stored data.

DNS Spoofing

The company may have a server that has been infected with forged Internet routing information. This false information may cause outgoing e-mails and other transmissions to be routed to a hacker's Web site rather than, or in addition to, the intended destination.

Session Hijacking

Session hijacking refers to a group of techniques by which an attacker can monitor, or even alter, communications between two computers using the Transfer Control Protocol. For purposes of acquiring sensitive data, the most useful form of session hijacking is the man-in-the-middle attack, which permits the intruder to intercept all communications in a session between two computers.

SQL Piggybacking

SQL piggybacking attacks are used to acquire sensitive data that are collected and stored by, or in connection with, a Web site or other online application. Hackers using this technique access the application (often through a technique known as "account harvesting"), then input false data and observe whether any of those data are mirrored in the system's response. Through trial and error, the hacker using this technique might find a key to obtaining customers' account information or other sensitive data.

Buffer Overflow Attacks

Buffer overflow attacks overwhelm the memory register—that is, the holding area for data awaiting processing—in a computer's central processing unit. If the amount of data in the memory register exceeds the register's defined capacity, the data may enter and corrupt other areas of the computer's random access memory, perhaps opening a back door into the system through which the company's data can be destroyed, altered, or acquired by outsiders.

Viruses

Viruses are programs introduced into a network by infected storage media, e-mail attachments, or file downloads. The defining characteristic of a virus is its quality of spreading from file to file on an infected system. Some viruses are harmless, but many are intended to overwhelm and disable the host system or corrupt or destroy data maintained on the system.

Worms

Worms are similar to viruses, but tend to spread from computer to computer rather than from file to file. A famous worm, and one that illustrates their properties well, was the "I love you" bug that infected the Internet over a few hours on May 4, 2000. The worm was propagated when users opened an e-mail attachment on Outlook. The worm overwrote files on the user's computer, then sent copies of itself to all of the addresses in the user's Outlook contacts file. This worm caused a number of corporate e-mail servers to "crash" and corrupted untold numbers of personal computers worldwide.

Trojan Horses

A Trojan horse can be more surreptitious and damaging than a virus or worm. After taking up residence on a system, a Trojan horse program can open a back door to the host network and send data, including the keystrokes of a user entering his or her password, to the hacker who placed the malicious program.

Attacks on State Maintenance

State maintenance is the back-and-forth transfer of identifying information between a browser and an on-line application during an online session. Depending on how the online server is storing and exchanging this information, an attacker can highjack this identifying information for its own purposes and execute online transactions on the user's behalf. Companies that engage in e-commerce, and their customers, are especially vulnerable to state maintenance attacks.

Sniffer Software

Sniffer software is a kind of computer network wiretap. A sniffer can pick off the keystrokes of information transmitted within or outside the victim company's network. E-mail is especially vulnerable to sniffer attacks.

2.7.3 Data Security Evalation

The data security evaluation is the process of measuring the risks of destruction, alteration, or disclosure of the company's information assets against the measures that are in place for managing those risks, and identifying any shortfalls in those measures that require correction.

Many risk assessment models, including those used by the very largest corporations and governmental organizations, set out elaborate techniques for conducting this stage of a data security risk assessment. Those models, like the approach set out in this document, measure the types and magnitude and loss the organization will incur if information assets of various values are compromised by adverse events. Those elaborate models also factor in the likelihood that a particular loss will occur (a calculation that often must be based on incomplete information), and conduct a cost-benefit analysis of the efficiency of implementing specific measures to control each risk.

For most organizations, the value of these elaborate models is questionable. For companies of ordinary size and complexity, the standard set of "best practice" security measures already is well understood and accepted, and regulators investigating a security incident will not be impressed if an elaborate statistical analysis is used, for example, to justify a failure to update antivirus software or change passwords at reasonable intervals. Accordingly, Icarus's data security evaluation should compare its existing security measures against best-practice measures in the areas of personnel, physical facilities, and information systems. That comparison should be made, not just as to overall security measures, but as to the treatment responsible companies ordinarily give to information assets in each of the categories we have identified as public, internal-use only, restricted, and highly restricted.

We will provide a proposed Data Security Program and Document Classification and Protection Program that reflect standard practices in industry and governmental organizations. Although those documents may not precisely reflect Icarus's business environment, they should provide a starting point for the risk security evaluation process.

We also will provide a sample Security Evaluation Worksheet. The sample will show a worksheet intended for information assets in the restricted category, and will recommend that Icarus protect those assets by implementing all of the general technical and administrative measures set out in the Data Protection Plan, supplemented by all of the measures required for restricted assets in the Data Classification and Protection Plan. In the "State of Compliance" column, we will make some hypothetical notations concerning differences between the recommended measures and the measures actually in place. Under "Required Actions," we will make some hypothetical notations concerning corrective measures.

The data security evaluation can be conducted before any new measures have been adopted, or can be conducted after a preliminary set of corrections to the existing data security measures has been made. The critical requirement, from the perspective of legal compliance, is that the complete risk assessment process be conducted and a record of that process made.

2.7.4 Risk Management

The final stage of the data security risk assessment is the implementation of the appropriate data protection measures in the areas of personnel, facilities, and information systems. As part of that implementation, Icarus should adopt written policies and training materials to ensure that data protection measures are understood and systematically implemented by all responsible personnel. Those documents will include the Data Protection Plan and Document Classification and Protection Plan. They also will include user and administrator security policies for the Icarus data network, written policies concerning the privacy of customer information, security policies for physical access to Icarus's premises, and other compliance materials as needed. To the extent the necessary materials do not already exist or should be updated, we are happy to assist with that process.

Notes

[1]Fair Credit Reporting Act, codified at 15 U.S.C. § 1681 et seq.

[2]*Id.*, 15 U.S.C. § 1681e(a).

[3]Children's Online Privacy Protection Act of 1998, 15 U.S.C. § 6501(b)(1)(D).

[4]Gramm-Leach-Bliley Financial Modernization Act of 1999, 15 U.S.C. § 6801(b)(1)–(3).

[5]Health Insurance Portability and Accountability Act of 1996 § 264; 45 C.F.R. Part 164, Subpart C (Dec. 28, 2000 as amended; May 31, 2002, Aug. 14, 2002, Feb. 20, 2003 and Apr. 17, 2003).

[6]15 U.S.C. § 45.

[7]*See* FTC Complaint in *Eli Lilly & Co.*, Docket No. C-4047, http://www.ftc.gov/os/2002/05/elilillycmp.htm (*Eli Lilly Complaint*); Agreement Containing Consent Order in *Eli Lilly & Co.*, http:www.ftc.gov/os/2002/01/lillyagree.pdf (*Eli Lilly Consent Agreement*); *Microsoft Corp.*, File No. 012-3240, http://www.ftc.gov/os/caselist/0123240/microsoftcmp.pdf (*MicrosoftComplaint*); *Microsoft Corp.*, http://www.ftc.gov/os/caselist/0123240/microsoftagree.pdf (*Microsoft Consent Agreement*); GUESS?, INC., and GUESS.COM, INC., File No. 022-3260, http://www.ftc.gov/os/os/2003/08/guesscmp.pdf (*Guess?, Inc. Complaint*); http://www.ftc.gov/os/2003/06/guessagree.htm (*Guess?, Inc. Consent Agreement*); *Petco Animal Supplies, Inc.*, Docket No. C-4133, http://www.ftc.gov/os/caselist/0323221/050308comp0323221.pdf (*Petco Complaint*); http://www.ftc.gov/os/caselist/0323221/041108agree0323221.pdf (*Petco Consent Agreement*). *MTS, Inc. doing business as Tower Records/Books/Video, and Tower Direct, LLC doing business as TowerRecords.com*, File No. 032-3209; http://www.ftc.gov/os/caselist/0323209/040602comp0323209.pdf (*Tower Complaint*); http:www.ftc.gov/os/caselist/0323209/040421agree0323209.pdf (*Tower Consent Agreement*).

[8]In the Matter of BJ's Wholesale Club, Inc., http://www.ftc.gov/os/caselist/0423160/092305comp0423160.pdf (*BJ's Complaint*); http://www.ftc.gov/os/caselist/0423160/05061agree0423160.pdf (*"BJ's Consent Agreement"*).

[9]It should be noted, however, that the Federal Trade Commission Act denies the FTC jurisdiction over some entities, including banks and telecommunications common carriers. The FTC also may not regulate insurance companies to the extent those companies actually are engaged in the business of insurance.

[10]*Tower Complaint* at ¶ 9. According to the FTC Complaint, when Tower redesigned the checkout portion of its Web site, the checkout process "generated an e-mail to consumers confirming their order and providing a URL that the user could use to check the status of their order online . . ." *Id.* at ¶ 8. Unfortunately, the "Order Status URL contained the order number in clear text"—a flaw the FTC characterized as a case of "broken account and session management." *Id.*

[11]The consent agreements also resemble, and appear largely to be based on, the Safeguards Rule adopted by the FTC to implement the information security requirements of the Gramm-Leach-Bliley Act. 16 C.F.R. Pt. 314 (2002). In fact, the FTC's data security campaign can fairly be viewed as an effort to expand the scope of the Safeguards Rule to apply to all U.S. businesses—not just the financial institutions subject to the Gramm-Leach-Bliley Act and the Safeguards Rule.

[12]*Eli Lilly Consent Agreement, supra*, sec. II.

[13]*Microsoft Consent Agreement, supra*, sec. I.

[14]*Guess?, Inc. Consent Agreement, supra*, sec. II.

[15]*Tower Consent Agreement, supra*, sec. II.B.

[16]*Eli Lilly Consent Agreement, supra*, secs. II.C.–II.D.

[17]*See, e.g., Guess?, Inc. Consent Agreement, supra*, sec. III.

[18]For example, in its complaint against BJ's Wholesale Club, the FTC noted that the respondent's practice of retaining credit card data "when it no longer had a need to keep the information" was a violation of "bank rules" (an apparent reference to the Payment Card Industry Data Security Standard, which sets security standards for merchants that honor credit and debit cards). As this reference demonstrates, the FTC will look to industry rules and standards for guidance as to the standard of care for a company that has come under Commission scrutiny.

[19]*See, e.g., Petco Complaint, supra*, where the FTC faulted Petco for failure to guard against a type of Web site attack that was "well known in the information technology industry." *Petco Complaint, supra*, para. 9. As the Complaint states: "Security experts have been warning the industry about these vulnerabilities since at least 1997; in 1998, at least one security organization developed, and made publicly available at no charge, a security measure that could prevent such attacks, and in June 2000 the industry began receiving reports of successful attacks on Web applications." *Id.*

[20]Information on NSIT publications can be found at http://csrc.nist.gov/publications/nistpubs.

[21]*See* http://www.sei.cmu.edu/publications/documents/04.reports/04hb003.html.

[22]*See* http://www.peltierassociates.com.

[23]*See* n. 19, *supra.*

[24]*See* http://www.fas.org/irp/offdocs/DCD_6-3_20Policy.htm.

[25]*See* Information Systems Audit and Control Association, http://www.isaca.org.

[26]*See* Information Systems Security Association, http://www.issa.org.

[27]*See* International Organization for Standardization, http://www.iso.org.

[28]*See, e.g.*, Cal. Bus. & Prof. Code § 17200, 17500; N.Y. Gen. Bus. Law § 349–350; 9 Vt. Stat. Ann. § 2451; Wis. Stat. Ann. § 426.110; Wyo. Stat. Ann. § 40-12-108.

[29]In the Matter of Ziff-Davis Media Inc., Assurance of Discontinuance effective Aug. 28, 2002 (Office of New York State Attorney General, www.oag.ny/us).

[30]*Id. See also* In re: InfoBeat LLC, Assurance of Discontinuance (Jan. 2000), at http://www.oag.state.ny.us/internet/litigation/infobeat.pdf. The language in the Ziff-Davis settlement, requiring implementation of security standards that have "gained sufficient industry acceptance and adoption such that Ziff-Davis' adherence to the standards would not unreasonably place Ziff-Davis at a competitive disadvantage" is a remarkably clear statement of the attitude of regulators—including the FTC—toward data security enforcement. Recognizing that they are not experts on the subject, regulators nonetheless expect companies to adopt safeguards that have become standard for their industries. This does not mean that a company must become an "early adopter" of costly technologies that might place them at a competitive disadvantage. It does mean, however, that if a safeguard has been generally adopted in your industry, your company also should adopt it unless there is a strong reason not to do so.

[31]*State of Ohio v. DSW, Inc.*, Case No. 05CV06-6128 (Complaint for Declaratory Judgment, Court of Common Pleas, Franklin County, Ohio, June 6, 2005), Press Release of Attorney General Jim Petro at http://www.ag.state.oh.us/press_releases/2005/pr20050606.htm.

[32]*See, e.g.*, A.R.S. § 44-7601; A.C.A. § 4-110-104; Cal. Civ. Code § 1798.81; C.R.S. § 6-1-713(1); O.C.G.A. § 10-15-2; KRS § 365.725; MCL § 445.72; N.J. Stat. § 56:8-162; NY CLS Gen. Bus. § 399-h; N.C. Gen. Stat. § 75.64; Tenn. Code Ann. § 39-14-150(g); Tex. Bus. & Com. Code § 48.102; 9 V.S.A. § 2445; Rev. Code Wash. § 19.215.010; Wis. Stat. § 895.505.

[33]Cal. Civ. Code § 1798.81 (2006).

[34]Maryland Regular Session, 422nd Session of the General Assembly, Senate Bill 194, § 14-3503(A).

[35]*Id.* § 14-3503(B). These provisions apply to written contracts that are entered into after January 1, 2009.

[36]A.C.A. § 4-110-104; Cal. Civ. Code § 1798.81; Nev. Rev. Stat. § 603A.210; R.I. Gen. Laws § 11-49.2-2; Tex. Bus. & Com. Code § 48.102; Utah Code Ann. § 13-44-201.

[37]Cal. Civ. Code § 1798.81, *supra.*

[38]*See, e.g.*, A.C.A. § 4-110-105; Cal. Civ. Code § 1798.29(a); Conn. Gen. Stat. § 36a-701; 6 Del. C. § 102(a); Fla. Stat. § 817.5681; O.C.G-A. § 10-1-912; HRS § 487N-2; 28 Idaho Code § 28-51-105; 815 ILCS 530/10(a); La.R.S. § 51:3074; Minn. Stat. § 13.055; Mont. Code Anno. § 30-14-1704; N.J. Stat. § 56:8-163; NY CLS Gen. Bus. § 899-aa; N.C. Gen. Stat. § 75-65; N.D. Cent. Code § 51-30-02; ORC Ann. § 1347.12; R.I. Gen. Laws § 1-49.2; Tex. Bus. & Com. Code § 48.103(b); 9 V.S.A. § 2435(6); Rev. Code Wash. § 19.255.010; Wis. Stat. § 895.507.

[39]*See, e.g.*, Minnesota Statutes § 325E.61(1)(a); Texas Business & Commercial Code § 48.103(b); Arkansas Code Annotated § 4-110-105.

[40]An "information broker" is defined in Maine as "a person who, for monetary fees or duties, engages in whole or in part in the business of collecting, assembling, evaluating, compiling, reporting, transmitting, transferring or communicating information concerning individuals for the primary purpose of furnishing personal information to nonaffiliated third parties." Maine Revised Statutes Annotated 210-B § 1347(3). *See also* Official Code of Georgia Annotated § 10-1-911(2).

[41]In Illinois, a data collector "may include, but is not limited to, government agencies, public and private universities, privately and publicly held corporations, financial institutions, retail operators, and any other entity that, for any purpose, handles, collects, disseminates, or otherwise deals with nonpublic personal information." Illinois H.B. 1633, Public Act 94-36, § 5.

[42]*See, e.g.*, California Civil Code § 1798/29(a); Burns Indiana Code Annotated 4-1-11-5(a); Minnesota Statutes § 13.055(2); Ohio Revised Code Annotated § 1347.12(B)(1).

[43]North Carolina General Statutes § 75-65(a).

[44]*See,.e.g.*, California Civil Code §1798.29(e); 6 Delaware Code §101(4); Florida Statutes §817.5681(5); Texas Business & Commercial Code §48.002(2) (defining "sensitive personal information").

[45]*See, e.g.*, A.C.A. §4-110-103(7); North Carolina General Statutes §75-65(a); North Dakota Century Code §51-30-01(2).

[46]California Civil Code §4-110-105(b).

[47]*Id.* §1798.82(d).

[48]*Remsburg v. Docusearch, Inc.*, 149 N.H. 148, 816 A.2d 1001 (Sup. Ct. N.H. 2003).

[49]*Id.*, 149 N.H. at 155, 816 A.2d at 1008.

[50]*Id. See also Cobell v. Norton*, 391 F.3d 251 (D.C. Cir. 2004).

[51]*See Fidelity & Deposit Co. of Maryland v. International Business Machines Co.*, 2005 WL 2665326, 2005 U.S. Dist. LEXIS 25420 (M.D. Pa. 2005).

[52]*See Stollenwerk v. Tri-West Healthcare Alliance*, 2005 WL 2465906, 2006 U.S. Dist. LEXIS 41054 (D. Az. 2005). Also, plaintiffs that allege only an increased risk of identity theft or other "speculative" harms may lack standing to bring lawsuits based on negligent handling of personal information. *Bell v. Acxiom Corporation*, 2006 U.S. Dist. LEXIS 72477 (E.D. Ark. 2006); *Key v. DSW, Inc.*, 454 F.Supp.2d 684 (D.D. Ohio, 2006); *Giordano v. Wachovia Securities, Inc.*, 2005 U.S. Dist. LEXIS 52266 (D. N.J. 2006).

[53]The proposed risk assessment set out here is intended to be appropriate for a company of Icarus's size and complexity, and is based generally on the model described by R. Peltier in his *Information Security Risk Analysis* (CRC Press 2001).

CHAPTER 3

If Your Organization Is a Financial Institution: The Gramm-Leach-Bliley Act and Other Financial Privacy Legislation

Because of its sensitivity and potential for misuse, personal financial information has enjoyed legal privacy protections of various kinds for many years. Banks and other financial institutions, which are the principal custodians of personal financial information, bear the primary legal obligations for fair use and protection of this information.

This chapter discusses four of the principal privacy statutes that give consumers rights in their financial information: the Gramm-Leach-Bliley Financial Modernization Act of 1999 (GLBA),[1] the Right to Financial Privacy Act (RFPA),[2] the Fair Credit Reporting Act (FCRA),[3] the Electronic Funds Transfer Act (EFTA),[4] and Section 326 of the USA PATRIOT Act.[5] We conclude with a brief discussion of state financial privacy protections.

3.1 The Gramm-Leach-Bliley Financial Modernization Act of 1999

The GLBA is not primarily a privacy statute. In fact, the principal effect of that statute is to permit banks to enter lines of business, such as securities brokerage and insurance, from which they formerly were barred under the Glass-Steagall Act and the 1982 amendments to the Bank Holding Company Act of 1956.[6]

The GLBA does, however, impose significant restrictions on financial institutions' sharing of their customers' personal financial information with outside entities, referred to in the statute as "nonaffiliated third parties." The privacy provisions of the GLBA are intended to give customers some control over such data transfers and uses, primarily by creating a right to receive notice of, and to "opt out" from, data sharing among financial institutions and third parties.

The GLBA privacy obligations are part of one of the most complex regulatory schemes in the U.S. economy—that is, the system of rules that govern banks, savings and loan associations, securities brokers, insurance companies, and other financial services providers. In order to determine your organization's GLBA obligations, if any, within this landscape, at least two preliminary questions must be answered: (1) is your organization a "financial institution" as that term is defined in the applicable statutes; and (2) if your organization *is* a financial institution, which regulator, or regulators, has enacted the rules that define your GLBA obligations?

Only when those questions are answered can you identify the precise GLBA requirements, if any, to which your organization is subject.

The next section considers these jurisdictional issues, followed by a section that describes the privacy obligations of institutions that are subject to the GLBA.

3.1.1 Financial Institutions and Activities Subject to the GLBA

Subtitle A of Title V of the GLBA declares that "each *financial institution* has an affirmative and continuing obligation to respect the privacy of its customers and to protect the security and confidentiality of those customers' nonpublic personal information."[7] Unfortunately, the GLBA does not directly identify the kinds of organizations and lines of business that qualify as "financial institutions" subject to the statute. Instead, the GLBA defines "financial institution" to include "any institution the business of which is engaging in financial activities as described in section 4(k) of the Bank Holding Company Act of 1956."[8] Section 4(k) of the Bank Holding Company Act, in turn, identifies certain activities as "financial in nature," and incorporates in that list other activities that the "Federal Reserve Board has determined, by order or regulation that is in effect on the date of the enforcement of the GLBA, to be so closely related to banking or managing or controlling banks as to be a proper incident thereto," and engaging "in the United States, in any activity that . . . a bank holding company may engage in outside of the United States; and . . . the Board has determined . . . to be usual in connection with the transaction of banking or other financial operations abroad."[9] Accordingly, an enterprise becomes a financial institution for GLBA purposes, not only by engaging in "the traditional financial activities specified in [section 4(k)] of the Bank Holding Company Act," but also by engaging in "those activities that the Federal Reserve Board has . . . found by regulation, order or interpretation to be either closely related to banking or usual in connection with the transaction of banking or other financial operations abroad."[10]

Putting the GLBA, the Bank Holding Company Act, and the Federal Reserve Board regulations, orders, and interpretations together, the financial activities subject or potentially subject to GLBA include:

1. Activities listed in the Bank Company Holding Act, including: "(A) Lending, exchanging, transferring, investing for others, or safeguarding money or securities. (B) Insuring, guaranteeing, or indemnifying against loss, harm, damage, illness, disability, or death, or providing and issuing annuities, and acting as principal, agent, or broker for purposes of the foregoing, in any State. (C) Providing financial, investment, or economic advisory services, including advising an investment company (as defined in section 3 of the Investment Company Act of 1940). (D) Issuing or selling instruments representing interests in pools of assets permissible for a bank to hold directly. (E) Underwriting, dealing in, or making a market in securities."[11]
2. Activities listed by the Federal Reserve Board as closely related to banking, including: "brokering or servicing loans, leasing real or personal property (or acting as agent, broker, or advisor in such leasing without operating, maintaining or repairing the property); appraising real or personal prop-

erty; check guaranty, collection agency, credit bureau, and real estate settlement services; providing financial or investment advisory activities including tax planning, tax preparation, and instruction on individual financial management; management consulting and counseling activities (including providing financial career counseling); courier services for banking instruments; printing and selling checks and related documents; community development or advisory activities; selling money orders, savings bonds, or traveler's checks; and providing financial data processing and transmission services, facilities (including hardware, software, documentation, or operating personnel), data bases, advice, or access to these by technological means."[12]

3. Activities the Federal Reserve Board has determined to be usual in connection with the transaction of banking and financial operations abroad, including: "leasing real or personal property (or acting as agent, broker, or advisor in such leasing) where the lease is functionally equivalent to an extension of credit; acting as fiduciary; providing investment, financial, or economic advisory services; and operating a travel agency in connection with financial services."[13]

Under this complex regulatory scheme, organizations that do not consider themselves traditional financial institutions might have GLBA obligations. Some travel agencies, for example, appear to be within the definition, as are retailers that offer their own installment payment accounts. The application of the GLBA privacy provisions to particular entities and activities, especially those outside traditional realms such as banking, brokerage, and insurance, has resulted in some confusion and even some litigation.[14] If your company or line of business falls outside the traditional financial service categories but is arguably within one or more items on the Federal Reserve Board lists described above, it might be advisable to obtain legal advice before assuming that GLBA obligations do *not* apply to your company or line of business.

Also, even where an activity plainly is subject to the GLBA, determining which agency's GLBA regulations apply to your institution or line of business can add another layer of confusion. Congress has directed eight separate agencies to adopt GLBA implementing regulations, and the various jurisdictions of those agencies are more a product of history than of logic. The jurisdiction of various agencies overlaps, and the traditional boundaries are tested by new types of financial institutions, offerings, and business models.[15] To the extent you are not already familiar with the financial "functional regulator" or regulators to which your organization is subject, therefore, a closer inquiry into the jurisdiction of the various agencies might be required. Table 3.1 is provided as a possible starting point for this process. (As that table points out, the "default regulator" for nontraditional financial institutions subject to the GLBA is the Federal Trade Commission. When in doubt, expect to be regulated by the FTC.)

Finally (and this is the good news), the GLBA regulations of the various agencies differ only slightly from one another, and do so only as needed to reflect the specific characteristics of the industries and activities those agencies regulate. Accordingly, compliance with the rules of one functional regulator is likely to

Table 3.1 Is My Organization Subject to GLBA Privacy Regulations?

Institutions that are subject to the GLBA privacy provisions include banks, savings and loan associations, credit unions, brokers, dealers, investment companies, investment advisers, insurance companies, and other financial institutions. If you are not certain concerning the status of your company under GLBA, section 509 directs you to the definitions of "activities that are financial in nature" set out in Section 4(k) of the Bank Holding Company Act of 1956.

If your company *is* a financial institution for purposes of GLBA, it must comply with privacy regulations enacted by at least one of the following agencies:

Office of the Comptroller of the Currency (OCC)

The OCC enforces the GLBA provisions as to national banks, Federal banks, and Federal agencies of foreign banks, and any subsidiaries of such entities. This authority is exercised under GLBA and Section 8 of the Federal Deposit Insurance act. If your company is a subsidiary of one of these entities but is a broker, dealer, insurance company, investment company, or investment adviser, GLBA regulations applicable to your company are not issued by OCC.

Board of Governors of the Federal Reserve System (FRS)

The FRS Board enforces the GLBA privacy requirements as to member banks of the Federal Reserve System (other than national banks), branches and agencies of foreign banks (other than Federal branches, Federal agencies, and insured State branches of foreign banks), commercial lending companies owned or controlled by foreign banks, organizations operating under section 25 or 25A of the Federal Reserve Act, and bank holding companies and their nonbank subsidiaries or affiliates. Again, the affected subdivisions or affiliates regulated by the FRS Board do not include brokers, dealers, insurance companies, investment companies and investment advisers. Like the OCC, the FRS Board's authority in this area is based on GLBA and section 8 of the Federal Deposit Insurance Act.

Board of Directors of the Federal Deposit Insurance Corporation

The FDIC issues GLBA privacy regulations to banks insured by the FDIC (other than members of the Federal Reserve System), insured State branches of foreign banks, and any subsidiaries of any such entities that are not brokers, dealers, insurance companies, investment companies, or investment advisers. The FDIC's authority also is based on GLBA and section 8 of the Federal Deposit Insurance Act.

Director of the Office of Thrift Supervision (OTS)

The OTC issues GLBA regulations for savings associations insured by the FDIC, and any of their subsidiaries (except brokers, dealers, insurance companies, investment companies, and investment advisers). The OTS's GLBA authority is based on the Act and section 8 of the Federal Deposit Insurance Act.

Board of the National Credit Union Administration

This agency issues GLBA rules for federally-insured credit unions and their subsidiaries.

Securities and Exchange Commission (SEC)

Under the Securities Act of 1934, the SEC issues GLBA privacy rules as to brokers and dealers. The SEC also issues GLBA regulations for investment companies under the Investment Company Act of 1940, and for investment advisers registered with the SEC pursuant to the Investment Advisers Act of 1940.

Commodity Futures Trading Commission (CFTC)

The CFTC has jurisdiction over trading in futures contracts pursuant to the Commodity Exchange Act. Under the terms of an agreement reached in 1981, the CFTC regulates "markets and instruments that serve a hedging and price discovery function," while the SEC regulates "markets and instruments with an underlying investment purpose."

State Insurance Regulators

Under section 104 of GLBA, persons "engaged in providing insurance" are subject to GLBA regulations issued by "the applicable State insurance agency of the State in which the person is domiciled . . . ."

Federal Trade Commission (FTC)

The FTC issues regulations under GLBA for any other financial institution or person that is not subject to the jurisdiction of any other agency or authority listed in section 505(a).

constitute substantial, if not necessarily perfect, compliance with the GLBA rules of other functional regulators.

3.1.2 Protecting Privacy Under the GLBA

The principal privacy obligations of financial institutions under the GLBA may be briefly stated: those institutions must give *notice* to *consumers* of the institutions' policies concerning disclosure of *nonpublic personal information* to *nonaffiliated third parties*, and must give those consumers an opportunity to *opt out of* such disclosures unless certain *exceptions* apply. Each element of these obligations requires some explanation.

3.1.2.1 Consumers and Customers

The GLBA privacy obligations apply to a financial institution's dealings with personal information of certain individuals. Those individuals are referred to in the statute as *consumers* and *customers*.

Whether an individual is your customer or merely a consumer determines the nature of your obligations to give that person notice of your privacy policies and an opportunity to opt out of information disclosures to third parties. If an individual is a consumer but not a customer, you are required only to notify that individual and provide the opt-out opportunity prior to actually *disclosing* his or her personal information to a third party.[16] If the individual is a customer as well as a consumer, you must provide that person with a notice of your privacy policies at the inception of the relationship and annually thereafter, even if you never disclose that customer's personal information to a third party.[17] Accordingly, it is important to know when a consumer relationship begins, and when such a relationship makes the transition to a customer relationship.

Consumers are any persons who purchase services from a financial institution, even on a one-time or occasional basis. For example, a person who uses the ATM of a bank at which he does not have an account is, for that purpose, a consumer of that bank's services. The casual ATM user is not, however, a *customer* of the bank providing the ATM. To become a customer of a financial institution, the consumer must have a continuing relationship with that institution.[18]

Consumer relationships can be formed with relative ease. As noted earlier, one-time or occasional use of a service, such as an ATM, creates a consumer relationship with the provider of that service. Similarly, a person who fills out an application for an account or other service creates a consumer relationship with a bank, even if no account is approved or opened. The bank does not have a consumer relationship, however, with a person to whom it sends an account application that is never completed or returned.

The line that divides a consumer relationship from a customer relationship is not always easy to draw, but savings accounts, checking accounts, brokerage accounts, and other services that involve continuing interaction—and exchanges of information—between the institution and an individual certainly qualify. Other transactions that involve a single transaction and little subsequent activity, such as purchase of a certificate of deposit, also may qualify.[19] Where the status of a consumer/customer relationship is uncertain, the rules of the institution's functional regulator should be consulted. If doubt remains, no harm can come from treating a doubtful case as a customer relationship and giving notice accordingly.

3.1.2.2 Nonpublic Personal Information

The GLBA privacy obligations address the financial institution's disclosures of "nonpublic personal information." This category is defined to include personally identifiable financial information that is: "(i) provided by a consumer to a financial institution; (ii) resulting from any transaction with the consumer or any service performed for the consumer; or (iii) otherwise obtained by the financial institution."[20] The category does not include publicly available information, but does include "any list, description, or other grouping of consumers (and publicly available information pertaining to them) that is derived using any nonpublic personal information other than publicly available information," except for "any list, description, or other grouping of consumers (and publicly available information pertaining to them) that is derived without using any nonpublic personal information."[21]

3.1.2.3 Content, Timing, and Mode of Delivery of Notices

As noted above, financial institutions must give all consumers notice of their privacy policies before disclosing nonpublic personal information to nonaffiliated third parties, and must give customers such notice at the inception of the customer relationship and annually thereafter.[22] The notices are intended to give customers and other consumers a meaningful opportunity to "opt out" of such disclosures before they are made.

The notice provided to consumers must be clear and conspicuous, and must indicate (among other things) the circumstances under which the institution will disclose nonpublic personal information to nonaffiliated third parties, and the types of information that may be disclosed. In order to protect consumers from long, verbose notices that may conceal more than they disclose, the functional regulators have simplified the process by specifying nine items that must be included in the notice where applicable. Those items are:[23]

1. The categories of nonpublic personal information that you collect;
2. The categories of nonpublic personal information that you disclose;
3. The categories of affiliates and nonaffiliated third parties to whom you disclose nonpublic personal information, other than those parties to whom you disclose information under §§ 216.14 and 216.15 [related to processing and servicing of transactions and certain other exceptions, discussed below];
4. The categories of nonpublic personal information about your former customers that you disclose and the categories of affiliates and nonaffiliated third parties to whom you disclose nonpublic personal information about your former customers, other than those parties to whom you disclose information under §§ 216.14 and 216.15;

5. If you disclose nonpublic personal information to a nonaffiliated third party under § 21613 [related to service providers and joint marketing] (and no other exception in § 216.14 or 216.15 applies to that disclosure), a separate statement of the categories of information you disclose and the categories of third parties with whom you have contracted;
6. An explanation of the consumer's right under § 216.10(a) to opt out of the disclosure of nonpublic personal information to nonaffiliated third parties, including the method(s) by which the consumer may exercise that right at that time;
7. Any disclosures that you make under section 603(d)(2)(A)(iii) of the Fair Credit Reporting Act (15 U.S.C. 1681a(d)(2)(A)(iii)) (that is, notices regarding the ability to opt out of disclosures of information among affiliates);
8. Your policies and practices with respect to protecting the confidentiality and security of nonpublic personal information; and
9. Any disclosure that you make under paragraph (b) of this section [stating that you make disclosures to other nonaffiliated third parties as permitted by law, where those disclosures are made pursuant to the exceptions set out in §§ 216.14 and 216.15].

When an institution has no affiliates and will make disclosures only pursuant to the various exceptions to the opt-out requirements, a "short form" notice may be used. The short form notice suggested by the Board of Governors of the Federal Reserve System reads as follows:[24]

> We collect nonpublic personal information about you from the following sources:
>
> - Information we receive from you on applications or other forms;
> - Information about your transactions with us or others; and
> - Information we receive from a consumer reporting agency.
>
> We do not disclose any nonpublic information about you to anyone, except as permitted by law. If you decide to close your account, we will adhere to the privacy policy and practices as described in the notice. We restrict access to your personal and account information to those employees who have a need to know that information to provide product or services to you. We maintain physical, electronic, and procedural safeguards that comply with Federal standards to guard your nonpublic personal information.

The initial notice to a customer must be given at the time the relationship between the consumer and the institution is established.[25] This requirement sometimes encounters practical obstacles, such as a potential delay in establishment of the relationship that the customer is willing to avoid by waiving the right to an immediate notice. The agency rules address some of these exceptional situations.[26]

Annual notices must be given to all customers, but need not be provided to former customers.[27]

Initial and annual notices may not be given orally, but may be provided electronically with the customer's agreement.[28] If customers use an electronic service of the institution to conduct transactions, notices may be posted on the Web site that is used for that purpose.[29]

3.1.2.4 Exceptions to Notice and Opt-Out Requirements

The GLBA and the agencies' implementing rules recognize a number of exceptions to the statute's notice and opt-out obligations. Because the exceptions are numerous and specific, and because they will be narrowly construed (that is, interpreted against the financial institution) in the event of a dispute concerning a particular disclosure, an institution proposing to rely on an exception should consult the statute and the specific rules of the appropriate functional regulator.

The principal (but not the only) exceptions are:

- *Disclosures to Service Providers and Joint Marketers.* Financial institutions must rely on outside vendors to process transactions and carry on their operations. Disclosures to such outside entities are not subject to notice and opt-out requirements. Financial institutions also enter into joint agreements with other such institutions for the marketing of products and services. Such information sharing is not subject to notice and opt-out requirements, but may be engaged in only after affected customers have received a privacy policy notice from the institution disclosing information under a joint agreement. Also, institutions that disclose nonpublic personal information pursuant to a joint agreement must require the receiving entity, by contract, to protect the confidentiality of that information.[30]
- *Disclosures That Are Necessary to a Transaction.* When a consumer has requested or authorized a transaction, that consumer is not entitled to notice and a chance to opt out from disclosures to third parties that are "necessary to effect, administer, or enforce the transaction."[31] Without this exception, the cost and difficulty of routine activities, such as processing of payments, would be prohibitive.
- *Disclosures with Consumer's Consent.* If a consumer has directed or consented to a particular disclosure of nonpublic personal information to a non-affiliated third party, the institution is not required to give specific notice of its intent to make that disclosure or give the consumer an opportunity to "opt out" of the disclosure that is already authorized. However, the consumer has the right to revoke consent by subsequently exercising the right to opt out of future disclosures of nonpublic personal information as permitted by the GBLA.[32] Also, the authority granted by this exception should not be taken as license to obtain general waivers of GLBA notice and opt-out rights.
- *Miscellaneous Exceptions.* A nonexhaustive list of other exceptions to the notice and opt-out requirements of GLBA will include: (1) to underwrite insurance or perform other functions in connection with a consumer's insurance;[33] (2) to protect the confidentiality or security of consumer records or prevent fraud, unauthorized transactions, or other liability;[34] (3) to provide information to insurance rate advisory organizations, guaranty funds or agencies, agencies that are rating you, persons that are assessing your compliance with industry standards, and your attorneys, accountants, and auditors;[35] and (4) to comply with Federal, State, or local laws, rules and other applicable legal requirements.[36]

3.1.2.5 Redistribution of Nonpublic Personal Information

Even when nonaffiliated third parties obtain nonpublic personal information lawfully under GLBA, the ability of those parties to disclose that information further is severely restricted by the GLBA and the agency rules.[37] As a general matter, an entity that obtains nonpublic personal information from a financial institution may not disclose that information to another nonaffiliated party unless the institution that furnished the information could lawfully have disclosed it to that party.

3.1.2.6 Enforcement of GLBA Obligations

The privacy obligations of the GLBA are enforced by the functional regulators that have adopted rules to implement those obligations. So, for example, violations by institutions subject to the Federal Reserve Board will be treated as violations of Federal Reserve regulations, violations by securities brokers will be dealt with by the Securities and Exchange Commission, and violations by financial institutions not subject to other agencies' jurisdiction will be addressed by the Federal Trade Commission.

The GLBA does not create a private right of action, which means that private persons may not successfully bring lawsuits based solely on violations of their privacy rights under the GLBA. However, financial institutions' disclosures of nonpublic personal information may be used as predicates for lawsuits against financial institutions based on other theories, such as negligence or violation of state consumer protection laws.

3.2 The Right to Financial Privacy Act

In 1976, the United States Supreme Court held that the Fourth Amendment's prohibition against unreasonable searches and seizures does not apply when law enforcement agencies attempt to obtain individuals' bank records.[38] As a result of the Court's decision, banks and their customers were left with no constitutional basis on which to demand a warrant or other process before banks released customers' financial records to government agencies.

Congress responded to the Court's decision with the Right to Financial Privacy Act (RFPA), which defines the circumstances under which financial institutions may be compelled to disclose customers' financial records to the federal government.[39] The RFPA permits records within its protection to be produced: (1) with the customer's authorization: (2) pursuant to a warrant;[40] (3) pursuant to administrative subpoena or summons; (4) pursuant to a judicial subpoena; or (5) in some circumstances, pursuant to a formal written request.[41] If a judicial warrant is not obtained, disclosure may be compelled only when there is reason to believe that the records sought are relevant to a legitimate law enforcement inquiry and after a copy of the subpoena, summons, or formal written request has been served on the customer.[42]

Although the RFPA is a significant source of rights for customers of financial institutions, the statute also contains many exceptions that protect the interest of government in obtaining access to individuals' financial records.[43] Notably, the RFPA does not prevent informal access to bank records by the Internal Revenue Service for the purpose of enforcing federal tax obligations.[44] In addition, banks remain subject to the Bank Secrecy Act of 1970, which requires them to create and hold records of their depositors' transactions that are deemed by the government to be useful to regulation and law enforcement.[45]

The RFPA does not restrict access to financial institution records by state and local governments. Many states, however, have enacted banking privacy statutes that restrict the ability of financial institutions to respond to state and local government demands for disclosure. Some of those statutes—such as those of California, Nevada, New Hampshire, and Oregon—are modeled closely on the RFPA.[46] Other state statutes differ from the RFPA in the range of institutions to which they apply[47] and the types of entities to which they limit disclosure. For example, the states of Connecticut, Illinois, Maine, and Maryland limit the right of disclosure, not only to governmental agencies, but to private persons and entities as well.[48]

Violations of the RFPA, by a financial institution or by an agency or department of the federal government, may result in civil penalties, injunctions, and (in the case of a willful or intentional governmental violation) disciplinary action against officers or employees of the department or agency involved.[49] Bank customers affected by a violation of the RFPA may recover statutory damages in the amount of $100 or may recover the amount of actual damages sustained.[50] If a violation is willful or intentional, the court may award punitive damages, and successful actions under RFPA may result in an award of costs and reasonable attorneys' fees.[51]

3.3 The Fair Credit Reporting Act

The U.S. economy depends heavily on consumer borrowing, and the process of granting consumer credit requires accurate, timely information concerning the creditworthiness of individuals. As a complex and pervasive industry grew up to support this process, the potential of that industry for abuse gave rise to the one of the first and most comprehensive privacy statutes affecting American business—the Fair Credit Reporting Act (FCRA).[52] Although FCRA primarily regulates the credit reporting industry, it also regulates the use of that industry's product by financial institutions. Accordingly, it is appropriate to address FCRA in this chapter.

FCRA imposes obligations on the producers and users of two types of reports, which the statute calls *consumer reports* and *investigative consumer reports*. The institutions that typically produce such reports, and that have the heaviest obligations under FCRA, are called *consumer reporting agencies*. An understanding of FCRA requires careful attention to the definitions of these terms.

A *consumer report* is "any written, oral, or other communication of any information by a consumer reporting agency bearing on a consumer's credit worthiness, credit standing, credit, capacity, character, general reputation, personal characteristics, or mode of living which is used or expected to be used or collected in whole or in part for the purpose of serving as a factor in establishing the consumer's eligibility for (A) credit or insurance to be used primarily for personal, family, or household purposes; (B) employment purposes; or (C) any other purpose authorized under [FCRA]."[53] This expansive definition is subject to a number of exclusions, including reports generated solely for purposes of a transaction between a consumer and the person making the report, and communication among persons related by common ownership or affiliated by corporate control.[54]

An *investigative consumer report* is a consumer report that contains information based on personal interviews. Specifically, an investigative consumer report is a "a consumer report or portion thereof in which information on a consumer's character, general reputation, personal characteristics, or mode of living is obtained through personal interviews with neighbors, friends or associates of the consumer reported on or with others with whom he is acquainted or who may have knowledge concerning any such items of information."[55] The definition does not include "specific factual information on a consumer's credit record obtained directly from a creditor of the consumer or from a consumer reporting agency when such information was obtained directly from a creditor of the consumer or from the consumer."[56]

Finally, a *consumer reporting agency* is "any person which, for monetary fees, dues, or on a cooperative nonprofit basis, regularly engages in whole or in part in the practice of assembling or evaluating consumer credit information or other information on consumers for the purpose of furnishing consumer reports to third parties, and which uses any means or facility of interstate commerce for the purpose of preparing or furnishing consumer reports."[57]

With these definitions in mind, what must consumer reporting agencies and users of their reports do in order to comply with FCRA?

3.3.1 Reporting Agencies May Furnish Reports Only as Permitted by FCRA

FCRA sets out a long list of purposes for which a consumer reporting agency may furnish a consumer report. That list is intended to be exclusive: it is unlawful to furnish reports for any purpose not specified in the statute.

The permitted circumstances are:[58]

1. In response to the order of a court having jurisdiction to issue such an order, or a subpoena issued in connection with proceedings before a Federal grand jury.
2. In accordance with the written instructions of the consumer to whom it relates.
3. To a person which it has reason to believe—
   a. intends to use the information in connection with a credit transaction involving the consumer on whom the information is to be furnished and involving the extension of credit to, or review or collection of an account of, the consumer; or
   b. intends to use the information for employment purposes; or
   c. intends to use the information in connection with the underwriting of insurance involving the consumer; or
   d. intends to use the information in connection with a determination of the consumer's eligibility for a license or other benefit granted by a governmental instrumentality required by law to consider an applicant's financial responsibility or status; or

e. intends to use the information, as a potential investor or servicer, or current insurer, in connection with a valuation of, or an assessment of the credit or prepayment risks associated with, an existing credit obligation; or
f. otherwise has a legitimate business need for the information—
   (1) in connection with a business transaction that is initiated by the consumer; or
   (2) to review an account to determine whether the consumer continues to meet the terms of the account.

4. In response to a request by the head of a State or local child support enforcement agency (or a State or local government official authorized by the head of such an agency), if the person making the request certifies to the consumer reporting agency that—
   a. the consumer report is needed for the purpose of establishing an individual's capacity to make child support payments or determining the appropriate level of such payments;
   b. the paternity of the consumer for the child to which the obligation relates has been established or acknowledged by the consumer in accordance with State laws under which the obligation arises (if required by those laws);
   c. the person has provided at least 10 days' prior notice to the consumer whose report is requested, by certified or registered mail to the last known address of the consumer, that the report will be requested; and
   d. the consumer report will be kept confidential, will be used solely for a purpose described in subparagraph (a), and will not be used in connection with any other civil, administrative, or criminal proceeding, or for any other purpose.
5. To an agency administering a State plan under section 454 of the Social Security Act (42 U.S.C. 654) for use to set an initial or modified child support award.
6. To the Federal Deposit Insurance Corporation or the National Credit Union Administration as part of its preparation for its appointment or as part of its exercise of powers, as conservator, receiver, or liquidating agent for an insured depository institution or insured credit union under the Federal Deposit Insurance Act or the Federal Credit Union Act, or other applicable Federal or State law, or in connection with the resolution or liquidation of a failed or failing insured depository institution or insured credit union, as applicable.

FCRA also limits the circumstances in which a consumer reporting agency may furnish consumer reports for employment purposes. Essentially, a report may be furnished for employment purposes only if the recipient certifies that it will comply with FCRA's requirements concerning notice to the consumer that the report will be obtained and, if applicable, notice to the consumer of intention to take adverse action based in whole or in part on the report. These user restrictions are discussed in more detail next.[59]

3.3.2 Reporting Agencies Must Maintain Accuracy of Information

FCRA is one of the few statutes that impose a duty of care with respect to the accuracy of information. Specifically, a consumer reporting agency that prepares a consumer report must "follow reasonable procedures to assure maximum possible accuracy of the information concerning the individual about whom the report relates."[60]

3.3.3 Reporting Agencies Must Police Users

Consumer reporting agencies may not simply rely on users' assurances that they will use consumer reports for purposes permitted by FCRA. The statute imposes on those agencies an affirmative duty to verify that entities requesting consumer reports are legitimate and will use the reports appropriately.[61] Although the statute does not prescribe specific verification measures, those measures reasonably will vary according to whether a user is known to the agency and has an established reputation as a responsible user of consumer report information.

3.3.4 Reporting Agencies Must Permit Consumers to Review Consumer Report Information

Consumer reporting agencies must permit consumers to review their files, and must specify the procedures to be followed in exercising that right.[62] Consumers also may place statements of dispute in their files, and may ask reporting agencies and entities that furnish information to those agencies to reinvestigate information the consumer believes to be inaccurate.[63] Where information in a consumer report is found to be inaccurate, the consumer is entitled to correction of that information, and in some circumstances the reporting agency must notify previous users of the consumers' reports of the correction.[64]

3.3.5 Reporting Agencies and Users Must Observe Rules Concerning Investigative Consumer Reports

As noted earlier, FCRA distinguishes investigative consumer reports, which are based in whole or in part on interviews, from ordinary consumer reports.

Investigative consumer reports bring into play additional obligations for both consumer reporting agencies and report users. Notably, preparers of such reports must re-verify information in an investigative report that is more than three months old, before including that information in a subsequent consumer report.[65] Also, users must advise consumers that an investigative consumer report may be made.[66]

3.3.6 Reporting Agencies Must Delete Obsolete Information

Some adverse information in consumer reports (but not nonadverse information) must be deleted after seven years.[67] A number of exceptions to this rule apply, including criminal convictions and information provided in connection with a proposed extension of credit in the amount of $150,000 or more.[68]

3.3.7 Reporting Agencies May Not Report Medical Information Without Consumer Consent

With certain exceptions, a consumer reporting agency may not furnish for employment purposes, or in connection with a credit or insurance transaction, a consumer report that contains medical information without the consumer's consent.[69] FCRA defines "medical information" to include "information or data, whether oral or recorded, in any form or medium, created by or derived from a health care provider of the consumer, that relates to . . . the past, present, or future physical, mental, or behavioral health or condition of any individual; . . . the provision of health care to an individual; or . . . the payment for the provision of health care to an individual."[70]

3.3.8 Users Must Comply with FCRA

In addition to its constraints on credit reporting agencies, the FCRA also imposes obligations on those that obtain and use consumer credit reports.[71] Specifically, when a merchant, employer, or other user takes action adverse to any person based on a credit report, the user must disclose that fact to the person as to whom adverse action is taken.[72] Users of credit reports also are criminally liable for obtaining information from credit agencies under false pretenses.[73]

Also, the FCRA, as interpreted by federal banking agencies and the Federal Trade Commission, has prevented financial institutions from sharing some types of customer information with affiliated companies. Recent amendments to the FCRA have addressed this problem by providing that "experience information"—that is, information concerning transactions between a customer and a company—may be shared with an affiliated company, either directly or through access by the affiliates to a central database.[74] The amended FCRA also permits affiliated entities to share other, nontransactional customer information if the customer has been given notice of that practice and has had an opportunity to refuse to permit information sharing with affiliates.[75]

3.3.9 FACTA Amendments

In 2003 the Congress passed the Fair and Accurate Credit Transactions Act (FACTA), which is intended to give consumers additional tools with which to detect and respond to identity theft.[76] FACTA's principal privacy-related provisions require businesses to respond to certain consumer reports of fraud or identity theft. Specifically, if a consumer "contacts a consumer reporting agency and expresses a belief that the consumer is a victim of fraud or identity theft . . . ," the agency must furnish the consumer with a "summary of rights." Pursuant to those rights, the consumer may request information from any of a defined group of businesses, including any business entity that has provided credit to "a person who has allegedly made unauthorized use of the means of identification of the victim," or (2) "provided for consideration products, goods, or services to, or accepted payment from, or otherwise entered into a commercial transaction for consideration with, a person who has allegedly made unauthorized use of the means of identification of the victim."[77] If the request is in writing and the victim has provided sufficient identifying information (or if the business "otherwise has a high degree of confidence that it knows the identity of the victim making a request"), the business must provide to the victim, without charge, "a copy of the application and business transaction records in its control, whether maintained by the business or by another person on its behalf."[78]

The privacy-related provisions of FACTA are complex, as is the question of the preemptive effect of FACTA on state identity theft legislation. If your company is presented with an apparent FACTA issue, you should consult the statute or seek expert advice on its requirements.[79]

3.3.10 FCRA Enforcement

Enforcement proceedings for violations of FCRA may be brought by the Federal Trade Commission and, as appropriate, by the functional regulators of financial institutions that use consumer reports.[80]

FCRA also authorizes civil lawsuits for willful, knowing, and negligent noncompliance with FCRA.

If a user obtains a consumer report under false pretenses, that user is liable for actual damages sustained by the consumer or $1,000, whichever is greater, as well as punitive damages, costs, and reasonable attorneys' fees as determined by the court.[81]

Finally, obtaining information from a consumer reporting agency under false pretenses, where that action is willful and knowing, is a criminal offense for which the user may be fined and imprisoned for up to two years.[82] Similar penalties may be imposed on reporting agency employees who knowingly and willfully provide information concerning an individual from the agency's files to a person who is not entitled to that information.[83]

3.3.11 State Regulation of Credit Reporting

A number of states also have enacted statutes limiting the disclosure and use of personal information by consumer credit reporting agencies. Most of the state statutes follow the overall approach of the FCRA, and most even adopt the FCRA's definitions of key statutory terms.[84]

Under state law, companies that prepare investigative reports may be identified as separately-defined entities (e.g., "investigative consumer reporting agencies") that are distinguished from consumer reporting agencies that do not perform these functions. State law definitions of these investigative firms and their activities may vary from the federal definition of an investigative consumer report. California, for example, defines an investigative consumer report as "a consumer report in which information on a consumer's character, general reputation, personal characteristics, or mode of living is obtained *through any means*."[85] California defines an investigative consumer reporting agency, in turn, as "any person who, for monetary fees or dues, engages in whole or in part in the practice of collecting, assembling, evaluating, compiling, reporting, transmitting, transferring, or communicating information concerning consumers for the purposes of furnishing investigative consumer reports to third parties, but does not include any governmental agency whose records are maintained primarily for traffic safety, law enforcement, or licensing purposes, or any licensed insurance agent, insurance broker, or solicitor, insurer, or life insurance agent."[86]

Any entity that prepares or uses consumer reports or investigative reports must be thoroughly familiar with the state and federal laws that affect those activities.

3.4 Section 326 of the USA PATRIOT Act

The USA PATRIOT Act includes a Title captioned "International Money Laundering Abatement and Anti-terrorist Financing Act of 2001." Section 326 of the statute amends the Bank Secrecy Act to require the Secretary of the Treasury to prescribe regulations "setting forth the minimum standards for financial institutions and their customers regarding the identity of the customer that shall apply in connection with the opening of an account at a financial institution."[87] The regulations mandated by Section 326 must at least require financial institutions to implement reasonable procedures for: (1) verifying the identify of any person seeking to open an account; maintaining records of the information used to verify the person's identity, including name, address, and other identifying information; and (2) determining whether the person appears on any list of known or suspected terrorists or terrorist organizations provided to the financial institution by any government agency.

Pursuant to Section 326, the various banking regulatory agencies adopted a set of regulations that require each financial institution to develop and implement a Customer Identification Program (CIP).[88] Each institution's CIP may be set up on a scale that is appropriate to the size and type of the institution's business, but must meet certain minimum requirements set out in the regulations.

3.5 Electronic Funds Transfer Act

The Electronic Funds Transfer Act (EFTA) requires financial institutions to disclose their privacy policies for electronic transfers of funds.

The Federal Reserve Board, EFTA's principal implementing agency, has adopted rules that require financial institutions to disclose to consumers the institutions' terms and conditions for electronic funds transfers. The required disclosures must be provided at the time the consumer contracts with the financial institution to use an electronic funds transfer service.[89]

3.6 State Financial Privacy Statutes

The privacy provisions of the GLBA, and other federal financial privacy statutes, generally do not preempt state laws that offer stronger consumer protections, and a number of states continue to enact and enforce their own financial privacy statutes.

California, for example, expressly has declared that "[t]he policies intended to protect financial privacy imposed by the Gramm-Leach-Bliley Act are inadequate to meet the privacy concerns of California residents."[90] Accordingly, the California Financial Information Privacy Act imposes stronger protections, including a requirement that financial institutions obtain affirmative "opt-in" consent to the sharing of consumers' nonpublic personal information with nonaffiliated third parties, rather than the "opt-out" approval permitted by the GLBA.[91]

States also regulate a myriad of financial institutions and uses of financial information. These state statutes and regulations are too numerous and varied to summarize here, but some California laws are illustrative:

- California prohibits bookkeepers from disclosing customer records without consent.[92]

- California restricts disclosures of federal and state tax return information without the affected consumer's consent.[93]
- Merchants that accept credit cards in California must ensure that electronic credit card payment receipts provided to the cardholder display only the last five digits of the credit account number or expiration date.[94]
- Credit card issuers in California must permit customers to "opt out" of disclosure of their marketing information to third parties. Card issuers must provide customers with written notice of their rights under this statute.[95]
- California, like other states, extensively regulates the privacy practices of insurance companies, agents, and insurance-supported institutions within its jurisdiction.[96]
- Credit card issuers must provide certain cardholder account information to cardholders or police agencies in connection with complaints of identity theft.[97]

As noted earlier, these California laws are merely illustrative of the limitations states may impose on the disclosure and use of financial information, or of personal information by financial institutions.

Notes

[1]Gramm-Leach-Bliley Financial Modernization Act, Pub. L. No. 106-102, 113 Stat. 1338 (1999), codified at various sections of 12 United States Code and 15 United States Code.

[2]12 U.S.C. §§ 3401–3422.

[3]15 U.S.C. § 1681.

[4]15 U.S.C. § 1693.

[5]Pub. L. No. 107-56, Title III, amending the Bank Secrecy Act, 31 U.S.C. § 3511 *et seq.*

[6]Pub. L. No. 73-66, 48 Stat. 162 (1933); Pub. L. No. 97-320, 96 Stat. 1469 (1982).

[7]15 U.S.C. § 6801(a) (emphasis added).

[8]*Id.* § 6809(4)(A).

[9]12 U.S.C. § 1843(k)(4).

[10]Patricia G. Micek, "New Privacy Requirements for Consumer Information under the Gramm-Leach-Bliley Act Apply to Financial Institutions and Many Other Businesses," 28 Westchester B. J. 53 (Spring, 2001).

[11]12 U.S.C. § 1843(k)(4)(A–E).

[12]12 C.F.R. §§ 225.28, 225.86(a), as summarized by the Federal Trade Commission at 65 FR 33646, 33647 (May 24, 2000).

[13]12 C.F.R. § 211.5(d). The reference to the transaction of banking and financial operations "abroad" does not mean that the GLBA will apply only to such banking and financial operations when they are conducted outside the United States. In fact, the Bank Holding Company Act expressly refers to engaging, *in the United States*, in activities that the bank holding company may engage in outside the United States and that the Board has determined to be usual in connection with the transaction of banking and financial operations abroad. 12 U.S.C. § 1843(k)(4)(G).

[14]*See American Bar Association v. Federal Trade Commission*, 386 U.S. App. D.C. 368, 430 F.3d 457 (D.C. Cir. 2005).

[15]The eight agencies and their implementing regulations are: the Board of Governors of the Federal Reserve System, 12 C.F.R. § 216; Office of the Comptroller of the Currency, 12 C.F.R. § 40; Federal Deposit Insurance Corporation, 12 C.F.R. § 332; Office of Thrift Supervision, 12 C.F.R. § 573; National Credit Union Administration, 12 C.F.R. § 716; Securities and Exchange Commission, 17 C.F.R. § 248; Commodity Futures Trading Commission, 17 C.F.R. § 160; Federal Trade Commission, 16 C.F.R. § 313. Also, GLBA privacy regulations applicable to insurance companies have been enacted by the states, which are the primary regulators of the business of insurance in the United States.

[16]12 C.F.R. § 216.4(a).

[17]12 C.F.R. § 216.4(a)(1).

[18]12 C.F.R. § 216.3(i)(1).

[19]12 C.F.R. § 216.3(i)(2)(i)(E).

[20]15 U.S.C. § 6809(4)(a).

[21]15 U.S.C. § 6809(4)(B), 6809(4)(C)(2).

[22]A financial institution may provide the notice jointly with its affiliates or with other financial institutions. 12 C.F.R. § 216.9(f).

[23]12 C.F.R. § 216.6(a). The list quoted here is taken from the regulations of the Board of Governors of the Federal Reserve System.

[24]12 C.F.R. pt. 216 App. A.

[25]12 C.F.R. § 216.4(a)(1).

[26]12 C.F.R. § 216.4(e)(1)(ii).

[27]12 C.F.R. § 216.4(e)(1)(i).

[28]12 C.F.R. § 216.9(a).

[29]12 C.F.R. § 216.9(b)(1)(iii).

[30]12 C.F.R. § 216.13(a).

[31]12 C.F.R. § 216.14(a).

[32]12 C.F.R. § 216.15(a).

[33]12 C.F.R. § 216.14(b)(v).

[34]12 C.F.R. § 216.15(2).

[35]12 C.F.R. § 216.15(a)(3).

[36]12 C.F.R. § 216.15(a)(7)(i).

[37]15 U.S.C. § 6802(c); 12 C.F.R. § 216.11.

[38]*United States v. Miller*, 425 U.S. 435 (1976).

[39]The RFPA defines "financial institution" to include "any office of a bank, savings bank, card issuer . . . , industrial loan company, trust company, savings association, building and loan, or homestead association (including cooperative banks), credit union, or consumer finance institution, located in any State or territory of the United States, the District of Columbia, Puerto Rico, Guam, American Samoa, or the Virgin Islands." 12 U.S.C. § 3401(1). The RFPA defines "financial record" to include "an original of, a copy of, or information known to have been derived from, any record held by a financial institution pertaining to a customer's relationship with the financial institution." 12 U.S.C. § 3401(2).

[40]12 U.S.C. § 3406.

[41]*Id.* § 3405.

[42]*Id.* Notice to the customer is intended to give the customer an opportunity to challenge production of his or her records. 12 U.S.C. § 3410. However, under certain circumstances specified in the statute, the court may order a delay in notice to the customer. 12 U.S.C. § 3409.

[43]12 U.S.C. § 3413.

[44]*Id.* § 3413(c); *see Raikos v. Bloomfield State Bank*, 703 F. Supp. 1365 (8th Cir. 1988).

[45]12 U.S.C. § 1829(a). Financial institutions and others engaging in electronic commerce also are subject to the Electronic Funds Transfer Act, which defines the rights and obligations of parties to electronic fund transfers and mandates notice to customers of the circumstances in which records of their transactions will be disclosed to others. 15 U.S.C. § 1693 *et seq.*

[46]Cal. Gov't Code §§ 7460–7493 (Deering Supp. 1990); Nev. Rev. Stat. Ann. § 239A (Michie 1986); NH Rev. Stat. Ann. § 359-C (1984); Or. Rev. Stat. §§ 192.550–192.595 (1989).

[47]Some statutes apply only to state-chartered banks, while others apply expansively to state banks, federal banks, savings and loan associations, credit card issuers, and credit reporting agencies.

[48]Conn. Gen. Stat. Ann. § 36-9k (West 1987); Ill. Ann. Stat. ch. 17, ¶ 360; ch. 17, ¶ 3303-8 (Smith-Hurd Supp. 1989); Me Rev. Stat. Ann. tit. 9-B, § 162 (1980); Md. Fin. Inst. Code Ann. §§ 1-301-1-305 (Michie Supp. 1989).

[49]12 U.S.C. § 3417. However, no recovery may be had, under the RFPA or any other state or federal law, against a financial institution that discloses financial records to a governmental authority in good faith. 12 U.S.C. § 3417(c).

[50]*Id.*

[51]*Id.*

[52]15 U.S.C. §§ 1681.

[53]15 U.S.C. § 1681a(d).

[54]15 U.S.C. § 1681a(d)(2).

[55]15 U.S.C. § 1681a(e).

[56]*Id.*

[57]15 U.S.C. § 1681a(f).

[58]15 U.S.C. § 1681b(a).

[59]Consumer reporting agencies that furnish reports for employment purposes also must provide the recipient with a statement of consumer rights in a form prescribed by the Federal Trade Commission.

[60]15 U.S.C. § 1681e(b).

[61]15 U.S.C. § 1681e(a).

[62]15 U.S.C. § 1681g, 1681 h.

[63]15 U.S.C. § 1681i(b), 1681h.

[64]15 U.S.C. § 1681i, 1681h.

[65]15 U.S.C. § 1681a(d)(1).

[66]15 U.S.C. § 1681l.

[67]15 U.S.C. § 1681c(a).

[68]15 U.S.C. § 1681c.

[69]15 U.S.C. § 1681b(g).

[70]15 U.S.C. § 1681a(i).

[71]With minor exceptions, credit reports may be furnished only to persons who are reasonably believed to intend to use those reports for extension of credit, employment decisions, underwriting of insurance, licensing, or other legitimate business needs involving transactions with the consumers to whom the reports pertain. *Id.* § 1681b.

[72]*Id.* § 1681m.

[73]*Id.* § 1681q.

[74]*Id.* § 1681a(d)(2)(A)(ii).

[75]*Id.* § 1681a(d)(2)(A)(iii).

[76]Fair and Accurate Credit Transactions Act of 2003, Pub. L. 109-159, 111 Stat. 1952, adding new sections to the Fair Credit Reporting Act, 15 U.S.C. § 1681 et seq.

[77]FACTA § 151, adding 15 U.S.C. § 1681g(e)(1).

[78]FACTA § 151, adding 15 U.S.C. 1681g(e)(1)–1681g(e)(2).

[79]FACTA also requires companies to exercise care in the disposal of information derived from credit reports.

[80]15 U.S.C. § 1681s.

[81]15 U.S.C. § 1681n.

[82]15 U.S.C. § 1681r.

[83]*Id.*

[84]*See, e.g.*, Cal. Civ. Code §§ 1785.1–1785.36; Ariz. Rev. Stat. Ann. §§ 44-1691–44-1696 (West 1989); NY Gen. Bus. Law § 380, as amended by 1979 NY Laws ch. 179 (McKinney Supp. 1990).

[85]Cal. Civ. Code § 1786.2(c) (*emphasis added*). Note that this definition is more inclusive than the FCRA definition, which defines investigative consumer reports to include only such reports as are based in whole or in part on personal interviews.

[86]*Id.* § 1786.2(d).

[87]31 U.S.C. § 5318(l).

[88]The regulations were adopted jointly by: Office of the Comptroller of the Currency, 12 C.F.R. Part 21; Federal Reserve System, 12 C.F.R. Parts 208 and 211; Federal Deposit Insurance Corporation, 12 C.F.R. Part 326; Office of Thrift Supervision, 12 C.F.R. Part 563; National Credit Union Administration, 12 C.F.R. Part 748; and Department of the Treasury, 12 C.F.R. Part 103.

[89]15 U.S.C. § 1693c; 12 C.F.R. § 205.7.

[90]California Financial Information Privacy Act, Cal. Fin. Code § 4051.5(a)(3).

[91]*Id.* § 4053(a).

[92]Cal. Civ. Code § 17991.1.

[93]*Id.* § 1799.1a.

[94]*Id.* § 1747.9.

[95]Cal. Civ. Code §§ 1748.10-1748.12.

[96]Cal. Ins. Code §§ 791-791.27.

[97]Cal. Civ. Code § 1748.95.

CHAPTER 4

If Your Organization Is an Electronic Communication Service Provider: The Electronic Communications Privacy Act and Stored Communications Act

In the United States, telephone companies, e-mail service providers, and other providers of communications services to the public have privacy obligations that do not apply to ordinary businesses. Among those obligations is the duty to protect the confidentiality of customer information, including communications that are transmitted or retained by those services.[1]

4.1 Disclosing Customer Information

The privacy obligations of communications service providers are set out primarily in the Electronic Communications Privacy Act (ECPA)[2] and the Stored Communications Act (SCA).[3] The ECPA defines the circumstances in which wire, oral, or electronic communications may be intercepted in "real time," by means of wiretapping or electronic eavesdropping. The SCA defines the circumstances in which service providers may disclose customer-related information in their possession, including the contents of communications that are stored on the provider's system.

The ECPA provides generally that no person, including a service provider, may acquire the contents of a wire, oral, or electronic communication as those communications are in transit rather than in storage on a service provider's system.[4] The statute includes numerous exceptions to the prohibition, however, including interceptions made with the consent of one party to the communication and interceptions that are necessary to protect legitimate interests of the service provider. The statute also sets out the minimum procedural requirements for any law enforcement agency, state or federal, to obtain a wiretap order.[5]

The SCA privacy obligations apply primarily to providers of "electronic communication service to the public."[6] The ECPA and SCA define "electronic communication service" as "any service which provides to users the ability to send or receive wire or electronic communications."[7] "Wire communications" and "electronic communications," in turn, are defined to include voice telephone conversations (whether wireline or wireless, and whether carried over traditional telephone lines or the Internet) and e-mail communications.[8] Accordingly, any company that offers public telephone or e-mail service is a provider of an "electronic communication service" under the SCA.

The SCA defines the circumstances in which a provider of electronic communication service to the public may divulge: (1) the contents of customer communications, (2) basic subscriber information, and (3) records or other information pertaining to a customer or subscriber. The following describes each of these sets of restrictions in turn.

4.1.1 Disclosing the Contents of Communications

The SCA defines the "contents" of a communication as "any information concerning the substance, purport, or meaning of that communication."[9] Congress first adopted this definition before e-mail became prevalent, to distinguish the contents of telephone calls from the telephone numbers used to dial those calls.[10] As e-mail has become more common, courts have had to decide which elements of an e-mail message constitute "content" and "noncontent" information for ECPA and SCA purposes. At the time of this writing, the better view seems to be that an e-mail address is noncontent information, but a subject line, like the body of the e-mail message itself, is part of the e-mail's contents and must be treated accordingly under the ECPA and SCA.

Subject to exceptions set out in the statute, a provider of electronic communication service to the public may not "knowingly divulge to any person or entity the contents of a communication while in electronic storage by that service."[11] The exceptions to this rule include disclosures with the consent of an originator or addressee of a communication, disclosures to governmental entities pursuant to warrant or other process, and disclosures that are "necessarily incident to the rendition of the service or to the protection of the rights or property of the provider of that service . . ."[12] Service providers also may disclose the contents of customer communications to law enforcement agencies where those communications were "inadvertently obtained" and appear to pertain to the commission of a crime.[13]

The SCA extensively addresses the methods by which a "governmental entity" may acquire the contents of stored communications from a service provider. Specifically, a governmental entity may compel such disclosure by: (1) obtaining a warrant from a court; (2) serving an administrative subpoena, grand jury or trial subpoena; or (3) obtaining a court order pursuant to a special procedure set out in Section 2703(d) of the SCA (sometimes referred to as a "2703(d) order").[14] The SCA also permits disclosure of customer information to the Federal Bureau of Investigation pursuant to the controversial "national security letter" procedure set out in section 2709 of the statute.

However, the SCA does not specify any method by which a private litigant may obtain the contents of a communication from a service provider pursuant to a subpoena or discovery request. In the absence of such provisions, the SCA should be read as prohibiting the release of customer communications to private litigants. A number of commentators and at least one court have expressly endorsed this interpretation, and no court has compelled a service provider to produce the contents of customer communications in response to a request from a private litigant.[15]

4.1.2 Disclosing Basic Subscriber Information

The SCA identifies specific types of basic subscriber information that may be produced to governmental entities without a warrant or Section 2703(d) order, so long as the governmental body presents an administrative, grand jury, or trial subpoena. Those categories of information are:[16]

A. name;
B. address;
C. local and long distance telephone connection records, or records of session times and durations;
D. length of service (including start date) and types of service utilized;
E. telephone or instrument number or other subscriber name or identity, including any temporarily assigned network address; and
F. means and source of payment for such service (including any credit card or bank account number) of a subscriber.

This information also may be produced to private parties voluntarily, or in response to a third-party subpoena or discovery request.[17] Before producing basic subscriber information voluntarily, however, a service provider should ensure that such a disclosure is consistent with its privacy policy. If the privacy policy does not permit such voluntary disclosures, the service provider should insist that the requesting party provide a subpoena or other process.

4.1.3 Disclosing Records or Other Information Pertaining to a Customer or Subscriber

In addition to basic subscriber information, the SCA permits the disclosure to governmental agencies of "a record or other information pertaining to a subscriber to or customer of such [electronic communication] service (not including the contents of such communications)."[18] As the U.S. Department of Justice has pointed out, this is a "catch-all category that includes all records that are not contents, including basic subscriber information."[19] Congress's purpose in creating this category was to give greater protection to noncontent information that reveals the history of a customer's electronic transactions.[20] Accordingly, noncontent information that is not contained within one of the enumerated categories of basic subscriber information, such as account logs, addresses of persons to whom e-mails were sent, and Internet sites visited, is classified as "records or other information pertaining to a customer or subscriber" under the SCA.[21]

This category of information, like basic subscriber information, may be provided to private parties voluntarily or pursuant to a subpoena or discovery request.[22] However, governmental entities may not obtain such information except pursuant to a Section 2703(d) order or a search warrant, with the customer's consent, or pursuant to a formal written request in connection with a telemarketing fraud investigation.[23]

Finally, the Federal Bureau of Investigation is empowered to demand disclosure by a wire or electronic communication service provider of "subscriber information and toll billing records information, or electronic communication transactional records in its custody or possession" by service on the provider of a so-called national security letter.[24] Such a letter may be accompanied by a demand that the service provider not disclose the existence of the request to the subscriber or any other person, except as necessary to comply with the request or obtain legal advice on the provider's compliance obligations.[25] The constitutional validity of the national security letter procedure has been challenged in various court actions, and service providers that are uncertain of their duty to comply with such a letter should obtain advice of counsel.

4.2 Disclosure of Customer Records Under the First Amendment

Lawsuits frequently are brought against persons who send e-mails or post to Web sites and online services anonymously. Those lawsuits (filed against "John Doe" and "Jane Doe" defendants) typically allege that a message or posting defamed the plaintiff, but some complaints allege trademark infringement or other offenses.

These lawsuits often are accompanied by third-party subpoenas to the defendant's communications service provider, demanding that the service provider disclose the defendant's identity. When presented with petitions to quash these subpoenas, courts have proved reluctant to enforce them because of the recognized right to anonymous speech under the First Amendment to the U.S. Constitution. The courts' concern is that the plaintiffs may be using a frivolous lawsuit as a means of exposing a speaker, as a means of informally punishing the speaker for exercising his or her First Amendment rights.[26]

In order to address this dilemma, several courts have required plaintiffs to demonstrate, before the subpoena requesting the defendant's identity may be enforced, that the complaint has merit. This can result in a "mini-trial" in which the plaintiff must come forward with sufficient facts to satisfy the court that the complaint is not frivolous.[27]

Customers might have no opportunity to exercise this right unless service providers notify their customers of the subpoena and give the customers a reasonable amount of time in which to bring a motion to quash. America Online, for example, has announced a policy of not complying with such subpoenas unless the customer has had notice and at least two weeks in which to respond. America Online also requests a copy of the complaint and any supporting documentation, so that it may, at its discretion, assess the validity of the underlying claim.[28]

Although service providers are under no legal obligation to accommodate their customers in this way (and should not commit themselves to do so, in their terms of use or elsewhere), helping customers to assert their First Amendment rights is good customer relations and might discourage plaintiffs from serving frivolous subpoenas on the service provider.

4.3 Disclosure in Circumstances That May Violate Foreign Law

Discovery demands may be upheld by a U.S. court, even where confidentiality laws of the country in which the data are stored, or of a country that otherwise has jurisdiction over the entity receiving the request, prohibit disclosure of the information demanded. For example, in a case involving data stored in the Cayman Islands by the Bank of Nova Scotia, the U.S. Court of Appeals for the Eleventh Circuit balanced a U.S. grand jury's need for information against the Cayman Islands' bank secrecy laws, and found in favor of compulsory disclosure of the account information demanded by the grand jury.[29] Accordingly, it is by no means certain that a U.S. court would decline to require disclosure of personal information of a communication service provider's customer simply because that disclosure would violate foreign law.[30]

In a specific case, a communications service provider faced with a subpoena for information that is protected by foreign law, but not U.S. law, can raise those concerns in a motion to quash the subpoena. The outcome of such an argument, however, is uncertain.

Notes

[1]Private companies also may have obligations as electronic communication service providers, even though they do not provide those services to the public. These subjects are covered in Chapters 9 and 13.

[2]18 U.S.C. § 2510 *et seq.*

[3]*Id.* § 2701 *et seq.*

[4]*Id.* § 2511.

[5]*Id.* §§ 2516, 2518.

[6]*Id.* § 2702. The SCA also sets out privacy obligations for providers of "remote computing service," such as data processing services provided over telephone lines or the Internet. *Id.*

[7]*Id.* § 2510(15). Most of the terms used in the SCA are defined in the ECPA, and those definitions are incorporated in the SCA by reference.

[8]*See id.* §§ 2510(1), 2510(12).

[9]*Id.* § 2510(8).

[10]Devices known as pen registers and trap and trace devices are used by law enforcement agencies to acquire the telephone numbers dialed, respectively, from and to telephones. The ECPA and SCA set out the requirements for acquisition of the contents of communications; a separate statute sets out the requirements for use of pen register and trap and trace devices by law enforcement to acquire noncontent information. *See* 18 U.S.C. § 3121 *et seq.*

[11]*Id.* § 2702(a)(1).

[12]*Id.*§ 2702(b).

[13]*Id.*

[14]*Id.* § 2703. If the communication has been in storage on the service provider's system for 180 days or less, the governmental agency must obtain a warrant in order to obtain the contents of the communication. *Id.* § 2703(a). Other forms of process may be used only if the communication has been stored on the system for more than 180 days. *Id.* § 2703(b). Except under circumstances prescribed in the statute, a request for the contents of a communication that is made pursuant to process other than a warrant requires notice to the customer. *Id.*

[15]*See O'Grady v. Superior Court*, 139 Cal. App. 4th 1423, 44 Cal. Rptr 3d 72 (Ct. App. Cal. 2006) (finding that the SCA "makes no exception for civil discovery" and "render[s] unenforceable the subpoenas" in that case); *see also* Stucky, *Internet and Online Law* § 5.03[1][a][i](2005) (stating that under SCA, "disclosures of content pursuant to a third party subpoena in civil litigation . . . are prohibited"); *see also* U.S. Internet Service Providers Association, *Electronic Evidence Compliance*, 18 Berkeley Tech. L. J. 945, 965 (2003).

[16] *Id.* § 2703(c)(2).

[17] *Id.* § 2702(c)(6). However, if the service provider is also a common carrier (e.g., a wireline or wireless telephone company), voluntary disclosure of this information might present issues under the privacy provisions of the Communications Act. 47 U.S.C. § 222.

[18] *Id.* § 2703(c)(1).

[19] United States Department of Justice, *Searching and Seizing Computers and Obtaining Electronic Evidence in Criminal Investigations*, p. 91 (July 2002) (available at www.cybercrime.gov).

[20] *Id.*, citing H.R. Rep. No. 103-827 (1994), reprinted in 1994 U.S.C.C.A.N. 3489, 3497, 3511.

[21] *Id.*

[22] 18 U.S.C. § 2702(c)(6). As with voluntary disclosure of basic subscriber information, service providers should ensure that such disclosure is consistent with their privacy policies.

[23] *Id.* § 2703(c)(1).

[24] 18 U.S.C. § 2709(a).

[25] *Id.* § 2709(c).

[26] *See Highfields Capital Management v. Doe (Highfields)*, 385 F.Supp.2d 969 (N.D. Cal. 1994); *Dendrite International, Inc., v. Doe (Dendrite)*, 775 A.2d 756 (N.J. App. Div. 2001); *Columbia Co. v. Seescandy.com (Seescandy)*, 185 F.R.D. 573 (N.D. Cal. 1999).

[27] *See John Doe No. 1 v. Cahill*, 884 A.2d 451 (Sup. Ct. Del. 2005); *see also Highifelds, supra; Dendrite, supra; Seescandy, supra.*

[28] AOL Civil Subpoena Policy, available at http://legal.aol.com/aol/aolpol/civilsubpoena.html.

[29] *In re Grand Jury Proceedings, The Bank of Nova Scotia United States v. The Bank of Nova Scotia*, 740 F.2d 817 (11th Cir. 1984).

[30] If the requested information is maintained in a foreign country rather than the United States, production still may be compelled if the entity receiving the subpoena has the legal right to obtain the information from its foreign office or affiliated entity. *See, e.g., Searock v. Stripling*, 736 F.2d 650, 653 (11th Cir. 1984).

CHAPTER 5

If Your Organization Is a Provider of Health Care, Health Insurance, or Related Services

Entities involved with the health care and health care insurance industries are subject to privacy obligations under the Health Insurance Portability and Accountability Act of 1996 (HIPAA) and the regulations adopted to implement that statute.[1] They also may be affected by privacy obligations imposed by other federal privacy requirements, and by state medical privacy laws.[2]

5.1 HIPAA

Like the Gramm-Leach-Bliley Act (GLBA), described in Chapter 3, HIPAA was not conceived primarily as a privacy statute. Just as GLBA was intended to make the financial services industry more competitive and efficient, HIPAA was intended to improve the efficiency and availability of health insurance coverage. The statute's Administrative Simplification title, in particular, which contains HIPAA's privacy obligations, streamlines the sharing of information among health insurers, health care providers, and other entities.[3]

Improved information sharing, however, can bring increased risks of misuse of patient and policyholder information. Accordingly, HIPAA gives patients and policyholders some control over the disclosure and use of personal information related to their health care. The HIPAA privacy provisions, in turn, are implemented by regulations of the United States Department of Health and Human Services (HHS).[4]

5.1.1 Entities Covered by HIPAA

HIPAA's privacy obligations apply to health plans, covered health care providers, health care clearinghouses and (indirectly) business associates of these so-called "covered entities" (see Figure 5.1).[5] They also apply to hybrid entities and organized health care arrangements. Each of these categories requires some explanation.

5.1.1.1 What Is a Health Plan?

A *health plan* is an individual or group plan that provides, or pays the cost of, medical care as defined in the Public Health Service Act (PHS).[6] A health plan includes, singly or in combination:

1. A group health plan, as described in the HHS regulation;[7]
2. A health insurance issuer, as described in the HHS regulation;[8]

HIPAA applies to health plans, health care providers, and health care clearinghouses. HIPAA also recognizes the categories of business associates, hybrid entities, affiliate covered entities, organized health care arrangements, and covered entities with multiple covered functions.

HEALTH PLANS INCLUDE:

- Health, dental, vision, and prescription drug insurers.
- Health maintenance organizations.
- Medicare, Medicaid, Medicare + Choice, and Medicare supplement insurers.
- Long-term care insurers (excluding nursing home fixed-indemnity policies).
- Employee-sponsored group health plans.
- Government and church-sponsored health plans.
- Multi-employer health plans.
- Exceptions to the health plan category include:
  - A group health plan with fewer than 50 participants that is administered solely by the employer that established and maintains the plan.
  - Certain government-funded programs.
  - Entities that provide only workers' compensation, automobile insurance, and property and casualty insurance.

HEALTH CARE PROVIDERS INCLUDE:

- Any health care provider that electronically transmits health information in connection with transactions for which HHS rules have been adopted.
- Covered transactions include claims, benefit eligibility queries, referral authorization requests, or other transactions for which HIPAA standards have been established.
- Health care provider is subject to HIPAA whether it electronically submits transactions directly or uses a billing service or other third party to do so.
- All providers of service are included, for example, institutional providers such as hospitals and noninstitutional providers such as physicians, dentists, and other practitioners as defined by Medicare. Also, any other organization that furnishes, bills, or is paid for health care.

HEALTH CARE CLEARINGHOUSES ARE:

- Entities that process nonstandard information that they receive from another entity into a standard format or content, or vice versa.
- Billing services, repricing companies, community health management information systems, and value-added networks and switches are included if these entities perform clearinghouse functions.

BUSINESS ASSOCIATES ARE:

- Persons or organizations, other than a member of a covered entity's workforce, that perform certain activities or functions on behalf of, or provide certain services to, covered entities that involve the use or disclosure of protected health information (PHI).
- Business associate activities include claims processing and billing, among other functions.
- A covered entity can be the business associate of another covered entity.
- Covered entities are responsible for entering into agreements with their business associates that impose written safeguards on the PHI used or disclosed by the business associate.

Figure 5.1 Is my organization subject to HIPAA privacy regulations?

A HYBRID ENTITY IS:

- A covered entity that is a single legal entity and collects both covered and non-covered functions.
- Entities that meet the definition *elect* to be treated as hybrid entities.
- The hybrid entity must specify, in writing, those elements of its operations that perform covered functions under HIPAA.
- Most Privacy Rule requirements will apply only to the covered functions of the hybrid entity.

AFFILIATED COVERED ENTITIES ARE:

- Covered entities that are legally separate but under common ownership or control.
- The affiliated entities must designate themselves in writing as affiliated covered entities.
- After designation, the affiliated entities will be treated as a single covered entity for Privacy Rule compliance purposes.

AN ORGANIZED HEALTH CARE ARRANGEMENT IS:

- A relationship in which participating covered entities share PHI to benefit their common enterprise.
- Types of organized health care arrangements recognized by the Privacy Rule are:
  - A clinically integrated setting in which individuals typically receive health care from more than one provider;
  - An organized system of health care in which the participating entities jointly hold themselves out to the public as part of a joint arrangement and jointly engage in utilization review, quality assessment, and improvement activities, or risk-sharing payment activities;
  - A group health plan and the health insurer or HMO that insures the plan's benefits, with respect to protected health information created or received by the insurer or HMO that relates to individuals who are or have been participants or beneficiaries of the group health plan;
  - All group health plans maintained by the same plan sponsor and all health insurers and HMOs that insure the plan's benefits, with respect to PHI created or received by the insurers or HMOs that relates to individuals who are or have been participants or beneficiaries in the group health plans.

COVERED ENTITIES WITH MULTIPLE COVERED FUNCTIONS

- If a covered entity performs multiple covered functions, it must operate its different covered functions in accordance with the provisions of the Privacy Rule that apply to those various covered functions.
- PHI of an individual may be shared between covered functions only if the individual to whom the PHI pertains is involved with both functions.

For additional information on entities subject to HIPAA, see the "decision tool" at http://www.cons.hhs.gov/hipaa/hipaa2/support/tools/decisionsupport/default.asp.

Figure 5.1 (Continued)

3. An HMO, as defined in the HHS regulation;[9]
4. Part A or B of the Medicare program under title XVIII of the [Social Security] Act;
5. The Medicaid program under title XIX of the Act, 42 U.S.C. 1396, et seq.;
6. An issuer of a Medicare supplemental policy (as defined in section 1882(g)(1) of the [Social Security] Act, 42 U.S.C. 1395ss(g)(1);
7. An issuer of a long-term care policy, excluding a nursing home fixed-indemnity policy;
8. An employee welfare benefit plan or any other arrangement that is established or maintained for the purpose of offering or providing health benefits to the employees of two or more employers;
9. The health care program for active military personnel under title 10 of the United States Code;
10. The veterans health care program under 38 U.S.C. chapter 17;
11. The Civilians Health and Medical Program of the Uniformed Services (CHAMPUS) (as defined in 10 U.S.C. 1072(4));
12. The Indian Health Service program under the Indian Health Care Improvement Act, 25 U.S.C. 1601, et seq.;
13. The Federal Employee Health Benefits Program under 5 U.S.C. 8902, et seq.;
14. An approved State child health plan under title XXI of the Act, providing benefits for child health assistance that meet the requirements of section 2103 of the [Social Security] Act, 42 U.S.C. 1397, et seq.;
15. The Medicare + Choice program under Part C of title XXVIII of the [Social Security] Act, 42 U.S.C. 1395w-21 through 1395w-28;
16. A high-risk pool that is a mechanism established under State law to provide health insurance coverage or comparable coverage to eligible individuals;
17. Any other individual or group plan, or combination of individual or group plans, that provides or pays for the cost of medical care . . .

The HHS definition of health plan excludes:

1. Any policy, plan, or program to the extent that it provides, or pays for the cost of, excepted benefits that are listed in section 2791(c)(1) of the PHS Act, 42 U.S.C. 300gg-91(c)(1);[10]
2. A government-funded program (other than one listed as eligible, above):
   a. Whose principal purpose is other than providing, or paying the cost of, health care; or
   b. Whose principal activity is (1) the direct provision of health care to persons; or (2) the making of grants to fund the direct provision of health care to persons.

5.1.1.2 What Is a Covered Health Care Provider?

Not all providers of medical and health-related services are regulated under HIPAA. Specifically, a health care provider is covered only if it "transmits any health care information in electronic form in connection with a transaction covered by [the HIPAA regulations]."[11]

Any health care provider that electronically transmits health care information in connection with one of the covered transactions, therefore, is a covered entity under HIPAA. A health care provider is defined in the HIPAA regulations as "a provider of services (as defined in section 1861(u) of the act, 42 U.S.C. 1395x(u)), a provider of medical or health services (as defined in section 1861(s) of the Act, 42 U.S.C. 1395x(s)), and any other person or organization who furnishes, bills, or is paid for health care in the normal course of business."[12]

5.1.1.3 What Is a Health Care Clearinghouse?

Health care clearinghouses are various entities that process health care information and related data for other entities. Specifically, the HHS regulations define a health care clearinghouse as "a public or private entity, including a billing service, repricing company, community health management information system or community health information system, and 'value added' networks and switches, that does either of the following functions: (1) Processes or facilitates the processing of health information received from another entity in a nonstandard format or containing nonstandard data content into standard data elements or a standard transaction; (2) Receives a standard transaction from another entity and processes or facilitates the processing of health information into nonstandard format or nonstandard content for the receiving entity."[13]

Health care clearinghouses sometimes act as business associates (see next section) of covered entities, and in such cases the clearinghouses generally do not create protected health information and are not subject to all of the HIPAA requirements.[14] However, if a clearinghouse is not acting as a business associate for a covered entity, it must comply with all HIPAA obligations.

5.1.1.4 What Are Business Associates?

A business associate is any entity that, on behalf of a covered entity or organized health care arrangement (discussed later), performs or assists in the performance of an activity involving the use or disclosure of individually identifiable health information.[15] The activities performed or assisted in may include, but are not limited to, "claims processing or administration, data analysis, processing or administration, utilization review, quality assurance, billing benefit management, practice management, and repricing . . ." or any other "function or activity regulated by" the HHS regulations.[16]

Business associates also are entities that provide certain services, including "legal, actuarial, accounting, consulting, data aggregation, . . . management, administrative, accreditation, or financial services to or for a covered entity, or to or for an organized health care arrangement in which the covered entity participates, where the provision of the service involves the disclosure of individually identifiable health information from such covered entity or arrangement or from another business associate of such covered entity or arrangement, to the person."[17]

Covered entities are permitted to use business associates to create or receive protected health information, but may do so only if the covered entity has a contract with the business associate that requires the associate to safeguard the protected information provided to it or created by it under the relationship. Specifically, the covered entity must ensure that the business associate has the following enforceable obligations:

(A) Not use or further disclose the information other than as permitted or required by the contract or as required by law;
(B) Use appropriate safeguards to prevent use or disclosure of the information other than as provided for by its contract;
(C) Report to the covered entity any use or disclosure of the information not provided for by its contract of which it becomes aware;
(D) Ensure that any agents, including a subcontractor, to whom it provides protected health information received from, or created or received by the business associate on behalf of, the covered entity agrees to the same restrictions and conditions that apply to the business associate with respect to such information;
(E) Make available protected health information in accordance with § 164.524;
(F) Make available protected health information for amendment and incorporate any amendments to protected health information in accordance with § 164.526;
(G) Make available the information required to provide an accounting of disclosures in accordance with § 164.528;
(H) Make its internal practices, books, and records relating to the use and disclosure of protected health information received from, or created or received by the business associate on behalf of, the covered entity available to the Secretary for purposes of determining the covered entity's compliance with this subpart; and
(I) At termination of the contract, if feasible, return or destroy all protected health information received from, or created or received by the business associate on behalf of, the covered entity that the business associate still maintains in any form and retain no copies of such information or, if such return or destruction is not feasible, extend the protections of the contract to the information and limit further uses and disclosures to those purposes that make the return or destruction of the information infeasible.
(iii) Authorize termination of the contract by the covered entity, if the covered entity determines that the business associate has violated a material term of the contract.
(3) Implementation specifications: Other arrangements. (i) If a covered entity and its business associate are both governmental entities:
(A) The covered entity may comply with paragraph (e) of this section by entering into a memorandum of understanding with the business associate that contains terms that accomplish the objectives of paragraph (e)(2) of this section.

(B) The covered entity may comply with paragraph (e) of this section, if other law (including regulations adopted by the covered entity or its business associate) contains requirements applicable to the business associate that accomplish the objectives of paragraph (e)(2) of this section.

(ii) If a business associate is required by law to perform a function or activity on behalf of a covered entity or to provide a service described in the definition of business associate in § 160.103 of this subchapter to a covered entity, such covered entity may disclose protected health information to the business associate to the extent necessary to comply with the legal mandate without meeting the requirements of this paragraph (e), provided that the covered entity attempts in good faith to obtain satisfactory assurances as required by paragraph (e)(3)(i) of this section, and, if such attempt fails, documents the attempt and the reasons that such assurances cannot be obtained.

(iii) The covered entity may omit from its other arrangements the termination authorization required by paragraph (e)(2)(iii) of this section, if such authorization is inconsistent with the statutory obligations of the covered entity or its business associate.

(4) Implementation specifications: Other requirements for contracts and other arrangements. (i) The contract or other arrangement between the covered entity and the business associate may permit the business associate to use the information received by the business associate in its capacity as a business associate to the covered entity, if necessary:

(A) For the proper management and administration of the business associate; or

(B) To carry out the legal responsibilities of the business associate.

(ii) The contract or other arrangement between the covered entity and the business associate may permit the business associate to disclose the information received by the business associate in its capacity as a business associate for the purposes described in paragraph (e)(4)(i) of this section, if:

(A) The disclosure is required by law; or

(B)(1) The business associate obtains reasonable assurances from the person to whom the information is disclosed that it will be held confidentially and used or further disclosed only as required by law or for the purpose for which it was disclosed to the person; and

(2) The person notifies the business associate of any instances of which it is aware in which the confidentiality of the information has been breached.[18]

5.1.1.5 Hybrid Entities

A hybrid entity is a single legal entity:

1. That is a covered entity;
2. Whose business activities include both covered and noncovered functions;
3. That designates health care components in accordance with paragraph § 164.105(a)(2)(iii)(c).[19]

An organization that meets the definition of a hybrid entity must designate the components of its organization that, if they were separate legal entities, would meet the definition of a covered entity. A designated health care component also may be designated only to the extent that it performs: (1) covered functions; or (2) activities that would make such component a business associate of a component that performs covered functions if the two components were separate legal entities.[20]

5.1.1.6 Organized Health Care Arrangements

The regulations refer to certain arrangements as "organized health care arrangements."[21] Five categories of such arrangements are recognized.

The first category is a "clinically integrated health care setting in which individuals typically receive health care from more than one health care provider."[22]

The second category is an organized "system of health care in which more than one covered entity participates and in which the participating covered entities: (i) hold themselves out to the public as participating in a joint arrangement; and (ii) participate in joint activities that include" at least one of the following: (A) utilization review; (B) quality assessment and improvement; or (C) payment activities.[23]

The third category is a "group health plan and a health insurance issuer or HMO with respect to such group health plan, but only with respect to protected health information created or received by such health insurance issuer or HMO that relates to individuals who are or who have been participants in such group health plan."[24]

The fourth category is a "group health plan and one or more other group health plans each of which are maintained by the same plan sponsor."[25]

Finally, the fifth category is defined as the group health plans described in category 4, "and health insurance issues or HMOs with respect to such group health plans, but only with respect to protected health information created or received by such health insurance issuers or HMOs that relates to individuals who are or have been participants or beneficiaries in any of such group health plans."[26]

Participants in organized health care arrangements are not business associates and are not required to operate under a business associate contract. The participants also may use joint notices and consents, subject to certain regulatory requirements.[27]

5.1.2 Information Protected by HIPAA

Under the HHS regulations, covered entities must take certain measures in their handling of protected health information (PHI), which includes all "individually identifiable health information" held or transmitted by a covered entity or its business associate in any form, whether electronic, paper, or oral.[28]

Specifically, PHI includes any information, including demographic data, that relates to:

- The individual's past, present, or future physical or mental health or condition;
- The provision of health care to the individual;
- The past, present, or future payment for the provision of health care to the individual, and that identifies the individual or for which there is a reasonable basis to believe it can be used to identify the individual.[29]

PHI does not include de-identified information, which is health care information that does not identify, and is unlikely to be usable to identify, an individual. A covered entity may demonstrate that information is de-identified by conducting a statistical analysis of the likelihood that the information can be used to identify individuals, or by removing certain identifiers listed in the regulations and meeting certain other requirements.[30]

5.1.3 When PHI May Be Disclosed

When a covered entity possesses or controls PHI, it may disclose that information only as permitted or required by the HIPAA rules or with the written authorization of—or on behalf of—the person to whom the PHI pertains. In broad outline, the categories of required and permitted PHI disclosures, and the rules governing authorization for PHI disclosures, are as follows.

5.1.3.1 Required Disclosures

The HIPAA rules recognize only two circumstances in which covered entities *must* disclose PHI. First, PHI must be disclosed to the persons to whom it pertains when those persons request access to their PHI or an accounting of past disclosures of their PHI.[31] Second, PHI must be disclosed to the U.S. Department of Health and Human Services when that agency is making a compliance review or pursuing an enforcement action.[32]

5.1.3.2 Permitted Uses and Disclosures

Permitted uses and disclosures are those a covered entity *may* make without the written permission of the individual to whom the PHI pertains. These include:

- To the individual, in cases other than requests for access or an accounting of disclosures;
- In connection with the covered entity's treatment;
- In connection with payment;
- In connection with health care operations;[33]
- For certain purposes, such as publication of patient directories and notification to family, relatives, or friends, *after the individual to whom the PHI pertains has been given an opportunity to agree or object*;[34]
- Incidental uses and disclosures, incident to an otherwise permitted use or disclosure, so long as the covered entity has adopted reasonable safeguards under the HIPAA rules and the PHI being shared was limited to the "minimum necessary;"[35]
- In connection with public interest and benefit activities such as abuse, neglect, health oversight, law enforcement, organ donation, and other purposes enumerated in the rules;[36]
- Release of "limited data sets," which are PHI from which specified identifiers have been removed and that are disclosed for research, health care operations, and public health purposes.[37]

5.1.3.3 Health Care Provider One-Time Consent

Subject to some exceptions, covered health care providers must obtain a one-time consent from an individual before using or disclosing that person's PHI. The consent must consist of at least the following:

(i) A description of the information to be used or disclosed that identifies the information in a specific and meaningful fashion;

(ii) The name or other specific identification of the person(s), or class of persons, authorized to make the requested use or disclosure;

(iii) The name or other specific identification of the person(s), or class of persons, to whom the covered entity may make the requested use or disclosure;

(iv) A description of each purpose of the requested use or disclosure. The statement "at the request of the individual" is a sufficient description of the purpose when an individual initiates the authorization and does not, or elects not to, provide a statement of the purpose;

(v) An expiration date or an expiration event that relates to the individual or the purpose of the use or disclosure. The statement "end of the research study," "none," or similar language is sufficient if the authorization is for a use or disclosure of protected health information for research, including for the creation and maintenance of a research database or research repository;

(vi) Signature of the individual and date. If the authorization is signed by a personal representative of the individual, a description of such representative's authority to act for the individual must also be provided;

(2) Required statements. In addition to the core elements, the authorization must contain statements adequate to place the individual on notice of all of the following:

(i) The individual's right to revoke the authorization in writing, and either:

(A) The exceptions to the right to revoke and a description of how the individual may revoke the authorization; or

(B) To the extent that the information in paragraph (c)(2)(i)(A) of this section is included in the notice required by § 164.520, a reference to the covered entity's notice.

(ii) The ability or inability to condition treatment, payment, enrollment, or eligibility for benefits on the authorization, by stating either:

(A) The covered entity may not condition treatment, payment, enrollment or eligibility for benefits on whether the individual signs the authorization when the prohibition on conditioning of authorizations in paragraph (b)(4) of this section applies; or

(B) The consequences to the individual of a refusal to sign the authorization when, in accordance with paragraph (b)(4) of this section, the covered entity can condition treatment, enrollment in the health plan, or eligibility for benefits on failure to obtain such authorization.

(iii) The potential for information disclosed pursuant to the authorization to be subject to redisclosure by the recipient and no longer be protected by this subpart.[38]

5.1.3.4 Authorization

If a use or disclosure of PHI is not for treatment, payment or health care operations or otherwise "required" or "permitted" for the purposes described above, that use or disclosure may be made only with the written authorization of the person to whom the PHI pertains.[39] Specifically, disclosures that require approval include "disclosures to a life insurer for coverage purposes, disclosures to an employer of the results of a pre-employment physical or lab test, or disclosures to a pharmaceutical firm for their own marketing purposes."[40]

5.1.4 The "Minimum Necessary" Principle

With some exceptions, covered entities must make reasonable efforts to request, use, and disclose only the minimum amount of PHI needed to accomplish the intended purpose.[41] The exceptions to this requirement are:

- In, or in response to, a health care provider's request in connection with treatment;
- Disclosure to the individual to whom the PHI pertains, or to that individual's representative;
- Use or disclosure pursuant to an authorization;
- Disclosure to the Department of Health and Human Services in connection with investigation, compliance, or enforcement activities;
- As required by law;
- As required for compliance with specified HIPAA rules.

So stated, the minimum necessary principle appears to place a heavy burden on covered entities that receive requests for PHI. How can the entity know that the request asks for no more information than is necessary to serve the requesting party's legitimate purpose? The Privacy Rule, adopted by the U.S. Department of Health and Human Services, gives some relief from this burden when it provides that a covered entity may (if reasonable under the circumstances) assume that the request complies with the minimum necessary principle. The assumption may be made when requests for PHI are received from: (a) public officials; (b) professionals that are business associates of the covered entity and are requesting the information in order to provide services to or on behalf of the covered entity; and (c) a researcher who provides the documentation required by the Privacy Rule.

Finally, in order to ensure compliance with the "minimum necessary" principle, each covered entity must develop policies and procedures that restrict access to PHI by the covered entity's workforce. Covered entities also must develop policies and procedures for responses to requests for disclosure that are designed to limit the information disclosed to the "minimum necessary."

5.1.5 Rights of Notice, Access, and Amendment

The Privacy Rule creates significant rights for individuals about whom PHI is collected, maintained, used, and disclosed.

Fundamental to this scheme is the right of notice. Each covered entity (with some exceptions set out in the Privacy Rule) must provide a notice of its privacy policies. If a covered health care provider has a direct treatment relationship with individuals, it must post the notice at each service delivery site and provide a copy of the privacy notice at the time of the first "service encounter" with the individual.[42] Covered entities must supply copies of their privacy notices to any person on request.[43]

Health care providers also are required to make a good-faith effort to obtain acknowledgement of receipt of the privacy notice from persons with whom those providers have a direct treatment relationship.[44] If no acknowledgement is obtained, the provider is required to document the reason for that failure.

Individuals also have a right of access to their PHI. Specifically, individuals have a right to inspect information known as a designated record set, which is information used by a covered entity to make decisions about payment and other matters.[45] Certain information, such as psychotherapy notes, is excluded from the designated data set, and access to the data set may be denied under certain circumstances set out in the Privacy Rule.[46]

HIPAA also gives individuals a right to obtain amendment of PHI that is inaccurate or incomplete.[47] Covered entities may deny the request for amendment, but must give the individual a written denial and permit him or her to place a statement of disagreement in the record.

5.1.6 Rights of Disclosure Accounting, Restriction, and Confidentiality

One of the most important HIPAA rights is the right of individuals to obtain, from covered entities or their business associates, an accounting of the disclosures of the individual's PHI that those covered entities or business associates have made.[48] The accounting is not required to be made for disclosures of certain kinds, including disclosures for treatment, payment, and health care operations and certain reports to corrections and law enforcement officials.

Individuals also may request that a covered entity restrict permitted uses or disclosures of PHI to persons involved in health care or payment, or disclosure "to notify family members or others about the individual's general condition, location, or death."[49] Covered entities may, but are not required to, agree to restriction requests.

Individuals also may ask health plans and covered health care providers to furnish PHI concerning the individual by an alternative means or to an alternative location.[50] Those requests must be honored if the individual represents that he or she will be endangered by disclosure of all or part of the subject PHI.

5.1.7 Covered Entity Compliance Measures

The HIPAA Privacy Rule requires covered entities to undertake a substantial range of compliance measures, which may be scaled to the size and complexity of those entities' operations. Notably, each covered entity must:

- Develop and implement written privacy policies and procedures;[51]
- Designate a privacy official and designate a person or office responsible for privacy-related complaints;[52]

- Train workforce members in privacy compliance;[53]
- Apply appropriate sanctions against workforce members who violate the entity's privacy policy or the HIPAA Privacy Rule;[54]
- Mitigate harmful effects caused by violations of the entity's privacy policy or the HIPAA Privacy Rule;[55]
- Maintain reasonable and appropriate administrative, physical and technical safeguards to prevent intentional or unintentional disclosures of PHI in violation of the Privacy Rule;[56]
- Maintain procedures for privacy-related complaints, including notice to individuals as to how to make complaints to the covered entity and the Department of Health and Human Services;[57]
- Maintain records concerning its privacy policies and procedures, privacy practices notices, disposition of complaints, and other documents for 6 years.[58]

5.1.8 HIPAA Data Security Obligations

Like the GLBA Safeguards Rule, the HIPAA regulations of the Department of Health and Human Services include obligations to safeguard the confidentiality and integrity of the personal information protected by the statute. The HIPAA rules, however, are somewhat more detailed that those promulgated by the FTC in its Safeguards Rule.

Like the GLBA Safeguards Rule in the case of financial information, the HIPAA rules require covered entities to implement administrative, technical, and physical safeguards to protect the confidentiality, integrity, and availability of PHI. The regulations also list a number of implementation specifications, each of which is designated as either "required" or "addressable." Covered entities must implement all required specifications, and may forego addressable specifications only if they can document why it would not be "reasonable and appropriate to implement the implementation specification."[59]

5.2 State Medical Privacy Statutes

One of the reasons for enactment of HIPAA was dissatisfaction with the inconsistent levels of medical privacy furnished by state laws. However, a number of states have such statutes and those are not preempted to the extent they provide equivalent or greater privacy protections.

The variety of state laws and regulations that affect the privacy of health care and health insurance information precludes exhaustive coverage of that subject here. For example, medical licensing boards impose confidentiality requirements, and courts recognize such evidentiary privacy protections as the physician-patient privilege and therapist-patient privilege. Other state laws restrict the collection, disclosure, or use of HIV status information, genetic information, participation in substance abuse programs, and other information.

California, for example, limits the ability of insurers to "disclose individually identifiable information concerning the health of, or the medical or genetic history of, a customer, to any affiliated or nonaffiliated depository institution, or to any other affiliated or nonaffiliated third party for use with regard to the granting of credit."[60] California also prohibits the disclosure of HIV test results to third parties, limits the disclosure of genetic test results, and requires "each employer who receives medical information [to] establish appropriate procedures to ensure the confidentiality and protection from unauthorized disclosure and use of that information."[61]

Organizations wishing to familiarize themselves with state privacy regulations affecting medical and related information should consult the laws and regulations of the individual states.

Notes

[1]Pub. L. No. 104-191, 110 Stat. 1936 (1996).

[2]Other federal privacy regulations that may apply to entities covered by HIPAA include the GLBA, the privacy provisions of the Public Health Service Act, and (for federal agencies) the Privacy Act of 1974. *See* Chapter 5, *supra; see also* 42 U.S.C. § 290dd-2; 5 U.S.C. § 552a. The subject of state medical privacy laws is discussed later in this chapter.

[3]The U.S. Department of Health and Human Services standards for electronic transmission of health care information are set out at 65 Fed. Reg. 50312 (Aug. 17, 2000).

[4]The HHS regulations are issued by that agency's Office for Civil Rights, and are set out at 45 C.F.R. Parts 160 and 164, "Safeguards for Privacy of Individually Identifiable Health Information; Security Standards for the Protection of Electronic Protected Health Information; General Administrative Requirements Including Civil Money Penalties; Procedures for Investigations, Imposition of Penalties, and Hearings."

[5]Figure 5.1 sets out an abbreviated list of HIPAA covered entities.

[6]45 C.F.R. § 160.103. The Public Health Service Act defines medical care as "amounts paid for—(A) the diagnosis, cure, mitigation, treatment, or prevention of disease, or amounts paid for the purpose of affecting any structure or function of the body, (B) amounts paid for transportation primarily for and essential to medical care referred to in subparagraph (A), and (C) amounts paid for insurance covering medical care referred to in subparagraphs (A) and (B)." 42 U.S.C. § 300gg-91(a)(2).

[7]The HHS regulations define a group health plan as "an employee welfare benefit plan (as defined in section 3(l) of the Employment Retirement Income and Security Act of 1974 (ERISA), 29 U.S.C. 1002(1)), including insured and self-insured plans, to the extent that the plan provides medical care . . . , including items and services paid for as medical care, to employees or their dependents directly or through insurance, reimbursement, or otherwise, that: (1) has 50 or more participants (as defined in section 3(7) of ERISA, 29 U.S.C. 1002(7)); or (2) is administered by an entity other than the employer that established and maintains the plan." 45 C.F.R. § 160.103.

[8]The regulation defines a health insurance issuer as "an insurance company, insurance service, or insurance organization (including an HMO) that is licensed to engage in the business of insurance in a State and is subject to State law that regulates insurance. Such term does not include a group health plan." *Id.* The regulations also incorporate by reference the definition of health insurance issuer set out in the Public Health Service Act at 300gg-91(b)(2).

[9]The regulations define an HMO, or health maintenance organization, as "a federally qualified HMO, an organization recognized as an HMO under State law, or a similar organization regulated for solvency under State law in the same manner and to the same extent as such an HMO." *Id.* The regulations also incorporate by reference the definition of health maintenance organization set out in the Public Health Service Act at 42 U.S.C. § 300gg-91(b)(3).

[10]"Excepted benefits" under the PHS Act include: (1) accident or disability income insurance; (2) coverage supplemental to liability insurance; (3) liability insurance, including general liability and automobile liability insurance; (4) workers' compensation or similar insurance; (5) automobile medical payment insurance; (6) credit-only insurance; and (7) coverage for on-site medical clinics. 42 U.S.C. 300gg-91(c)(1).

[11]45 C.F.R. § 160.103.

[12]*Id.* The definitions of "medical and other health services" and "provider of services" referred to in this definition, as set out at 42 U.S.C. 1395x(s) and 1395x(u), are:

(s) Medical and other health services. The term "medical and other health services" means any of the following items or services:

(1) physicians' services;

(2)

(A) services and supplies (including drugs and biologicals which are not usually self-administered by the patient) furnished as an incident to a physician's professional service, or kinds which are commonly furnished in physicians' offices and are commonly either rendered without charge or included in the physicians' bills (or would have been so included but for the application of section 1847B);

(B) hospital services (including drugs and biologicals which are not usually self-administered by the patient) incident to physicians' services rendered to outpatients and partial hospitalization services incident to such services;

(C) diagnostic services which are—

(i) furnished to an individual as an outpatient by a hospital or by others under arrangements with them made by a hospital, and

(ii) ordinarily furnished by such hospital (or by others under such arrangements) to its outpatients for the purpose of diagnostic study;

(D) outpatient physical therapy services and outpatient occupational therapy services;

(E) rural health clinic services and Federally qualified health center services;

(F) home dialysis supplies and equipment, self-care home dialysis support services, and institutional dialysis services and supplies;

(G) antigens (subject to quantity limitations prescribed in regulations by the Secretary) prepared by a physician, as defined in section 1861(r)(1), for a particular patient, including antigens so prepared which are forwarded to another qualified person (including a rural health clinic) for administration to such patient, from time to time, by or under the supervision of another such physician;

(H) (i) services furnished pursuant to a contract under section 1876 to a member of an eligible organization by a physician assistant or by a nurse practitioner (as defined in subsection (aa)(5)) and such services and supplies furnished as an incident to his service to such a member as would otherwise be covered under this section if furnished by a physician or as an incident to a physician's service; and

(ii) services furnished pursuant to a risk-sharing contract under section 1876(g) to a member of an eligible organization by a clinical psychologist (as defined by the Secretary) or by a clinical social worker (as defined in subsection (hh)(2)), and such services and supplies furnished as an incident to such clinical psychologist's services or clinical social worker's services to such a member as would otherwise be covered under this part if furnished by a physician or as an incident to a physician's service;

(I) blood clotting factors, for hemophilia patients competent to use such factors to control bleeding without medical or other supervision, and items related to the administration of such factors, subject to utilization controls deemed necessary by the Secretary for the efficient use of such factors;

(J) prescription drugs used in immunosuppressive therapy furnished, to an individual who receives an organ transplant for which payment is made under this section;

(K) (i) services which would be physicians' services and services described in subsection (ww)(1) if furnished by a physician (as defined in subsection (r)(1)) and which are performed by a physician assistant (as defined in subsection (aa)(5)) under the supervision of a physician (as so defined) and which the physician assistant is legally authorized to perform by the State in which the services are performed, and such services and supplies furnished as incident to such services as would be covered under subparagraph (A) if furnished incident to a physician's professional service, but only if no facility or other provider charges or is paid any amounts with respect to the furnishing of such services, [and]

(ii) services which would be physicians' services and services described in subsection (ww)(1) if furnished by a physician (as defined in subsection (r)(1)) and which are performed by a nurse practitioner or clinical nurse specialist (as defined in subsection (aa)(5)) working in collaboration (as defined in subsection (aa)(6)) with a physician (as defined in subsection (r)(1)) which the nurse practitioner or clinical nurse specialist is legally authorized to perform by the State in which the services are performed, and such services and supplies furnished as an incident to such services as would be covered under subparagraph (A) if furnished incident to a physician's professional service, but only if no facility or other provider charges or is paid any amounts with respect to the furnishing of such services;

(L) certified nurse-midwife services;

(M) qualified psychologist services;

(N) clinical social worker services (as defined in subsection (hh)(2));

(O) erythropoietin for dialysis patients competent to use such drug without medical or other supervision with respect to the administration of such drug, subject to methods and standards established by the Secretary by regulation for the safe and effective use of such drug, and items related to the administration of such drug;

(P) prostate cancer screening tests (as defined in subsection (oo));

(Q) an oral drug (which is approved by the Federal Food and Drug Administration) prescribed for use as an anticancer chemotherapeutic agent for a given indication, and containing an active ingredient (or ingredients), which is the same indication and active ingredient (or ingredients) as a drug which the carrier determines would be covered pursuant to subparagraph (A) or (B) if the drug could not be self-administered;

(R) colorectal cancer screening tests (as defined in subsection (pp));

(S) diabetes outpatient self-management training services (as defined in subsection (qq));

(T) an oral drug (which is approved by the Federal Food and Drug Administration) prescribed for use as an acute anti-emetic used as part of an anticancer chemotherapeutic regimen if the drug is administered by a physician (or as prescribed by a physician)—

(i) for use immediately before, at, or within 48 hours after the time of the administration of the anticancer chemotherapeutic agent; and

(ii) as a full replacement for the anti-emetic therapy which would otherwise be administered intravenously;

(U) screening for glaucoma (as defined in subsection (uu)) for individuals determined to be at high risk for glaucoma, individuals with a family history of glaucoma, and individuals with diabetes;

(V) medical nutrition therapy services (as defined in subsection (vv)(1)) in the case of a beneficiary with diabetes or a renal disease who—

(i) has not received diabetes outpatient self-management training services within a time period determined by the Secretary;

(ii) is not receiving maintenance dialysis for which payment is made under section 1881; and

(iii) meets such other criteria determined by the Secretary after consideration of protocols established by dietitian or nutrition professional organizations;

(W) an initial preventive physical examination (as defined in subsection (ww));

(X) cardiovascular screening blood tests (as defined in subsection (xx)(1));

(Y) diabetes screening tests (as defined in subsection (yy));

(Z) intravenous immune globulin for the treatment of primary immune deficiency diseases in the home (as defined in subsection (zz)); and

(AA) ultrasound screening for abdominal aortic aneurysm (as defined in subsection (bbb)) for an individual—

(i) who receives a referral for such an ultrasound screening as a result of an initial preventive physical examination (as defined in section 1861(ww)(1));

(ii) who has not been previously furnished such an ultrasound screening under this title; and

(iii) who—

(I) has a family history of abdominal aortic aneurysm; or

(II) manifests risk factors included in a beneficiary category recommended for screening by the United States Preventive Services Task Force regarding abdominal aortic aneurysms;

(3) diagnostic X-ray tests (including tests under the supervision of a physician, furnished in a place of residence used as the patient's home, if the performance of such tests meets such conditions relating to health and safety as the Secretary may find necessary and including diagnostic mammography if conducted by a facility that has a certificate (or provisional certificate) issued under section 354 of the Public Health Service Act, diagnostic laboratory tests, and other diagnostic tests;

(4) X-ray, radium, and radioactive isotope therapy, including materials and services of technicians;

(5) surgical dressings, and splints, casts, and other devices used for reduction of fractures and dislocations;

(6) durable medical equipment;

(7) ambulance service where the use of other methods of transportation is contraindicated by the individual's condition, but, subject to section 1834(l)(14), only to the extent provided in regulations;

(8) prosthetic devices (other than dental) which replace all or part of an internal body organ (including colostomy bags and supplies directly related to colostomy care), including replacement of such devices, and including one pair of conventional eyeglasses or contact lenses furnished subsequent to each cataract surgery with insertion of an intraocular lens;

(9) leg, arm, back, and neck braces, and artificial legs, arms, and eyes, including replacements if required because of a change in the patient's physical condition;

(10) (A) pneumococcal vaccine and its administration and subject to section 4071(b) of the Omnibus Budget Reconciliation Act of 1987, influenza vaccine and its administration; and

(B) hepatitis B vaccine and its administration, furnished to an individual who is at high or intermediate risk of contracting hepatitis B (as determined by the Secretary under regulations); and

(11) services of a certified registered nurse anesthetist (as defined in subsection (bb));

(12) subject to section 4072(e) of the Omnibus Budget Reconciliation Act of 1987, extra-depth shoes with inserts or custom molded shoes with inserts for an individual with diabetes, if—

(A) the physician who is managing the individual's diabetic condition (i) documents that the individual has peripheral neuropathy with evidence of callus formation, a history of preulcerative calluses, a history of previous ulceration, foot deformity, or previous amputation, or poor circulation, and (ii) certifies that the individual needs such shoes under a comprehensive plan of care related to the individual's diabetic condition;

(B) the particular type of shoes are prescribed by a podiatrist or other qualified physician (as established by the Secretary); and

(C) the shoes are fitted and furnished by a podiatrist or other qualified individual (such as a pedorthist or orthotist, as established by the Secretary) who is not the physician described in subparagraph (A) (unless the Secretary finds that the physician is the only such qualified individual in the area);

(13) screening mammography (as defined in subsection (jj);

(14) screening pap smear and screening pelvic exam; and

(15) bone mass measurement (as defined in subsection (rr)).

No diagnostic tests performed in any laboratory, including a laboratory that is part of a rural health clinic, or a hospital (which, for purposes of this sentence, means an institution considered a hospital for purposes of section 1814(d)) shall be included within paragraph (3) unless such laboratory—

(16) if situated in any State in which State or applicable local law provides for licensing of establishments of this nature, (A) is licensed pursuant to such law, or (B) is approved, by the agency of such State or locality responsible for licensing establishments of this nature, as meeting the standards established for such licensing; and

(17) (A) meets the certification requirements under section 353 of the Public Health Service Act; and

(B) meets such other conditions relating to the health and safety of individuals with respect to whom such tests are performed as the Secretary may find necessary.

There shall be excluded from the diagnostic services specified in paragraph (2)(C) any item or service (except services referred to in paragraph (1)) which would not be included under subsection (b) if it were furnished to an inpatient of a hospital. None of the items and services referred to in the preceding paragraphs (other than paragraphs (1) and (2)(A)) of this subsection which are furnished to a patient of an institution which meets the definition of a hospital for purposes of section 1814(d) shall be included unless such other conditions are met as the Secretary may find necessary relating to health and safety of individuals with respect to whom such items and services are furnished.

. . .

(u) Provider of services. The term "provider of services" means a hospital, critical access hospital, skilled nursing facility, comprehensive outpatient rehabilitation facility, home health agency, hospice program, or, for purposes of section 1814(g) and section 1835(e), a fund.

[13]45 C.F.R. § 160.103.

[14]Health care clearinghouses that also are business associates must comply with all obligations under their contracts with covered entities, and must comply with certain HIPAA obligations. However, clearinghouses that act as business associates are not subject to consent, authorization, and notice obligations, and are not required to give individuals access to or an opportunity to amend their records.

[15]*Id.* § 160.102.

[16]*Id.* § 160.103. Business associates are distinct from affiliated covered entities, which are separate covered entities that share common ownership or control. These organizations are permitted to designate themselves as single covered entities, and may issue single privacy notices and consent forms.

[17]*Id.*

[18]45 CFR § 164.504.

[19]*Id.* § 164.103.

[20]*Id.* § 164.105(a0(2)(iii)(C).

[21]*Id.*

[22]*Id.*

[23]*Id.*

[24]*Id.*

[25]*Id.*

[26]*Id.*

[27]*See id.* §§ 164.506, 164.520(d).

[28]*Id.*

[29]*Id.* PHI does not include "de-identified information" from which the identities of individuals cannot be determined.

[30]45 CFR § 164.514.

[31]*Id.* § 164.502(a)(2).

[32]*Id.*

[33]*Id.* § 164.506(c).

[34]*Id.* § 164.510.

[35]*Id.* § 164.502(a)(1)(iii).

[36]*Id.* § 164.512.

[37]*Id.* § 164.514(e).

[38]*Id.* § 164.508.

[39]*Id.*

[40]Department of Health and Human Services, "Summary of the HIPAA Privacy Rule" at 9 (HHS Summary).

[41]*Id.* § 164.502(b), 164.514(d).

[42]*Id.* §§ 164.520(a), (b).

[43]*Id.* § 164.520(c).

[44]*Id.* § 164.520(c).

[45]*Id.* § 164.501.

[46]*Id.* § 164.524.

[47]*Id.* § 164.526.

[48]*Id.* § 164.528.

[49]HHS Summary at 13; *id.* § 164.522(a).

[50]*Id.* § 164.522(b).

[51]*Id.* § 164.530(i).

[52]*Id.* § 164.530(a).

[53]*Id.* § 164.530(b).

[54]*Id.* § 164.530(e).

[55]*Id.* § 164.530(f).

[56]*Id.* § 164.530(c).

[57]*Id.* §§ 164.530(d), 164.520(b)(1)(vi).

[58]*Id.* § 164.530(j).

[59]*Id.* § 164.306(d)(3).

[60]Cal. Civ. Code § 56.265. Entities that furnish administrative services to health care payment services also must limit their disclosures and use of medical information in their possession. *Id.*§ 56.26.

[61]Cal. Health and Safety Code § 120975 *et seq.* (HIV testing); Cal. Civ. Code § 56.17 (genetic testing); *id.* §§ 56.20–56.245 (employer disclosure of employee medical information).

CHAPTER 6

Doing Business in—or with—Europe: The European Union Data Protection Directive

Europe's privacy law regime is very different from that of the United States. Notably, the Data Protection Directive of the European Union (EU), adopted at Cambridge, England in 1995 (Directive), affects all governmental and private compilations of personal data that are made for more than personal use. The Directive is implemented by statutes of the EU member states and prescribes the minimum protections that those national statutes must provide.[1]

The Directive prevents the collection and processing of personal information, with certain exceptions, unless the subject has given his or her "unambiguous consent" to those activities.[2] Where data gathering falls within a recognized exception to the right of unambiguous consent, the subject of the data collection still has a "right to object" to that activity.[3]

The requirement of unambiguous consent, and the companion right to object, would be useless without a mechanism to notify individuals of data collection activity. Accordingly, when a data controller or representative collects information directly from the subject, the collector's and representative's identity must be disclosed to the subject along with the purpose of the data collection.[4] If information about an individual is not obtained from the subject, the duty to disclose is not triggered until the controller or processor of the information first discloses it to a third party, and does not arise at all under certain circumstances.[5]

The Directive also imposes significant minimization, accuracy, and use standards on collectors and processors of personal data. Notably, a data controller must collect data for a specified purpose and may not use it in a way not compatible with that purpose.[6] Individuals have a right to know what personal data are maintained in a data controller's database and to access that personal data and obtain correction of errors and elimination of information that exceeds the purpose of collection or otherwise violates the Directive. The Directive also requires data controllers to implement adequate security and confidentiality procedures, and limits the use of stored personal data to make automated decisions concerning credit and other decisions with direct effects on individual welfare.[7]

In order to comply with the Directive, each EU country not only was required to enact the substantive and procedural protections just described, but was required to create an appropriate regulatory body and provide for civil remedies for persons aggrieved by violations of data protection laws, including a right to damages.[8]

The stringent privacy obligations of the Directive have obvious implications for European subsidiaries or affiliates of U.S. companies that collect or maintain personal information in Europe. Failure to conduct data collection or related activities in Europe, in compliance with the Directive, may subject such subsidiaries or affiliates to legal action under the laws of the countries in which those companies operate. Because the Directive is only a "floor"—not a ceiling—for privacy protections in Europe, individual member states' laws may be more restrictive than the requirements of the Directive.

However, the impact of the Directive on U.S. companies goes beyond its direct effect on the operations of those companies in Europe. The Directive also provides that computerized personal data may be transferred to another country only if that country ensures an "adequate" level of protection for personal data.[9] Although this provision does not require transferee countries to offer protection at a level precisely equivalent to that of the Directive, European authorities took the position that the Unites States, with its patchwork of privacy laws, did not offer adequate protection to personal data transferred from Europe.

The attitude of the European authorities posed a significant threat to both U.S. and European businesses. The EU countries are among the most important trading partners of the United States, and transborder data flows from Europe to the United States—whether from European companies or the European subsidiaries of U.S. companies—are vital to the conduct of business in an era of global trade.

In an effort to avoid wholesale disruption of data flows from Europe to the United States, the U.S. Department of Commerce negotiated with the European Commission a so-called "Safe Harbor" framework for compliance with the Directive.

The Safe Harbor regime requires a company to publicly declare its intention to observe the Safe Harbor principles. The company or other organization also must: (1) join a self-regulatory private program that adheres to the Safe Harbor's requirements; or (2) implement a self-regulatory program that conforms to the Safe Harbor principles. In order to ensure enforceability, the company must be subject to the jurisdiction of the Federal Trade Commission or the Department of Transportation.[10]

The Safe Harbor principles are:

- *Notice.* Individuals have a right to notice of the purposes for which data are collected and used, how to contact the organization with any inquiries and complaints, the types of third parties to which it discloses the information, and the means the organization offers for limiting the use and disclosure of information.
- *Choice.* Individuals have a right to "opt out" of disclosure of their personal data for a purpose inconsistent with the purpose for which the information was collected. Affirmative, rather than opt-out, consent is required before information classified as sensitive may be disclosed to third parties.
- *Onward Transfers.* Before information may be transferred to a third party acting as an agent for the transferor, the transferor must ensure that the transferee subscribes to the Safe Harbor principles or otherwise provides adequate levels of protection as required by the Directive.
- *Access.* Individuals have a right, on reasonable terms, to obtain access to their personal information. Individuals also have the right to obtain correction,

amendment, or deletion of inaccurate personal information concerning them, except when the burden or expense of providing access would be disproportionate to the risks to the individual's privacy, or when such correction, amendment, or deletion would violate the rights of another party.

- *Security.* Companies and other organizations must employ reasonable measures to protect personal data from unauthorized access, disclosure, alteration, and destruction.
- *Data Integrity.* Personal information may not be used in a way that is incompatible with the purposes for which it has been collected, or the purposes that subsequently were authorized by the individual to which the information pertains. Organizations must take reasonable measures to ensure that personal information they maintain is current, accurate, and relevant to its intended use.
- *Enforcement.* An enforcement mechanism must be in place, and must include means of verifying compliance, resolving disputes, and providing remedies when the Safe Harbor principles are violated. The mechanism for dispute resolution must be readily available and must not impose excessive costs on individuals that seek remedies and dispute resolution concerning their personal information

Although participation in the Safe Harbor program by U.S. companies has been uneven, companies that receive, or intend to receive, personal information from European affiliates or third parties should seriously consider participating.

Notes

[1]Council Directive 95/46/EC of the European Parliament and of the Council of 24 October 1995 on the Protection of Individuals with Regard to the Processing of Personal Data and on the Free Movement of Such Data, 1995 O.J. (L281) (Directive).

[2]*Id.* art.7. Most data protection obligations under the Directive are imposed on "data controllers," which are defined to include any "natural or legal person, public authority, agency or any other body which alone or jointly with others determines the purposes and means of the processing of personal data . . ." *Id.* art 2(d). A data "processor" under the Directive is a "natural or legal person, public authority, agency or any other body which processes personal data on behalf of the controller." *Id.* art. 2(f).

[3]*Id.* art. 14.

[4]*Id.* art. 10.

[5]*Id.* art. 15.

[6]*Id.*, Recitals § 28.

[7]*Id.* art. 7.

[8]*Id.* arts. 22, 23, 28.

[9]*Id.* art. 25.

[10]Entities not subject to the jurisdiction of those agencies may comply with the Safe Harbor by entering into an EU-approved "Model Contract" with the European transferor of personal information.

PART II
Information About Job Applicants and Employees

The privacy rights of employees are defined by both state and federal law. Accordingly, for many of the subjects covered in the following three chapters, there is no substitute for familiarity with the specific requirements of each jurisdiction in which your company has employees.

In order to give some idea of the interplay between the state and federal law of employee privacy, the following chapters discuss federal statutes and regulations and the counterpart laws of selected states.

In Chapter 7, we discuss issues typically encountered during the hiring process, including background checks, inquiries into credit history and criminal records, and areas of inquiry that are limited by civil rights and other laws.

In Chapter 8, we discuss privacy rights that typically become relevant after employees are hired.

Finally, Chapter 9 addresses the special problems posed by employer surveillance of employee activities, including video surveillance and monitoring of employees' telephone calls, e-mail, and Internet use.

CHAPTER 7

The Hiring Process

Poor hiring decisions often are based on inadequate information. In order to avoid hiring personnel who will fail to perform or even expose the employer to liability, employers want to know as much as possible about an applicant's work record, qualifications, and character. Much of that information can be obtained in interviews, but checks with outside sources also are necessary in order to confirm applicants' credentials or obtain other information that the interviews might not have disclosed. In some lines of business, such due diligence may be required by law; in all businesses, failure to screen applicants adequately may lead to claims of negligent hiring brought by persons who are harmed by employees' subsequent actions.[1]

These legitimate concerns notwithstanding, employers are restricted in their ability to collect and use personal information about prospective employees in the course of pre-employment interviews and post-offer screening. Failure to observe these restrictions, like failure to screen applicants adequately, can subject employers to legal liability. Navigating these treacherous waters has become an increasing part of the Human Resources specialist's workload.

The following sets out some of the principal legal constraints on information-gathering about prospective employees. Because so many federal and state statutes and regulations affect this process, and because employee privacy law is developing rapidly, employers should supplement the information in this chapter with specific legal advice tailored to the jurisdictions in which they do business and the lines of business in which they are engaged.

7.1 The Americans with Disabilities Act

The Americans with Disabilities Act (ADA) strongly affects the rights of employers to acquire and disclose medical information concerning job applicants and employees.[2] Specifically, the ADA prohibits employers from requiring medical examinations or making medical inquiries concerning a prospective employee before an offer of employment is made.[3] After an offer is made, a medical examination may be required if all entering employees are subjected to the same examination regardless of disability.[4] The ADA also requires that all "information obtained regarding the medical condition or history of the applicant [be] collected and maintained on separate forms and in separate medical files and [be] treated as a separate medical record."[5]

After a person is employed, the employer may not "require a medical examination and shall not make inquiries of an employee as to whether such employee is an individual with a disability or as to the nature or severity of the disability, unless such examination or inquiry is shown to be job related and consistent with business necessity."[6] However, an employer may conduct voluntary medical examinations and take medical histories if those activities are part of an employee health program. Also, an employer may inquire into an employee's ability to perform job-related functions.[7]

Certain exceptions to the ADA preserve important rights of employers. Notably, tests for illegal drug use are not "medical examinations" for purposes of the ADA's restrictions on such examinations.[8] Also, although there is some disagreement among courts and commentators on this point, the mere fact that an employer has made inquiries or required medical examinations not permitted by the ADA may not give rise to a private cause of action if the aggrieved applicant or employee does not, in fact, have a disability.[9]

7.2 Fair Credit Reporting Act

In the course of pre-employment screening, employers may find it helpful to obtain consumer report data that is subject to the Fair Credit Reporting Act (FCRA).[10]

Employers are permitted to obtain consumer reports "for the purpose of evaluating a consumer for employment, promotion, reassignment or retention as an employee,"[11] and a consumer reporting agency may furnish a consumer report to a person the agency has reason to believe intends to use the information for employment purposes.[12] However, the agency may not furnish a consumer report for employment purposes unless the employer first certifies that it has made "a clear and conspicuous disclosure" to the employee or applicant, in writing, that a consumer report may be obtained for employment purposes.[13] Also, the employee or applicant must have authorized, in writing, the employer's procurement of the report; and the employer must have certified that "information from the consumer report will not be used in violation of any applicable Federal or State equal employment opportunity law or regulation. . . ."[14] The consumer reporting agency also must provide to the applicant or employee, with the report or at an earlier time, a summary of applicable FCRA rights.[15]

Employers also might wish to obtain so-called "investigative credit reports" (sometimes referred to as "character reports") on applicants.

An investigative consumer report is something like an investigation for a government security clearance. When performed by a consumer reporting agency, such investigations are subject to the FCRA. An investigative consumer report is defined in the FCRA as "a consumer report or portion thereof in which information on a consumer's character, general reputation, personal characteristics, or mode of living is obtained through neighbors, friends, or associates of the consumer reported on or with others with whom he is acquainted or who may have knowledge concerning any such items of information."[16]

An employer may request and obtain an investigative consumer report, but only after certifying to the consumer reporting agency that it has disclosed to the applicant or employee the fact that such an investigative consumers report may be prepared.[17] The employer also must certify to the agency that it will, "on written request by the consumer within a reasonable period of time after the receipt by him of the disclosure [that an investigative consumer report may be made], make a complete and accurate disclosure of the nature and scope of the investigation requested."[18] The required disclosure must be made "in a writing mailed, or otherwise delivered, to the consumer not later than five days after the date on which the request for such disclosure was received from the consumer or such report was first requested, whichever is the later."[19]

The taking of adverse employment-related action, on the basis of a consumer report or investigative consumer report, triggers certain employee rights under the FCRA.

Notably, if an employer intends to use a consumer report as the basis for adverse action, the employer must provide the applicant or employee with a written description of his or her rights under the FCRA, and should give the applicant or employee a reasonable time in which to respond. After adverse action is taken on the basis of a consumer report, the employer must furnish the applicant or employee with a written notice of his or her rights to obtain a free copy of the consumer report from the agency and dispute the accuracy or completeness of any information furnished by the agency. Roughly similar rights must be extended to applicants when adverse action will be taken or has been taken on the basis of an investigative consumer report.

Finally, if a consumer report is or will be based on personal interviews with third parties, additional FCRA requirements apply. Specifically, within three days after requesting the report, the employer must advise the applicant or employee of the fact that such a report is being sought, and must give the applicant or employee a summary of his or her rights under the FCRA. The notice must specifically refer to the applicant's or employee's right to request additional information concerning the scope of the investigation. If such a request is made within a reasonable time, the employer must make a complete and accurate disclosure within five days of receiving the request or initiating procurement of the report, whichever is later.

7.3 State Laws Restricting Employer Use of Credit Reports

The FCRA is not the exclusive source of restrictions on employers' use of information gathered by consumer reporting agencies. State laws also may apply and in some cases may be more restrictive than the FCRA. California, for example, has two applicable statutes: the Investigative Consumer Reporting Agencies Act (ICRAA) and the Consumer Credit Reporting Agencies Act (CCRAA).

A few observations about the California statutes show why the laws affecting employer background checks and investigations are some of the most complex requirements to which businesses are subject.

For example, although the federal FCRA does not apply to internal investigations conducted by the employer's own staff, California's ICRAA does regulate such investigations. Specifically, California employers must provide notice to employees when they obtain information contained in public records in the course of an internal investigation. If the investigation is for purposes other than investigating allegations of misconduct or wrongdoing, the employer must provide a copy of the record to the applicant or employee within seven days after receipt of the information, unless the right to such notice was previously waived. If the investigation involves possible misconduct or wrongdoing, the employer must provide a copy of the public record to the applicant/employee after the investigation is completed, unless that right has previously been waived. If the employer takes adverse action as a result of an internal investigation that uses a public record, a copy of that record must be provided to the applicant/employee even if rights under the ICRAA were previously waived.

California's statutes also define key terms in ways that overlap with, but are confusingly different from, their approximate counterparts in the FCRA. For example, as noted in Chapter 2, the FCRA defines an "investigative consumer report" as a report in which information concerning "character, general reputation, personal characteristics, or mode of living is obtained through *personal interviews* . . ." California's ICRAA, however, defines an "investigative consumer report" as one in which "information on a person's character, general reputation, personal characteristics or mode of living is obtained through *any means*," including review of public records and other documents. Accordingly, a California corporation that obtains character reports by any means must comply with both the FCRA and ICRAA regulations applicable to investigative consumer reports.

Similarly, disclosure and other requirements in the FCRA, ICRAA, and CCRAA are highly duplicative, but California employers must be careful to comply with all of them. In order to ensure compliance, employers must stay abreast of changes in the law, whether those changes come from Washington or Sacramento.

Employers doing business in other states must be equally alert to new legal requirements that come from their state capitals concerning the use of credit reports, and to the interplay between those requirements and federal law.

7.4 Laws Restricting Use of Criminal Records

Few concerns are more rational than an employer's desire *not* to hire criminals, but federal and state authorities limit the ability of employers to rely on criminal records in their hiring decisions. Because criminal records are public, these restrictions have more to do with civil rights concerns than privacy.

At the federal level, reliance on criminal records is limited primarily by policy statements and guidelines of the Equal Employment Opportunity Commission (EEOC), adopted under Tile VII of the 1964 Civil Rights Act.[20] The EEOC, which regulates employers with 15 or more employees, distinguishes between arrest records, which "are not reliable evidence that a person has committed a crime," and convictions, which are based on a process requiring a high burden of proof.[21] Broad inquiries into an applicant's arrest record will be hard to justify, and adverse decisions based on arrest records may not be made unless the applicant has been given an opportunity to explain the circumstances, the employer concludes that the applicant committed the offense, the underlying conduct is related to the job for which the applicant is applying, and the arrest is reasonably recent.[22] The EEOC's limitations on use of conviction records are less severe, but the employer still must be prepared to demonstrate a "business necessity" for refusal to hire based on a past conviction, and should accompany the request for information with a statement that past convictions will not immediately result in an adverse decision.[23]

State laws and regulations concerning reliance on criminal records vary widely in their terms. Where state law permits criminal records to be expunged, employers generally are prohibited from inquiring about those expunged records and job applicants need not disclose the incidents on which they are based.[24] A number of states forbid any inquiry into arrest records, but others allow such inquiries if the events are recent and related to job requirements.[25] Employers generally may inquire into nonexpunged conviction records under state laws, but still may be limited in their ability to rely on those records in making adverse hiring decisions.[26]

State laws, like federal law, create a tension in this area by *requiring* inquiries into criminal records, or at least those records that relate to some types of offenses, before applicants may be hired for dependent care, daycare, or other positions. Also, under both state and federal law, government agencies may be subject to hiring restrictions that differ from those to which private employers are subject.

7.5 Requesting and Giving References

Employers have strong reasons to contact former employers, schools, and other persons and organizations that have information about an applicant's past job performance and educational credentials. Those persons and organizations are in the best position to confirm that the applicant has truthfully represented his or her qualifications for the job. Complete and truthful references also help the prospective employer spot problems in the applicant's background that suggest a risk of misconduct or poor performance in the new job. Failure to make such inquiries might lend support to claims of negligent hiring in the event third parties are harmed by an employee's misdeeds.

Prospective employers increasingly find, however, that past employers are reluctant to give detailed references. The reluctance is based on concerns about lawsuits from past employees based on defamation, invasion of privacy, or claims that unfavorable references were given in retaliation for civil rights complaints or other protected conduct. Because of these concerns, some employers who are asked for references will only confirm the former employees' dates of employment or give other neutral, factual information.

Even this level of caution, however, does not give the past employer a complete bar to liability. For example, if a past employer gives a reference that fails to disclose an applicant's history of workplace violence, a plaintiff who is injured by the employee's misconduct in the new job might name the past employer as a defendant. Obviously, there is a strong public interest in encouraging employers to give candid, complete, and truthful responses to requests for references.

Most states have responded to this problem by enacting statutes that immunize employers from liability for references unless they make statements known to be false, made with intent to mislead, or made with reckless disregard as to its falsity.[27] However, employers who are asked to give references might want additional assurance that they will not be sued by the subjects of those references. Prospective employers should obtain written consent from the applicants, authorizing the prospective employer to obtain references and releasing past employers from liability for giving those references.

7.6 Other Restrictions on Pre-Employment Screening

A complex web of statutes, regulations, and potential causes of action limits the subjects that employers should address when screening applicants for employment. Among other legal constraints, employers must take into account the Civil Rights Act of 1964 and the implementing regulations of the EEOC (some of which we already have discussed); the Age Discrimination in Employment Act of 1967;[28] and the Americans with Disabilities Act, discussed above in Section 7.1. Employers also must be aware of developments in the courts, which have defined the legal environment concerning sexual harassment and other issues.

Subjects that should be avoided in the interview and pre-employment screening process include:

- Age;
- Marital status;
- Sexual orientation;
- Disability, beyond capacity to perform specific job-related tasks;
- History of filing lawsuits or other claims against employers;
- Past union affiliation;
- Race or ethnicity;
- Religion;
- National origin;
- Genetic information;
- Medical history;
- Medical history or plans to become pregnant.

Where pre-employment screening and interviewing practices are concerned, the best approach is to have a policy that is applied consistently, and to limit inquiries to questions that are clearly related to job requirements.

Notes

[1]Federal and state laws require employers to conduct background checks on applicants for a variety of jobs, including employment as commercial drivers, childcare or adult care workers, and teachers. Employers also are subject to immigration laws concerning the eligibility of job applicants to work in the United States.

[2]Americans with Disabilities Act, Pub. L. 101-336, 42 U.S.C. §§ 12101–12213.

[3]ADA § 102(d)(2)(A), 42 U.S.C. § 12112(d)(2)(A). An employer may, however, inquire generally at this stage as to the applicant's ability to perform job-related functions.

[4]*Id.* § 102(d)(3)(A), 42 U.S.C. § 12112(d)(3)(A).

[5]*Id.* § 102(d)(2)(B), 42 U.S.C. § 12112(d)(2)(B). Under certain defined circumstances, such information may be disclosed to supervisors and managers, first aid and safety personnel, and government officials. *Id.*

[6]*Id.* § 102(d)(4)(A), 42 U.S.C. § 12112(d)(4)(A).

[7]*Id.* § 102(d)(4)(B), 42 U.S.C. § 12112(d)(4)(B).

[8]*Id.* § 104(d), 42 U.S.C. § 12114(d).

[9]*See, e.g., Griffin v. Steeltech, Inc.*, 160 F.3d 591 (10th Cir. 1998), *cert. denied*, 526 U.S. 1065 (1999); *Adler v. L&M Rail Link*, 13 F.Supp.2d 912 (N.D. Iowa 1998), abrogated by *Cossette v. Minn. Power & Light*, 188 F.3d 964, 970 n. 4 (8th Cir. 1999); *Armstrong v. Turner Indus., Inc.*, 141 F.3d 554 (5th Cir. 1998).

[10]15 U.S.C. §§ 1681 *et seq*. For a longer discussion of the Fair Credit Reporting Act, *see* Chapter 3.

[11]FCRA § 603(h), 15 U.S.C. § 1681a(h).

[12]*Id.* § 604(a)(3)(B), 15 U.S.C. § 1681b(a)(3)(B).

[13]*Id.* § 604(b), 15 U.S.C. § 1681b(b).

[14]*Id.*

[15]*Id.*

[16]*Id.* § 603(e), 15 U.S.C. § 1681a(e). The definition excludes "specific factual information on a consumer's credit record obtained directly from a creditor of the consumer or from a consumer reporting agency when such information was obtained directly from a creditor of the consumer or from the consumer." *Id.*

[17] *Id.* § 606(d)(1), 15 U.S.C. § 1681d(d)(1).

[18]*Id.* § 606(b), 15 U.S.C. § 1681d(b). The FCRA does not apply to investigations conducted by the employer's staff.

[19]*Id.* The FCRA also includes requirements that consumer reporting agencies must follow in order to ensure the accuracy of information they obtain in the course of preparing investigative consumer reports. *Id.* § 606(d), 19 U.S.C. § 1681d(d).

[20]42 U.S.C. § 2000e *et seq.*; Equal Employment Opportunity Commission, *Policy Guidelines on the Consideration of Arrest Records in Employment Decisions under Title VII of the Civil Rights Act of 1964* (1990), available at http://www.eeoc.gov/*policy*/docs/arrest_records.html (last visited Nov. 17, 2007) *(EEOC Arrest Guidelines) Equal Employment Opportunity Commission Policy Statement on the Issue of Conviction Records under Title VII of the Civil Rights Act of 1964* (1987), available at http://www.eeoc.gov/policy/docs/convict1.html (last visited Nov. 17, 2007) (*EEOC Conviction Guidelines).*

[21]EEOC Arrest Guidelines, supra.

[22]*Id.*

[23]EEOC Conviction Guidelines, supra.

[24]*See, e.g.*, Conn. Gen. Stat. Ann. § 54-142; 47 Okla. Stat. Ann. § 2-129; Va. Code § 19.2-392.4(a).

[25]*See, e.g.*, Cal. Labor Code § 432.7; Colo. Rev. Stat. § 24-72-301; Wash. Rev. Code Ann. § 43.43.710, 43.43.810.

[26]*See, e.g.*, Haw. Rev. Stat. § 846.1; N.Y. Exec. Law § 296.16; 18 Pa. Stat. Ann. § 9124.

[27]*See, e.g.*, Cal. Civ. Code § 47(c); Fla. Stat. Ann. § 768.095; Md. Labor & Emp. Code § 5-399.7; Wis. Stat. § 895.487.

[28]29 U.S.C. § 621–634.

CHAPTER 8

Internal Investigations and Other Aspects of the Employment Relationship

After the hiring process is complete and an applicant has joined the workforce, the relationship between employer and employee continues to be affected by a number of privacy laws. Some of those restrictions are based on statutes and regulations discussed in the previous chapter. For example, the Americans with Disabilities Act, the Fair Credit Reporting Act and counterpart state laws, and statutes and regulations limiting the use of criminal records apply to posthiring as well as pre-employment inquiries and decisions. In this chapter, we discuss these and other constraints in the context of the ongoing relationship between employer and employee.

8.1 Internal Investigations

Employers typically conduct internal investigations to determine responsibility for suspected misconduct. Such investigations may be necessary, not just to identify employees who should be disciplined or removed from the workforce, but to examine internal procedures that need strengthening in order to reduce the risk of future incidents.

The events and concerns that give rise to internal misconduct investigations vary. They include thefts of tangible or intellectual property, threats of workplace violence, sexual harassment, and suspected violations of antitrust or securities laws. The fact-gathering methods used, and the privacy issues they present, will vary according to the nature of the suspected offense. Some of those methods and issues are discussed in this section.

8.1.1 Workplace Searches

When an employer is a governmental agency or involves itself with governmental activity to an extent that makes it a state actor, a search conducted by that employer might be subject to the U.S. Constitution's prohibition against unreasonable searches and seizures,[1] or to similar protections set out in state constitutions.[2] Under those constitutional provisions, if a workplace search involving state action concerns a place or situation in which the employee has a reasonable expectation of privacy, a court might rule that the search should not have been conducted, or should have been carried out by law enforcement agents pursuant to a warrant.

Private employers generally are not subject to constitutional constraints, but searches conducted by private businesses might trigger claims for invasion of privacy under common law. If those searches are conducted in a discriminatory manner, they also will give rise to claims under civil rights laws.

Searches of employees' persons, in particular, should be conducted only on reasonable grounds and in such a way as not to humiliate or embarrass the employee.[3] Searches of employees' briefcases, purses, bookbags, and other personal property often are justifiable, especially if the employer has reason to believe that an employee may be carrying drugs or weapons into the workplace, or may be taking the business's property out of the workplace without authorization. Employers should be careful to obtain employees' consent to such searches, however, by reserving that right in the employee handbook or elsewhere, and should ensure that searches are conducted in a reasonable and nondiscriminatory manner.[4] Attempts to search employees' belongings outside the employer's premises should be avoided.

Searches of desks, file cabinets, lockers, and other work areas are easiest to justify because employees have little or no expectation of privacy in facilities provided by their employers for work-related use. Employers can weaken their case for such searches, however, by permitting personnel to secure lockers and other facilities with their own locks, or by giving assurances that employees might interpret as recognizing a right to privacy in their work areas. Also, as with other types of searches, employers should be careful not to engage in random, discriminatory, or unnecessarily invasive searches of work areas, and should obtain consent to searches by posting an appropriate policy or making the policy part of the employee handbook.

8.1.2 Labor Law Considerations in Internal Investigations

Employers with union workforces already should be aware of any limitations on internal investigations in their collective bargaining agreements. Those limitations might include a right of employees to have union representatives present when they are questioned as part of a misconduct investigation. The collective bargaining agreement also may limit the employer's right to use particular investigative methods.

In addition to any provisions of the company's collective bargaining agreement that might apply, the National Labor Relations Board (NLRB) requires that union employees be permitted, on request, to have a coworker present as a witness during any investigatory interview that might lead to disciplinary action.

8.1.3 Civil Rights Laws and Regulations

The previous chapter discussed the impact of civil rights–related laws, such as the Civil Rights Act of 1964, the Age Discrimination in Employment Act, and the Americans with Disabilities Act, on pre-employment interviews and background investigations. These same statutes, and the regulations that implement them, must be observed in the conduct of internal investigations. Notably, decisions to investigate possible misconduct, methods used to conduct investigations, and the disciplinary and other actions that result from investigations must be even-handed and must not single out employees based on race, color, religion, national origin, age, disability, sex, or any protected activity under the antidiscrimination laws.

As we also discussed in the previous chapter, the states have their own civil rights statutes that may provide additional protections in all of these areas.

8.1.4 Sexual Harassment Investigations

The law of sexual harassment, as defined by the courts and implemented by the Equal Employment Opportunity Comission (EEOC) and state agencies, requires employers to develop and carry out effective procedures for investigation of harassment complaints. The employer's duty to investigate must be understood in the full context of sexual harassment law, which makes employers *strictly liable* for the unlawful actions of their supervisors that result in tangible employment actions.[6] In other words, if an employee's refusal of, or acquiescence in, a supervisor's unwelcome sexual demands results in termination, promotion, demotion, or other tangible action, the employer is responsible *even if it took reasonable measures to prevent sexual harassment.*

The only exception to this harsh rule comes into play when a supervisor's harassment does not result in tangible employment action. In such a case, the employer may establish an affirmative defense to a harassment claim based on two elements: (1) that the employer exercised reasonable care to prevent and promptly correct any harassing behavior; and (2) that the employee unreasonably failed to take advantage of any preventive or corrective opportunities provided by the employer to avoid harm otherwise.[7]

The employer's conduct of investigations is central to establishing the affirmative defense. Employers must maintain a complaint process and must conduct prompt investigations in response to those complaints. Specifically:

- The employer must establish, publicize, and enforce a complaint policy that clearly explains prohibited conduct. The policy must provide that harassment based on sex, sexual conduct, race, color, religion, national origin, age, disability, or protected activity will not be tolerated.[8] The policy should cover harassment by all employees and express the employer's intention to deal with harassment before it rises to the level of a violation of law.[9]
- The policy must assure employees that retaliation against personnel who exercise their rights under the complaint policy will not be tolerated.[10]
- The policy must be flexible, so that employees will not be discouraged from taking advantage of the complaint process. Notably, employers should avoid requiring that complaints be taken up the usual chain of supervision. Ideally, a neutral party within the company, such as the Human Resources department, will be designated as the point of contact so that employees can avoid lodging complaints with supervisors who might, themselves, be involved in the incidents that gave rise to the complaint. The policy also should advise employees of deadlines for filing complaints with the EEOC or state agencies.[11]
- The policy should promise to keep complaints confidential to the extent possible. This assurance cannot be absolute, because witnesses and persons against whom claims are directed must be advised of the complaint. However, the existence and nature of the complaint should not be disclosed to persons who have no need for that information.[12]
- The employer should implement an effective process for prompt investigation of harassment complaints. If the accused harasser denies the charge and a factual investigation is necessary, the investigation should start immediately.

Other measures, such as reassignment of the alleged harasser or placing the accused on leave with pay, might be necessary while the investigation is in progress. Persons conducting the investigation should be qualified for the task and should not be subject to the supervision of the accused harasser.[13]

- If the investigation concludes with a finding that harassment occurred, the employer must take prompt, appropriate action. Such action might include disciplinary measures against the offender, but also should include measures designed to prevent future harassment. Remedial measures should not adversely affect the complainant.

Sexual harassment law subjects employers to contradictory pressures. Internal investigations of harassment claims are necessary if the employer wishes to minimize its exposure to legal claims; at the same time, investigations raise the usual risk of invasion of privacy, defamation, and other claims that may be brought by the accused harasser if the proceeding is not handled with appropriate discretion. Accordingly, as with all investigations, employers must keep the details of sexual harassment inquiries confidential to the extent possible.

8.1.5 Other Considerations in Internal Investigations

Internal investigations—especially those that result in disciplinary action—present a number of additional risks that employers can minimize by following some commonsense guidelines.

Notably, employers should avoid taking disciplinary actions that might be construed as retaliation for an employee's exercise of rights guaranteed by law. Particular risk areas include: (1) employee complaints to the Equal Employment Opportunity Commission or other agencies for alleged employer civil rights violations; (2) testifying or making statements on behalf of fellow employees who have brought such complaints; (3) "whistle-blowing" reports by employees to regulators or other official agencies concerning the employer's possible violations of law; (4) union organizing activity; and (5) making claims under minimum wage and overtime laws.

Employers also should understand the potential of investigations to give rise to various tort claims.

For example, statements that employers make to others (orally or in writing) may give rise to defamation claims if the statements were untrue, the employer knew the statements to be untrue (or was at least indifferent as to their truth or falsity), and the statements harmed the reputation of the employee.[14] In order to avoid defamation complaints, employers conducting investigations should make statements about employee conduct only to persons involved in the investigation or who otherwise have a legitimate need for the information, and should avoid making any statements that go beyond the available facts.

Similarly, an investigation that is especially intrusive, or that results in needlessly wide dissemination of sensitive information about an employee, may give rise to claims for invasion of privacy, which is "not one tort but a complex of four . . ."[15] The privacy torts are: (1) intrusion into a person's solitude or seclusion; (2) publicity that places a person in a false light; (3) public disclosure of private facts; and

(4) appropriation of a person's image, signature, likeness, or name for a commercial purpose.

In the employment context, most invasion-of-privacy claims involve one or more of the first three torts.

In order to bring a successful action for the first of these privacy torts—that is, intrusion into solitude or seclusion—the employee must prove that the intrusion involved a place in which he had a privacy expectation and was unreasonable under the circumstances. Such actions are likely to succeed if the employer's intrusion involved the employee's home, and are less likely to succeed if the intrusion involved the workplace.[16] Even an intrusion that might otherwise be reasonable will support a lawsuit if the use made of the "fruits of the intrusion" is needlessly invasive of the employee's privacy.[17]

Claims of false light publicity require proof that the defendant made public statements about the plaintiff that placed the person in a false light and would be objectionable to a reasonable person.[18] Objectionable statements that satisfy the requirements for this tort also are likely to support defamation claims.

Public disclosure of private facts occurs when an employer makes statements about an employee to third parties, whereby those statements would be offensive and objectionable to a reasonable person. Public disclosure cases differ from defamation and false light claims. For a public disclosure charge to succeed, it is not necessary to prove that the employer's statement was untrue or placed the employee in a false light.[19] In the Michigan case of *Beaumont v. Brown*, for example, the court held that an employer could be liable to an employee for embellishing an otherwise legitimate inquiry letter to the Army, concerning the employee's absence from work for military duty, with "derogatory remarks" that disclosed "embarrassing private facts" about the employee.[20] The truth or falsity of the employer's statements was irrelevant to the employee's claim.

In order to avoid tort claims for invasion of employees' privacy, employers should confine searches to workplace areas in which employees have a low expectation of privacy, and should disclose information gained in the course of investigations only to persons with a valid interest in those proceedings. Employers also should avoid any dissemination of personal information about employees that is irrelevant to an investigation or other legitimate business purpose, especially when that information has not been verified or would cause embarrassment to a reasonable person.

8.2 Use of Credit Reports

Section 7.2 of the previous chapter discussed the limitations the Fair Credit Reporting Act (FCRA) places on uses of consumer reports as part of the pre-employment screening process. Those same limitations, and many counterpart restrictions in state law, apply to the use of consumer reports in connection with posthiring personnel decisions, including the conduct of internal investigations. If in doubt about the permissible uses of credit reports concerning employees, employers should consult counsel.

8.3 Privacy of Employee Medical Records

A number of state and federal laws and regulations affect employers' handling of employees' medical records. Those laws and regulations include the Americans with Disabilities Act (ADA), the Family and Medical Leave Act (FMLA), the Health Insurance Portability and Accountability Act (HIPAA), the Fair Credit Reporting Act (FCRA), and the Occupational Safety and Health Act (OSHA).

The ADA is intended primarily to prevent discrimination against persons on the basis of disabilities. In support of that goal, the ADA imposes both record-keeping and confidentiality obligations. Employers must keep records of medical examinations and inquiries concerning a disability confidential, and must maintain that information in files that are separate from other personnel records. Medical information required by state workers' compensation laws may be provided to the agencies that administer those laws.[21]

Employees' requests for family and medical leave, and documentation supporting those requests, are subject to the Family and Medical Leave Act. According to the implementing regulations of the Department of Labor, records and documents "relating to medical certifications, recertifications or medical histories of employees or employees' family members, created for purposes of FMLA, shall be maintained as confidential medical records in separate files/records from the usual personnel files, and if ADA is also applicable, such records shall be maintained in conformance with ADA confidentiality requirements . . ."[22] However, supervisors and managers may be informed "regarding necessary restrictions on the work or duties of an employee and necessary accommodations." Also, first aid and safety personnel may be advised if the employee's condition may require emergency treatment, and government officials investigating legal compliance "shall be provided relevant information upon request."[23]

HIPAA privacy regulations, which are discussed in detail in Chapter 5, apply primarily to health insurance companies, health care providers, and other "covered entities" to the extent those entities maintain and use personal health information (PHI). Employers are covered entities if they self-insure, but otherwise are not subject to all of the HIPAA privacy obligations. Notably, an employer may maintain medical information needed to carry out legal obligations, including requirements of the ADA, FMLA, OSHA and other statutes, without complying with the HIPAA privacy regulations described in Chapter 5. However, an employer that sponsors a group health plan likely will acquire and maintain PHI in connection with that plan, and should protect the confidentiality of that information. At a minimum, PHI acquired in this way should be kept in files separate from other personnel records and secured by reasonable data security procedures.[24]

The Fair Credit Reporting Act, discussed in detail at Chapter 3, contains some provisions that relate to medical records. Specifically, FCRA limits the circumstances in which consumer reporting agencies may provide medical information to employers, and the circumstances in which employers may disclose that information to others. Consumer reports containing medical information may be furnished in connection with employment with the applicant's or employee's written consent, or when the information concerns debts incurred for medical services and does not identify (or permit identification of) the service provider. Also, with limited exceptions, FCRA does not permit employers to disclose medical information derived from consumer reports to third parties.

Finally, the Occupational Safety and Health Act (OSHA) requires employers to keep records of work-related injuries and illnesses. However, in the event of injuries and illnesses that raise privacy concerns, such as mental disorders and injuries resulting from sexual assault, employers must maintain a file concerning those injuries and illnesses that is separate from their usual OSHA medical files.

8.4 Employees' Rights of Access to Personnel Files

Most of the laws that give employees the right to see and review their personnel files are state laws. At the federal level, limited access rights to some categories of personnel data are provided under HIPAA,[25] OSHA,[26] and regulations of the Department of Transportation.[27]

Many states give employees extensive rights to examine their personnel files. In California, for example, every employee "has the right to inspect the personnel records that the employer maintains relating to the employee's performance or to any grievance concerning the employee."[28] The employer is not required to make those records available during the employee's regular working hours, but must "make the contents of those personnel records available at reasonable intervals and at reasonable times."[29]

California, like other states that mandate employee access to personnel records, permits some exceptions. These include records of criminal investigations, references, and certain records or ratings that were obtained prior to the employee's employment.[30]

Many of the state statutes that mandate employees' access to their personnel files are listed in Appendix A.

8.5 Lie Detectors, Drug Tests, and Medical Tests

Employers use, or attempt to use, a number of testing procedures that raise privacy concerns. These tests range from polygraphs, to general physical exams, to specialized tests for drugs and alcohol, HIV, and genetic characteristics. Each of these types of testing is subject to some degree of regulation.

8.5.1 Lie Detectors

A number of devices and techniques measure, or purport to measure, physiological phenomena associated with statements that the speaker knows to be untruthful. The most famous such device is the polygraph, which measures changes in heart rate, blood pressure, and other vital signs of a person as he or she answers a series of questions. Voice stress analyzers also are used to measure reactions that are said to correlate with the truth or falsity of a subject's statements.

Until state and federal legislation curtailing their use was enacted, polygraphs and voice stress analyzers became popular tools of pre-employment screening and internal misconduct investigations.

The Employee Polygraph Protection Act (EPPA), passed by Congress in 1988, prohibits nearly all uses of lie detection tests by private employers. Under the EPPA, it is generally unlawful "directly or indirectly, to require, request, suggest, or cause any employee or prospective employee to take or submit to a lie detector test."[31] It also is unlawful under EPPA to "use, accept, refer to, or inquire concerning the results of any lie detector test of any employee or prospective employee," or to take any adverse action against an applicant or employee who refuses such a test or makes a complaint about an employer's violation of EPPA. Adverse action based on the results of a lie detector test also is forbidden.

There are some exceptions to the EPPA prohibitions. Notably, the statute does not apply to governmental employers, contains exceptions for national defense and security matters, and has a limited exemption for ongoing investigations "involving economic loss or injury to the employer's business, such as theft, embezzlement, misappropriation, or an act of unlawful industrial espionage or sabotage."[32]

EPPA does not preempt state laws that offer equal or greater protections against use of lie detectors, and a number of states have their own statutes regulating the use of these devices. Most of these statutes, like EPPA, regulate only lie detection techniques that measure physiological responses, but at least two states also limit the use of written honesty tests.[33]

As with other investigative techniques, employers that examine applicants and employees on matters of truthfulness and honesty must do so in a manner consistent with civil rights and, when the business is unionized, the collective bargaining agreement. Employers also should be aware that disclosure of the results of such tests, except as necessary for a legitimate business or public safety purpose, may result in claims of defamation or invasion of privacy.

8.5.2 Drug Tests

Drug testing has become common in the U.S. workplace, and employers generally are permitted to test applicants and employees for recent use of drugs and alcohol. Certain employers, in fact, may be required to administer drug tests.

The employer's right to test for drug and alcohol use is not unlimited, however. Constraints on the practice include the Drug-Free Workplace Acts, the Americans with Disabilities Act, and the Transportation Employee Testing Act.

The first federal Drug-Free Workplace Act was enacted in 1988. The statute applies to organizations and individuals with federal grants or contracts. Although the 1988 Act does not require drug testing, it encourages the practice by requiring government contractors and grantees to publish antidrug policies and administer a drug awareness program. The 1988 Act also requires employers to report employees' criminal convictions for workplace drug use, and either terminate these employees or require them to undergo drug treatment.

The 1998 Drug-Free Workplace Act is aimed at small businesses (not necessarily government contractors or grantees) and authorizes Small Business Administration grants to employers that want to start workplace antidrug programs. A qualifying program will include employee drug testing, but employers are prohibited as a condition of the grants from disclosing test results, or disclosing the fact that an employee is enrolled in a drug treatment program, to fellow employees or other third parties.

The ADA addresses both alcohol testing and drug rehabilitation. An alcohol test is classified as a "medical examination" for ADA purposes, meaning that such a test may not be administered to an applicant until a conditional offer of employment has been made. The ADA does not prohibit or restrict testing of employees for illegal drug use. Employers should be aware, however, that alcoholics and persons who have been treated for drug use have disabilities for ADA purposes and are protected from discrimination based on those disabilities. Notably, an employer may not ask a job applicant questions that are likely to elicit information about alcoholism or drug rehabilitation.

The Department of Transportation and its various agencies, including the U.S. Coast Guard and the Federal Aviation Administration, require employers in the transportation field to test all employees that perform "safety-sensitive functions" for drug and alcohol use. Each agency has published its own drug and alcohol testing regulations for employers subject to its jurisdiction. Records of drug and alcohol test results must be kept confidential and maintained separately from other personnel records.

Finally, a large number of states have statutes that regulate drug testing, most of which include some confidentiality requirements. Employers should be aware of these state laws before implementing a program of drug and alcohol testing for applicants and employees.

8.5.3 Medical Tests

Private employers might have legitimate reasons to require applicants and employees to undergo various types of medical tests, but their discretion to require such tests is significantly constrained by federal and state law.

The most important such constraint is the Americans with Disabilities Act, which limits medical testing and inquiries related to disabilities at three points in the employer–employee relationship.

The first point at which the ADA and the implementing regulations of the EEOC apply to a covered employer is the pre-offer stage. When an applicant has not received an offer or conditional offer of employment, the prospective employer is not permitted to require any medical tests at all, and is not permitted to ask questions that might elicit information about a disability. The employer is permitted to ask about the applicant's ability to do tasks that are directly related to the job, but more general questions about the applicant's capacities or incapacities are not permitted. The employer may ask questions about the applicant's lifestyle, but only if the questions are not likely to elicit responses about disabilities. (Inquiries into lifestyle might, of course, create other problems if they have to do with religion or other suspect categories relevant to civil rights laws.)

The second stage, for ADA purposes, is the point at which the employer has made a bona fide offer or conditional offer of employment to the applicant. At this point, the employer may require a medical examination and inquire into disabilities, medical history, and history of workers' compensation claims, but only if those examinations and inquiries are applied equally to all candidates for jobs of the kind offered. The results of medical examinations must not be disclosed to third parties or used to discriminate on the basis of disability. Employers at this stage also may require reasonable follow-up medical examinations related to the results of initial examinations.

In order for a conditional offer to be used as the basis for medical examinations or inquiries, all other conditions to the applicant's hiring must have been met. In other words, if the employer is still waiting for references, approvals from superiors, or other events that might result in a decision not to hire, medical tests and inquiries concerning disabilities are premature and unlawful.

The third stage to which ADA regulations are addressed is the ongoing employment relationship. Existing employees may be subjected to medical examinations to the extent those are job-related and necessary. Employees also may lawfully be examined or questioned on medical matters in defined circumstances, including as required by regulations or as part of the employee's voluntary participation in employer-sponsored health programs. Finally, employers may require medical information when an employee returns from sick leave, subject to restrictions in the Family and Medical Leave Act.

The full scope of state and federal regulation of medical testing is beyond the scope of this book, but employers should seek legal advice before requiring any medical examination, including testing for HIV status and genetic predispositions to illnesses and disabilities.[34]

Notes

[1]U.S. Const. Am. IV.

[2]Many state constitutions restrict unreasonable searches and seizures, and some state constitutions recognize rights of privacy that can extend to workplace searches. Most of these protections, like those of the Bill of Rights in the U.S. Constitution, restrict only governmental conduct. California's constitution, however, restricts both private and public conduct.

[3]*See Bodewig v. K-Mart, Inc.*, 635 P.2d 657 (Ct. App. Or. 1981).

[4]In some workplaces, such as defense contractors that handle classified material, employers might reasonably search briefcases, purses, and book bags every time employees enter or leave the premises. Like other searches, these activities should be nondiscriminatory and supported by notice to employees.

[5]*See, e.g., Wal-Mart Stores, Inc. and United Food and Commercial Workers Union International Union, AFL-CIO*, 343 NLRB 127 (2004); *see also IBM Corporation*, 341 NLRB 1288 (2004). The *IBM Corporation* decision overruled a previous finding that even nonunion employees have a right to a coworker witness in investigatory interviews. However, employers still are not permitted to discipline employees for making such a request. *IBM Corporation*, 341 NLRB at 1295.

[6]*Burlington Industries, Inc. v. Ellerth*, 524 U.S. 742 (1998); *Farragher v. City of Boca Raton*, 524 U.S. 775 (1998). For the EEOC's detailed guidance on sexual harassment law enforcement, *see* U.S. Equal Employment Opportunity Commission, "Enforcement Guidance: Vicarious Employer Liability for Unlawful Harassment by Supervisors," available at http://www.eeoc.gov/policy/docs/harassment.html (last visited Nov. 25, 2007) (*EEOC Guidance*). Employers also may be liable for harassment by nonsupervisory personnel when the complaint establishes the elements

of a hostile environment claim. However, employers do not have the kind of strict liability for coworker harassment that they face when supervisors sexually harass subordinates.

[7]*EEOC Guidance, supra* at 3.

[8]*Id.* at 10. Protected activity is "opposition to prohibited discrimination or participation in the statutory complaint process." *Id.*

[9]*Id.*

[10]*Id.*

[11]*Id.* at 10–11.

[12]*Id.* at 11.

[13]*Id.* 11–12.

[14]Employers' statements to outside investigators and others with a legitimate interest in the subject of a statement enjoy a qualified privilege, but the privilege may be lost if the statements are not made in good faith or are inappropriate under the circumstances. *See* William Prosser, Handbook of the Law of Torts § 115 (5th ed. 1984); O. Lee Reed & Jan W. Henkel, Facilitating the Flow of Truthful Personnel Information: Some Needed Change in the Standard Required to Overcome the Qualified Privilege to Defame, 26 Am. Bus. L.J. 305, 311–315 (1988).

[15]W. Page Keeton, et al., Prosser and Keeton on the Law of Torts § 113 at 804 (5th ed. 1984) (*Prosser and Keaton*).

[16]*See Love v. Southern Bell Tel. & Tel. Co.*, 263 So.2d 460 (La. Ct. App. 1972), *cert. denied*, 266 So.2d 429 (La. 1972), in which the employer made repeated entry into the employee's home.

[17]*See Lambert v. Dow Chemical Co.*, 215 So.2d 673 (La. Ct. App. 1968), in which the employer obtained photographs of an employee's injured leg and displayed them as part of the company's safety program.

[18]*Prosser and Keeton, supra*, at 813.

[19]*See, e.g., Beaumont v. Brown*, 257 N.W.2d 522 (Mich. 1977).

[20]*Id.*

[21]*See* U.S. Equal Employment Opportunity Commission, "The ADA: Your Responsibilities as an Employer," available at http://www.eeoc.gov/facts/ada17.html (last visited Nov. 25, 2007).

[22]29 CFR § 825.500(g).

[23]*Id.*

[24]Employers also should be aware of the medical privacy statutes and regulations of the states in which they do business, some of which are listed in Appendix A. To the extent those statutes and regulations provide employees with protections that are at least as strong as those of federal law, they are not preempted by HIPAA and other federal statutes. Employers should obtain expert legal advice on the possible application of those statutes.

[25]HIPAA's requirements that persons be granted access to their medical records apply to employers that are self-insurers.

[26]Under OHSA, employees are entitled to request and receive medical records maintained by the employer, including records concerning exposure to hazardous substances. OSHA permits some exceptions to this obligation. *See* 29 C.F.R. § 1910.20.

[27]The Department of Transportation includes a number of agencies, such as the United States Coast Guard, the Federal Railway Administration, the Federal Aviation Administration, and the Federal Motor Carrier Safety Association, that regulate "safety-sensitive transportation employers and employees." *See* U.S. Department of Transportation, Office of the Secretary of Transportation, Office of Drug & Alcohol Policy & Compliance, http://www.dot.gov/ost/dapc/odapc_faq.html (last visited Nov. 28, 2007). These agencies' regulations on alcohol and drug testing include certain confidentiality provisions, and require a medical review officer or service agent involved in alcohol and drug testing to provide copies and test results and other information to an employee on request. 49 CFR Part 40, § 40.329.

[28]Cal. Labor Code § 1198.5(a).

[29]*Id.* § 1198.5(b).

[30]*Id.* § 1198.5(d).

[31]29 U.S.C. § 2001(1).

[32]*Id.* § 2006.

[33] State statutes that restrict use of lie detection tests are listed in Appendix A.

[34] Many of the relevant state laws are listed in Appendix A.

CHAPTER 9

Surveillance of Employees and Employee Communications

Although the subject is controversial, businesses have legitimate reasons to monitor their employees' workplace activities, including the communications those employees make and receive over employer-provided systems and facilities. Surveillance cameras can capture criminal activities, not only of employees, but of intruders on the business's premises. Monitoring of communications can ensure that employees are dealing properly with customers and other third parties; are using employer-provided telephones, e-mail, and Internet access for work-related purposes; and are not engaged in communications that may subject the employer to liability. Under some circumstances, in fact, employers might have an affirmative duty to monitor the communications of personnel who are believed to be involved in illicit activities with the potential to harm others.[1]

However, employer surveillance of employees is subject to a number of state and federal privacy laws and may also be the subject of collective bargaining. Accordingly, business owners and managers should conduct surveillance with care, and only after obtaining up-to-date legal advice.

This chapter surveys the applicable law as it affects three activities: monitoring of employees' telephone and e-mail communications, monitoring of employees' Internet usage, and video surveillance of the workplace.

9.1 Telephone and E-Mail Communications

In especially egregious circumstances, an employer's monitoring of employee telephone calls and e-mail messages might support causes of action for the various privacy torts discussed earlier in this chapter. By far the most important sources of law in this area, however, are the federal Electronic Communications Privacy Act (ECPA) and the wiretapping/eavesdropping laws of the states.

9.1.1 The ECPA and SCA

As we discussed in Chapter 4, the federal law governing interceptions of telephone calls in real-time is the ECPA, and the federal law governing the acquisition of stored communications is the Stored Communications Act (SCA).[2] The first statute applies when employers "listen in" on or record employee telephone conversations while those conversations are in progress; the second applies when employers retrieve employee's e-mail messages from storage and review them.[3]

Of the two federal laws, the ECPA is by far the more important constraint on employer conduct. Courts have held that the SCA permits an employer, as the provider of e-mail service for its employees, to read stored e-mails of its personnel for any purpose; accordingly, unless a collective bargaining agreement or other commitment made to employees prevents it, employers generally will not be liable to employees for reading their e-mail.[4]

The ECPA generally prohibits anyone from using a mechanical, electronic, or other device to "intercept"—that is, intentionally overhear or record—a telephone conversation.[5] Of the several exceptions to this federal prohibition, two are of particular value to employers: (1) the "business extension" exemption for interception of calls on the employer's premises for a business purpose; and (2) the "one party consent" exception for interceptions made with the consent of one party to the conversation.[6] The following discusses each of these exceptions.

9.1.1.1 Business Extension Exception

The ECPA includes a definitional provision that gives employers (or persons authorized by employers) some latitude to eavesdrop on, and perhaps even record, employee conversations when those acts of eavesdropping and recording are in the ordinary course of the employer's business. Specifically, the ECPA states that an interception has not taken place if the device by which the contents of a conversation are acquired is a "telephone instrument equipment or facility, or any component thereof . . . furnished to the subscriber or user by a provider of wire or electronic communication service in the ordinary course of its business and being used by the subscriber or user in the ordinary course of its business or furnished by such subscriber or user for connection to the facilities of such service and used in the ordinary course of its business . . ."[7]

This exception, as interpreted by the courts, consists of two principal elements: first, the interception must be accomplished by use of an extension telephone or other common device; and second, the interception must be in the course of the employer's business.

The courts have had some difficulty deciding whether a device attached to a telephone line or instrument by the employer qualifies as a permitted "telephone instrument equipment or facility" under the business extension exception. In *Epps v. Saint Mary's Hospital of Athens, Inc.*, for example, the Eleventh Circuit Court of Appeals held that an employer's use of a double-reeled tape recorder, attached to an ambulance dispatch console on which emergency telephone calls were terminated, qualified under the exception.[8] In *Williams v. Poulos*, however, the First Circuit Court of Appeals found that alligator clips placed on a telephone line on the employer's premises were not devices of the kind contemplated by the business extension exception.[9] Similarly, in *Deal v. Spears*, the Eighth Circuit Court of Appeals found that a recording device connected to the employer's extension telephone did not qualify for the exception.[10] Taken together, these cases suggest that the business telephone exception may not immunize the use of a recording device to preserve the contents of employee conversations. However, simple use of an extension telephone, or of a second headset used by a job candidate to monitor a service representative's conversation, should come within the exception.

Defendants relying on the business extension exception also must demonstrate that their use of interception and recording equipment was "in the ordinary course of business." In interpreting this language, the courts distinguish employees' business calls, which may be extensively monitored if necessary to serve the employer's business purpose, and personal calls, which ordinarily may be monitored only to the extent needed to ascertain that those calls are, in fact, personal.[11] In *Ali v. Douglas Cable Communications*, for example, the court found that an employer who listened in extensively on his sales representatives' business conversations in order to "monitor [representatives] in the use of proper skills and to assist the [representatives] with difficult customers" acted in the ordinary course of business within the exception.[12] In *Deal v. Spears*, however, the court found that an employer's interest in preventing use of her telephones for personal calls might justify limited monitoring, but did not support "recording twenty-two hours of calls" and listening to all of them.[13] Similarly, in *United States v. Harpel*, the court found "as a matter of law that a telephone extension used without authorization or consent to surreptitiously record a private telephone conversation is not used in the ordinary course of business."[14] As these examples show, reliance on the business extension exception to support a practice of automatically recording all of an employees' telephone conversations, both business and personal, may prove difficult to sustain. However, as long as the employer is listening to business-related conversations as part of the hiring process, the second element of the business extension exception should be satisfied.

9.1.1.2 One-Party Consent

In defending a suit brought under the ECPA, the proof of one party's consent (presumably, the employee's consent) to the interception of his or her calls has substantial advantages over a defense based on the business extension exception. Notably, an employee's consent may immunize the use of recording devices that would not pass muster as "business extensions." Similarly, there is proof that an employee's consent will foreclose any inquiry into the relationship between the interception activity and the employer's "business purpose." Fortunately, the ECPA, like the wiretap statutes of most states, permits a telephone conversation to be intercepted or recorded so long as only "one of the parties to the communication has given prior consent to such interception . . ."[15]

Under the one-party consent exemption as interpreted by the courts, an employer may base a consent defense on the employee's express or implied agreement to the interception activity. An employee gives express consent when he or she makes an oral or written statement of assent to interception of the employee's calls. An employee gives implied consent by making telephone calls after being informed that those calls will be intercepted. Regardless of how consent is obtained, the employer must convey its policy clearly and in reasonable detail. One court, for example, rejected an employer's consent defense on the ground that the employee was not "informed (1) of the manner (i.e., the intercepting and recording of telephone conversations) in which this monitoring was conducted; and (2) that he himself would be subjected to such monitoring."[16] Similarly, a court rejected a defense based on consent when the employee was not informed "that [the employer was] monitoring the phone, but only [that the employer] *might* do so . . ."[17] Accordingly, notice to employees should be prominently given, in the employee handbook or elsewhere, and receipt of that notice should be acknowledged by the employee in writing if possible.[18]

9.1.2 Compliance with State "Two-Party Consent" Statutes

Like the ECPA, most state wiretapping/eavesdropping statutes permit conversations to be monitored with the consent of one party. However, several states permit interception of telephone calls only with the consent of both parties to the conversation, and provide for civil suits and criminal prosecutions against those who intercept calls without such two-party consent.[19] The state at either end of a conversation might assert jurisdiction if the call is recorded or monitored in violation of that state's laws, and the state with the more restrictive statute might be found to have the greater interest in the matter for purposes of choice of law.[20]

In order to minimize the risk of litigation arising out of a candidate's monitoring of conversations with customers in two-party consent states, employers should advise nonemployee parties to employee conversations that their calls may be monitored or taped for quality management, training, or customer protection purposes. This is typically accomplished by a recorded message at the beginning of each call.

Finally, although state wiretapping statutes vary in the prohibitions and penalties they prescribe, those statutes typically classify violations as felonies and permit private plaintiffs to recover their actual damages or, in the alternative, a specified statutory award. In Connecticut, for example, a successful plaintiff may recover actual damages, liquidated damages at the rate of $100 per day for each day a violation occurred, or $1,000—whichever is higher.[21] State statutes also may allow a successful plaintiff to recover punitive damages, attorneys' fees, and the costs of litigation.[22]

9.2 Monitoring Employees' Internet Use

Employees use employer-provided Internet access for a number of purposes, including sending and receiving Web-based e-mails and instant messages, posting content to blogs and newsgroups, and retrieving and viewing material from Web sites. Whether some or all of these activities constitute the receipt or transmission of electronic communications for purposes of the ECPA and SCA has not been conclusively determined by the courts. However, the courts have found that an employer may monitor an employee's workplace Internet use pursuant to a technology use policy or similar guidance disseminated to the workforce.[23] In cases in which the employer is reasonably on notice that the employee is using workplace Internet access for unlawful purposes, the employer may have a duty to conduct such surveillance.[24] Accordingly, employers should give their personnel clear, unambiguous notice that all use of the employers' communications facilities, including Internet access, is for business purposes only and will be monitored at the employer's discretion. The notice also should make clear that unauthorized use of the employer's system for unlawful, improper, or otherwise harmful purposes may result in disciplinary action. If employers permit their personnel to access the company network from home, or otherwise assist employees to do business-related work on home computers or laptops, their policies should reserve the right to monitor or review such remote use of the Internet, as well.

9.3 Video Surveillance of the Workplace

Video surveillance of the workplace should not give rise to legal concerns when it does not intrude on restrooms, locker rooms, or other places where employees might have an expectation of privacy. Surveillance of these "private" areas, however, could support actions for invasion of privacy and might run afoul of numerous statutes, including the federal Video Voyeurism Protection Act of 2004 and various state laws.[25]

Finally, video surveillance of the workplace, like monitoring of electronic communications and Internet usage, may be the subject of collective bargaining, and a collective bargaining agreement may contain restrictions more severe than those imposed by federal and state law.

Notes

[1]*See Doe v. XYC Corp.*, 887 A.2d 1156 (Sup. Ct. N.J. 2005).

[2]The ECPA is codified at 18 U.S.C. § 2510 *et seq.*; the SCA is codified at 18 U.S.C. 2701 *et seq.*

[3]A number of courts have considered whether, under various circumstances, the acquisition of an e-mail message constitutes a real-time interception of that message, which would implicate the ECPA, or an acquisition of those messages from storage under the SCA. *See, e.g., United States v. Councilman*, 418 F.3d 67 (1st Cir. 2005). Without pursuing the intricacies of those cases here, it is sufficient to say that when an employer reads an employee's stored e-mail on the company's server, a finding that that conduct is an interception under the ECPA, rather than an acquisition of a stored electronic communication, is very unlikely.

[4]*See Bohach v. City of Reno*, 932 F.Supp. 1232 (D. Nev. 1996).

[5]18 U.S.C. § 2511(1)(a). Violation of this prohibition may result in criminal prosecution, possibly resulting in a fine, imprisonment for not more than five years, or both. *Id.* § 2511(4). Persons aggrieved by a violation also may bring civil suits for injunctive relief, damages, or both. *Id.* § 2520.

[6]Under the ECPA, "intercept" means the "aural [i.e., with the human ear] or other acquisition of the contents of any wire, electronic, or oral communication through the use of any electronic, mechanical, or other device." *Id.* §2510(4).

[7]*Id.* § 2510 (5)(a).

[8]*Epps v. St. Mary's Hospital of Athens, Inc.*, 802 F.2d 412 (11th Cir. 1986).

[9]*Williams v. Poulos*, 11 F.3d 271 (1st Cir. 1993).

[10]*Deal v. Spears*, 980 F.2d 1153, 1158 (8th Cir. 1992). *See also United States v. Harpel*, 493 F.2d 346, 350 (10th Cir. 1974) (finding that a tape recorder connected to a telephone receiver is not within the exception).

[11]*Watkins v. L. M. Berry & Co.*, 704 F.2d 577, 581 (11th Cir. 1983).

[12]*Ali v. Douglas Cable Communications*, 929 F.Supp. 1362, 1373 (D. Kan. 1996).

[13]*Id.* In *Epps v. St. Mary's Hospital of Athens, Inc.*, however, the court found that even a personal call may lawfully be monitored in its entirety if the call "concerned scurrilous remarks about supervisory employees" and therefore threatened "contamination of a working environment . . ." *Epps v. St. Mary's Hospital of Athens, Inc., supra*, 802 F.2d at 417.

[14]*United States v. Harpel, supra*, 493 F.2d at 351.

[15]*Id.* § 2511 (2)(d). This exemption is lost, however, if the interception is made "for the purpose of committing any criminal or tortious act . . ." *Id.*

[16]*Williams v. Poulos, supra*, 11 F.3d at 281.

[17]*Deal v. Spears*, 980 F.2d 1153, 1157 (8th Cir. 1992) (emphasis added).

[18]At the time of this writing, two states—Connecticut and Delaware—have statutes that expressly require written notice to employees of workplace communications monitoring. Those statutes likely apply to monitoring of Internet use, discussed below, as well as telephone and e-mail communications.

[19]At least 13 states now prohibit interceptions without the consent of both parties. *See, e.g.*, Cal. Penal Code § 631, 632; Conn. Gen. Stat. Ann. 52-570(d); Del. Code Ann. tit. 11, § 2402; Fla. Stat. ch. 934.03; Ill. Comp. Stat. 5/14-2, 5/14-3; Md. Code Ann., Cts & Jud. Proc. 10-402; Mass Ann. Laws ch. 272, § 99; Mich. Comp. Laws § 750.539a *et seq.;* Mont. Code Ann. § 45-8-213; Nev. Rev. Stat. Ann. § 200.620-650; N.H. Rev. Stat. Ann. § 570-A; 18 Pa. Cons. Stat. § 5703-5704; Wash. Rev. Code § 9.73.030.

[20]*See Kearney v. Salomon Smith Barney, Inc.*, 137 P.3d 914 (Sup. Ct. Cal. 2006).

[21]Conn. Gen. Stat. Ann. § 54-41(r).

[22]*Id.*

[23]*See., e.g., United States v. Simons*, 206 F.3d 392 (4th Cir. 2000).

[24]*Doe v. XYC Corp., supra.*

[25]18 U.S.C. § 1801; *see, e.g.*, Cal. Labor Code § 453; Conn. Gen. Stat. § 31-48; N.Y. Penal Law §§ 250.40–250.60; Tex. Penal Code § 21.15.

PART III
Communicating with Customers and Consumers

The laws and practices we have described so far involve one kind of privacy: the rights of individuals to control the acquisition, use, and disclosure of their personal communications and information. But privacy law also protects another set of interests, often referred to broadly as "the right to be left alone." This vague right is the basis for a great deal of common-law, statutory, and constitutional law, ranging from abortion rights to the tort of invasion of privacy.

Legislators also have reacted when their constituents demand that marketers "leave them alone." The laws resulting from these demands restrict the ability of U.S. businesses to use a number of important sales channels, notably including telemarketing, facsimile advertising, and e-mail. The following describes the statutes and regulations affecting each of these marketing channels.

CHAPTER 10
Telemarketing

In our relentlessly competitive market economy, no potential method of commercial communication is neglected for long. Marketing messages adorn our public places and permeate our entertainment. The inundation is so complete that most people learn to ignore most of the din of advertising that surrounds them. This consumer resistance is matched by the marketers' quest for advertising channels that seize and hold a consumer's attention, however briefly.

Telemarketing is such a channel. Many people tune out television commercials and throw out bulk mail without reading it, but reflexively answer telephone calls. If the potential customer can be kept on the telephone for as little as a full minute, the caller can deliver a substantial sales pitch to a prospect who might actually be listening. For these reasons, telemarketing is a high-value medium for the advertiser.

Unfortunately, telemarketing also is an enduring source of public complaints, partly rooted in the nature of telephone calls themselves. Unlike letters and e-mails, telephone calls do not arrive quietly and do not wait patiently until their recipients have found a convenient time to retrieve them. Each telephone call arrives at a time of the caller's choosing, accompanied by a more or less strident noise. If the pleasure of the resulting conversation does not outweigh these negatives, the recipient might be left with a feeling of deep annoyance; and few telemarketing calls are received or recalled with pleasure.[1]

As privacy intrusions go, telemarketing calls cause little harm. Telemarketers do not ruin reputations, steal identities, destroy data, or commit any of the other destructive practices at which much of privacy law is aimed. But the cumulative annoyance caused by untold millions of telemarketing calls, and the resulting complaints to legislators and regulators, have had their effect.

Both federal and state laws now regulate telemarketing activities, and the requirements of those laws often conflict. In fact, in order to understand the obligations to which your organization's telemarketing activities are subject, it may be necessary to consult the rules of at least two federal agencies (the Federal Communications Commission (FCC) and the (FTC) Federal Trade Commission) and the laws of any states to which, or from which, telemarketing calls are placed.

10.1 Conflicting Rules and Overlapping Jurisdiction

Federal efforts to regulate telemarketing began with the Telephone Consumer Protection Act (TCPA) in 1991.[2] The TCPA created some definite rules for telemarketers and delegated to a single federal agency—the FCC—the authority to make additional regulations as the public interest required. Unfortunately, the TCPA sowed the first seeds of confusion by failing to preempt inconsistent state laws in plain, unmistakable language. That failure contributed to today's bewildering patchwork of state and federal telemarketing rules.

The confusion increased drastically with enactment of the Telemarketing Consumer Fraud and Abuse Prevention Act in 1994.[3] In this legislation, Congress gave the FTC authority to "prescribe rules prohibiting deceptive telemarketing acts or practices and other abusive telemarketing acts or practices."[4] As the hearings and reports preceding the enactment of this law show, Congress's main concern was with fraudulent marketing schemes, of the kind the FTC already was accustomed to regulating in other contexts, that happened to be perpetrated over the telephone. Although the statute also directed the FTC to adopt time-of-day restrictions and caller identification and disclosure requirements, it did not expressly authorize the FTC to address other matters, such as prerecorded messages and do-not-call requests, that were well within the FCC's existing jurisdiction under the TCPA and the Communications Act. Unfortunately, the statute's broad mandate to the FTC to regulate "abusive" telemarketing practices blurred the boundary between the two agencies' authority. In other words, the federal-state mess was compounded by an interagency mess.

Of these two bad decisions—the failure to preempt state law and the delegation of rulemaking authority to two federal agencies rather than one—the creation of parallel regimes of telemarketing regulation at the federal level is especially hard to justify. If the FCC's jurisdiction under the TCPA had been somehow incomplete, supplemental regulation by the FTC might have made sense; but the FCC already had all the authority it needed to deal with telemarketing campaigns in all segments of the U.S. economy. In fact, it was the FTC, with its lack of jurisdiction over banks, common carriers, and various other businesses, that lacked the necessary authority to regulate all telemarketers.[5]

The state preemption issue came to a head in 2003, when the FCC adopted its rules implementing the FTC's national do-not-call (DNC) registry.[6] Although the TCPA expressly gave the states continuing authority to regulate intrastate telemarketing calls, and gave the FCC jurisdiction to regulate both interstate *and* intrastate telemarketing, the TCPA was less clear on the subject of state regulation of interstate calls.[7] Many states already had adopted their own DNC lists and a number of those states imposed restrictions on telemarketers that were more severe than those of the TCPA and the FCC's existing rules. If the states' authority extended only to intrastate calling, telemarketers might avoid the more restrictive state rules by placing all of their calls on an interstate basis. But, if the states insisted on regulating calls placed to their residents from points outside their states, then the compliance burden would increase dramatically, and Congress's effort to create a uniform, nationwide regulatory regime would be frustrated.

The FCC responded to this challenge with apparent resolution. Stating that more restrictive state laws governing interstate calls were almost certainly preempted by the TCPA and the FCC's rules, the Commission invited telemarketers that faced state threats of enforcement action based on interstate calls to seek relief from the FCC.[8]

Unfortunately, when preemption petitions were duly brought, the FCC simply failed to act. Political pressure from the states, and perhaps from Congress, apparently had weakened the Commission's resolve. At the time of this writing, over eight such petitions remain pending, including a joint petition from 33 parties that was filed in April 2005.[9]

The effect of all of this confusion can be briefly summarized.

First, on the state-federal front, telemarketers are forced to tailor their marketing campaigns around a patchwork of state laws that differ widely in critical provisions. As the joint petition filed with the FCC in 2005 pointed out, the differences include:[10]

- Failure of many states to recognize established business relationships as an exception to calling restrictions, or state existing business relationships (EBR) definitions that are more restrictive than the EBR definition in federal law.
- Widely varying requirements concerning disclosures that telemarketers must make to persons answering telephones.
- Differences in time-of-day and holiday calling restrictions.
- Widely varying rules concerning solicitation calls by nonprofit organizations.
- Differing rules concerning the use of automatic dialing and announcing devices.
- Various requirements for registration of telemarketers and purchase of state DNC lists.

On the federal interagency front, two examples of FCC/FTC inconsistency will suggest the scope of the problem.

The first example concerns so-called company-specific do-not-call requests. According to the telemarketing regulations of both the FCC and the FTC, telemarketers may not call consumers who previously have asked those callers not to call again.[11] Such company-specific requests must be honored, even if the consumers' telephone numbers are not listed on the national DNC registry and even if the consumers have EBRs with the callers. (An EBR exists when the consumer has made a purchase from the caller within 18 months before the call or has inquired about the caller's product or service within 3 months before the call.)[12]

But the duty to honor such requests may not last forever. In fact, under the FCC's rules, the residential telephone numbers of consumers who have asked a company not to call them again can be put back on the company's calling list after 5 years.[13] But the FTC provides for no such time limit, and therefore requires company-specific requests to be honored until rescinded.

The issue is complicated by limitations on the FTC's jurisdiction under the Federal Trade Commission Act, which denies the FTC power to regulate banks, common carriers, and certain other businesses.[14] The FTC has acknowledged that where its rules and those of the FCC differ, the FCC rules control those entities not subject to FTC jurisdiction.[15] Logically, this means that if a bank, common carrier, or other exempt organization has a list of company-specific DNC requests that are more than 5 years old, it should be able to retire those numbers after 5 years as the FCC permits.

But the FTC is an aggressive agency that does not hesitate to push the envelope of its jurisdiction. Where telemarketing is concerned, the FTC has announced that it *will* act against telemarketing firms that violate its rules, even when those firms are working for companies that are themselves exempt from FTC jurisdiction.[16] Effectively, this means that a company can only enjoy the benefit of its exemption from FTC telemarketing jurisdiction if it conducts its telemarketing campaigns in-house rather than through a telemarketing vendor.

Company-specific DNC requests are not the only point of disagreement between the FTC's rules and those of the FCC. The two agencies also differ in their treatment of calls that deliver prerecorded marketing messages (sometimes referred to in the press as "robo-calls"). The FCC permits such calls to persons with whom the caller has an EBR; the FTC does not.

The FTC's prohibition on robo-calls has always been a concealed rather than an open obstacle. In fact, the FTC's Telemarketing Sales Rule (TSR) does not mention prerecorded messages at all. However, a careful reading of the TSR's "call abandonment" provisions shows that calls that deliver prerecorded sales messages effectively are classified as unlawful "abandoned calls" under the TSR, even when those calls are made to persons with whom the caller has an EBR. In order to understand this result, which directly contradicts the parallel regulations of the FCC, it is necessary to know more about the two agencies' call abandonment rules.

Both agencies define "abandoned calls" as calls not answered by a live sales representative within 2 seconds of the called person's completed greeting.[17] If a sales representative is not available to speak with the person answering the call, that person must receive, within 2 seconds after the called person's completed greeting, a prerecorded identification message that states only the name and telephone number of the business, entity, or individual on whose behalf the call was placed. The identification message may not contain a sales pitch.

The agencies' rules deal differently, however, with calls that deliver prerecorded sales messages. The FCC rules expressly state that a call placed to someone with whom the caller has an EBR is not "abandoned" when it connects to a prerecorded sales message rather than a live representative, so long as the recording begins within 2 seconds of the called party's greeting.[18] The FTC's rules, however, do not contain this qualification. As a result, the FTC defines a call that does not connect to a live representative within 2 seconds as an abandoned call, even when that call delivers a prerecorded sales message within 2 seconds of a greeting from a person with whom the caller has an EBR.

In November 2003, Voice Mail Broadcasting Corporation (VMBC) asked the FTC to confirm that delivery of a prerecorded message to a residential telephone subscriber with whom the caller has an EBR is permitted under the TSR.[19] VMBC argued that by granting its petition, the FTC would conform its rules to those of the FCC without inviting the "dead air" and call hang-up problems that were the source of the call abandonment restrictions.[20] VMBC also argued that callers are unlikely to abuse existing customers by using prerecorded messages excessively.[21]

The Commission asked for comments on the VMBC proposal and announced that until the proceeding was concluded, it would "forbear" from enforcement actions against marketers who delivered prerecorded messages to persons with whom they had an EBR.

In an order published October 4, 2006, the FTC rejected VMBC's arguments, finding that the proposed EBR-based "safe harbor" for prerecorded calls would not serve the public interest. Among other findings, the Commission concluded that permitting EBR-based prerecorded calls would lead to greater intrusions on consumer privacy, would interfere with consumers' ability to make and receive health and safety-related calls, and would erode the effectiveness of the federal Do-Not-Call Registry. More generally, the FTC found that encouraging wider use of inexpensive "prerecorded" telemarketing would increase commercial calling volumes and upset the "delicate balance" the Commission had struck between the privacy interests of consumers and the legitimate interests of businesses in contacting their existing customers. (The Commission also brushed aside the argument that it should harmonize its rules with those of the FCC.)[22]

The FTC went beyond denial of the VMBC petition, however, and affirmatively decided to propose an amendment to its rules that would expressly prohibit "any outbound telemarketing call that delivers a prerecorded message when answered by a person, unless the seller has obtained the express agreement, in writing, of such person to place prerecorded calls to that person."[23] Far from resolving the conflict between its rules and those of the FCC, the Commission proposed to carve that conflict in stone.

Finally, the FTC proposed to drop its policy of forbearance as to prerecorded sales messages delivered to persons with whom the caller has an EBR. Specifically, the FTC announced that, no later than January 2, 2007, it would resume active enforcement of its prohibition.[24] In December, 2006, the FTC extended that deadline until the conclusion of the pending proceeding to amend its rules.

At the time of this writing, companies subject to FTC jurisdiction may continue to deliver prerecorded marketing messages to consumers with whom they have an EBR. When the present rulemaking concludes, however, with the FTC's expected adoption of a clear prohibition on robo-calls, companies subject to the FTC must cease making those calls. Companies not subject to FTC jurisdiction will be free to make such calls to consumers with whom they have an EBR, so long as those marketing campaigns are carried on in-house rather than through third-party vendors.

In the face of this regulatory confusion, no summary of the telemarketing obligations of U.S. business can anticipate all of the scenarios an organization will face. The following outline of those obligations should be supplemented by legal advice before decisions concerning a telemarketing campaign are made.

10.2 The Federal Communications Commission's Telemarketing Regulations

The FCC issues telemarketing regulations pursuant to the authority granted in the TCPA, codified at Section 227 of the Communications Act of 1934.[25] Some of the principal provisions of those regulations follow.

10.2.1 Autodialers, Artificial Voices, Prerecorded Messages, and Other Issues

The FCC limits the use of autodialers, artificial voices, and prerecorded messages. In order to comply with the FCC regulations, you first must ensure that you do not make any calls (not just telemarketing calls) using an automatic telephone dialing system or artificial or prerecorded voice to an emergency telephone line,[26] hospital guest room, or patient room,[27] or any mobile telephone.[28] These prohibitions do not apply if the call is made for emergency purposes or with the express prior consent of the called party.[29] Also, the rules provide a "safe harbor" period for calls to mobile telephone numbers that only recently have been ported from wireline numbers.[30]

The rules also impose specific prohibitions on the use of artificial or prerecorded voices in calls to residential telephone numbers. Specifically, unless the caller has the express prior consent of the called party, no such call may be made unless it is made for emergency purposes, is not made for a commercial purpose, or (if the call is made for a commercial purpose) it does not include or introduce an unsolicited advertisement or constitute a telephone solicitation.[31] An exception also is made (by the FCC, but not the FTC) for calls to residential customers with whom the caller has an EBR. The FCC also exempts calls made on behalf of a tax-exempt nonprofit organization.[32]

The rules also impose other restrictions on autodialers, artificial voices, and prerecorded voices. Notably, it is unlawful to use an automatic dialing system in such a way that two or more telephone lines of a multiline business are engaged simultaneously.[33] Also, all artificial or prerecorded telephone messages must include certain information, including the identity of the entity making the call, the name under which a business caller is registered to do business, and (during or after the message) the telephone number of the business that placed the call.[34]

The FCC imposes restrictions on abandoned calls—that is, calls that are disconnected after the called party answers. Specifically, a call is "abandoned" if "it is not connected to a live sales representative within two (2) seconds of the called person's completed greeting."[35] If a live salesperson is not available after 2 seconds, that person must receive a prerecorded identification message that "that states only the name and telephone number of the business, entity, or individual on whose behalf the call was placed, and that the call was for "telemarketing purposes."[36] The telephone number provided must be useable for the placement of a do-not-call request placed during regular business hours.[37]

A variant of the "abandoned call" rule applies to telemarketing calls that deliver artificial or prerecorded voice messages. If such a call is made to a person "who either has granted prior express consent for the call to be made or has an EBR with the caller," that call is not an abandoned call "if the message begins within two (2) seconds of the called person's completed greeting."[38] As noted earlier, this rule differs from the FTC's TSR, which does not recognize an EBR exception to the abandoned call requirements.

The FCC also provides that an unanswered telemarketing call may not be disconnected prior to at least 15 seconds or four (4) rings.[39] Putting this rule together with the abandoned call rules, we can summarize by saying that it is generally unlawful to *disconnect* a telemarketing call before 15 seconds or four (4) rings; and that if a live person answers the call, it is generally unlawful to *wait* more than two (2) seconds, after the live party completes his or her greeting, before connecting the called party to a live sales representative or leaving an identification message.

10.2.2 Time-of-Day Restrictions

The FCC regulations also limit the times of day within which a caller may make a *telephone solicitation*, which is defined as "the initiation of a telephone call or message for the purpose of encouraging the purchase or rental of, or investment in, property, goods, or services . . ."[40] Telephone solicitations do not include calls made with the called party's "prior express invitation or permission," or to persons with whom the caller has an EBR, or made by or on behalf of a tax-exempt nonprofit organization.[41] A call that comes within this definition may not be made to a residential subscriber before 8:00 A.M. or after 9:00 P.M.[42]

10.2.3 The Federal Do-Not-Call List

Some of the most important provisions of the telemarketing regulations involve the federal do-not-call (DNC) list authorized by legislation enacted in March 2003.[43] The DNC list restricts calls that meet the definition of telephone solicitation—that is, commercial calls to residential subscribers who have not given permission for such calls, with whom the caller does not have an EBR, and that lack tax-exempt nonprofit status. Under the statute and the implementing regulations, it is unlawful to place a telephone solicitation call to a residential telephone number that has been placed on the federal DNC list.[44] DNC registrations must be honored for five (5) years (although, at this writing, bills pending in Congress would make the registrations permanent). Liability for placing calls that violate the DNC rules can be avoided only if the caller demonstrates that the violation "is the result of error" and that, as part of its routine business practice, the caller:

- Has established and implemented written procedures to comply with the DNC rules;
- Has trained its personnel, and any entity assisting in its compliance, in procedures established pursuant to the DNC rules;
- Has maintained and recorded a list of telephone numbers that the seller may not contact;
- Uses a process to prevent telephone solicitations to any telephone number on any list established pursuant to the DNC rules, employing a version of the DNC registry obtained from the administrator of the registry no more than three months prior to the date any call is made, and maintains records documenting this process;
- Uses a process to ensure that it does not sell, rent, lease, purchase, or use the DNC database, or any part thereof, for any purpose except compliance with the telemarketing regulations and other applicable law;
- Purchases access to the DNC list from its administrator and does not participate in any arrangements to share the cost of accessing the DNC list, including any such arrangement with telemarketers.[45]

10.2.4 Company-Specific DNC Lists

Telemarketers also must maintain so-called "company-specific" DNC lists. Specifically, the rules provide that "[n]o person or entity shall initiate any call for telemarketing purposes to a residential telephone subscriber unless such person or entity has instituted procedures for maintaining a list of persons who request not to receive telemarketing calls made by or on behalf of that person or entity."[46] When a telemarketer receives a request to be placed on the company-specific DNC list, it must honor that request within a reasonable time (not to exceed 30 days).[47] Persons or entities that make telemarketing calls "must have a written policy, available on demand, for maintaining a [company-specific] do-not-call list," and personnel "engaged in any aspect of telemarketing must be informed and trained on the existence and use of the do-not-call list."[48]

10.2.5 The EBR Exception

One of the most important features of the FCC's telemarketing rules is the set of exceptions that apply to calls placed to persons with whom the caller has an EBR. If your company's relationship with the called party falls within the EBR definition, your company may:

- Call a residential subscriber at a telephone number that has been placed on the federal DNC list;
- Delivery autodialed, prerecorded, or artificial voice messages within two (2) seconds of a called party's greeting without violating the "abandoned call" restrictions;
- Avoid classification of your call as a "telephone solicitation," thereby permitting your company to place the call before 8:00 A.M. or after 9:00 P.M.

Accordingly, the EBR definition is one of the central provisions of the FCC's telemarketing rules. Specifically, an EBR is "a prior or existing relationship formed by a voluntary two-way communication between a person or entity and a residential subscriber with or without an exchange of consideration, on the basis of the subscriber's purchase or transaction with the entity within the eighteen (18) months immediately preceding the date of the telephone call or on the basis of the subscriber's inquiry or application regarding products or services offered by the entity within the three months immediately preceding the date of the call, which relationship has not been previously terminated by either party."[49]

This federal EBR definition, which is substantially broader than the counterpart provisions of many state telemarketing laws, is subject to some limitations. Notably, a request from a consumer to be placed on the caller's company-specific DNC list terminates an EBR with that caller. Also, an EBR between a telephone subscriber and an affiliate of your company does not create an EBR with your company unless the subscriber would reasonably expect your company to be included in the EBR with the affiliate.

10.2.6 The "Caller ID" Requirements

The FCC's telemarketing rules also address the common tactic of blocking transmission of the caller's Caller Identification (Caller ID) data as a means of defeating the called party's efforts to screen incoming calls. Under the rules, telemarketers must pass on Caller ID data, which must at least include the Calling Party Number (CPN) or the Automatic Number Identification (ANI) number assigned by the caller's telephone company for billing purposes. When it is available from the serving telephone company, the name of the telemarketer or seller also must be transmitted to the called party. The number transmitted must permit the called party to make a DNC request during normal business hours.

Finally, it is unlawful to block the transmission of Caller ID information when making a telemarketing call.

10.3 The Federal Trade Commission's Telemarketing Regulations

As noted earlier, the FTC adopted its Telemarketing Sales Rule, or TSR, pursuant to the authority granted by the Telemarketing Consumer Fraud and Prevention Act. That authority was augmented by provisions of the USA PATRIOT Act of 2001, which extended the coverage of the TSR to include charitable fund-raising by non-profit organizations as well as the solicitation of commercial transactions.[50]

Many provisions of the TSR are aimed at fraudulent practices rather than intrusions on privacy, and therefore are beyond the scope of this book. Notably, the TSR requires disclosure of the costs and other terms of a transaction proposed by a telemarketer, prohibits credit card laundering, and addresses other practices that would be equally deceptive if engaged in through other marketing channels.[51]

The TSR also prohibits "abusive" practices, some of which duplicate prohibitions in the FCC regulations. These include calling after 9:00 P.M. or before 8:00 A.M., calling residential numbers on the national DNC registry, making abandoned calls, and calling residential customers who have previously asked the caller not to contact them.[52]

As noted earlier, some inconsistencies between the TSR and the FCC's rules remain unresolved.

10.4 Other Sources of Telemarketing Regulation

Organizations that propose to engage in telemarketing should be aware, not only of FCC, FTC, and state requirements, but of industry-specific statutes and regulations to which they might be subject. For example, some of the functional regulators of the financial services industry have addressed telemarketing, and private associations, such as the National Association of Securities Dealers, also may have rules that address telemarketing activities by their members.

Finally, Tables 10.1 to 10.3 suggest some decisions that telemarketers might make, consistent with applicable regulations, under various circumstances. Obviously, these tables do not take all relevant considerations into account and should not be relied on as the sole basis for any decision.

Table 10.1 When May I Make a Marketing Call Using an Autodialer?

Facts	*Decision*
Residential line	Call, but observe abandoned/disconnected call rules and other telemarketing requirements.
Guest or patient room of health care facility	Do not call except in emergency or with prior express permission.
Emergency line	Do not call except in emergency or with prior express permission.
Pager or mobile number	Do not call except in emergency or with prior express permission.
Multiline business number	Call, but do not engage two or more lines simultaneously.

Table 10.2 When May I Make a Marketing Call Using an Artificial or Prerecorded Voice?

Facts	*Decision*
Residential line	Call only if you have an EBR or prior consent, in emergency, or for noncommercial purpose. Observe identification requirements.
Emergency line	Call only with prior consent or in emergency.
Guest room or patient room of health care facility	Call only with prior consent or in emergency.
Pager or mobile phone	Call only with prior consent or in emergency.

Table 10.3 When May I Make a Marketing Call Using a Live Agent?

Facts			*Decision*
Number called on National DNC List: no prior consent to call	EBR	Not on company-specific DNC list	Call
		On company-specific DNC list	Do not call
	No EBR	Not on company-specific DNC list	Do not call
		On company-specific DNC list	Do not call
Number called not on National DNC List: no consent to call	EBR	Not on company-specific DNC list	Call
		On company-specific DNC list	Do not call
	No EBR	Not on company-specific DNC list	Call
		On company-specific DNC list	Do not call

Notes

[1]The intrusiveness of telephone calls can be avoided simply by refusing to answer the telephone when taking the call is inconvenient, and services such as voice mail and Caller ID enable telephone subscribers to screen calls or retrieve them at their leisure. Not all subscribers, however, have purchased those services or use them consistently.

[2]47 U.S.C. § 227.

[3]15 U.S.C. §§ 6101–6108.

[4]*Id.* § 6102(a)(1).

[5]*See* 15 U.S.C. § 45(a)(2).

[6]*Rules and Regulations Implementing the Telephone Consumer Protection Act of 1991,* Report and Order, 18 F.C.C. Rcd 14014 (2003) (*TCPA Order*).

[7]47 U.S.C. § 227(e).

[8]*TCPA Order,* ¶ 84.

[9]Petition of Alliance Contract Services, *et al.* for Declaratory Ruling that the FCC has Exclusive Regulatory Jurisdiction over Interstate Telemarketing (filed in FCC CG Docket No. 02-278, April 29, 2005) (*Joint Petition)*.

[10]*Joint Petition, supra.*

[11]47 C.F.R. § 64.1200(d); 16 C.F.R. § 310.4(b)(1)(iii)(A).

[12]47 C.F.R. § 64.1200(f)(5); 16 C.F.R. § 310.2(n).

[13]47 C.F.R. § 64.1200(d).

[14]15 U.S.C. § 45(a)(2).

[15]68 FR 4580, 4586–4587 (Jan. 29, 2003).

[16]*Id.; see also* 60 FR at 43843 (Aug. 23, 1995).

[17]47 C.F.R. § 64.1200(a)(6); 16 C.F.R. § 310.4(b)(1)(iv).

[18] 47 C.F.R. § 64.1200(a)(6).

[19] *See* 71 FR 58716, 58717 (Oct. 4, 2006).

[20]*Id.*

[21]*Id.*

[22]71 FR 58716, *supra.*

[23]*Id.* at 58726.

[24]*Id.*

[25]47 U.S.C. § 227.

[26]An emergency telephone line includes "any 911 line and any emergency line of a hospital, medical physician or service office, health care facility, poison control center, or fire protection or law enforcement agency . . ." 47 C.F.R. § 64.1200(a)(1)(i).

[27]Specifically, no such call may be made to "the telephone line of any guest room or patient room of a hospital, health care facility, elderly home, or similar establishment . . ." *Id.* §64.1200(a)(1)(ii).

[28]Such calls are not permitted to "any telephone number assigned to a paging service, cellular telephone service, specialized mobile radio service, or other radio common carrier service, or any service for which the called party is charged for the call." *Id.* §64.1200(a)(1)(iii).

[29]*Id.* §64.1200(a)(i). "A person will not be liable for violating the prohibition in paragraph (a)(1)(iii) when the call is placed to wireless number that has been ported from wireline service and such call is a voice call; not knowingly made to a wireless number; and made within 15 days of the porting of the number from wireline to wireless service, provided the number is not already on the national do-not-call registry or caller's company-specific do-not-call list."

[30]*Id.* §64.1200(a)(1)(4).

[31]*Id.* §64.1200(a)(2)(i)–(iii).

[32]*Id.* §64.1200(a)(2)(iv)–(v).

[33]*Id.* §64.1200(a)(4).

[34]*Id.* §64.1200(b). When the call is to a residence, the caller must leave a telephone number that the called party can use to make a do-not-call request.

[35]*Id.* §64.1200(a)(6).

[36]*Id.*

[37]*Id.* The telephone number also may not be a 900 number or other number "for which charges exceed local or long distance transmission charges."

[38]*Id.* §64.1200(a)(6)(i). The definition of "established business relationship" is discussed below. Also, the "abandoned call" rules do not apply to calls placed by tax-exempt, nonprofit organizations.

[39]*Id.* § 64.1200(a)(5).

[40]*Id.* § 64.1200(f)(9).

[41]*Id.*

[42]*Id.* § 64.1200(c)(1).

[43]Do-Not-Call Implementation Act, Pub. L. No. 108-10, 117 Stat. 557 (2003), codified at 15 U.S.C. § 6101.

[44]*Id.* § 64.1200(c)(2).

[45]*Id.* § 64.1200(c)(2). Telephone solicitation calls may be made to numbers on the DNC list to persons with whom the caller has a personal relationship and to persons who have given the caller prior express, signed, written permission to make the call. *Id.* § 64.1200(c)(2)(ii).

[46]*Id.* § 64.1200(d).

[47]*Id.*

[48]*Id.*

[49]*Id.* § 64.1200(f)(3).

[50]Pub. L. No. 107-56, 115 Stat. 272 (Oct. 26, 2001).

[51]16 C.F.R. § 310.3.

[52]*Id.* § 310.4.

CHAPTER 11

Fax Advertising

Some of the most restrictive rules governing electronic marketing are aimed at facsimile (fax) advertising. Under section 227 of the Communications Act and the implementing regulations of the Federal Communication Commission (FCC) (which we'll refer to here as the "Junk Fax Rules"), it is unlawful to "use any telephone facsimile machine, computer, or other device to send, to a telephone facsimile machine, an unsolicited advertisement . . ."[1] The exceptions to this prohibition are narrow, and anyone planning to use faxes as an advertising channel should review the FCC regulations carefully before proceeding with such a program.

11.1 Communications Covered by the Junk Fax Rules

The FCC's Junk Fax Rules apply to any "unsolicited advertisement" sent to a "telephone facsimile machine" through the use of a "telephone facsimile machine, computer, or other device."[2] The FCC has found that this category includes not just traditional fax messages, but also "faxes sent to personal computers equipped with, or attached to, modems and to computerized fax servers . . ."[3] However, the Junk Fax Rules do not apply to faxes that are sent as e-mail over the Internet.[4]

The term "unsolicited advertisement" is defined in the Communications Act as "any material advertising the commercial availability of or quality of any property, goods, or services which is transmitted to any person without that person's prior express invitation or permission."[5] A message that does not promote a commercial product or service, including a request for a donation to a political campaign, political action committee, or charitable organization, is not classified as an unsolicited advertisement by the Junk Fax Rules.[6]

According to the FCC, the requirement of prior express invitation or permission to send a commercial fax may be satisfied by oral, written, or electronic methods, but the recipient "must clearly indicate that he or she consents to receiving such faxed advertisements from the company to which permission is given, and provide the individual or business's fax number to which faxes may be sent."[7]

11.2 The EBR Exception to the Junk Fax Rules

The most important exception to the prohibition on sending unsolicited fax advertisements is the established business relationship, or EBR, exception. For this purpose, the definition of an EBR is similar to the one set out in the telemarketing rules (see Chapter 10). Specifically, an EBR for Junk Fax Rule purposes is "a prior or existing relationship formed by a voluntary two-way communication between a person or entity and a business or residential subscriber with or without an exchange of consideration, on the basis of an inquiry, application, purchase or transaction by the business or residential subscriber regarding products or services offered by such person or entity, which relationship has not been previously terminated by either party."[8] Although written evidence of the EBR is not required, the FCC has made it clear that in the event of a dispute, the burden is on the sender of a fax to prove the existence of the relationship.[9] The EBR does not extend to affiliates of the entity with which the recipient engaged in voluntary communication.[10]

The FCC also is unwilling to assume that an EBR alone creates an expectation, in the customer, that he or she will be contacted by fax. Accordingly, the Junk Fax Rules provide that an EBR-based advertisement may not be sent to a fax number unless the sender obtained that number by means of voluntary communication from the recipient,[11] or through a "directory, advertisement, or site on the Internet to which the recipient voluntarily agreed to make available its facsimile number for public distribution."[12] If the sender "obtains the facsimile number from other sources, the sender must take reasonable steps to verify that the recipient agreed to make the number available for public distribution."[13]

11.3 Notice and Opt-Out Requirements

Even when a fax advertisement is permitted under the EBR exception, the sender must give the recipient an opportunity to opt out of further commercial faxes from that sender. This obligation includes giving the recipient a clear and conspicuous notice of the opt-out right,[14] including a "domestic contact telephone and facsimile machine number for the recipient to transmit [an opt-out] request to the sender," and "a cost-free mechanism for a recipient to transmit a request pursuant to such notice . . ."[15] The telephone numbers, fax numbers, and cost-free mechanisms required by the statute must permit a recipient to make an opt-out request at any time on any day of the week. The sender must honor the opt-out request within 30 days.[16]

11.4 Senders and Broadcasters

The FCC recognizes that a fax advertising campaign can involve many players. Notably, the Junk Fax Rules distinguish between senders, which are the businesses on behalf of which fax ads are sent, and "fax broadcasters" that transmit those messages on behalf of senders. The Rules make clear that senders, not broadcasters and other third parties, are responsible for ensuring that opt-out notices appear on commercial faxes and opt-out requests are honored within 30 days.[17] A fax broadcaster will be responsible for Junk Fax violations only if "it demonstrates a high degree of involvement in, or actual notice of, the unlawful activity and fails to take steps to prevent such facsimile advertisements . . ."[18]

11.5 Transactional Communications

Businesses often use fax machines to send copies of documents that require review and signature or that otherwise facilitate transactions in which the parties already are engaged. The FCC agrees that such messages are not advertisements for purposes of the Junk Fax Rules.[19] However, a message that refers to transactions to which the recipient has not yet agreed, or that has as its primary purpose the conveyance of an advertising message, will not come within this exception.[20]

11.6 Conclusion

The fax advertising prohibitions are among the most aggressively enforced of the FCC's regulations. Besides FCC enforcement actions, which often result in substantial monetary forfeitures, aggrieved recipients of unlawful fax advertising may bring civil suits, and state authorities may bring actions to recover damages on behalf of their citizens.[21] The private actions must be brought in state court and must be "otherwise permitted by the laws or rules of court of a State . . ."[22] Actions by the states are brought in federal courts.[23]

Notes

[1]47 U.S.C. § 227(b)(1)(C).

[2]*Id.*

[3]*Rules and Regulations Implementing the Telephone Consumer Protection Act of 1991*, CG Docket No. 02-278, Report and Order, ¶ 200 (July 3, 2003) (*TCPA Order*).

[4]*Id.*

[5]47 U.S.C. § 227(a)(4).

[6]*Rules and Regulations Implementing the Telephone Consumer Protection Act of 1991; Junk Fax Prevention Act of 2005*, CG Docket No. 02-278, Report and Order and Third Order on Reconsideration, ¶ 43 (April 6, 2006) (*Junk Fax Order*).

[7]*TCPA Order, supra* at ¶ 187.

[8]47 C.F.R. § 64.1200(f)(5).

[9]*Junk Fax Order, supra*, n. 54.

[10]*Id.* ¶ 20.

[11]*Id.* § 227(b)(1)(C)(i).

[12]47 C.F.R. § 64.1200(a)(3)(ii)(B).

[13]*Id.* The Rules assume that a recipient intends public distribution of a fax number that appears on the recipient's own directory, advertisement, or Internet site unless those materials explicitly state that advertisements will not be accepted at the number. *Id.*

[14]*Id.* § 227(b)(1)(C)(iii).

[15]*Id.* § 227(b)(2)(D).

[16]*Junk Fax Order, supra*, ¶ 31.

[17]*Id.* ¶ 38.

[18]*Id.* ¶ 40.

[19]*Id.* ¶ 49.

[20]*Id.* ¶ 51.

[21]*Id.* § 227(b)(3).

[22]*Id.*

[23]*Id.* § 227(f)(2).

CHAPTER 12

Spam: Regulation of Commercial E-Mail

E-mail continues to be an economically attractive, yet much-reviled, form of advertising. It is possible to send "spam" lawfully, but companies that use this marketing channel must navigate both the federal CAN-SPAM Act of 2003 and a growing variety of state laws that affect this practice.

12.1 Federal Antispam Law: The CAN-SPAM Act of 2003

The federal CAN-SPAM Act does not prohibit the use of e-mail advertising.[1] It does, however, prohibit certain fraudulent and misleading practices and requires senders of commercial e-mails to label those messages as commercial and give recipients a means to opt out of future mailings from those senders. The Act also authorizes the Federal Trade Commission (FTC) and state authorities to bring enforcement proceedings against violators.

The CAN-SPAM Act is a complex set of prohibitions and definitions that leave businesses with a number of ambiguities and possible pitfalls to confront. This chapter sets out the Act's principal provisions and the FTC rulemaking proceedings that have attempted to clarify some—but not all—of the Act's ambiguities.

12.1.1 The Act Applies Primarily to "Commercial Electronic Mail Messages"

The CAN-SPAM Act applies primarily to any "commercial electronic mail message," which is defined as "any electronic mail message the *primary purpose* of which is the commercial advertisement or promotion of a commercial product or service (including content on an Internet Web site operated for a commercial purpose)."[2] (In the discussion that follows, we sometimes refer to commercial electronic mail messages as "CEMMs.")

As we discuss further below, this definition covers the most common forms of today's spam e-mail, which have no purpose but to solicit the purchase of commercial products and services. The use of the undefined terms "advertisement" and "promotion," however, and above all the undefined expression "primary purpose," have caused considerable confusion. If my law firm sends a newsletter to clients about recent legal developments, is the primary purpose of the mailing to inform clients or to promote the firm's services? If a car dealer sends a notice of a safety recall that includes a pitch for its new car models, is the e-mail a "transactional or relationship message" (as defined in the next section of this chapter), or is the primary purpose of the message commercial?

In January 2005, the FTC brought some clarity to the meaning of "primary purpose" as used in the CAN-SPAM Act.[3] Specifically, the Commission considered three categories of message: (1) those that contain only commercial content; (2) those that contain a combination of commercial content and "transactional or relationship" content, as described in the next section; and (3) those that contain both commercial content and noncommercial content that does not meet the definition of a "transactional or relationship" message.

As to messages in the first category, the Commission found that the primary purpose of those messages always would be deemed to be commercial.[4]

For messages in the second category, the FTC determined that the primary purpose of the message will be commercial if: (1) a recipient reasonably interpreting the subject line of the message would likely conclude that the message contains a commercial advertisement; or (2) the transactional or relationship content does not appear, in whole or in substantial part, at the beginning of the body of the message.[5]

As to the third category of message, the FTC found that the primary purpose of such a message is commercial if: (1) a recipient reasonably interpreting the subject line would likely conclude that the message contains an advertisement; or (2) a recipient reasonably interpreting the body of the message would likely conclude that the message contains an advertisement. *Id.* § 316.3(a)(3). In determining how the body of a message would reasonably be interpreted, the FTC will consider a number of factors, including the placement of commercial content at the beginning of the message, the proportion of the message that is dedicated to commercial content, and "how color, graphics, type size, and style are used to highlight commercial content."[6]

12.1.2 Transactional or Relationship Messages

One of the Act's surprising features is its failure to create a broad exemption for e-mails sent to recipients with whom the sender has a preexisting or current business relationship. Such an exemption, which was common in state antispam laws and is a feature of federal telemarketing law, permits businesses to contact their past and present customers without observing all of the restrictions that apply to e-mails sent to strangers.

Instead of creating a preexisting or current business relationship exemption, the CAN-SPAM Act recognizes only a narrow category of "transactional or relationship messages," which include:

> an electronic mail message the primary purpose of which is—
>
> to facilitate, complete, or confirm a commercial transaction that the recipient has previously agreed to enter into with the sender;
>
> to provide warranty information, product recall information, or safety or security information with respect to a commercial product or service used or purchased by the recipient;

> to provide—
>
> > notification concerning a change in the terms or features of;
> >
> > notification of a change in the recipient's standing or status with respect to; or
> >
> > at regular periodic intervals, account balance information or other type of account statement with respect to,
> >
> > a subscription, membership, account, loan, or comparable ongoing commercial relationship involving the ongoing purchase or use by the recipient of products or services offered by the sender;
>
> to provide information directly related to an employment relationship or related benefit plan in which the recipient is currently involved, participating, or enrolled; or
>
> to deliver goods or services, including product updates or upgrades, that the recipient is entitled to receive under the terms of a transaction that the recipient has previously agreed to enter into with the sender.

The Act authorizes the FTC to modify this definition of "transactional or relationship message" as needed to accommodate changes in technology and e-mail practices and to accomplish the purpose of the Act.[7] The FTC has so far declined to modify the statutory definition.

12.1.3 Opt-Out Requirements

All recipients of commercial electronic mail messages must be given an effective opportunity to refuse the receipt of future CEMMs from the senders of those e-mails. In order to ensure this "opt-out" right, the Act makes it unlawful to "initiate the transmission to a protected computer of any [CEMM] that does not contain a functioning return electronic mail address or other Internet-based mechanism, clearly and conspicuously displayed," that a recipient may use to request "not to receive future [CEMMs] from that sender at the electronic mail address where the message was received . . ."[8] The opt-out opportunity must be effective, as to each CEMM transmitted, for at least 30 days after transmission of the original message.[9]

An alert reader will have noticed that these opt-out requirements involve three players: the recipient, who must be given the right to opt-out; the person who "initiates" the CEMM, who must provide the opt-out mechanism that the recipient will use; and the "sender," from whom the recipient requests not to receive further CEMMs. An understanding of the opt-out provisions (and many other elements of the Act) requires familiarity with these terms.

First, to "initiate" a CEMM is to "originate or transmit such message or to procure the origination or transmission of such message, but [it does] not include actions that constitute routine conveyance of such message."[10] To "procure" initiation of a CEMM, in turn, is "intentionally to pay or provide other consideration to, or induce, another person to initiate such a message on one's behalf."[11] Under this definition, when a company with a product or service to promote hires a vendor to run an e-mail marketing campaign, both that company and its vendor are initiators.

A "sender," on the other hand, is a specific kind of initiator. A sender is "a person who initiates [a CEMM] and whose product, service, or Internet Web site is advertised or promoted by the message."[12] Accordingly, although both an e-mail advertising vendor and the company whose product is advertised initiate a CEMM, only the company whose product is advertised is a sender of that CEMM.[13]

Finally, the Act defines the "recipient" of a CEMM as "an authorized user of the electronic mail address to which the message was sent or delivered."[14]

Putting all of these players together, the opt-out scheme of the Act appears to make both e-mail advertising vendors and their clients responsible for ensuring that an effective opt-out mechanism is implemented. The opt-out mechanism mandated by the Act, however, must permit recipients to refuse future CEMMs from the sender—that is, the person whose product or service is advertised—rather than from any nonsender initiator.

The opt-out requirements of the Act include a number of additional refinements. For example, the Act allows the recipient to be provided with a list or menu that allows the recipient to choose which types of CEMMs it does not wish to receive from the sender, as long as this menu also includes an option to opt out from receiving *all* CEMMs from the sender.[15] If the recipient only opts out from receiving certain types of CEMMs, the sender is only prohibited from sending that recipient CEMMs that fall within the scope of the opt-out request.[16]

A sender's receipt of an opt-out request also starts the clock running on a 10-business-day window within which CEMMs may continue to be sent to that recipient. After 10 business days, however, the sender may not initiate the transmission to the recipient of any CEMM that falls within the scope of the opt-out request.[17]

The duty to honor opt-out requests also extends to persons that may act on behalf of the sender. Specifically, no one acting on behalf of a sender may initiate the transmission of a CEMM to an opted-out recipient, if, more than 10 days after the receipt of the opt-out request, the person acting on behalf of the sender has actual or constructive knowledge that the message falls within the scope of the opt-out request.[18] It also is unlawful for anyone acting on behalf of the sender to provide or select an e-mail address to which a CEMM will be sent, if the person providing or selecting the address has actual or constructive knowledge that a resulting message would violate the opt-out provisions of the Act.[19]

Finally, the Act prohibits any sender, or any other person who is aware of an opt-out request, from selling, leasing, exchanging, or otherwise transferring the e-mail address of the recipient.[20] The only exceptions to this restriction are cases in which the recipient has given express consent to such a transfer of his or her e-mail address, and cases in which the transfer is made for purposes of legal compliance.[21]

Opt-out requests also may be withdrawn by "affirmative consent" of the recipient, when that affirmative consent is given subsequent to the opt-out request.[22]

12.1.4 Labeling Requirements

The Act requires senders of CEMMs to label those messages, by providing in each message a "clear and conspicuous identification that the message is an advertisement or solicitation."[23] Initiators of CEMMs also must provide clear and conspicuous notice of the recipient's opportunity to opt out of further CEMMs from the sender, and must include a "valid physical postal address of the sender."[24]

If the recipient has given "prior affirmative consent" to the receipt of a message, then the message need not bear the "clear and conspicuous identification that the message is an advertisement or solicitation." Even when affirmative consent was given, however, the message still must include notice of the opt-out opportunity and a valid postal address of the sender.[25]

Finally, the Act requires a special subject heading, specified by the FTC, for any CEMM that includes sexually oriented material.[26] The FTC has adopted implementing requirements and has brought enforcement actions against e-mail pornographers that have failed to comply.

12.1.5 Aggravated Violations

Certain kinds of conduct, in relation to the initiation of CEMMs, are defined as aggravated violations that will incur heightened penalties. Specifically, penalties may be increased for violations of the Act that are accompanied by any of the following:

- Initiating or assisting in the initiation of a CEMM with actual or constructive knowledge that the recipient's e-mail address was obtained by an automated process from an online site with a posted policy of not giving out addresses for purposes of third-party e-mailings;[27]
- Initiating or assisting in the initiation of a CEMM with actual or constructive knowledge that the recipient's e-mail address was obtained by the use of a program for random generation of e-mail addresses;[28]
- Use of scripts or other automated means to register for multiple e-mail accounts or online user accounts from which to transmit an unlawful CEMM;[29]
- Relaying or retransmitting an unlawful CEMM from a protected computer or computer network that was accessed without authorization.[30]

12.1.6 Fraudulent or Misleading Practices

A number of provisions of the Act are intended to control the use of e-mail to mislead recipients. Some of these antifraud and antideception provisions apply only to transmissions of multiple commercial electronic mail messages, other provisions apply even to the transmission of a single CEMM, and still other provisions apply even to transactional or relationship messages. Some of these antifraud provisions are defined by amendment to the U.S. Criminal Code and carry criminal penalties.

12.1.7 Antifraud Provisions Applicable to Multiple CEMMs

The antifraud provisions affecting multiple e-mails, which carry significant penalties, address methods by which large-scale spammers obscure the origin of their messages. These "multiple CEMM" antifraud provisions consist of amendments to the chapter of the U.S. Criminal Code that prohibits various forms of criminal fraud.[31]

Two of the prohibited methods involve the routing or originating of spam messages through computers, other than the originating computer, by hacking or other means. Specifically, it is unlawful knowingly to access a protected computer without authorization and intentionally initiate the transmission of multiple CEMMS from or through that computer, or knowingly to access a protected computer to relay or transmit multiple CEMMs with the intent to deceive recipients or any Internet access service as to the origin of such message.[32]

Another prohibited method is the material falsification of header information in multiple CEMMs and the intentional initiation of the transmission of such messages.[33]

Finally, these multiple CEMM antifraud provisions of the Act prohibit the use of e-mail accounts and domain names that have been obtained through the use of falsified registration information. Specifically, it is unlawful to register under a false identity for five or more e-mail accounts or online user accounts or two or more domain names, and intentionally initiate multiple CEMMs from any combination of such accounts or domain names; or to falsely claim to be the registrant or legitimate successor in interest to the registrant of five or more Internet protocol addresses, and intentionally initiate the transfer of multiple CEMMs from such addresses.[34]

The Act also contains specific penalty provisions for violation of the multiple-CEMM antifraud prohibitions. A fine and imprisonment for up to five years, or both, may be imposed if the offense is committed in furtherance of a state or federal felony, or if the defendant has previously been convicted of one of the multiple-CEMM fraud offenses, the federal Computer Fraud and Abuse Act, or the law of any state for similar conduct. A fine and imprisonment of up to 3 years, or both, are prescribed if the offense involves access to a protected computer without authorization; the offense involves 20 or more falsified e-mail or online user account registrations, or 10 or more falsified domain name registrations; the volume of messages involved exceeded 2,500 during any 24-hour period, 25,000 during any 30-day period, or 250,000 during any 1-year period; the offense caused loss to one or more persons aggregating $5,000 or more in value during any one-year period; the offense resulted in the person committing the offense obtaining anything of value aggregating $5,000 or more during any 1-year period; or the offense was undertaken by the defendant in concert with three or more other persons with respect to whom the defendant occupied a position of organizer or leader.[35] In all other cases, a fine or imprisonment of not more than 1 year, or both, may be imposed.[36]

Violations of the multiple-CEMM antifraud provisions may result in forfeiture of property used in committing, or acquired from the proceeds of, the offense.[37]

12.1.8 Antifraud Provisions Applicable to All CEMMs

As noted earlier, some antifraud provisions of the Act apply even to a single transmission of a commercial electronic mail message. Notably, it is unlawful for any person to initiate the transmission, to a protected computer, of a CEMM if the initiator has actual or constructive knowledge that a subject heading of the message likely would mislead a reasonable recipient as to the contents or subject matter of the message.[38]

12.1.9 Antifraud Provisions Applicable to CEMMs and Transactional or Relationship Messages

Some antifraud provisions apply, not only to all CEMMs, but also to transactional and relationship messages. Specifically, such a message may not be sent to a protected computer if the message contains, or is accompanied by, "header information that is materially false or materially misleading."[39] The Act defines the expression "materially false or materially misleading" to include header information that is "technically accurate" but includes an originating e-mail address, domain name, or Internet protocol address that was obtained by false or fraudulent pretenses.[40] The expression also includes messages that fail to identify a protected computer used to initiate the message because the initiator knowingly used another protected computer to relay or retransmit the message for purposes of disguising its origin.[41]

12.1.10 How the Act Is Enforced

The CAN-SPAM Act's prohibitions are enforced by a combination of FTC proceedings, criminal prosecutions, state attorney general actions, and private suits brought by Internet service providers.

The FTC has the leading role. The Act specifically provides that violations of the Act may be enforced as unfair or deceptive acts or practices under the Federal Trade Commission Act.[42] Pursuant to its enforcement authority, the FTC investigates violations, enters into consent decrees, imposes monetary penalties, and refers violations to the Department of Justice for criminal prosecution.

The states may bring actions against entities believed to have violated the provisions of the Act regarding false or misleading transmission information or deceptive subject headings, or that have engaged in a pattern or practice that violates the opt-out provisions of the Act.[43] A state may bring its action in a U.S. district court and may demand injunctive relief, an award of damages equal to the actual monetary loss suffered, or statutory damages as set out in the Act. (Statutory damages may be increased by a factor of three if the court finds that the violation was committed willfully and knowingly, or involved one or more of the aggravating violations.)

Also, before bringing an action to enforce the Act, a state must serve prior written notice on the FTC or other appropriate federal agency.[44] The FTC or other federal agency may intervene in the case, remove the action to the appropriate United States district court and file petitions for appeal. Also, states may not bring enforcement actions under the Act while a federal civil or administrative enforcement action is pending.[45]

Finally, a provider of Internet access service may bring a private action if it has been adversely affected by a use of false or misleading transmission information, by one of the defined aggravating violations or by failure to comply with the requirements concerning sexually oriented material.[46] An Internet access provider also may bring an action when it has been adversely affected by a pattern or practice that violates the opt-out provisions of the Act. If an Internet access provider is successful, the plaintiff may recover the greater of its actual monetary loss or statutory damages. The plaintiff may recover up to three times the amount otherwise available if the defendant's conduct was willful or knowing or involved aggregated conduct, and reasonable costs and attorneys' fees may be awarded.

12.1.11 State Antispam Laws Are Partially Preempted

A driving force behind the passage of the Act was concern about more restrictive state antispam laws, particularly the stringent antispam legislation that would have taken effect in California on January 1, 2004. Thus, an integral provision of the Act is its preemption of any state law that "expressly regulates the use of electronic mail to send commercial messages, except to the extent that any such statute, regulation or rule prohibits falsity or deception in any portion of a commercial electronic mail message or information attached thereto."[47] However, the Act does not preempt state laws that are not specific to electronic mail, including common law causes of action and laws that "relate to acts of fraud or computer crime."[48]

12.1.12 FTC Rulemaking Proceedings

Since the CAN-SPAM Act was enacted, the FTC has undertaken rulemaking proceedings that are intended to clarify some the statute's requirements. Notably, the Commission has prescribed the label that must be provided with e-mails containing adult content, and has set out some guidelines (described in Section 12.1.1) for determining the "primary purpose" of an e-mail message. The FTC also has reported to Congress on the advisability of adopting a national "Do-Not-E-mail" list, recommending that such a list not be adopted. The Commission has declined, however, to take some of the discretionary actions permitted by the statute, including expansion of the category of "transactional or relationship message."

In a Notice of Proposed Rulemaking dated May 12, 2005, the FTC proposed additional rules, including shortening of the time during which opt-out requests must be honored from 10 days to 3 days.[49] The Commission also proposes some guidelines for determining which initiator of an e-mail is a "sender" for purposes of the CAN-SPAM Act, and for determining when obligations under the Act attach to so-called "forward to a friend" scenarios. At the time of this writing, those proposed rules have not been officially adopted.

12.2 State Antispam Laws

When the CAN-SPAM Act of 2003 was enacted, most states already had passed laws that regulated some aspect of e-mail advertising. Most provisions of those state statutes now are preempted by the CAN-SPAM Act, but state prohibitions against fraudulent e-mail advertising, including false routing information and misleading subject lines, still may be enforced.

Perhaps the most ambitious state antispam laws are the child registry statutes enacted by the legislatures of Utah and Michigan.[50] Both states have created lists of online "contact points" or Internet domains to which messages may not be sent if they advertise products, such as tobacco, pornography, alcohol, lotteries, firearms, and illegal drugs, that minors may not lawfully purchase. The Utah statute also prohibits the sending of messages that advertise materials "harmful to minors" to any contact point on the registry.

The registries are populated by submissions from individuals. E-mail advertisers that promote products and materials prohibited by the Utah and Michigan statutes must "scrub" their electronic mailing lists against the registries every 30 days.

Notes

[1]Controlling the Assault of Non-Solicited Pornography and Marketing Act of 2003, Pub. L. No. 108-187, 117 Stat. 2699 (2003), codified at 15 U.S.C. §§ 7701-13; 18 U.S.C. §§ 1001, 1037; 28 U.S.C. § 994; and 47 U.S.C. § 227 (CAN-SPAM Act, or Act).

[2]CAN-SPAM Act § 3(2)(A) (emphasis added).

[3]70 FR 3110 (Jan. 19, 2005).

[4]16 C.F.R. § 316.3(a)(1).

[5]*Id.* § 316.3(a)(2).

[6]*Id.*

[7]*Id.* § 3(17)(B).

[8]*Id.* § 5(a)(3). "Protected computer," a term borrowed from the federal Computer Fraud and Abuse Act, is defined in that statute so as to include any computer connected to the public Internet.

[9]*Id.* § 5(a)(3)(A)(ii).

[10]*Id.* § 3(9). The "routine conveyance" language is an exemption for e-mail providers, Internet service providers, and other entities that process the automatic transmission and routing of CEMMs to addresses provided by an initiator or other party. *See Id.* § 3(19).

[11]*Id.* § 3(12).

[12]*Id.* § 3(16).

[13]Companies that advertise on behalf of "separate lines of business or divisions" must keep track of which line of business sent a particular CEMM. Under the Act, if a company "operates through separate lines of business or divisions and holds itself out to the recipient throughout the message as that particular line of business or division rather than as the entity of which such line of business or division is a part, then the line of business or the division shall be treated as the sender of such message for purposes of this Act." *Id.* § 3(16)(B). Among other things, this provision appears to mean that a recipient's opt-out applies only to future messages from the line of business or division that sent the original CEMM. However, this provision also appears to mean that a recipient's prior affirmative consent to receive CEMMs from a sender, which permits the sender to send subsequent CEMMs without labeling them as advertisements or solicitations, may apply only to messages from the line of business or division that held itself out to the recipient as the sender of the original CEMM.

[14]*Id.* § 3(14).

[15]*Id.* § 5(3)(B).

[16]*Id.* § 5(4). Note that compliance with this requirement falls *primarily* on the sender, and not on any other initiator or participant in the CEMM process.

[17]*Id.* § 5(a)(4)(A).

[18]*Id.* § 5(a)(4)(A)(ii).

[19]*Id.* § 5(a)(4)(A)(iii).

[20]*Id.* § 5(a)(4)(A)(iv).

[21]*Id.*

[22] *Id.* § 5(a)(4)(B).

[23] *Id.* § 5(a)(5)(A).

[24] *Id.*

[25] *Id.* § 5(a)(5)(B).

[26] *Id.* § 5(d).

[27] *Id.* § 5(b).

[28] *Id.* The term "constructive knowledge" is used here, and elsewhere in this chapter, as shorthand for the statutory phrase "knowledge fairly implied on the basis of objective circumstances." *Id.*

[29] *Id.*

[30] *Id.*

[31] *Id.* § 4. These provisions are codified as a new section 1037 of Chapter 47 of Title 18, U.S. Code.

[32] To be codified at 18 U.S.C. sec. 1037 (a)(1)–(2).

[33] *Id.* § 1037(a)(3).

[34] *Id.* § 1037(a)(4)–(5).

[35] *Id.* § 1037(b)–(c).

[36] *Id.* § 1037(b)(3).

[37] *Id.* § 1037(c). The Act also directs the U.S. Sentencing Commission to review its guidelines and consider sentencing enhancements for persons convicted of multiple-CEMM antifraud violations who obtained e-mail addresses from Web sites or other online locations without consent of the persons holding those addresses, or who randomly generated e-mail addresses. Sentencing enhancements also are to be considered for persons who commit multiple-CEMM antifraud violations in connection with fraud, identity theft, obscenity, child pornography, sexual exploitation of children, and other offenses. The Act also urges the Department of Justice to "use all existing law enforcement tools to investigate and prosecute those who send bulk commercial e-mail to facilitate the commission of Federal crimes . . ." CAN-SPAM Act § 4.

[38] *Id.* § 5(a)(2).

[39] *Id.* § 5(a)(1).

[40] *Id.* § 5(a)(1)(A).

[41] *Id.* § 5(a)(1)(C).

[42] *Id.* § 7(a). Other, industry-specific agencies also may bring actions under the Act. Those agencies include the Office of the Comptroller of the Currency, the Securities and Exchange Commission, and the insurance regulators of the various states. *Id.* § 7(b).

[43] *Id.* § 7(f).

[44] *Id.* § 7(f)(5).

[45] *Id.* § 7(f)(8).

[46] *Id.* § 7(g).

[47] *Id.* § 8(b)(1).

[48] *Id.* § 8(b)(2).

[49] 70 FR 25426 (May 12, 2005).

[50] Utah Child Protection Registry Act, U.C.A. 1953 § 13-39-101-401 (2004), *amended by* Utah Laws ch. 336; Michigan Children's Protection Registry Act, M.C.L.A. §§ 752.1061–752.1068 (2004).

CHAPTER 13

Monitoring and Recording Customer Communications

In Chapter 9, we discussed at some length the legal challenges posed by monitoring of employee communications, including conversations with customers and other third parties. As we noted in that chapter, employees may have rights under the Electronic Communications Privacy Act (ECPA), state wiretapping/eavesdropping laws, and collective bargaining agreements if their conversations with third parties are intercepted by employers without a clear policy, disseminated to employees in advance, that permits such monitoring.

As we also pointed out in Chapter 9, under federal law and the laws of most states, conversations may be intercepted with the prior consent of one party to those conversations. Under those laws, conversations between employees and customers or consumers are covered by the employees' prior consent to monitoring.

A number of states, however, require the consent of all parties to a conversation before those conversations may lawfully be intercepted. Also, those states are likely to assert jurisdiction over conversations that either involve residents of those states, or that are recorded or otherwise intercepted in those states. Accordingly, employers that intend to monitor employee/customer conversations should either avoid monitoring conversations with persons in those two-party consent states, or should announce, at the start of the conversation, that the call may be recorded for quality control or other purposes.[1]

Note

[1]At least 13 states now prohibit interceptions without the consent of both parties. *See, e.g.*, Cal. Penal Code § 631, 632; Conn. Gen. Stat. Ann. 52-570(d); Del. Code Ann. tit. 11, § 2402; Fla. Stat. ch. 934.03; Ill. Comp. Stat. 5/14-2, 5/14-3; Md. Code Ann., Cts & Jud. Proc. 10-402; Mass Ann. Laws ch. 272, § 99; Mich. Comp. Laws § 750.539a et seq.; Mont. Code Ann. § 45-8-213; Nev. Rev. Stat. Ann. § 200.620-650; N.H. Rev. Stat. Ann. § 570-A; 18 Pa. Cons. Stat. § 5703-5704; Wash. Rev. Code § 9.73.030.

PART IV
Other U.S. Privacy Laws

Appendices A and B of this book list a large number of federal and state privacy laws, some of which are not specifically discussed in the body of the book. The inclusion of those appendices should give fair notice to readers that the variety and proliferation of privacy-related laws make expert legal counsel critically important before making any business decisions that might affect the privacy interests of employees, customers, or others.

The following should give some idea of the variety of privacy-related laws not already discussed at length in this book.

A. Educational Institutions

The Family Educational Rights and Privacy Act[1] (FEPA) applies to educational institutions that receive funding from the federal government. The FEPA prohibits those institutions from disclosing student records except in response to a subpoena, or to the student, the student's parents, school officials who have a legitimate need for information contained in the files, organizations engaged in research, or public officials with responsibility for education. The FEPA does not create a private right of action for persons aggrieved by violations of the statute; the only penalty for noncompliance is withdrawal of federal funds from the offending institution.[2]

B. Video Rental Stores

A federal statute gives customers a civil cause of action against any video tape service provider (i.e., video rental store) that knowingly discloses personal information concerning the customer to any person.[3] The statute contains exceptions for disclosures to law enforcement agencies pursuant to warrant, grand jury subpoena, or court order;[4] and also permits video stores to disclose the names and addresses of customers if the customer has had a prior opportunity to prohibit such disclosure.[5]

C. Cable Television Operators

The Communications Act of 1934 includes extensive provisions limiting the collection and use by cable television operators of so-called "personally identifiable information" concerning cable television customers.[6] Notably, the Communications Act requires cable operators to notify subscribers of the nature of any personal information that will be collected by the operators, the uses to which that information may be put, and the circumstances under which that information may be disclosed to third parties.[7] The statute also provides, subject to certain exceptions, that cable operators may not use their facilities to collect personal information concerning subscribers, or disclose such information to others, without the subscribers' consent;[8] and that cable operators must make personal information available to subscribers and give subscribers an opportunity to correct inaccurate personal information maintained by the operator.[9]

D. Insurance Companies

Insurance companies are subject primarily to state, rather than federal, regulation in the United States. As part of their regulatory oversight of the insurance industry, many states have enacted statutes recognizing privacy rights in the collection and use of personal information by insurance companies. These statutes may impose data protection obligations, not only on insurance companies themselves, but also on medical care institutions, medical professionals, insurance industry information clearinghouses, consumer reporting agencies, and other entities that routinely share personal information with insurers.[10] Notably, California's Insurance Information and Privacy Protection Act controls the collection, use, and disclosure of personal information by insurance companies, agents, and insurance-support companies.[11]

Also, as we discussed in Chapter 3, the Gramm-Leach-Bliley Act (GLBA) provides that insurers are subject to state regulations implementing the GLBA privacy provisions. All insurers authorized to do business in the various states are subject to such GLBA privacy regulations.[12]

E. Doctors, Lawyers, and Other Professionals

The courts recognize that persons may not be compelled to disclose the substance of their dealings with their attorneys, physicians, clergy, and (in some states) their accountants.[13] These testimonial privileges are reinforced by professional codes of conduct and, in some states, by common law and statutory requirements.[14]

F. Automobile Manufacturers and Rental Car Companies

Some states restrict privacy practices of auto manufacturers and car rental companies. For example, California requires auto manufacturers to disclose, in the owner's manual, the fact that a car is equipped with an event recorder, and must observe restrictions on the use of those devices and the data they retrieve and record.[15] Also, California limits the ability of car rental companies lawfully to obtain, access, or use information about the renter's use of a vehicle by means of onboard surveillance technology, and prohibits such companies from disclosing information about the renter's use of the vehicle without the renter's consent.[16]

G. Merchants That Issue "Club Cards"

Some supermarkets and other retailers offer cards that make shoppers eligible for lower prices in exchange for permitting the store to track and record the shoppers' purchases. California has imposed some restrictions on these practices. Specifically, under the Supermarket Club Card Act, issuers of these cards may not collect shoppers' driver's license information or Social Security numbers or, subject to some exceptions, disclose personal information to third parties.[17]

H. Users and Providers of Computer "Spyware"

As online marketing and data collection techniques have grown more sophisticated, consumers have become increasingly aware of Internet-borne programs that monitor their browsing habits, alter the appearance of their desktops, plague them with pop-up ads, and cause their computers to slow down or even crash.

These programs, which range from the harmless to the annoying to the truly malicious, have been the target of bills introduced in the Congress. So far, no federal antiadware or antispyware bills have become law. California and at least 15 other states, however, have enacted legislation intended to control spyware.[18]

Because of California's particular economic importance, that state's spyware law is worth examining in detail (we'll refer to it simply as the Spyware Act). The law is aimed at a number of activities, all of which are unlawful only if engaged in knowingly, with conscious avoidance of knowledge, or willfully. Those activities include causing, without authorization, software to be copied onto the computer of a consumer in California and using the software to do any of the following:

(a) Modify, through intentionally deceptive means, any of the following settings related to the computer's access to, or use of, the Internet:
  (1) The page that appears when an authorized user launches an Internet browser or similar software program used to access and navigate the Internet;
  (2) The default provider or Web proxy the authorized user uses to access or search the Internet;
  (3) The authorized user's list of bookmarks used to access Web pages.

(b) Collect, through intentionally deceptive means, personally identifiable information that meets any of the following criteria:
  (1) It is collected through the use of a keystroke-logging function that records all keystrokes made by an authorized user who uses the computer and transfers that information from the computer to another person;

   (2) It includes all or substantially all of the Web sites visited by an authorized user, other than Web sites of the provider of the software, if the computer software was installed in a manner designed to conceal from all authorized users of the computer the fact that the software is being installed;
   (3) It is a data element . . . that is extracted from the consumer's computer hard drive for a purpose wholly unrelated to any of the purposes of the software or service described to an authorized user.

(c) Prevent, without the authorization of an authorized user, through intentionally deceptive means, an authorized user's reasonable efforts to block the installation of, or to disable, software, by causing software that the authorized user has properly removed or disabled to automatically reinstall or reactivate on the computer without the authorization of an authorized user.

(d) Intentionally misrepresent that software will be uninstalled or disabled by an authorized user's action, with knowledge that the software will not be so uninstalled or disabled.

(e) Through intentionally deceptive means, remove, disable, or render inoperative security, antispyware, or antivirus software installed on the computer.

It also is unlawful, under the Spyware Act, to download software to a California consumer's computer and use that software (again, knowingly or willfully) to do any of the following:

(a) Take control of the consumer's computer by doing any of the following:
   (1) Transmitting or relaying commercial electronic mail or a computer virus from the consumer's computer, where the transmission or relaying is initiated by a person other than the authorized user and without the authorization of an authorized user;
   (2) Accessing or using the consumer's modem or Internet service for the purpose of causing damage to the consumer's computer or of causing an authorized user to incur financial charges for a service that is not authorized by an authorized user;
   (3) Using the consumer's computer as part of an activity performed by a group of computers for the purpose of causing damage to another computer, including, but not limited to, launching a denial of service attack;
   (4) Opening multiple, sequential, stand-alone advertisements in the consumer's Internet browser without the authorization of an authorized user and with knowledge that a reasonable computer user cannot close the advertisements without turning off the computer or closing the consumer's Internet browser.

(b) Modify any of the following settings related to the computer's access to, or use of, the Internet:
   (1) An authorized user's security or other settings that protect information about the authorized user for the purpose of stealing personal information of an authorized user;

(2) The security settings of the computer for the purpose of causing damage to one or more computers.

(c) Prevent, without the authorization of an authorized user, an authorized user's reasonable efforts to block the installation of, or to disable, software, by doing any of the following:

(1) Presenting the authorized user with an option to decline installation of software with knowledge that, when the option is selected by the authorized user, the installation nevertheless proceeds;

(2) Falsely representing that software has been disabled.

The Spyware Act imposes other restrictions, including prohibitions against inducing California consumers to download software by falsely representing that the software is necessary for security reasons, for privacy reasons, or to open, view, or play a particular type of content.

The Spyware Act's prohibitions are subject to some exceptions. Notably, it does not forbid a hardware, communications service, or software provider from monitoring or interacting with a computer for the purpose of diagnostics, technical support, or other lawful activities.

More antispyware legislation is likely to be enacted and some of that legislation may be at the federal level. Among other challenges, the drafters of such legislation must avoid sweeping benign or helpful activities, such as automatic transmission of "cookies" to facilitate interaction with a Web site, into the same unlawful category as malicious and harmful code.

Once again, these illustrative statutes are intended to convey the scope of the privacy law compliance task, and to encourage U.S. businesses to address that problem in a systematic way, with the guidance of expert counsel.

Notes

[1]20 U.S.C. § 1232(g).

[2]At least one court, however, has found an implied private right of action under FEPA. *Faye v. South Colonie Central School District*, 802 F.2d 21 (2d Cir. 1986).

[3]18 U.S.C. § 2710.

[4]*Id.* § 2710(b)(20(C).

[5]*Id.* § 2710(b)(2)(D).

[6]47 U.S.C. § 551.

[7]*Id.* § 551(a)(1)–(2).

[8]*Id.* § 551(b)–(c).

[9]*Id.* § 551(d). Cable operators also must destroy personally identifiable information that no longer is needed for the purpose for which it was collected. *Id.* § 551(e).

[10]*See* Conn. Gen. Stat. Ann. § 38A-976 (West 1987); Mass. Gen. Laws Ann. ch. 751 (West Supp. 1994).

[11]Cal. Ins. Code §§ 791–791.27.

[12]*See, e.g.*, 10 CCR 2689.1 (2005); Colo. Ins. Reg. 6-4-1 § 3; Florida Admin. Code 69J-128.001; 50 Ill. Admin. Code 400150; N.J. Admin. Code 11:1-44.1; 31 Pa. Code § 146a.1 (2005).

[13]The accountant-client privilege did not exist at common law. Although more than 20 states recognize the privilege by statute, several of those statutes limit the privilege by permitting disclosure of accountant-client communications in response to a summons or subpoena. More importantly, the U.S. Internal Revenue Service does not recognize the accountant-client privilege. Denzil Causey and Frances McNair, *An Analysis of State Accountant-Client Privilege Statutes*, 27 AM. BUS. L.J. 535, 538 (1990).

[14]*See, e.g.*, *Behringer v. Medical Center at Princeton*, 592 A.2d 1251 (N.J. Super Ct. Law Div. 1991).

[15]Cal. Veh. Code § 9951.

[16]Cal. Civ. Code § 1936.

[17]*Id.* § 1749.60.

[18]Cal. Bus. and Prof. Code §§ 22947–22947.6.

APPENDIX A

Selected Federal and State Privacy Statutes and Regulations

Federal Statutes And Regulations

- **Privacy Act of 1974, 5 U.S.C. § 552a.** Limits collection, use, and disclosure of personal data by agencies of federal government. Includes restrictions on use of "computer matches" to suspend, reduce, or deny payments to an individual.
- **Federal Information Security Management Act of 2002, Pub.L. No. 107-347, 116 Stat. 2899.** Authorizes the adoption of minimum data security and integrity standards for federal agencies; establishes a Chief Information Officer with the Office of Management and Budget.
- **Restrictions on Disclosure of Information in Possession of Social Security Administration or Department of Health and Human Services, 42 U.S.C. § 1306.** With exceptions, prohibits the disclosure of tax returns, files, records, reports, papers, or other information obtained by the Social Security Administration and the Department of Health and Human Services. Violations may be punished by fines and imprisonment.
- **Confidentiality Rights of Participants in Research Projects of Public Health Service, 42 U.S.C. § 241(d).** Secretary of Health and Human Services is authorized to empower persons engaged in biomedical, behavioral, clinical, or other research to protect the privacy of individuals who are the subject of such research. Where so authorized, those persons may not be compelled to identify those individuals in criminal, administrative, legislative, or other proceedings.
- **Privacy Protection Provisions Applicable to Federally Funded Alcohol and Drug Treatment Programs, 42 U.S.C. § 290dd-2.** With some exceptions, records of the identity, diagnosis, prognosis, or treatment of any patient maintained in connection with the performance of any program related to substance abuse education, prevention, training, treatment, rehabilitation, or research which is conducted, regulated, or directly or indirectly assisted by any department or agency of the United States must be kept confidential.
- **Confidentiality Protections for Records in Veterans' Medical Centers, 38 U.S.C. § 5701.** With some exceptions, all files, records and other papers and documents pertaining to any claims by veterans and their dependents are confidential and privileged and may not be disclosed.
- **Confidentiality of Letters, Post Cards and Packages, 18 U.S.C.§ 1702.** Fines and imprisonment for persons who take undelivered mail to "pry into the business or secrets of another" or for other purposes.

- **Restrictions on Use and Dissemination of Social Security Numbers, *e.g.*, 42 U.S.C. § 405(c)(2)(c)(viii), 5 U.S.C. § 552a (note), 31 U.S.C. § 3327.** Authorized persons who obtain Social Security Account Numbers shall not disclose them; Privacy Act restrictions on disclosure of records held by federal agencies; Secretary of the Treasury to ensure that Social Security Account Numbers are not visible through envelopes used to mail government checks.
- **Confidentiality of Federal Tax Returns, 26 U.S.C. § 6103.** Except as specifically authorized, tax returns and information therein are confidential.
- **Requirement that Federal Agencies Conduct a "Privacy Impact Assessment" before Acquiring Certain Technologies or Taking Certain Actions, 44 U.S.C. §§ 3501, 3601.** These requirements are part of a broad statutory effort to improve federal government information practices.
- **Computer Fraud and Abuse Act, 18 U.S.C. § 1030.** Prohibits various harmful intrusions into computer systems.
- **Electronic Communications Privacy Act, 18 U.S.C. § 2510 *et seq*.** The federal wiretap statute. Governs both private and governmental interceptions of wire, oral, and electronic communications.
- **Stored Communications Act, 18 U.S.C. § 2701 *et seq*.** Limits the rights of both public and private entities to acquire the contents of stored communications and information concerning subscribers to electronic communication services and remote computing services.
- **Drivers Privacy Protection Act, 18 U.S.C. §§ 2721–2725.** Limits the ability of state Motor Vehicles authorities to sell or otherwise disclose vehicle registration and other data.
- **Privacy Protections Applicable to Federally Funded Alcohol and Drug Treatment Programs, 42 U.S.C. § 290dd-2.** With some exceptions, records of the identity, diagnosis, prognosis, or treatment of any patient maintained in connection with the performance of any program related to substance abuse education, prevention, training, treatment, rehabilitation, or research which is conducted, regulated, or directly or indirectly assisted by any department or agency of the United States must be kept confidential.
- **Privacy Restrictions on States that Records for HIV Testing, Counseling and Treatment, 42 U.S.C. § 300ff-61.** Federal grants for HIV early intervention services must be conditioned on grant recipients' agreement to ensure individual privacy.
- **Prohibition Against Denial of Government Benefits for Failure to Provide a Social Security Number, 5 U.S.C. § 552a (note), 42 U.S.C. § 405(a)(c)(2)(c)(i) (exempting certain state agencies).** Under the Privacy Act of 1974, it is unlawful for any federal, state, or local government agency to deny to any individual any right, benefit, or privilege because of such person's refusal to disclose his Social Security Account Number. Exceptions are provided for states or political subdivisions thereof in the administration of tax, general public assistance, driver's license, or motor vehicle registration laws.
- **Fair and Accurate Credit Transactions Act of 2003, P.L. No. 108-159, 117 Stat. 1952 (2003), amending 15 U.S.C. § 1681; 20 U.S.C. §§ 9701–9708; 30 U.S.C. § 5318.** The Fair and Accurate Credit Transactions Act (FACTA)

amends the Fair Credit Reporting Act (FCRA) for the purpose of strengthening the FCRA's privacy and consumer protection provisions and discouraging identity theft. Among other requirements, FACTA authorizes responsible agencies to enact regulations that require entities maintaining information derived from credit reports to dispose of such information properly.

- **FACTA Disposal Rule, 16 C.F.R. § 682.3.** The Federal Trade Commission (FTC) is one of several agencies that have enacted regulations implementing the records disposal requirements of the Fair and Accurate Credit Transactions Act. Organizations that fail to dispose of records properly, and fail to select records disposal vendors with care, may be charged with unfair or deceptive practices under the Federal Trade Commission Act.
- **Federal Trade Commission Act, 15 U.S.C. § 45(a).** Prohibits unfair or deceptive acts or practice. The Federal Trade Commission uses this statute to bring enforcement actions against companies and organizations that fail to secure customer information against unauthorized acquisition or loss.
- **Employee Polygraph Protection Act, 29 U.S.C. § 2001, *et seq*.** Limits the ability of most employers to administer polygraph tests on employees and applicants for employment.
- **Telephone Consumer Protection Act, 47 U.S.C. § 227.** Federal statute regulating telemarketing and facsimile advertising practices.
- **Federal Communications Commission regulations implementing provisions of the Telephone Consumer Protection Act, 47 C.F.R. § 64.1200.** Regulations that restrict telemarketing and facsimile advertising practices, including use of autodialers and artificial or prerecorded voices, calls made to mobile telephones and residential numbers on the national do-not-call registry, and other practices.
- **Federal Trade Commission Telemarketing Sales Rule, 16 C.F.R. § 312.** For entities subject to Federal Trade Commission jurisdiction, sets conditions for lawful telemarketing, including compliance with the national do-not-call registry.
- **CAN-SPAM Act of 2003, P.L. No. 108-107, 117 Stat. 2699 (2003), codified at 15 U.S.C. § 7701-13; 18 U.S.C. §§ 1001, 1037; 28 U.S.C. § 994; 47 U.S.C. § 227.** Federal statute regulating the initiation of commercial electronic mail messages (spam) and related practices.
- **Payment Card Industry Data Security Standard, see https://www/pcisecuritystandards.org/index.html.** Failure to abide by the data security requirements of this standard can result in monetary penalties and loss of ability to honor credit cards or process credit card data.

State Statutes and Regulations

Alabama

- Right of Access to Criminal Records, Code of Ala. § 41-9-643.
- Confidentiality of Criminal Records, Code of Ala. 41-9-636.

- Alabama Computer Crime Act, Code of Ala. § 13A-8-01.
- Alabama Eavesdropping Law, Code of Ala. § 13A-11-30.
- Confidentiality of Library Records, Code of Ala. § 41-8-10.
- Telemarketing Statute, § 8-19C-2 of Ala. Code.
- Privacy and Security of Nonpublic Personal Information Collected and Maintained by Insurers (Implementing Requirements of Gramm-Leach-Bliley Act), 17 Ala. Code §§ 27-7-44 *et seq.*
- Genetic Testing, Discrimination and Other Privacy Restrictions, Ala. Code § 27-53-2.
- Privacy of Customer Bank Records, Ala. Code § 5-5A-43.

Alaska

- Privacy Right in State Constitution, Art. 1, § 22.
- Sealing of Arrest and Conviction Records, Alaska Stat. § 12.62.180.
- Privacy of Criminal Justice Information Systems, Alaska Stat. §§ 12.62.010, 12.63.030(a).
- Fair Information Practices of State Agencies, Alaska Stat. § 44.99.300.
- Confidentiality of Library Records, Alaska Stat. § 09.25.140.
- Employee Access to Employee Records, Alaska Stat. § 23.10.430.
- Wiretapping/Eavesdropping/Electronic Surveillance, Alaska Stat. § 42.20.310.
- Privacy of Tax Records, Alaska Stat. § 9.25.100.
- Alaska Statutes Governing Theft of Stored Data and Computer Service, Alaska Stat. §§ 11.81.900(b)(48), 11.46.200(a)(3).
- Telemarketing Statute, Alaska Stat. § 45.50.475.
- Privacy and Security of Nonpublic Personal Information Collected and Maintained by Insurers (Implementing Requirements of Gramm-Leach-Bliley Act), 3 AAC §§ 26.605 *et seq.*
- Privacy of Bank Customer Records, Alaska Stat. §§ 06.30.120, 06.05.175.
- Patient Privacy Rights, Alaska R. Civ. Pro. § 43(h)(4) and 8, Alaska Stat. § 47.30.260.
- Limits on Use of Polygraph Tests, Alaska Stat. §23.10.037.

Arizona

- Privacy Right in State Constitution, Art. II, § 8.
- Right to Notation on Criminal Record in Cases of Wrongful Arrest, Indictment or Conviction, A.R.S. § 13-1761.
- Sharing of Criminal Record Information, A.R.S. § 41.750.
- Confidentiality of Library Records, A.R.S. § 41.1354.
- Use of Social Security Numbers by State Colleges and Universities, A.R.S. § 15-1823.
- Privacy of Student Records, A.R.S. § 15-151.
- Wiretapping/Eavesdropping/Electronic Surveillance, A.R.S. § 13-3004.

- Privacy of Tax Records, A.R.S. § 42.108.
- Arizona Statute Governing Computer Crimes, Ariz. Rev. Stat. §§ 13-2301E, 13-2316.
- Arizona "Must-Shred" Law, A.R.S. § 44-7601.
- Notification for Compromised Personal Information (Arizona Data Security Breach Notification Statute), 2006 Ariz. Session Laws 232.
- Telemarketing Statute, Ariz. Rev. Stat. § 45.50.475.
- Consumer Credit Reporting and/or Credit Card Information and Transactional Privacy, Ariz. Rev. Stat. § 44-1693(A)(4).
- Privacy and Security of Nonpublic Personal Information Collected and Maintained by Insurers (Implementing Requirements of Gramm-Leach-Bliley Act), 20 A.S.A. §§ 20-2104 *et seq.*
- Genetic Testing, Discrimination and Other Privacy Restrictions, Ariz. Rev. Stat. § 20-1379.
- Patient Privacy Rights, Ariz. Rev. Stat. §§ 12-2292 through 12-2294.
- Limits on Use of Polygraph Tests, Ariz. Rev. Stat. § 32-2701.
- Restrictions on Certain Tests, Ariz. Rev. Stat. § 41-1463.
- Privacy Rights of Students or Parents, Ariz. Rev. Stat. § 15-151.

Arkansas

- Arkansas Computer Crime Statute, Ark. Code Ann. § 5-41-104.
- Protection of Privacy of Criminal Records Database, Ark. Code Ann. §§ 12-12-201 to 12-12-207.
- Confidentiality of Library Records, Ark. Code Ann. § 13-2-701.
- Wiretapping/Eavesdropping/Electronic Surveillance, Ark. Code. Ann. § 5-60-120.
- Arkansas Computer Crime Statute, Ark. Code Ann. §§ 5-41-103, 5-41-104.
- Arkansas "Must Shred" and Breach Notification Statute, A.C.A. §4-110-104.
- Personal Information Protection Act (Arkansas Data Security Breach Notification Statute), A.C.A. § 4-110-103.
- Telemarketing Statute, Ark. Code Ann. §§ 29-30-178, 5-63-204, 4-99-302.
- Privacy and Security of Nonpublic Personal Information Collected and Maintained by Insurers (Implementing Requirements of Gramm-Leach-Bliley Act), A.C.A. §§ 23-61-113 *et seq.*
- Physician-Patient Privilege, A.C.A. § 47.30.260.

California

- Privacy Right in State Constitution, Art. I, § 1.
- Right to Have Criminal Records Sealed or Destroyed in Certain Cases, Cal. Pen. Code § 851.8, Cal. Health & Safety Code § 11361.5.
- Restrictions on Disclosure of Criminal History, Cal. Labor Code § 432.7.
- Privacy of Criminal Justice Records, Cal. Pen. Code §§ 11075-81.

- Fair Information Practices of State Agencies, Cal. Civ. Code § 1798.
- Department of Motor Vehicles Records, Cal. Civ. Code §§ 1798.26, Cal. Vehicle Code § 12-80.5.
- Privacy of Voters' Registration Records, Cal. Election Code § 2194.
- Confidentiality of Library Records, Cal. Gov. Code § 6254(j).
- Use of Social Security Numbers for Driver Licensing, Cal. Vehicle Code § 12801.
- Privacy of Student Records, Cal. Pen. Code § 626.11; Cal. Edu. Code §§ 49060, 76200.
- Right of Employee to Inspect Employee Records, Cal. Labor Code § 1198.5, Cal. Edu. Code §§ 24317, 92612.
- Use by Employers of Applicants' Medical Histories, Cal. Civ. Code §§ 56.05(b), 56.20(a).
- Wiretapping/Eavesdropping/Electronic Surveillance, Cal. Pen. Code §§ 631-637.
- California Statutes Concerning Computer-Related Crimes, Cal. Pen. Code §§ 5502, 2702.
- California "Must Shred" Statute, Cal. Civ. Code § 1798.80.
- Accounting of Disclosures (California Data Security Breach Notification Statute), Cal. Civ. Code § 1798.29.
- California Statute concerning Automobile "Black Box" Tracking Devices, Cal. Pen. Code § 637.7.
- Use of Concealed Cameras, Cal. Pen. Code § 647.
- Telemarketing Statute, Pub. Util. Code §§ 2873-2874, 2875.
- Privacy and Security of Nonpublic Personal Information Collected and Maintained by Insurers (Implementing Requirements of Gramm-Leach-Bliley Act), 10 Cal. Regulations §§ 2689.2 *et seq*. See also Cal. Ins. Code § 791.
- Genetic Testing, Discrimination and Other Privacy Restrictions, Cal. Ins. Code §§ 10140, 10147.
- Customer Privacy Rights and Requirements, Cal. Pen. Code § 637.5.
- Rights of Subjects of Credit Reports, Cal. Civ. Code § 1785, § 1786.
- Credit Card Customer Privacy Rights, Cal. Civ. Code § 1748.12.
- Customer Privacy Rights, Video Stores, Cal. Civ. Code § 1799.3; *see also* federal video rental store privacy provisions, 18 U.S.C. § 2710.
- Patient Privacy Rights, Cal. Health and Safety Code §§ 1795, 123110, 103850, 103885, 128735.
- Limits on Use of Polygraph Tests, Cal. Lab. Code § 432.2.
- Employee Rights in Employment Records, Cal. Labor Code § 1198.5, Cal. Edu. Code § 49060, 92612.
- Privacy Rights of Students or Parents, Cal. Edu. Code § 49060.

Colorado

- Right to Petition to Seal Criminal Record, Colo. Rev. Stat. § 24-72-308.
- Privacy of Criminal Records, Colo. Rev. Stat. § 24-72-301.

- Privacy of Medical, Personnel, Library and Public School Student Records, Colo. Rev. Stat. §§ 24-72-204(3)(a) and 24-90-119.
- Confidentiality of Library Records, Colo. Rev. Stat. §§ 24-72-204(3)(a) and 24-90-119.
- Privacy of Student Records, Colo. Rev. Stat. § 24-72-204.
- Employee Access to Job References, Colo. Rev. Stat. § 8-2-114.
- Wiretapping/Eavesdropping/Electronic Surveillance, Colo. Rev. Stat. §§ 16-15-101, 18-9-301.
- Privacy of Tax Records, Colo. Rev. Stat. § 39-21-113(4)(a).
- Colorado Computer Crimes Statue, C.R.S. § 18-5.5.-101.
- Colorado "Must Shred" Statute, C.R.S. § 6-1-713.
- Concerning Security Breaches Regarding Personal Identifying Information (Colorado Data Security Breach Notification Statute), House Bill 06-1119 (2006).
- Telemarketing Statute, C.R.S. § 18-9-311.
- Privacy and Security of Nonpublic Personal Information Collected and Maintained by Insurers (Implementing Requirements of Gramm-Leach-Bliley Act), 3 CCR §§ 702.6 *et seq.*
- Genetic Testing, Discrimination and Other Privacy Restrictions, C.R.S. §§ 10-3-1140.7 and 10-3-1108.
- Rights of Subjects of Credit Reports, C.R.S. § 12-14.3-101.
- Patient Privacy Rights, C.R.S. § 25-1-801.
- Employee Rights in Employment Records, C.R.S. § 8-2-114.

Connecticut

- Erasure of Court and Police Records in Certain Circumstances, Conn. Gen. Stat. Ann. § 54-142a.
- Privacy of Criminal Records Database, Conn. Gen. Stat. Ann. § 54-142-(g)-(p).
- Privacy of Individual Information held by State and Local Agencies, Conn. Gen. Stat. Ann. § 4-190.
- Confidentiality of Library Records, Conn. Gen. Stat. Ann. 11-25.
- Confidentiality of Student Records, Conn. Gen. Stat. Ann. § 10-156.
- Employee Right to Inspect Employee Records, Conn. Gen. Stat. Ann. § 31-128a.
- Restrictions on Camera Surveillance of Employees, Conn. Gen. Stat. Ann. § 31-486.
- Wiretapping/Eavesdropping/Electronic Surveillance, Conn. Gen. Stat. Ann. §§ 53a-107, 54-14.
- Privacy of Tax Records, Conn. Gen. Stat. Ann. § 12-15.
- Connecticut Computer Crime Statute, Conn. Gen. Stat. § 53a-250.
- Connecticut "Must-Shred" Statute, Conn. Gen. Stat. 6-1-713(1).
- Connecticut Data Security Breach Notification Statute, Conn. Gen. Stat. § 36a-701b.

- Video Surveillance, Conn. Gen. Stat. § 54-14a *et seq.*
- Telemarketing Statute, Conn. Gen. Stat. § 42-288a.
- Privacy, Conn. Gen. Stat. Ann. § 53-421.
- Employee Rights in Employment Records, Conn. Gen. Stat. Ann. § 31-12a.
- Privacy and Security of Nonpublic Personal Information Collected and Maintained by Insurers (Implementing Requirements of Gramm-Leach-Bliley Act), Conn. Gen. Stat. §§ 38a-8a *et seq.*, Conn. Regs. §§ 38a-8-105 *et seq.*
- Genetic Testing, Discrimination and Other Privacy Restrictions, Conn. Gen. Stat. Ann. § 38a-816(19).
- Privacy of Bank Customer Records, Conn. Gen. Stat. Ann. §§ 36a-41 through 36a-42.
- Rights of Subjects of Credit Reports, Conn. Gen. Stat. Ann. § 36a-699a.
- Customer Privacy Rights, Video Rental Stores, Conn. Gen. Stat. Ann. § 53-450, *see also* federal video rental store privacy provisions, 18 U.S.C. § 2710.
- Patient Privacy Rights, Conn. Gen. Stat. Ann. §§ 4-105, 52-146h, 19A-581.
- Limits on Use of Polygraph Tests, Conn. Gen. Stat. Ann. § 31-51g.
- Restrictions on Certain Tests, Conn. Gen. Stat. Ann. § 31-51t.
- Privacy Rights of Students or Parents, Conn. Gen. Stat. Ann. § 10-15b.

Delaware

- Rights to Obtain Copy or Destruction of Criminal Records in Certain Circumstances, 11 Del. Code § 8511(4), 11 Del. Code § 4371, 11 Del. Code § 3904.
- Privacy of Criminal Records Database, 11 Del. Code § 8513.
- Confidentiality of Library Records, 29 Del. Code § 10002d(12).
- Privacy of Student Records, 14 Del. Code § 4111.
- Employee Right to Inspect Employee Files, 19 Del. Code §§ 719, 723.
- Wiretapping/Eavesdropping/Electronic Surveillance, 11 Del. Code § 1335.
- Privacy of Tax Records, 30 Del. Code § 368.
- Delaware Computer Crime Statute, 11 Del. Code §§ 931-39.
- Computer Security Breaches (Delaware Data Security Breach Notification Statute), 6 Del. C. § 101.
- Surveillance in Private Places, 11 Del. Code § 1335(a)(2).
- Employee Rights in Employment Records, 19 Del. Code § 719, 721.
- Privacy and Security of Nonpublic Personal Information Collected and Maintained by Insurers (Implementing Requirements of Gramm-Leach-Bliley Act), Del. Regs §§ 18.900.904 *et seq.*
- Genetic Testing, Discrimination and Other Privacy Restrictions, 18 Del. Code Ann. § 2317.
- Limitations on Right to Demand Credit Card Data, 11 Del. Code §§ 914-915.
- Customer Privacy Rights, Video Stores, 11 Del. Code § 925, *see also* federal video rental store privacy provisions, 18 U.S.C. § 2710.

- Patient Privacy Rights, 16 Del. Code §§ 711, 1204.
- Limits on Use of Polygraph Tests, 19 Del. Code § 704.
- Restrictions on Certain Tests, 19 Del. Code § 711.

Florida

- Privacy Right in State Constitution, Art. I, § 23.
- Right to Have Criminal Records Expunged in Certain Circumstances, Fla. Stat. Ann. § 901.33.
- State and local agencies limited in their right to base public employment decisions on criminal record. Fla. Stat. Ann. § 112.011.
- Privacy of Criminal Records, Fla. Stat. Ann. § 934.056.
- Data Security Obligations of State Government Departments, Fla. Stat. Ann. § 282.318.
- Confidentiality of Library Records, Fla. Stat. Ann. § 257.261.
- Privacy of Student Records, Fla. Stat. Ann. § 232.23.
- Right of School Employees to Inspect Personnel Records, Fla. Stat. Ann. § 231.291.
- Wiretapping/Eavesdropping/Electronic Surveillance, Fla. Stat. Ann. § 934.01.
- Florida Computer Crime Statute, Fla. Stat. Ann. § 815.01.
- Breach of Security Concerning Confidential Information in Third-Party Possession (Florida Data Security Breach Notification Statute), Fla. Stat. § 817.5681.
- Surveillance of Private Places by Merchants, Fla. Stat. Ann. § 877.26.
- Telemarketing Statute, Fla. Stat. Ann. §§ 501.059, 365.165, 365.1657.
- Privacy and Security of Nonpublic Personal Information Collected and Maintained by Insurers (Implementing Requirements of Gramm-Leach-Bliley Act), Fla. Stat. Ann. §§ 626.9651 *et seq.*, Fla. Regs. §§ 69J-128-001 *et seq.*
- Genetic Testing, Discrimination and Other Privacy Restrictions, Fla. Stat. Ann. § 627.429.
- Privacy of Customer Records, Fla. Stat. Ann. § 659.062.
- Limitations on Right to Demand Credit Card, Fla. Stat. Ann. § 832.075.
- Patient Privacy Rights, Fla. Stat. Ann. §§ 455.241, 395.017, 395.202, 381.606.
- Restrictions on Certain Tests, Fla. Stat. Ann. §§ 440.102, 760.40.
- Privacy Rights of Students or Parents, Fla. Stat. Ann. § 232.23.

Georgia

- Limitations on Disclosure of Arrest Information, Ga. Code Ann. § 35-3-34.
- Privacy of Criminal Records Database, Ga. Code Ann. §§ 35-3-37, 35-3-38.
- Confidentiality of Department of Motor Vehicles Records, Ga. Code Ann. §§ 40-2-130, 40-3-23.
- Confidentiality of Library Records, Ga. Code Ann. § 24-9-46.

- Wiretapping/Eavesdropping/Electronic Surveillance, Ga. Code. Ann. § 16-1162.
- Privacy of Tax Records, Ga. Code Ann. § 48-7-60.
- Georgia Computer Crime Statute, O.C.G. § 16-9-90.
- Georgia "Must Shred" Statute, O.C.G. § 10-15-1.
- Georgia Data Security Breach Notification Statute, O.C.G. § 10-1-911.
- Telemarketing Statute, O.C.G. §§ 46-5-23, 46-5-27.
- Privacy and Security of Nonpublic Personal Information Collected and Maintained by Insurers (Implementing Requirements of Gramm-Leach-Bliley Act), Ga. Regs. §§ 120-2-87-01 *et seq.*
- Genetic Testing, Discrimination and Other Privacy Restrictions, O.C.G. § 33-54.1.
- Rights of Subjects of Credit Reports, O.C.G. § 10-1-392.
- Limitations on Right to Demand Credit Card, O.C.G. § 10-1-393.3.
- Patient Privacy Rights, O.C.G. §§ 31-33-2, 29-9-49, 24-9-42.
- Limits on Use of Polygraph Tests, O.C.G. § 43-36-1.

Hawaii

- Privacy Right in State Constitution, Art. 1, § 6.
- Arrest Records May be Expunged on Request to Attorney General, Haw. Rev. Stat. § 831-3-2.
- Limitations on Denial of Public Employment based on Criminal History, Haw. Rev. Stat. § 831-3.01.
- Privacy of Criminal Records, Haw. Rev. Stat. § 846.1.
- State Agency Information Practices (Uniform Information Practices Act), Haw. Rev. Stat. § 92F.
- Privacy of Motor Vehicle Records, Haw. Rev. Stat. § 286-172.
- Wiretapping/Eavesdropping/Electronic Surveillance, Haw. Rev. Stat. §§ 711-1111, 803.41-803.48.
- Privacy of Tax Records, Haw. Rev. Stat. § 235.116.
- Hawaii Computer Fraud Statute, Haw. Rev. Stat. §§ 708-890.
- Hawaii "Must-Shred" Statute, Hawaii Senate Bill 2292, effective Jan. 1, 2007.
- Hawaii Security Breach Notification Statute, Haw. Rev. Stat. § 487N.
- Telemarketing Statute, Haw. Rev. Stat. § 445-184.
- Privacy and Security of Nonpublic Personal Information Collected and Maintained by Insurers (Implementing Requirements of Gramm-Leach-Bliley Act), Haw. Rev. Stat. §§ 431:3A-101 *et seq.*
- Genetic Testing, Discrimination and Other Privacy Restrictions, Haw. Rev. Stat. § 431:10a-118.
- Patient Privacy Rights, Haw. Rev. Stat. §§ 323C, 334-5, 622-57, 621-20.
- Limits on Use of Polygraph Tests, Haw. Rev. Stat. § 378.21.
- Restrictions on Certain Tests, Haw. Rev. Stat. § 329B.

Idaho

- Idaho Computer Crime Statute, Idaho Code § 18-2202.
- Disclosure of Criminal Records, Idaho Code § 67-3008.
- Confidentiality of Library Records, Idaho Code § 9-340.
- Wiretapping/Eavesdropping/Electronic Surveillance, Idaho Code § 18-6701.
- Privacy of Tax Records, Idaho Code § 63-3076.
- Idaho Computer Crime Statute, Idaho Code § 18-2202.
- Idaho Data Security Breach Notification Statute, Idaho Code § 28-51-104.
- Telemarketing Statute, Idaho Code § 48-1003A.
- Privacy and Security of Nonpublic Personal Information Collected and Maintained by Insurers (Implementing Requirements of Gramm-Leach-Bliley Act), IDAPA ch. 18.01.48.
- Patient Privacy Rights, Idaho Code §§ 54-1810(h)(2), 9-420, 9-203(4).
- Limits on Use of Polygraph Tests, Idaho Code § 44-903.
- Privacy Rights of Students or Parents, Idaho Code § 9-203(6).

Illinois

- Privacy Right in State Constitution, Art I, § 6.
- Arrest Records May be Expunged under Certain Circumstances, 20 ILCS 2630/5 and 7.
- Agency may not inquire into arrest history of applicant for public employment, 775 ILCS 5/4-103.
- Privacy of Criminal Records, 20 ILCS § 2630/7.
- Confidentiality of State Records, 5 ILCS 160/2.
- Confidentiality of Motor Vehicle Records, 624 ILCS 5/2-123.
- Confidentiality of Library Records, 75 ILCS 70/2.
- Release of Social Security Numbers by Secretary of State, 625 ILCS 5/2-1239(h).
- Privacy of Student Records, 105 ILCS 10/1.
- Wiretapping/Eavesdropping/Electronic Surveillance, 720 ILCS §§ 360/1, 5/14-1.
- Privacy of Tax Records, 35 ILCS § 5/917.
- Illinois Computer Crime Statute, 750 ILCS 5/16D-1.
- Illinois Criminal "Must-Shred" Statute, 720 ILCS 5/16G-21.
- Personal Information Protection Act (Illinois Data Security Breach Notification Statute), 815 ILCS § 530/5.
- Telemarketing Statute, § 815 ILCS 413/15.
- Employee Rights in Employment Records, 820 ILCS § 40/1.
- Privacy and Security of Nonpublic Personal Information Collected and Maintained by Insurers (Implementing Requirements of Gramm-Leach-Bliley Act), 50 Ill. Regs. §§ 4001.10 *et seq.*
- Genetic Testing, Discrimination and Other Privacy Restrictions, 410 ILCS § 50/3.

- Customer Privacy Rights and Requirements for Cable Television Operators, 720 ILCS § 110/2.
- Privacy of Bank Customer Records, 205 ILCS § 5/48.1.
- Patient Privacy Rights, 410 ILCS §§ 50/3, 735 ILCS 5/8-802, 740 ILCS 110/1.
- Limits on Use of Polygraph Tests, 225 ILCS § 430/14/1.
- Restrictions on Certain Tests, 410 ILCS § 513/25.
- Privacy Rights of Students or Parents, 105 ILCS 10/1.

Indiana

- Right to Destruction of Arrest Record in Certain Circumstances, Ind. Code Ann. § 35-4.8.
- Privacy of Criminal Records, Ind. Code Ann. § 5-2-4.
- Indiana Fair Information Practices Act for State Agencies, Ind. Code. Ann §§ 5-14-3-1, 4-1-6-3.
- Privacy of Motor Vehicle Records, Ind. Code Ann. § 9-1-1-8.
- Confidentiality of Library Records, Ind. Code Ann. § 5-14-3-4(16).
- Acquisition of Social Security Numbers by State Agencies, Ind. Code Ann. § 4-1-8-1.
- Wiretapping/Eavesdropping/Electronic Surveillance, Ind. Code. Ann. § 35-33.5-5-1.
- Indiana Computer Crime Statute, Ind. Code § 35-43-1-2.
- Indiana "Must Shred" and Data Security Breach Notification Statute, Indiana Code § 24-4-14.
- Telemarketing Statute, Ind. Code §§ 24-5-12-24, 24-4.7-4-1.
- Privacy and Security of Nonpublic Personal Information Collected and Maintained by Insurers (Implementing Requirements of Gramm-Leach-Bliley Act), 760 IAC §§ 1-67-1 *et seq.*
- Genetic Testing, Discrimination and Other Privacy Restrictions, Ind. Code § 27-8-26-5.
- Patient Privacy Rights, Ind. Code §§ 16-39-5-1, 16-39-1-1, 16-18-2-195, 34-43-1-3, 34-1-14-5.

Iowa

- Iowa Computer Crime Statute, Iowa Code Ann. § 716A.
- Privacy of Criminal Justice Information Systems, Iowa Code Ann. § 692.1-5.
- Confidentiality of Library Records, Iowa Code Ann. § 22.7(13).
- Use of Social Security Number for Driver Identification, Iowa Code Ann. § 321.182.
- Privacy of Student Records, Iowa Code Ann. § 68A.7.
- Right of Public Employees to Inspect Personnel Files, Iowa Code Ann. § 91B.1.
- Limits on Disclosure of Information from Public Employees' Personnel Records, Iowa Code Ann. § 68A.7.

- Wiretapping/Eavesdropping/Electronic Surveillance, Iowa Code Ann. §§ 716.7-8, 727.8. Iowa Computer Crime Statute, Iowa Code Ann. § 716A.
- Telemarketing Statute, Iowa Code Ann. § 708.7.
- Employee Rights in Employment Records, Iowa Code Ann. § 91B.1.
- Privacy and Security of Nonpublic Personal Information Collected and Maintained by Insurers (Implementing Requirements of Gramm-Leach-Bliley Act), Iowa Code Ann. §§ 505.8 *et seq.*, 11 1AC §§ 4-14 *et seq.*
- Privacy of Bank Customer Records, Iowa Code Ann. § 527.10.
- Limitations on Right to Demand Credit Card, Iowa Code Ann. § 537.8101.
- Customer Privacy Rights, Video Rental Stores, Iowa Code Ann. § 727.11.
- Patient Privacy Rights, Iowa Code Ann. §§ 622.10, 140.1-4, 139.41.
- Limits on Use of Polygraph Tests, Iowa Code Ann. § 730.4.
- Restrictions on Certain Tests, Iowa Code Ann. § 73.5.
- Privacy Rights of Students or Parents, Iowa Code Ann. § 68A.7.

Kansas

- Security Requirements for and Right of Access to State Police Database, Kan. Stat. Ann. § 22-4704.
- Review of Criminal History as Condition of Employment, Kan. Stat. Ann. § 22-4710.
- Privacy of Motor Vehicles and Other State Records, Kan. Stat. Ann. §§ 21-3914 and 74-2012.
- Confidentiality of Library Records, Kan. Stat. Ann. § 45-221(a)(23).
- Wiretapping/Eavesdropping/Electronic Surveillance, Kan. Stat. Ann. § 22-2514.
- Privacy of Tax Records, Kan. Stat. Ann. § 79-3234.
- Kansas "Must Shred" and Data Security Breach Notification Statute, 2006 Kansas Session Laws 149.
- Kansas Computer Crime Statute, Kan. Stat. Ann.§ 21-3755.
- Telemarketing Statute, Kan. Stat. Ann. § 50-670.
- Privacy and Security of Nonpublic Personal Information Collected and Maintained by Insurers (Implementing Requirements of Gramm-Leach-Bliley Act), Kan. Stat. Ann. §§ 40-2404 *et seq.*
- Genetic Testing, Discrimination and Other Privacy Restrictions, Kan. Stat. Ann. § 40-2111.
- Rights of Subjects of Credit Reports, Kan. Stat. Ann. § 50-270.
- Limitations on Right to Demand Credit Card, Kan. Stat. Ann. § 50-669.
- Patient Privacy Rights, Kan. Stat. Ann. §§ 59-2931, 60-427, 65-2837(f), 74-5323.
- Restrictions on Certain Tests, Kan. Stat. Ann. § 44-1009.

Kentucky

- Right of Access to Arrest Records, Ky. Rev. Stat. Ann. § 61.884.
- Privacy of Criminal Records, Ky. Per. Stat. Ann. § 17.150.

- Open Records Statute, Ky. Rev. Stat. Ann. §§ 61.870 to 61.884.
- Use of Social Security Numbers in Driver's Licensing, Ky. Rev. Stat. §§ 186.412(2) and 196.412.(3).
- Privilege for Communications between Student and Counselor, Ky. Rev. Stat. § 421.216.
- Wiretapping/Eavesdropping/Electronic Surveillance, Ky. Rev. Stat. § 526.010.
- Privacy of Tax Records, Ky. Rev. Stat. § 131.190. Kentucky Computer Crimes Statute, Ky. Rev. Stat. § 434.840.
- Kentucky "Must-Shred" Statute, Ky. Rev. Stat. § 365.725.
- Telemarketing Statute, Ky. Rev. Stat. §§ 367.469, 367.461.
- Privacy and Security of Nonpublic Personal Information Collected and Maintained by Insurers (Implementing Requirements of Gramm-Leach-Bliley Act), 806 KAR §§ 3:210 *et seq.*
- Genetic Testing, Discrimination and Other Privacy Restrictions, Ky. Rev. Stat. § 304.12-090.
- Rights of Subjects of Credit Reports, Ky. Rev. Stat. § 431.350.
- Patient Privacy Rights, Ky. Rev. Stat. §§ 313.200, 421.215.
- Privacy Rights of Students or Parents, Ky. Rev. Stat. § 421.216.

Louisiana

- Privacy Right in State Constitution, Art. I, § 5.
- Right to Destruction of Criminal Misdemeanor Records, La. Rev. Stat. Ann. § 44:9.
- Security of Criminal Justice Information System, La. Rev. Stat. Ann. § 15.575.
- Confidentiality of Library Records, La. Rev. Stat. Ann. § 44:13.
- Wiretapping/Eavesdropping/Electronic Surveillance, La. Rev. Stat. Ann. § 14:322.
- Privacy of Tax Records, La. Rev. Stat. Ann. § 47:1508.
- Louisiana Computer Crime Statute, La. R.S. §§ 14:73.1-5.
- Database Security Breach Notification Law (Louisiana Data Security Breach Notification Statute), La. R.S. § 51:3074.
- Surreptitious Video Surveillance, La. R.S. § 14:283.
- Telemarketing Statute, La. R.S. § 45:844-14.
- Privacy and Security of Nonpublic Personal Information Collected and Maintained by Insurers (Implementing Requirements of Gramm-Leach-Bliley Act), Title 37 of Louisiana Regulations, Part XIII, Ch. 99, Reg. 76, §§ 9903 *et seq.*
- Genetic Testing, Discrimination and Other Privacy Restrictions, La. R. S. 22:213.7
- Privacy of Bank Customer Records, La. R.S. § 9:3571.
- Customer Privacy Rights, Video Rental Stores, La. R.S. § 37:1746, *see also* federal video rental store privacy provisions, 18 U.S.C. § 2710.
- Patient Privacy Rights, La. R.S. §§ 15:476, 40:2014.1.
- Limits on Use of Polygraph Tests, La. R.S. § 36-A:2848.

Maine

- Maine Computer Crime Statute, 17A Me. Rev. Stat. Ann. § 432.
- Privacy of Criminal Records, 16 Me. Rev. Stat. Ann. §§ 611, 620.
- Confidentiality of Library Records, 27 Me. Rev. Stat. Ann. § 121.
- Privilege for Communications between Student and Counselor, 20 Me. Rev. Stat. Ann. § 805.
- Public Employees' Rights of Access to Personnel Records, 5 Me. Rev. Stat. § 7071.
- Wiretapping/Eavesdropping/Electronic Surveillance, 15 Me. Rev. Stat.; 17 Me. Rev. Stat. § 511.
- Privacy of Tax Records, 36 Me. Rev. Stat. § 191. Maine Computer Crime Statute, 17A M.R.S § 432.
- Notice of Risk to Personal Data (Maine Data Security Breach Notification Statute), 10 M.R.S. § 1347.
- Telemarketing Statute, 69A M.R.S. § 4690A, 19 M.R.S. § 1498.
- Employee Rights in Employment Records, 26 M.R.S. § 631.
- Privacy and Security of Nonpublic Personal Information Collected and Maintained by Insurers (Implementing Requirements of Gramm-Leach-Bliley Act), 24A Maine Ins. Code §§ 2203 *et seq.*
- Genetic Testing, Discrimination and Other Privacy Restrictions, 24 A Maine Ins. Code § 2159-C.
- Privacy of Bank Customer Records, 9-B M.R.S. § 161.
- Rights of Subjects of Credit Reports, 10 M.R.S. § 1312.
- Patient Privacy Rights, 22 M.R.S. § 1711; 32 M.R.S. § 3153.
- Limits on Use of Polygraph Tests, 32 M.R.S. §§ 7154, 7166.
- Restrictions on Certain Tests, 26 M.R.S. §§ 681-690.
- Privacy Rights of Students or Parents, 20 M.R.S. § 805.

Maryland

- Petition to Court to Seal Arrest Records, 27 Md. Ann. Code § 735-41, 27 Md. Ann. Code § 292(a).
- Privacy of Criminal Records Database, 27 Md. Ann. Code §§ 742, 13.03(3).
- Confidentiality of Library Records, Md. State Gov. Code Ann. § 10-616.
- Privacy of Student Records, Md. State Gov. Code Ann. § 10-616.
- Privilege for Certain Statements by Students to Professional Educator, Md. Ed. Code Ann. § 7-410.
- Wiretapping/Eavesdropping/Electronic Surveillance, Md. Ct. & Jud. Proc. Code Ann. § 10-402.
- Privacy of Tax Records, Md. Tax-Gen. Code Ann. § 13-207. Maryland Computer Crime Statute, 27 Md. Ann. Code § 146.
- Telemarketing Statute, 78 Md. Ann. Code § 55C.
- Privacy and Security of Nonpublic Personal Information Collected and Maintained by Insurers (Implementing Requirements of Gramm-Leach-Bliley Act), Tit. 31 Maryland Regulations, subtitle 16, ch. 8.

- Genetic Testing, Discrimination and Other Privacy Restrictions, 48A Md. Ann. Code § 223.1, Md. Ins. Code § 27-909.
- Privacy of Bank Customer Records, Md. Fin. Inst. Code § 1-302.
- Rights of Subjects of Credit Reports, Md. Comm. Law Code § 14-209.
- Customer Privacy Rights, Video Rental Stores, 27 Md. Ann. Code § 583, *see also* federal video rental store privacy provisions, 18 U.S.C. § 2710.
- Patient Privacy Rights, Md. Health Gen. Code §§ 4-102, 19-1507.
- Limits on Use of Polygraph Tests, Md. Ann. Code of Labor and Empl. § 3-702.
- Restrictions on Certain Tests, Md. Gen. Health Law § 17-214.1.
- Privacy Rights of Students or Parents, Md. State Gov. Code § 10-616; Md. Edu. Code § 7-410.

Massachusetts

- Provisions for Sealing of Criminal Records, Mass. Gen. Laws ch. 276, § 100.
- Restrictions on Employer Inquiries concerning Arrest Records and Similar Inquiries by College/University Admissions Officials, Mass. Gen. Laws ch. 276, § 100 and ch. 94, § 34.
- Privacy of Criminal Records, Mass. Gen. Laws ch. 6, §§ 167-179B.
- Privacy of Records of State Agencies, Mass. Gen. Laws ch. 66A.
- Expunging Child Abuse Reports, Mass. Gen. Laws ch. 119, § 51E.
- Destruction of Welfare Records, Mass. Gen. Laws ch. 66, § 17A.
- Confidentiality of Library Records, Mass. Gen. Laws ch. 4, § 7.
- Use of Social Security Number in Drivers' Licensing, Mass. Gen. Laws Ann. ch. 30A, § 13A.
- Privacy, Inspection and Destruction of Student Records, Mass. Gen. Laws Ann. ch. 71, § 34.
- Right of Pubic Employees to Inspect Personnel Records, Mass. Gen. Laws Ann. ch. 149, § 52C.
- Wiretapping/Eavesdropping/Electronic Surveillance, Mass. Gen. Laws Ann. ch. 272, § 99.
- Privacy of Tax Records, Mass. Gen. Laws Ann. ch. 62C, §§ 21, 74. Massachusetts Statutes re Theft of Computer Data and Services, Mass. Gen. Laws Ann. ch. 26 §§ 30(2), 33-A.
- Surveillance of Private Places by Retailers, Mass. Gen. Laws Ann. ch. 93 § 89.
- Telemarketing Statute, Mass. Gen. Laws Ann. ch. 159, § 19B-E.
- Employee Rights in Employment Records, Mass. Gen. Laws Ann. ch. 151B, § 4.
- Privacy and Security of Nonpublic Personal Information Collected and Maintained by Insurers (Implementing Requirements of Gramm-Leach-Bliley Act), Mass. Gen. Laws Ann. ch. 1751.
- Genetic Testing, Discrimination and Other Privacy Restrictions, Mass. Gen. Laws ch. 175 § 108H.
- Privacy of Bank Customer Records, Mass. Gen. Laws ch. 167B, §§ 7, 16.
- Rights of Subjects of Credit Reports, Mass. Gen. Laws ch. 93, §§ 51-58.

- Limitations on Right to Demand Credit Card, Mass. Gen. Laws ch. 93 § 104.
- Patient Privacy Rights, Mass. Gen Laws ch. 111, § 70E.
- Limits on Use of Polygraph Tests, Mass. Gen. Laws ch. 149, § 19B.
- Restrictions on Certain Tests, Mass. Gen. Laws ch. 149, § 19B.
- Privacy Rights of Students or Parents, Mass. Gen. Laws ch. 71, §§ 34D, 34E.

Michigan

- Employers may not inquire into arrests that do not result in convictions, Mich. Comp. Laws Ann. § 37.2205(a).
- Return of Arrest Information to Persons not Convicted, Mich. Comp. Laws Ann. § 28.243.
- Confidentiality of Library Records, Mich. Comp. Laws Ann. § 397.601.
- Privacy of Student Records and Communications, Mich. Comp. Laws Ann. § 600.2165.
- Right of Employee to Inspect Personnel File, Mich. Comp. Laws Ann. § 423.501.
- Wiretapping/Eavesdropping/Electronic Surveillance, Mich. Comp. Laws Ann. § 750.539. Michigan Computer Crime Statute, Mich. Comp. Laws Ann. § 752.791.
- Michigan "Must-Shred" Statute, MCL § 445.63, § 12.
- Michigan Security Breach Notification Statute, MCL § 445.72.
- Telemarketing Statute, Mich. Comp. Laws Ann. §§ 445.111a, 484.125.
- Employee Rights in Employment Records, Mich. Comp. Laws Ann. §§ 423.501, 37.2205a.
- Privacy and Security of Nonpublic Personal Information Collected and Maintained by Insurers (Implementing Requirements of Gramm-Leach-Bliley Act), Department of Labor and Economic Growth, Office of Financial and Insurance Services, Standards for Safeguarding Customer Information, R. 500.551.
- Genetic Testing, Discrimination and Other Privacy Restrictions, Mich. Comp. Laws Ann. §§ 550.1401(e), 333.21072a, 500.3407b.
- Customer Privacy Rights, Video Rental Stores, Mich. Comp. Laws Ann. § 445.1712, *see also* federal video rental store privacy provisions, 18 U.S.C. § 2710.
- Patient Privacy Rights, Mich. Comp. Laws Ann. § 600.2157.
- Limits on Use of Polygraph Tests, Mich. Comp. Laws Ann. § 37.201.
- Restrictions on Certain Tests, Mich. Comp. Laws Ann. § 37.1202.
- Privacy Rights of Students or Parents, Mich. Comp. Laws Ann. § 600.2165.

Minnesota

- Restrictions on Use of Certain Criminal Records in Connection with Public Employment and Licensing, Minn. Stat. Ann. § 364.04.
- Privacy of Law Enforcement Data, Minn. Stat. Ann. § 13.82.

- Data Practices Act, Governing Privacy Obligations of State Agencies, School Boards, State University, Local Commissions and Authorities (Townships Excluded), Minn. Stat. Ann. § 13.01.
- Computer Matching, Minn. Stat. Ann. § 13B.01.
- Confidentiality of Library Records, Minn. Stat. Ann. § 13.40.
- Use of Social Security Numbers in Drivers' Licensing, Minn. Stat. Ann. § 171.06.
- Privacy of Student Records, Minn. Stat. Ann. § 13.32.
- Right of Employees to Inspect Personnel Records, Minn. Stat. Ann. § 181.960.
- Wiretapping/Eavesdropping/Electronic Surveillance, Minn. Stat. Ann. § 626A.01. Minnesota Computer Crime Statute, Minn. Stat. §§ 609.87, 609.89.
- Minnesota Must-Shred Statute, Minn. Stat. § 13.05(5)(b).
- Minnesota Data Security Breach Notification Statute, Minn. Stat. § 325E.61.
- Telemarketing Statute, Minn. Stat. § 325E.26-31.
- Employee Rights in Employment Records, Minn. Stat. § 181.960.
- Privacy and Security of Nonpublic Personal Information Collected and Maintained by Insurers (Implementing Requirements of Gramm-Leach-Bliley Act), Minn. Stat. §§ 60A.98 *et seq.*
- Genetic Testing, Discrimination and Other Privacy Restrictions, Minn. Stat. § 72A-499.
- Rights of Subjects of Credit Reports, Minn. Stat. § 13C.01.
- Limitations on Right to Demand Credit Card, Minn. Stat. §§ 325F.981 and 982.
- Patient Privacy Rights, Minn. Stat. §§ 595-02(4), 144.651.
- Limits on Use of Polygraph Tests, Minn. Stat. § 181.75.
- Restrictions on Certain Tests, Minn. Stat. § 181.93.
- Privacy Rights of Students or Parents, Minn. Stat. § 13.32.

Mississippi

- Mississippi Computer Crime Statute, Miss. Code Ann. § 97-45-1.
- Correction of Errors in Criminal Records Database, Misc. Code Ann. § 45-27-11.
- Confidentiality of State Agency Information, Miss. Code Ann. §§ 25-53-53 and 25-53-55.
- Confidentiality of Library Records, Miss. Code Ann. § 39-3-365.
- Confidentiality of Student Records, Miss. Code Ann. § 37-15-3.
- Wiretapping/Eavesdropping/Electronic Surveillance, Miss. Code Ann. §§ 41-29-501, 41-39-531, 41-29-701. Mississippi Computer Crime Statute, Miss. Code Ann. § 97-45-1.
- Video Surveillance of Private Places, Miss. Code Ann. § 97-29-63.
- Privacy and Security of Nonpublic Personal Information Collected and Maintained by Insurers (Implementing Requirements of Gramm-Leach-Bliley Act), Miss. Code Ann. §§ 83-1-45 *et seq.*, Miss Dept of Insurance Reg. No. 2000-6.

- Patient Privacy Rights, Miss. Code Ann. § 13-1-21.
- Limits on Use of Polygraph Tests, Miss. Code Ann. § 73-29-31.
- Privacy Rights of Students or Parents, Miss. Code Ann. § 37-15-3.

Missouri

- Arrest records may be sealed and kept confidential under certain circumstances, Mo. Ann. Stat. § 610.100.
- Confidentiality of Library Records, Mo. Ann. Stat. § 182.817. Missouri Statute Prohibiting Tampering with Intellectual Property, Mo. Ann. Stat. § 569.093.
- Recording of Images of Persons in Private Places, Mo. Ann. Stat. § 565.253.
- Telemarketing Statute, Mo. Ann. Stat. §§ 407.1098, 407.1104.
- Privacy and Security of Nonpublic Personal Information Collected and Maintained by Insurers (Implementing Requirements of Gramm-Leach-Bliley Act), Mo. Ann. Stat. §§ 375.918 *et seq.*, Regulations, Tit. 20, Div. 100, ch. 6, §§ 100-6.100 *et seq.*
- Genetic Testing, Discrimination and Other Privacy Restrictions, Mo. Ann. Stat. § 375.1303.
- Patient Privacy Rights, Mo. Ann. Stat. § 491.060.
- Restrictions on Certain Tests, Mo. Ann. Stat. § 375.1306.

Montana

- Privacy Right in State Constitution, Art. II, § 10.
- Montana Computer Crime Statute, Mont. Code Ann. § 45-6-310.
- Privacy of Criminal Records, Mont. Code Ann. § 44-5-101.
- Confidentiality of Library Records, Mont. Code Ann. § 22-1-1103.
- Privilege for Communications between Student and Counselor, Mont. Code Ann. § 93-701-4.
- Wiretapping/Eavesdropping/Electronic Surveillance, Mont. Code Ann. § 45-8-213. Montana Computer Crime Statute, Mont. Code Ann. § 45-6-310.
- Montana "Must Shred" Statute, Mont. Code. Ann. § 30-14-702.
- Montana Data Security Breach Notification Statute, Mont. Code Ann. § 30-14-1704.
- Telemarketing Statute, Mont. Code Ann. § 45-8-216.
- Privacy and Security of Nonpublic Personal Information Collected and Maintained by Insurers (Implementing Requirements of Gramm-Leach-Bliley Act), Mont. Code Ann. §§ 33-19-409, Regulations Tit. 6, ch. 6, subch. 69, §§ 6.6.6902 *et seq.*
- Rights of Subjects of Credit Reports, Mont. Code Ann. §§ 31-3-101 through 31-3-153.
- Patient Privacy Rights, Mont. Code Ann. § 93-70104(4).
- Limits on Use of Polygraph Tests, Mont. Code Ann. § 39.2-304.
- Restrictions on Certain Tests, Mont. Code Ann. §§ 39-2-304, 50-16-1009.
- Privacy Rights of Students or Parents, Mont. Code Ann. § 93-701-4.

Nebraska

- Nebraska Computer Crime Statute, Neb. Rev. Stat. § 28-1343.
- Privacy of Criminal Records, Neb. Rev. Stat. § 29-3523.
- Confidentiality of Library Records, Neb. Rev. Stat. § 84-712.05.
- Privacy of Student Records, Neb. Rev. Stat. §§ 79-4, 157 and 79-4, 158.
- Wiretapping/Eavesdropping/Electronic Surveillance, Neb. Rev. Stat. § 86-701.
- Privacy of Tax Records, Neb. Rev. Stat. §§ 77-27, 119(1). Nebraska Computer Crime Statute, Neb. Rev. Stat. § 28-1343.
- Nebraska Data Security Breach Notification Statute, 2005 Bill Text NE L.B. 876.
- Telemarketing Statute, Neb. Rev. Stat. § 87-307.
- Privacy and Security of Nonpublic Personal Information Collected and Maintained by Insurers (Implementing Requirements of Gramm-Leach-Bliley Act), Neb. Rev. Stat. §§ 44-902 *et seq.*
- Limits on Use of Polygraph Tests, Neb. Rev. Stat. § 81-1932.
- Restrictions on Certain Tests, Neb. Rev. Stat. § 48-1901.
- Privacy Rights of Students or Parents, Neb. Rev. Stat. § 79-4, 157.

Nevada

- Petitions to Seal Criminal Records, Nev. Rev. Stat. § 179.245, 179.255.
- Right to Inspect Criminal Records, Nev. Rev. Stat. § 179A.150.
- Confidentiality of Library Records, Nev. Rev. Stat. § 239.13.
- Privilege for Communications Between Student and Counselor, Nev. Rev. Stat. §§ 49.290, 49.291.
- Right of Employee to Inspect Personnel Files, Nev. Rev. Stat. § 613.075.
- Wiretapping/Eavesdropping/Electronic Surveillance, Nev. Rev. Stat. § 200.610. Nevada Computer Crime Statute, Nev. Rev. Stat. § 205.473.
- Nevada "Must Shred" Statute, Nev. Rev. Stat. § 603A.200.
- Security of Personal Information (Nevada Data Security Breach Notification Statute), Nev. Rev. Stat. § 603A.020.
- Telemarketing Statute, Nev. Rev. Stat. § 207.325 (unsolicited faxes).
- Employee Rights in Employment Records, Nev. Rev. Stat. § 613.075.
- Privacy and Security of Nonpublic Personal Information Collected and Maintained by Insurers (Implementing Requirements of Gramm-Leach-Bliley Act), Nevada Regulations §§ 679B.61 *et seq.*
- Genetic Testing, Discrimination and Other Privacy Restrictions, Nev. Rev. Stat. § 689A.417.
- Limitations on Right to Demand Credit Card, Nev. Rev. Stat. § 598.088.
- Patient Privacy Rights, Nev. Rev. Stat. §§ 49.215-245, 629.061.
- Limits on Use of Polygraph Tests, Nev. Rev. Stat. §§ 648A.190, 613.480.
- Restrictions on Certain Tests, Nev. Rev. Stat. § 613.345.
- Privacy Rights of Students or Parents, Nev. Rev. Stat. § 49.290, 49.291.

New Hampshire

- New Hampshire Computer Crime Statute, N.H. Rev. Stat. Ann. § 638.16.
- Disclosure of Certain Criminal Records, N.H. Rev. Stat. Ann. § 648.9.
- Information Practices Act for State Agencies, N.H. Rev. Stat. Ann. § 7-A.
- Use of Social Security Numbers in Drivers' Licensing, N.H. Rev. Stat. Ann. § 263:40-a.
- Right of Employee to Inspect Personnel File, N.H. Rev. Stat. Ann. § 275.56.
- Wiretapping/Eavesdropping/Electronic Surveillance, N.H. Rev. Stat. Ann. § 570-A:1. New Hampshire Computer Crime Statute, N.H. Rev. Stat. Ann. § 638:16.
- New Hampshire Breach Notification Statute, N.H. Rev. Stat. Ann. § 359-C:20(I).
- Telemarketing Statute, N.H. Rev. Stat. Ann. §§ 359-E:1 through 359-E:6.
- Employee Rights in Employment Records, N.H. Rev. Stat. § 275.56.
- Privacy and Security of Nonpublic Personal Information Collected and Maintained by Insurers (Implementing Requirements of Gramm-Leach-Bliley Act), New Hampshire Ins. Dept. ch. Ins. 3000, §§ 3001.04 *et seq.*
- Genetic Testing, Discrimination and Other Privacy Restrictions, N.H. Rev. Stat. Ann. §§ 141-H:4 through 141-H:5.
- Privacy of Customer Records, N.H. Rev. Stat. Ann. § 359-C.
- Rights of Subjects of Credit Reports, N.H. Rev. Stat. Ann. § 359-B.
- Patient Privacy Rights, N.H. Rev. Stat. Ann. §§ 329:26, 330-A:19.
- Restrictions on Certain Tests, N.H. Rev. Stat. Ann. § 141-H:3.

New Jersey

- Petitions to Expunge Criminal Record, N.J. Rev. Stat. § 2A:164-28.
- Confidentiality of Library Records, N.J. Rev. Stat. § 18A:73-43.2.
- Privacy of Student Records, N.J. Rev. Stat. § 18A:36-19.
- Wiretapping/Eavesdropping/Electronic Surveillance, N.J. Rev. Stat. § 2A:156A-1. New Jersey Computer Fraud Statute, N.J. Stat. §§ 2A:38A-1 and 2C:20-1.
- New Jersey "Must Shred" Statute, N.J. Stat. § 56:8-161.
- New Jersey Data Security Breach Notification Statute, N.J. Stat. § 56:8-163.
- Telemarketing Statute, N.J. Stat. § 17-48.
- Privacy and Security of Nonpublic Personal Information Collected and Maintained by Insurers (Implementing Requirements of Gramm-Leach-Bliley Act), N.J. Stat. §§ 17.23A-2 *et seq.*
- Genetic Testing, Discrimination and Other Privacy Restrictions, N.J. Stat. § 17B:30-12.
- Customer Privacy Rights and Requirements, Cable Television Operators, N.J. Stat. § 48:5A-1.
- Rights of Subjects of Credit Reports, N.J. Stat. § 56:11-29.

- Limitations on Right to Demand Credit Card, N.J. Stat. §§ 56:11-17, 358-M:1.
- Patient Privacy Rights, N.J. Stat. § 2A:84A-22.2-9.
- Limits on Use of Polygraph Tests, N.J. Stat. § 2C:40A-1.
- Restrictions on Certain Tests, N.J. Stat. § 17B:30-12.

New Mexico

- Certain criminal records may not be used in connection with applications for public employment or licenses, N.M. Stat. Ann. § 28-2-3.
- Privacy of Criminal Records Database, N.M. Stat. Ann. §§ 15-1A-11, 29-10-6.
- Confidentiality of Library Records, N.M. Stat. Ann. §§ 18-9-3 through 18-9-5.
- Wiretapping/Eavesdropping/Electronic Surveillance, N.M. Stat. Ann. § 30-12-2. New Mexico Computer Crime Statute, N.M. Stat. Ann. § 30-45-1.
- Telemarketing Statute, N.M. Stat. Ann. § 57-12-22.
- Privacy and Security of Nonpublic Personal Information Collected and Maintained by Insurers (Implementing Requirements of Gramm-Leach-Bliley Act), New Mexico Regulations Tit. 13, §§ 13.1.3.7 *et seq.*
- Genetic Testing, Discrimination and Other Privacy Restrictions, N.M. Stat. Ann. § 24-21-4.
- Rights of Subjects of Credit Reports, N.M. Stat. Ann. § 56-3-1.
- Patient Privacy Rights, N.M. Stat. Ann. §§ 43-1-19, 24-2B-6.
- Restrictions on Certain Tests, N.M. Stat. Ann. § 28-10A-1.

New York

- Sealing of Criminal Records, N.Y. Crim. Proc. Law § 160.50, § 170.56.
- Limitations on Employer Inquiries into Arrest Records, N.Y. Exec. Law § 296.16.
- Information practices for State Agencies, N.Y. Pub. Office Law §§ 89(2), 91.
- Confidentiality of Library Records, N.Y. Civ. Prac. Law and Rules § 4509.
- Use of Social Security Numbers as Identification at Schools and Colleges, N.Y. Ed. Code § 52-b.
- Restrictions on Employee Surveillance by Employers, N.Y. Lab. Law § 704(1).
- Restrictions on Disclosure of Employment and Medical Data, N.Y. Pub. Off. Law § 89(2)(b)(i).
- Wiretapping/Eavesdropping/Electronic Surveillance, N.Y. Crim. Proc. Law § 700.05.
- Privacy of Tax Records, N.Y. Tax Law § 697. New York Computer Crime Statute, N.Y. Pen. Law § 156.
- New York "Must-Shred" Statute, NY CLS Gen Bus § 399-h.
- New York Data Security Breach Notification Statute, NY CLS Gen Bus § 899-aa.
- Visual Surveillance in Private Places, N.Y. Gen. Bus. Law § 395-b.
- Telemarketing Statute, N.Y. Gen. Bus. Law § 399-Z.

- Privacy and Security of Nonpublic Personal Information Collected and Maintained by Insurers (Implementing Requirements of Gramm-Leach-Bliley Act), New York Insurance Regulations, Tit. 11 §§ 242.1 *et seq.*
- Genetic Testing, Discrimination and Other Privacy Restrictions, N.Y. Ins. Code § 2612.
- Rights of Subjects of Credit Reports, N.Y. Gen. Bus. Law § 380.
- Limitations on Right to Demand Credit Card, N.Y. Gen. Bus. Law § 520-a.
- Customer Privacy Rights, Video Rental Stores, N.Y. Gen. Bus. Law § 670, *see also* federal video rental store privacy provisions, 18 U.S.C. § 2710.
- Patient Privacy Rights, N.Y. Pub. Health Law §§ 17, 18.
- Limits on Use of Polygraph Tests, N.Y. Labor Law § 733.
- Restrictions on Certain Tests, N.Y. Exec. § 296.

North Carolina

- North Carolina Computer Crimes Statute, N.C. Gen. Stat. § 14-453.
- Confidentiality of Library Records, N.C. Gen. Stat. § 125-19.
- Privilege for Communications between Student and Counselor, N.C. Gen. Stat. § 8-53-4.
- Right of State, County and Local Employees to Inspect Personnel Records, N.C. Gen. Stat. §§ 126-22, 153A-98, 160A-168.
- Wiretapping/Eavesdropping/Electronic Surveillance, N.C. Gen. Stat. § 14-155.
- Privacy of Tax Records, N.C. Gen. Stat. § 105-259. North Carolina Computer Crime Statute, N.C. Gen. Stat. 14-453.
- North Carolina "Must Shred" and Data Security Breach Notification Statute, N.C. Gen. Stat. § 75-61.
- Telemarketing Statute, N.C. Gen. Stat. § 75-30.
- Privacy and Security of Nonpublic Personal Information Collected and Maintained by Insurers (Implementing Requirements of Gramm-Leach-Bliley Act), N.C. Gen. Stat. §§ 58-39-1 *et seq.*
- Genetic Testing, Discrimination and Other Privacy Restrictions, N.C. Gen. Stat. § 58-39-55.
- Privacy of Bank Customer Records, N.C. Gen. Stat. § 53B-1.
- Restrictions on Certain Tests, N.C. Gen. Stat. §§ 95-28.1A, 130A-148(i).
- Privacy Rights of Students or Parents, N.C. Gen. Stat. § 8-53.4.

North Dakota

- North Dakota Computer Crime Statute, N.D. Cent. Code § 12.1-06.1-08.
- Confidentiality of Library Records, N.D. Cent. Code § 40-38-12.
- Privilege for Communications between Student and Counselor, N.D. Cent. Code § 31-06.1.
- Right of Public Employees to Inspect Personnel Files, N.D. Cent. Code § 54-06-21.

- Wiretapping/Eavesdropping/Electronic Surveillance, N.D. Cent. Code § 12.1-15-02.
- Privacy of Tax Records, N.D. Cent. Code § 57-38-57. North Dakota Computer Fraud Statute, N.D. Cent. Code § 12.1-06.1-08.
- Notice of Security Breach for Personal Information (North Dakota Data Security Breach Notification Statute), N.D. Cent. Code § 51-30-01.
- Telemarketing Statute, N.D. Cent. Code § 49-21-01.6.
- Privacy and Security of Nonpublic Personal Information Collected and Maintained by Insurers (Implementing Requirements of Gramm-Leach-Bliley Act), N.D. Cent. Code §§ 26.1-02-27 *et seq.*, Insurance Regulations, Tit. 45, §§ 45-14-01-02 *et seq.*
- Privacy of Bank Customer Records, N.D. Cent. Code § 6-08.1-03.
- Limitations on Right to Demand Credit Card, N.D. Cent. Code § 51-14.1-03.
- Patient Privacy Rights, N.D. Cent. Code § 31-01-06(3).
- Restrictions on Certain Tests, N.D. Cent. Code § 23-07.5-01.
- Privacy Rights of Students or Parents, N.D. Cent. Code § 31-06.1.

Ohio

- Expunging Criminal Records, Ohio Rev. Code Ann. § 2953.32.
- Restrictions on Inquiries by Employers and Licensing Bodies into Criminal Records, Ohio Rev. Code Ann. § 2953.43.
- Privacy of Criminal Records, Ohio Rev. Code Ann. § 109.57.
- Information Practices of State Agencies, Ohio Rev. Code Ann. § 1347.01.
- Privacy of Student Records, Ohio Rev. Code Ann. § 3319.321.
- Privacy of Employee Medical Records, Ohio Rev. Code Ann. § 4113.23.
- Wiretapping/Eavesdropping/Electronic Surveillance, Ohio Rev. Code Ann. §§ 2933.51–2933.66, 4931.28.
- Privacy of Tax Records, Ohio Rev. Code § 5101.18.2. Ohio Statute Affecting Theft of Computer Media, ORC Ann. §§ 2901.01 and 2913.01.
- Ohio Data Security Breach Notification Statute, ORC Ann. § 1347.12.
- Surreptitious Video Surveillance, ORC Ann. § 2907.08.
- Privacy and Security of Nonpublic Personal Information Collected and Maintained by Insurers (Implementing Requirements of Gramm-Leach-Bliley Act), ORC Ann. §§ 3904.01 *et seq.*
- Genetic Testing, Discrimination and Other Privacy Restrictions, ORC Ann. §§ 1742 and 3901.49.
- Limitations on Right to Demand Credit Card, ORC Ann. § 1349.17.
- Patient Privacy Rights, ORC Ann. §§ 3701.74, 2151-42.1.
- Privacy Rights of Students or Parents, ORC Ann. § 3319.321.

Oklahoma

- Oklahoma Computer Crime Statute, 21 Okla. Stat. Ann. §§ 1951-56.
- Privacy of Criminal Records, 47 Okla. Stat. Ann. § 2-129.

- Security of Data in State Database, 74 Okla. Stat. Ann. § 118.17.
- Confidentiality of Library Records, 65 Okla. Stat. Ann. § 1-105.
- Requirement or Use of Social Security Numbers by State Agencies, 74 Okla. Stat. Ann. § 3111.
- Restriction on Disclosure of Student Information by Teachers, 70 Okla. Stat. Ann. § 6-115.
- Wiretapping/Eavesdropping/Electronic Surveillance, 21 Okl. Stat. Ann. § 1782; 3 Okl. Stat. Ann. § 176.1.
- Privacy of Tax Records, 68 Okl. Stat. Ann. § 205. Oklahoma Computer Crime Statute, 21 Okla. Stat. Ann. §§ 1951-56.
- Oklahoma Breach Notification Statute, Okla. Stat. Ann. § 3113.1.
- Privacy and Security of Nonpublic Personal Information Collected and Maintained by Insurers (Implementing Requirements of Gramm-Leach-Bliley Act), 36 Okla. Stat. Ann. §§ 307.2 *et seq.*
- Genetic Testing, Discrimination and Other Privacy Restrictions, 36 Okla. Stat. Ann. § 3614-1.
- Privacy of Customer Records, 6 Okla. Stat. Ann. § 2201-2206.
- Rights of Subjects of Credit Reports, 24 Okla. Stat. Ann. § 82.
- Customer Privacy Rights, Video Rental Records, 5 Okla. Stat. Ann. § 776, *see also* federal video rental store privacy provisions, 18 U.S.C. § 2710.
- Patient Privacy Rights, 76 Okla. Stat. Ann. § 19, 12 Okla. Stat. Ann. § 385(6).
- Limits on Use of Polygraph Tests, 36 Okla. Stat. Ann. § 1468.
- Restrictions on Certain Tests, 36 Okla. Stat. Ann. § 3414.2.
- Privacy Rights of Students or Parents, 70 Okla. Stat. Ann. § 6-115.

Oregon

- Petition for Conviction to Be Set Aside, Or. Rev. Stat. § 137.225.
- Confidentiality of Library Records, Or. Rev. Stat. § 192.500(i)(j).
- Privacy of Student Records, Or. Rev. Stat. § 336.195.
- Privilege for Communications to Elementary and Secondary School Teachers, Or. Rev. Stat. § 44.040.
- Opportunity for Employee to View Personnel Records, Or. Rev. Stat. § 652.750.
- Right of Employer to Inquire into Past Arrest of Applicants or Employees, Or. Rev. Stat. § 181.010.
- Wiretapping/Eavesdropping/Electronic Surveillance, Or. Rev. Stat. §§ 133.721, 165.540.
- Privacy of Tax Records, Or. Rev. Stat. § 314.835. Oregon Computer Fraud Statute, Or. Rev. Stat. § 164.377.
- Video Surveillance in Private Places, Or. Rev. Stat. § 163.700.
- Telemarketing Statute, Or. Rev. Stat. § 646.561, 646.611.
- Privacy and Security of Nonpublic Personal Information Collected and Maintained by Insurers (Implementing Requirements of Gramm-Leach-Bliley Act), Or. Rev. Stat. §§ 746.606, Oregon Ins. Regs. §§ 836-080-0506.

- Genetic Testing, Discrimination and Other Privacy Restrictions, Or. Rev. Stat. § 659.036.
- Privacy of Bank Customer Records, Or. Rev. Stat. § 192.550.
- Patient Privacy Rights, Or. Rev. Stat. §§ 192.525, 44.040(I)(d), 433.075.
- Limits on Use of Polygraph Tests, Or. Rev. Stat. § 659.335.
- Restrictions on Certain Tests, Or. Rev. Stat. §§ 438.435, 659.036, 659.225.
- Employee Rights in Personnel Records, Or. Rev. Stat. § 652.750.
- Privacy Rights of Students or Parents, Or. Rev. Stat. § 336.195.

Pennsylvania

- Restrictions on Use of Criminal Records in Employment and Licensing Decisions, 18 Pa. Stat. Ann. § 9124.
- Review and Correction of Criminal Records, 18 Pa. Stat. Ann. § 9151.
- Confidentiality of Library Records, 24 Pa. Stat. Ann. § 4428.
- Right of Employee to Inspect Personnel Files, 43 Pa. Stat. Ann. § 1321. Pennsylvania Computer Fraud Statute, 18 Pa. Stat. Ann. § 3933.
- Breach of Personal Information Notification Act (Pennsylvania Data Security Breach Notification Statute), 73 P.S. § 2302.
- Telemarketing Statute, 66 Pa. Stat. Ann. § 2906.
- Employee Rights in Employment Records, 43 Pa. Stat. Ann. § 1321.
- Privacy and Security of Nonpublic Personal Information Collected and Maintained by Insurers (Implementing Requirements of Gramm-Leach-Bliley Act), Pennsylvania Insurance Regulations, Tit. 31, §§ 146a.1 *et seq.*
- Limitations on Right to Demand Credit Card, 69 Pa. Stat. Ann. § 2602.
- Patient Privacy Rights, 28 Pa. Stat. Ann. § 328.
- Limits on Use of Polygraph Tests, 18 Pa. Stat. Ann. § 7321.
- Restrictions on Certain Tests, 35 Pa. Stat. Ann. §§ 7601-12.

Rhode Island

- Destruction of Certain Criminal Records Required, R.I. Gen. Laws § 12-1-12.
- Restrictions on Employer Inquiry into Arrest Records, R.I. Gen. Laws § 28-5-7(7).
- Confidentiality of Library Records, R.I. Gen. Laws § 38-2-2(U).
- Use of Social Security Number as Identification at Schools, Public Colleges and Public Universities, R.I. Gen. Laws §§ 16-38-5.1, 42-72.5-2(6).
- Invasion of Student Privacy, R.I. Gen. Laws § 16-38-5.
- Right of Employees to Inspect Personnel Records, R.I. Gen. Laws § 28-6.4-1.
- Restrictions on Surveillance of Employees, R.I. Gen. Laws § 28-7-13.
- Wiretapping/Eavesdropping/Electronic Surveillance, R.I. Gen. Laws Ann. § 12-5.1-1.
- Privacy of Tax Records, R.I. Gen. Laws § 44-30-95(c). Rhode Island Computer Crime Statute, R.I. Gen. Laws § 11-52-1.
- Rhode Island "Must-Shred" Statute, R.I. Pub. Laws 225.

- Rhode Island Security Breach Notification Statute, R.I. Gen. Laws § 1-49.2-3.
- Telemarketing Statute, R.I. Gen. Laws § 11-35-26, 5-61-1.
- Employee Rights in Employment Records, R.I. Gen. Laws § 28-6.4-1.
- Privacy and Security of Nonpublic Personal Information Collected and Maintained by Insurers (Implementing Requirements of Gramm-Leach-Bliley Act), Rhode Island Insurance Regulations §§ 02-030-099 *et seq.*
- Genetic Testing, Discrimination and Other Privacy Restrictions, R.I. Gen. Laws §§ 23-6-11 through 23-6-24.
- Rights of Subjects of Credit Reports, R.I. Gen. Laws § 6-13.1-21.
- Limitations on Right to Demand Credit Card, R.I. Gen. Laws § 6-13-16, § 6-13-17 (may not record Social Security numbers on checks).
- Customer Privacy Rights, Video Rental Records, R.I. Gen. Laws § 11-18-32, *see also* federal video rental store privacy provisions, 18 U.S.C. § 2710.
- Patient Privacy Rights, R.I. Gen. Laws §§ 5-37.3-3, 5-37-22.
- Limits on Use of Polygraph Tests, R.I. Gen. Laws § 28-6.1-1.
- Restrictions on Certain Tests, R.I. Gen. Laws §§ 28-6.5-1, 28-6-7.1.
- Privacy Rights of Students or Parents, R.I. Gen. Laws § 16-38-5.

South Carolina

- Privacy Right in State Constitution, Art. 1, § 10.
- Certain Criminal Records Must Be Destroyed if No Conviction Results, S.C. Code § 17-4.
- Privacy of Driver's License Data, S.C. Code § 3D-4-160.
- Confidentiality of Library Records, S.C. Code § 60-4-10.
- Wiretapping/Eavesdropping/Electronic Surveillance, S.C. Code §§ 16-17-470, 46-740.33.
- Privacy of Tax Records, S.C. Code § 12-7-1680. South Carolina Computer Crime Statute, S.C. Code § 16-16-10.
- Privacy and Security of Nonpublic Personal Information Collected and Maintained by Insurers (Implementing Requirements of Gramm-Leach-Bliley Act), S.C. Code §§ 30-2-30 *et seq.*, South Carolina Ins. Regs. §§ 69-58 *et seq.*
- Limits on Use of Polygraph Tests, S.C. Code § 40-53-180.

South Dakota

- South Dakota Computer Crime Statute, S.D. Cod. Laws Ann. § 43-43B-1.
- Right to Review Criminal Records, S.D. Cod. Laws Ann. § 23-5-12.
- Confidentiality of Library Records, S.D. Cod. Laws Ann. § 14-2-51.
- Privilege for Communications between Student and Counselor, S.D. Cod. Laws Ann. §§ 19-2-5.1, 19-2-5.2.
- Right of State Employees to Inspect Personnel Records, S.D. Cod. Laws Ann. § 3-6A-31.
- Wiretapping/Eavesdropping/Electronic Surveillance, S.D. Cod. Laws Ann. § 23A-35A-1.

- Privacy of Tax Records, S.D. Cod. Laws Ann. § 10-1-28.1. South Dakota Computer Hacking Statute, S.D. Cod. Laws Ann. § 43-43B-1.
- Privacy and Security of Nonpublic Personal Information Collected and Maintained by Insurers (Implementing Requirements of Gramm-Leach-Bliley Act), South Dakota Ins. Regs. §§ 20:06:45:01 *et seq.*
- Privacy Rights of Students or Parents, S.D. Cod. Laws §§ 19-2-5.1, 19-2-5.2.

Tennessee

- Petitions to Destroy Arrest Records, Tenn. Code Ann. § 40-32-101.
- Privacy of Criminal Records, Tenn. Code Ann. § 10-7-504.
- Confidentiality of Library Records, Tenn. Code Ann. § 10-8-101.
- Privacy of Student Records, Tenn. Code Ann. § 10-7-504.
- Right of State Employees to Inspect Personnel Records, Tenn. Code Ann. § 8-50-108.
- Wiretapping/Eavesdropping/Electronic Surveillance, Tenn. Code Ann. § 65-21-110.
- Privacy of Tax Records, Tenn. Code Ann. § 67-1-110(5). Tennessee Computer Crime Statute, Tenn. Code Ann. § 39-14-602.
- Tennessee "Must Shred" Statute, Tenn. Code Ann. § 39-14-150.
- Tennessee Data Security Breach Notification Statute, Tenn. Code Ann. § 47-18-2107.
- Tennessee Wiretapping Statute, Tenn. Code Ann. § 65-21-110.
- Telemarketing Statute, Tenn. Code Ann. §§ 65-4-405, 64-5-403, 47-18-1501, 47-18-1602, 39-6-1102.
- Privacy and Security of Nonpublic Personal Information Collected and Maintained by Insurers (Implementing Requirements of Gramm-Leach-Bliley Act), Tenn. Code Ann. §§ 56-8-119 *et seq.*, Tenn. Ins. Regs. §§ 0780-1-72.
- Genetic Testing, Discrimination and Other Privacy Restrictions, Tenn. Code Ann. § 56-7-2703.
- Limitations on Right to Demand Credit Card, Tenn. Code Ann. § 47-22-104.
- Patient Privacy Rights, Tenn. Code Ann. §§ 53-1322, 10-7-504, 24-1-207.
- Limits on Use of Polygraph Tests, Tenn. Code Ann. § 62-27-123.
- Privacy Rights of Students or Parents, Tenn. Code Ann. § 10-7-504.

Texas

- Texas Computer Crime Statute, Tex. Pen. Code Ann. § 3301.
- Security of Legislative Records, Tex. Civ. Stat. Ann. Art. 54296.
- Right to Review Criminal Records, Tex. Gov. Code § 552.023.
- Privacy of Student Records, Tex. Gov. Code § 552.114.
- Wiretapping/Eavesdropping/Electronic Surveillance, Tex. Pen. Code Ann. § 16.02; Tex. Rev. Stat. of Crim. Proc. §§ 18.20-18.21. Texas Computer Crime Statute, Tex. Pen. Code Ann. § 33.01.

- Texas "Must Shred" Statute, Tex. Bus. & Com. Code § 48-102.
- Texas Data Security Breach Notification Statute, Tex. Bus. & Com. Code § 48-103.
- Telemarketing Statute, 4 Tex. Bus. & Com. Code § 43.051, 43.101, 35.47.
- Privacy and Security of Nonpublic Personal Information Collected and Maintained by Insurers (Implementing Requirements of Gramm-Leach-Bliley Act), Tex. Ins. Regs. Tit. 28 §§ 22.1 *et seq.*
- Genetic Testing, Discrimination and Other Privacy Restrictions, Tex. Ins. Code Ann. Art. 21.73.
- Rights of Subjects of Credit Reports, Tex. Fin. Code § 391.002.
- Patient Privacy Rights, Tex. Health & Safety Code §§ 161.0213, 81-102.
- Limits on Use of Polygraph Tests, Tex. Occ. Code §§ 1703.351(a)(7)(B), 1703.204.
- Restrictions on Certain Tests, Tex. Labor Code § 24.402.
- Privacy Rights of Students or Parents, Tex. Gov. Code § 552.114.

Utah

- Provisions to Seal or Expunge Arrest Records, Utah Code Ann. §§ 77-18-9 to 14, 77-26-16.
- Privacy of Criminal Records, Utah Code Ann. § 53-5-214.
- Government Records Access and Management Act, Utah Code Ann. § 63-2-103.
- Right of State and Local Employees to Inspect Personnel Records, Utah Code Ann. § 67-18-1.
- Wiretapping/Eavesdropping/Electronic Surveillance, Utah Code Ann. §§ 76-9-401, 77-23a-1.
- Privacy of Tax Records, Utah Code Ann. § 59-1-403. Utah Computer Crime Statute, Utah Code Ann. § 76-6-701.
- Utah "Must Shred" Statute, Utah Code § 13-44-201.
- Utah Data Security Breach Notification Statute, Utah Code Ann. § 13-44-102.
- Telemarketing Statute, Utah Code Ann. §§13-25-1, 13-25a-103(6).
- Privacy and Security of Nonpublic Personal Information Collected and Maintained by Insurers (Implementing Requirements of Gramm-Leach-Bliley Act), Utah Code §§ 31A-23a-417 *et seq.*, Utah Ins. Regs. §§ R590-205-2.
- Rights of Subjects of Credit Reports, Utah Code Ann. § 70C-7-107.
- Patient Privacy Rights, Utah Code Ann. §§ 78-24-8(4), 78-25-25.
- Limits on Use of Polygraph Tests, Utah Code Ann. § 34-37-16.
- Restrictions on Certain Tests, Utah Code Ann. § 34-38-1.

Vermont

- Vermont Computer Crime Statute, 12 Vt. Stat. Ann. § 4101.
- Confidentiality of Library Records, 1 Vt. Stat. Ann. § 317(b)(19).
- Confidentiality of Student Records, 1 Vt. Stat. Ann. § 317(11).

- Right of State Employee to Inspect Personnel File, 1 Vt. Stat. Ann. § 317(b)(7).
- Privacy of Tax Records, 32 Vt. Stat. Ann. § 3102. Vermont Computer Crime Statute, 13 Vt. Stat. § 4101.
- Vermont "Must-Shred" Statute, 9 Vt. Stat. § 2445.
- Vermont Security Breach Notification, 9 Vt. Stat. § 2435.
- Privacy and Security of Nonpublic Personal Information Collected and Maintained by Insurers (Implementing Requirements of Gramm-Leach-Bliley Act), 8 Vt. Stat. §§ 10201 *et seq.*
- Genetic Testing, Discrimination and Other Privacy Restrictions, 18 Vt. Stat. § 9334.
- Rights of Subjects of Credit Reports, 9 Vt. Stat. § 2480b and 2480e.
- Patient Privacy Rights, 12 Vt. Stat. § 1608.
- Limits on Use of Polygraph Tests, 21 Vt. Stat. § 5a.
- Restrictions on Certain Tests, 18 Vt. Stat. §§ 9333, 21 Vt. Stat. § 51, 21 Vt. Stat. § 495.
- Privacy Rights of Students or Parents, 1 Vt. Stat. § 317(11).

Virginia

- Petitions to Seal Criminal Records, Va. Code § 19.2-392.4(a) and (c).
- Adverse employer action may not be taken on basis of certain arrest information, *id.*
- Privacy of Criminal Records, Va. Code §§ 9-192 and 19.2-309.
- Privacy Protection Act for State Agencies, Va. Code § 2.1-377.
- Confidentiality of Library Records, Va. Code § 2.1-342(b)(8).
- Use of Social Security Number for Drivers' Licensing, Va. Code §§ 46.2-323, 46.2-342.
- Demanding Disclosure of Social Security Number as Condition of Participation in Activity or Acquisition of Good or Service, Va. Code § 2.1-385.
- Privacy of Student Records, Va. Code § 2.1-342(b)(3).
- Wiretapping/Eavesdropping/Electronic Surveillance, Va. Code § 19.2-61.
- Privacy of Tax Records, Va. Code §§ 58-46, 2.1-342(B)(3). Virginia Computer Crime Statute, Va. Code § 18.2-152.2.
- Surreptitious Videotaping, Va. Code § 181.2-386.
- Telemarketing Statute, Va. Code § 18.2-425.1, 29.1-513.
- Privacy and Security of Nonpublic Personal Information Collected and Maintained by Insurers (Implementing Requirements of Gramm-Leach-Bliley Act), Va. Code §§ 38.2-221.2 *et seq.*
- Genetic Testing, Discrimination and Other Privacy Restrictions, Va. Code § 38.2-613.
- Rights of Subjects of Credit Reports, Va. Code §§ 38.1-52(11), 6.1-366.
- Limitations on Right to Demand Credit Card Data, Va. Code § 62.A-512.
- Patient Privacy Rights, Va. Code §§ 32.1-127.1:03, 8.01-413, 32.1-36.1, 8.01-399, 2.1-342(b).

- Restrictions on Certain Tests, Va. Code §§ 32.1-36.1, 32.1-37.2.
- Privacy Rights of Students or Parents, Va. Code § 2.1-342(b)(3).

Washington

- Privacy Right in State Constitution, Art. I, § 7.
- Petition for Destruction of Criminal Records, Wash. Rev. Code Ann. § 43.43.730.
- Privacy of Criminal Records, Wash. Rev. Code Ann. §§ 43.43.710, 43.43.810.
- State Agency Information Practices, Wash. Rev. Code Ann. § 43.105.070.
- Confidentiality of Library Records, Wash. Rev. Code Ann. § 42.17.310(1).
- Privacy of Student Records, Wash. Rev. Code Ann. § 42.17.310.
- Right of Employees to Inspect Personnel Files, Wash. Rev. Code Ann. § 49.12.250.
- Wiretapping/Eavesdropping/Electronic Surveillance, Wash. Rev. Code Ann. § 9.73.030.
- Privacy of Tax Records, Wash. Rev. Code Ann. § 42.17.310(1)(c). Washington Computer Crime Statute, Wash. Rev. Code §§ 9A.52.110, 9A.52.120.
- Washington "Must Shred" Statute, Rev. Code Wash. § 19.215.020.
- Washington Data Security Breach Notification Statute, Rev. Code Wash. § 19.255.010.
- Telemarketing Statute, Rev. Code Wash. § 80.36.390.400.
- Employee Rights in Employment Records, Rev. Code Wash. § 49.12.250.
- Privacy and Security of Nonpublic Personal Information Collected and Maintained by Insurers (Implementing Requirements of Gramm-Leach-Bliley Act), WAC §§ 284-04-120.
- Rights of Subjects of Credit Reports, Rev. Code Wash. § 19.182.090.
- Limitations on Right to Demand Credit Card, Rev. Code Wash. § 62.A-512.
- Patient Privacy Rights, Rev. Code Wash. §§ 70.02.020-030, 70.170.010, 5.60.050.
- Limits on Use of Polygraph Tests, Rev. Code Wash. § 49.44.120.
- Restrictions on Certain Tests, Rev. Code Wash. § 49.60.172.
- Privacy Rights of Students or Parents, Rev. Code Wash. §42.17.310.

West Virginia

- Certain records and items must be returned on acquittal, W.Va. Code § 15-2-24(h).
- Right to Inspect Criminal Records, W.Va. Code § 29B1-3.
- Confidentiality of Library Records, W.Va. Code § 10-1-22.
- Wiretapping/Eavesdropping/Electronic Surveillance, W. Va. Code § 62-1D-1.
- Privacy of Tax Records, W. Va. Code § 11-10-5. West Virginia Computer Crime Statute, W.Va. Code §§ 61-3c-4 to 12.
- Privacy and Security of Nonpublic Personal Information Collected and Maintained by Insurers (Implementing Requirements of Gramm-Leach-Bliley Act), West Virginia Ins. Regs. §§ 114-57-1 *et seq.*

- AIDS Discrimination, W. Va. Code §§ 33-15-13 and 33-16-9.
- Patient Privacy Rights, W. Va. Code, §§ 50-6-10, 33-15-13, 33-16-9.
- Limits on Use of Polygraph Tests, W. Va. Code, § 21-5-5a.

Wisconsin

- Restrictions on Employer Inquiries into Arrest Records, Wis. Stat. Ann. § 111.335.
- Right to Inspect Criminal Records, Wis. Stat. Ann. § 19.35(1)(a).
- Information Practices of State Agencies, Wis. Stat. Ann. §§ 19.69 and 19.365.
- Confidentiality of Library Records, Wis. Stat. Ann. § 43.30.
- Use of Social Security Number as Identifier by Schools and Universities, Wis. Stat. Ann. § 118.169.
- Privacy of Student Records, Wis. Stat. Ann. § 118.125.
- Employees' Right to Inspect Personnel Records, Wis. Stat. Ann. § 103.13.
- Limits on Surveillance of State Health Care Workers, § Wis. Stat. Ann. § 230.86.
- Wiretapping/Eavesdropping/Electronic Surveillance, Wis. Stat. Ann. §§ 968.27, 230.86.
- Privacy of Tax Records, Wis. Stat. Ann. § 71.78. Wisconsin Computer Crime Statute, Wis. Stat. § 943.70.
- Wisconsin "Must Shred" Statute, Wis. Stat. § 895.505.
- Wisconsin Security Breach Notification Statute, Wis. Stat. § 859.507.
- Telemarketing Statute, Wis. Stat. §§ 134.72, 196-207.
- Employee Rights in Employment Records, Wis. Stat. § 103.13.
- Privacy and Security of Nonpublic Personal Information Collected and Maintained by Insurers (Implementing Requirements of Gramm-Leach-Bliley Act), Wis. Ins. Regs. §§ 25.02 *et seq.*
- Genetic Testing, Discrimination and Other Privacy Restrictions, Wis. Stat. § 631.89.
- Customer Privacy Rights and Requirements, Cable Television Operators, Wis. Stat. § 134.42, § 968.27(1)
- Limitations on Right to Demand Credit Card, Wis. Stat. §§ 423.402, 423.401.
- Patient Privacy Rights, Wis. Stat. §§ 146.82, 146.83, 146.025, 885.21.
- Limits on Use of Polygraph Tests, Wis. Stat. §§ 111.37, 942.06.
- Restrictions on Certain Tests, Wis. Stat. §§ 111.372, 111.39, 103.15.
- Privacy Rights of Students or Parents, Wis. Stat. § 118.125.

Wyoming

- Wyoming Computer Crime Statute, Wyo. Stat. § 6-3-501 to 504.
- Right to Inspect Criminal Records, Wyo. Stat. § 7-19-109.
- Confidentiality of Library Records, Wyo. Stat. § 16-4-203(d).

- Wiretapping/Eavesdropping/Electronic Surveillance, Wyo. Stat. §§ 7-3-601 through 7-3-611. Wyoming Computer Crime Statute, Wyo. Stat. §§ 6-3-501 to 6-3-504.
- Privacy and Security of Nonpublic Personal Information Collected and Maintained by Insurers (Implementing Requirements of Gramm-Leach-Bliley Act), Wyo. Stat. §§ 26-2-133, Wyo. Ins. Regs. ch. 054.
- Patient Privacy Rights, Wyo. Stat. § 1-139(1).

District of Columbia

- D.C. employment records must be maintained in a way that protects the privacy of applicants and employees, D.C. Code Ann. § 1-632.1.
- Confidentiality of Library Records, D.C. Code Ann. § 37-106.2.
- Wiretapping/Eavesdropping/Electronic Surveillance, D.C. Code Ann. § 23-541. D.C. employment records must be maintained in a way that protects the privacy of applicants and employees, D.C. Code Ann. § 1-632.1.
- Privacy and Security of Nonpublic Personal Information Collected and Maintained by Insurers (Implementing Requirements of Gramm-Leach-Bliley Act), D.C. Code Ann. § 26-3622.
- D.C. Data Security Breach Notification Regulation, 54 D.C. Reg. 393.

APPENDIX B

Key Provisions of State Secure Disposal Laws, Data Security Laws, and Data Security Breach Notification Laws

1. State Secure Disposal Statutes

A number of state laws require the proper disposal of records that contain personal information. At this writing, 26 such statutes are on the books. Excerpts from those statutes are set out below.

Arizona

"An entity shall not knowingly discard or dispose of records or documents without redacting the information or destroying the records or documents if the records or documents contain an individual's first and last name or first initial and last in combination with a corresponding complete:

1. Social security number.
2. Credit card, charge card or debit card number.
3. Retirement account number.
4. Savings, checking or securities entitlement account number.
4. Driver license number or nonoperating identification license number."

A.R.S. § 44-7601(A).

"This section applies only to paper records and paper documents."

A.R.S. § 44-7601(F).

"For the purposes of this section, 'entity' includes a corporation, foreign corporation, not for profit corporation, profit and not for profit unincorporated association, nonprofit corporation, sole proprietorship, close corporation, corporation sole or limited liability company, a professional corporation, association or limited liability company, a business trust, estate, partnership, registered limited liability partnership, trust or joint venture, government, governmental subdivision or agency or any other legal or commercial entity."

A.R.S. § 44-7601(G).

Arkansas

"A person or business shall take all reasonable steps to destroy or arrange for the destruction of a customer's records within its custody or control containing personal information that is no longer to be retained by the person or business by shredding, erasing, or otherwise modifying the personal information in the records to make it unreadable or undecipherable through any means." A.C.A. §4-110-104(a).

"A person or business that acquires, owns, or licenses personal information about an Arkansas resident shall implement and maintain reasonable security procedures and practices appropriate to the nature of the information to protect the personal information from unauthorized access, destruction, use, modification, or disclosure." *Id.* §4-110-104(b).

" 'Business' means a sole proprietorship, partnership, corporation, association, or other group, however organized and whether or not organized to operate at a profit, including a financial institution organized, chartered, or holding a license or authorization certificate under the law of this state, any other state, the United States, or of any other country or the parent or subsidiary of a financial institution." *Id.* §4-110-103(2)(A).

" 'Business' includes:

(i) An entity that destroys records; and
(ii) A state agency." *Id.* §4-110-103(2)(B).

" 'Owns or licenses' includes, but is not limited to, personal information that a business retains as part of the internal customer account of the business or for the purpose of using the information in transactions with the person to whom the information relates." *Id.* §4-110-103(6).

" 'Personal information' means an individual's first name or first initial and his or her last name in combination with any one (1) or more of the following data elements when either the name or the data element is not encrypted or redacted:

(A) Social security number;
(B) Driver's license number or Arkansas identification card number;
(C) Account number, credit card number, or debit card number in combination with any required security code, access code, or password that would permit access to an individual's financial account; and
(D) Medical information."

Id. §4-110-103(7).

California

"A business shall take all reasonable steps to destroy, or arrange for the destruction of a customer's records within its custody or control containing personal information which is no longer to be retained by the business by (1) shredding, (2) erasing, or (3) otherwise modifying the personal information in those records to make it unreadable or undecipherable through any means." Cal. Civ. Code §1798.81.

" 'Business' means a sole proprietorship, partnership, corporation, association, or other group, however organized and whether or not organized to operate at a profit, including a financial institution organized, chartered, or holding a license or authorization certificate under the law of this state, or any other state, the United States, or of any other country, or the parent or subsidiary of a financial institution. The term includes an entity that destroys records." *Id.* §1798.80(a).

" 'Personal information' means any information that identifies, relates to, describes, or is capable of being associated with, a particular individual, including, but not limited to, his or her name, signature, social security number, physical characteristics or description, address, telephone number, passport number, driver's license or state identification card number, insurance policy number, education, employment, employment history, bank account number, credit card number, debit card number, or any other financial information." *Id.* §1798.80(e).

Colorado

"Each public and private entity in the state that uses documents during the course of business that contain personal identifying information shall develop a policy for the destruction or proper disposal of paper documents containing personal identifying information." C.R.S. 6-1-713(1).

"Unless an entity specifically contracts with a recycler or disposal firm for destruction of documents that contain personal identifying information, nothing herein shall require a recycler or disposal firm to verify that the documents contained in the products it receives for disposal or recycling have been properly destroyed or disposed of as required by this section." *Id.* §6-1-713(4).

"For the purpose of this section, 'personal identifying information' means: A social security number; a personal identification number; a password; a pass code; an official state or government-issued driver's license or identification card number; biometric data; an employer, student, or military identification number; or a financial transaction device." *Id.* 6-1-713(2).

Connecticut

"A business shall take all reasonable steps to destroy or arrange for the destruction of a customer's records within its custody or control containing personal information which is no longer to be retained by the business, by shredding, erasing or otherwise modifying the personal information in those records to make it unreadable or indecipherable through any means . . ."

Conn. House Bill 5694, § 1(b).

" 'Business' means a sole proprietorship, partnership, corporation, association, limited liability company or other entity, whether or not organized to operate for profit, including, but not limited to, a financial institution organized or chartered, or holding a license or authorization to conduct business under the laws of this state, any other state, the United States or any other country, or the parent, affiliate or a subsidiary of such financial institution."

Id. § 1(a)(1).

" 'Personal information' means the following information that identifies, relates to, describes, or is capable of being associated with a particular individual:

(A) Signature, (B) Social Security number, (C) physical characteristics or description, (D) passport number, (E) driver's license or state identification card number, (F) insurance policy number, (G) bank account number, (H) credit or debit card number, or (I) individual financial information. "

Id. § 1(a)(3).

" 'Customer' means a person who provides personal information to a business for the purpose of purchasing or leasing a product or obtaining a service from such business."

Id. § 1(a)(2).

" 'Record' means any material, regardless of physical form, on which information is recorded or preserved by any means, including in written or spoken words, graphically depicted, printed or electromagnetically transmitted. 'Record' does not include publicly available directories containing information a person has voluntarily consented to have publicly disseminated or listed, such as name, address or telephone number." *Id.* § 1(a)(4).

"A disposal business that conducts business in this state or disposes of personal information of residents of this state shall take all reasonable measures to dispose of records containing personal information by implementing and monitoring compliance with policies and procedures that protect against unauthorized access to or use of personal information during or after the collection and transportation and disposal of such information."

Id. § 1(c).

Georgia

"A business may not discard a record containing personal information unless it:

(1) Shreds the customer's record before discarding the records;
(2) Erases the personal information contained in the customer's record before discarding the record;
(3) Modifies the customer's record to make the personal information unreadable before discarding the record; or
(4) Takes actions that it reasonably believes will ensure that no unauthorized person will have access to the personal information contained in the customer's record for the period between the record's disposal and the record's destruction." O.C.G.A. §10-15-2.

" 'Business' means a sole proprietorship, partnership, corporation, association, or other group, however organized and whether or not organized to operate at a profit. The term includes a financial institution organized, chartered, or holding a license or authorization certificate under the laws of this state, any other state, the United States, or any other country, or the parent or subsidiary of any such financial institution. The term also includes an entity that destroys records. However, the term shall not include any bank or financial institution that is subject to the privacy and security provisions of the Gramm-Leach-Bliley Act . . . , nor shall it include any hospital or health care institution licensed under Title 31 which is subject to the privacy and security provisions of [HIPAA], nor any other entity which is governed by federal law, provided that the federal law governing the business requires the business to discard a record containing personal information in the same manner as Code Section 10-15-2." *Id.* §10-15-1(2).

" 'Discard' means to throw away, get rid of, eliminate." *Id.* §10-15-1(5).

" 'Dispose' means the sale or transfer of a record for value to a company or business engaged in the business of record destruction." *Id.* §10-15-1(6).

" 'Personal information' means:

(A) Personally identifiable data about a customer's medical condition, if the data are not generally considered to be public knowledge;
(B) Personally identifiable data which contain a customer's account or identification number, account balance, balance owing, credit balance, or credit limit, if the data relate to a customer's account or transaction with a business;
(C) Personally identifiable data provided by a customer to a business on opening an account or applying for a loan or credit; or
(D) Personally identifiable data about a customer's federal, state, or local income tax return." *Id.* §10-15-1(9).

" 'Personally identifiable' means capable of being associated with a particular customer through one or more identifiers, including, but not limited to, a customer's fingerprint, photograph, or computerized image, social security number, passport number, driver identification number, personal identification card number, date of birth, medical information, or disability information." *Id.* §10-15-1(10)(A).

"A customer's name, address, and telephone number shall not be considered personally identifiable data unless one or more of them are used in conjunction with one or more of the identifiers listed in subparagraph (A) of this paragraph." *Id.* §10-15-1(10)(B).

" 'Customer' means an individual who provides personal information to a business for the purpose of purchasing or leasing a product or obtaining a service from the business." *Id.* §10-15-1(4).

Hawaii

"Any business or government agency that conducts business in Hawaii and any business or government agency that maintains or otherwise possesses personal information of a resident of Hawaii shall take reasonable measures to protect against unauthorized access to or use of the information in connection with or after its disposal.

(b) The reasonable measures shall include:
(1) Implementing and monitoring compliance with policies and procedures that require the burning, pulverizing, recycling, or shredding of papers containing personal information so that information cannot be practicably read or reconstructed;
(2) Implementing and monitoring compliance with policies and procedures that require the destruction or erasure of electronic media and other nonpaper media

containing personal information so that the information cannot practicably be read or reconstructed; and
(3) Describing procedures relating to the adequate destruction or proper disposal of personal records as official policy in the writings of the business entity.
(c) A business or government agency may satisfy its obligation hereunder by exercising due diligence and entering into a written contract with, and thereafter monitoring compliance by, another party engaged in the business of record destruction to destroy personal information in a manner consistent with this section. Due diligence should ordinarily include one or more of the following:
(1) Reviewing an independent audit of the disposal business's operations or its compliance with this statute or its equivalent;
(2) Obtaining information about the disposal business from several references or other reliable sources and requiring that the disposal business be certified by a recognized trade association or similar third party with a reputation for high standards of quality review; or
(3) Reviewing and evaluating the disposal business's information security policies or procedures, or taking other appropriate measures to determine the competency and integrity of the disposal business."

Hawaii Senate Bill No. 2292, § 2, effective Jan. 1, 2007.

" 'Business' means a sole proprietorship, partnership, corporation, association, or other group, however organized and whether or not organized to operate at a profit. Except as provided in section ____-2(e) [sic], the term includes a financial institution organized, chartered, or holding a license or authorization certificate under the laws of the State, any other state, the United States, or any other country, or the parent or the subsidiary of any such financial institution. The term also includes an entity whose business is records destruction.

'Disposal' means the discarding or abandonment of records containing personal information or the sale, donation, discarding, or transfer of any medium, including computer equipment or computer media, containing records of personal information, or other nonpaper media on which records of personal information are stored, or other equipment for nonpaper storage of information.

'Government agency' means any department, division, board, commission, public corporation, or other agency or instrumentality of the State or any county.

'Personal information' means an individual's first name or first initial and last name in combination with any one or more of the following data elements, when either the name or the data elements are not encrypted:

(1) Social security number;
(2) Driver's license number or Hawaii identification card number; or
(3) Account number, credit or debit card number, access code, or password that would permit access to an individual's financial account.

'Personal information' shall not include publicly available information that is lawfully made available to the general public from federal, state, or local government records.

'Records' means any material on which written, drawn, spoken, visual, or electromagnetic information is recorded or preserved, regardless of physical form or characteristics."

Id. § 1.

"(d) A disposal business that conducts business in Hawaii or disposes of personal information of residents of Hawaii shall take reasonable measures to dispose of records containing personal information by implementing and monitoring compliance with policies and procedures that protect against unauthorized access to, or use of, personal information during or after the collection, transportation, and disposing of such information."

Id. § 2.

Illinois

Illinois has enacted a criminal statute that makes it an offense, with intent to facilitate identity theft, to dispose of personal information without shredding the record in which it is contained or otherwise making it unintelligible to unauthorized persons.

"A person commits the offense of facilitating identity theft when he or she, in the course of his or her employment or official duties, has access to the personal information of another person in the possession of the State of Illinois, whether written, recorded, or on computer disk and knowingly, with the intent of committing identity theft, aggravated identity theft, or any violation of the Illinois Financial Crime Law, disposes of that written, recorded, or computerized information in any receptacle, trash can, or other container that the public could gain access to, without shredding that information, destroying the recording, or wiping the computer disk so that the information is either unintelligible or destroyed."

720 ILCS 5/16G-21

Indiana

"Chapter 14. Persons Holding a Customer's Personal Information

Sec. 1. This chapter does not apply to the following:

(1) The executive, judicial, or legislative department of State government or any political subdivision.
(2) A unit (as defined in IC 36-1-2-23).
(3) The Office of County Auditor.
(4) The Office of County Treasurer.
(5) The Office of County Recorder.
(6) The Office of County Surveyor.
(7) A County Sheriff's Department.
(8) The Office of County Coroner.
(9) The Office of County Assessor.

(10) A person who engages in the business of waste collection, except to the extent the person holds a customer's personal information directly in connection with the business of waste collection.
(11) A person who maintains and complies with a disposal program under:
   (A) The Federal USA PATRIOT Act (P.L. 107-56);
   (B) Executive Order 13224;
   (C) The Federal Driver's Privacy Protection Act (18 U.S.C. 2721 *et seq.*);
   (D) The Federal Fair Credit Reporting Act (15 U.S.C. sec. 1681 *et seq.*);
   (E) The Federal Financial Modernization Act of 1999 (15 U.S.C. sec. 6801 *et seq.*):
   (F) The Federal Health Insurance Portability and Accountability Act (HIPAA) (P.L. 104-191).

Sec. 2. As used in this chapter, "customer" means a person who:

(1) has received or contracted for the direct or indirect provision of goods or services from another person holding the person's personal information; or
(2) provides the person's personal information to another person in connection with a transaction with a nonprofit corporation or charitable organization.
The term includes a person who pays a commission, a consignment fee, or another fee contingent on the completion of a transaction.

Sec. 3. As used in this chapter, 'dispose of' means to discard or abandon the personal information of a customer in an area accessible to the public. The term includes placing the personal information in a container for trash collection.

Sec. 4. For purposes of this chapter, personal information is 'encrypted' if the personal information:

(1) has been transformed through the use of an algorithmic process into a form in which there is a low probability of assigning meaning without a confidential process or key; or
(2) is secured by another method that renders the personal information unreadable or unusable.

Sec. 5. As used in this chapter, 'person' means an individual, a partnership, a corporation, a limited liability company, or another organization.

Sec. 6. As used in this chapter, 'personal information' has the meaning set forth in IC 24-4.9-2-10. The term includes information stored in a digital format.

Sec. 7(A). For purposes of this chapter, personal information is 'redacted' if the personal information has been altered or truncated so that not more than the last four (4) digits of:
(1) a driver's license number;
(2) a state identification number; or
(3) an account number; is accessible as part of personal information.
(B) For purposes of this chapter, personal information is 'redacted' if the personal information has been altered or truncated so that not more than five (5) digits of a Social Security number are accessible as part of personal information.

Sec. 8. A person who disposes of the unencrypted, unredacted personal information of a customer without shredding, incinerating, mutilating, erasing, or otherwise rendering the information illegible or unusable commits a Class C infraction. However, the offense is a Class A infraction if:

(1) the person violates this section by disposing of the unencrypted, unredacted personal information of more than one hundred (100) customers, or
(2) the person has a prior unrelated judgment for a violation of this section."
Indiana 114th General Assembly, Second Regular Session, House Enrolled Act No. 1101; codified at Burns Ind. Code Ann. § 24-4-14-1.

Kansas

"Unless otherwise required by federal law or regulation, a person or business shall take reasonable steps to destroy or arrange for the destruction of a customer's records within its custody or control containing personal information which is no longer to be retained by the person or business by shredding, erasing or otherwise modifying the personal information in the records to make it unreadable or undecipherable through any means."

Kansas 81st Legislature, 2005 Regular Session, Senate Bill 196.

" 'Personal information' means a consumer's first name or first initial and last name linked to any one or more of the following data elements that relate to the consumer, when the data elements are neither encrypted nor redacted:

(1) Social Security number;
(2) driver's license number or state identification number; or
(3) financial account number, or credit or debit card number, alone or in combination with any required security code, access code or password that would permit access to a consumer's financial account. The term 'personal information' does not include publicly available information that is lawfully made available to the general public from federal, state or local government records." *Id.*

" 'Encrypted' means transformation of data through the use of algorithmic process into a form in which there is a low probability of assigning meaning without the use of a confidential process or key, or securing the information by another method that renders the data elements unreadable or unusable."

Id.

" 'Redact' means alteration or truncation of data such that no more than the following are accessible as part of the personal information:

(1) Five digits of a Social Security number; or
(3) the last four digits of a driver's license number, state identification card number or account number."

Id.

Kentucky

"When a business disposes of, other than by storage, any customer's records that are not required to be retained, the business shall take reasonable steps to destroy, or arrange for the destruction of, that portion of the records containing personally identifiable information by shredding, erasing, or otherwise modifying the personal information in those records to make it unreadable or indecipherable through any means."

KRS § 365.725(5).

" 'Business' means a sole proprietorship, partnership, corporation, limited liability company, association, or other entity, however organized, and whether or not organized to operate at a profit . . . The term includes an entity that destroys records."

KRS § 365.720.

" 'Personally identifiable information' means data capable of being associated with a particular customer through one (1) or more identifiers, including but not limited to a customer's name, address, telephone number, electronic mail address, fingerprints, photographs or computerized image, social security number, passport number, driver identification number, personal identification card number or code, date of birth, medical information, financial information, tax information, and disability information."

Id.

" 'Records' means any material, regardless of the physical form, on which information is recorded or preserved by any means, including in written or spoken words, graphically depicted, printed, or electromagnetically transmitted."

Id.

Maryland

Excerpts from Personal Information Protection Act

(B) (1) "Business" means a sole proprietorship, partnership, corporation, association, or any other business entity, whether or not organized to operate at a profit.
(2) "Business" includes a financial institution organized, chartered, licensed, or otherwise authorized under the laws of this state, any other state, the United States, or any other country, and the parent or subsidiary of a financial institution.
(3) "Business" does not include an entity that has an annual gross income of less than $1,000,000.
(C) "Encrypted" means the transformation of data through the use of an algorithmic process into a form in which there is a low probability of assigning meaning without use of a confidential process or key.
(C) (D) (1) "Personal information" means an individual's first name or first initial and last name in combination with any one or more of the following data elements,

when the name or the data elements are not encrypted, redacted, or otherwise protected by another method that renders the information unreadable or unusable:
(I) a Social Security number;
(II) a driver's license number; or
(III) a financial account number, including a credit card number or debit card number, that in combination with any required security code, access code, or password, would permit access to an individual's financial account; or
(IV) an individual taxpayer identification number; or
(IV) a consumer report, as defined in Section 14-1201 of this title.
(2) "Personal information" does not include:
(I) publicly available information that is lawfully made available to the general public from federal, state, or local government records;
(II) information that an individual has consented to have publicly disseminated or listed; or
(III) information that is disseminated or listed in accordance with the Federal Health Insurance Portability and Accountability Act.
(D) (E) "Records" means information that is inscribed on a tangible medium or that is stored in an electronic medium and is retrievable in perceivable form.

14-3502.

(A) In this section, "Customer" means an individual residing in the State who provides personal information to a business for the purpose of purchasing or leasing a product or obtaining a service from the business.
(B) When a business is destroying a customer's records that contain personal information of the customer, the business shall take reasonable steps to protect against unauthorized access to or use of the personal information, taking into account:
(1) the sensitivity of the records;
(2) the nature and size of the business and its operations;
(3) the costs and benefits of different destruction methods; and
(4) available technology.

14-3503.

(A) To protect personal information from unauthorized access, use, modification, or disclosure, a business that owns or licenses personal information of an individual residing in the State shall implement and maintain reasonable security procedures and practices that are appropriate to the nature of the personal information owned or licensed and the nature and size of the business and its operations.
(B) (1) A business that uses a nonaffiliated third party as a service provider to perform services for the business and discloses personal information about an individual residing in the State under a written contract with the third party shall require by contract that the third party implement and maintain reasonable security procedures and practices that:
(I) are appropriate to the nature of the personal information disclosed to the nonaffiliated third party; and
(II) are reasonably designed to help protect the personal information from unauthorized access, use, modification, disclosure, or destruction.

(2) This subsection shall apply to a written contract that is entered into on or after January 1, 2009.
A violation of this subtitle:
(1) is an unfair or deceptive trade practice within the meaning of Title 13 of this Article; and
(2) is subject to the enforcement and penalty provisions contained in Title 13 of this Article.

SECTION 2. AND BE IT FURTHER ENACTED, That this Act shall take effect January 1, 2008.

Michigan

Michigan's Senate Bill 309, summarized here, was signed by Governor Granholm on January 3, 2007, and took effect 180 days after that date.

"A person or agency that maintains a database that includes personal information regarding multiple individuals shall destroy any data that contain personal information concerning an individual when that data is removed from the database and that person or agency is not retaining the data elsewhere for another purpose not prohibited by state or federal law."

MCL § 445.72a.

"As used in this section, 'destroy' means to destroy or arrange for the destruction of data by shredding, erasing, or otherwise modifying the data so that they cannot be read, deciphered, or reconstructed through generally available means."

MCL § 445.63.

" 'Data' means computerized personal information."

Id.

" 'Personal identifying information' means a name, number, or other information that is used for the purpose of identifying a specific person or providing access to a person's financial accounts, including, but not limited to, a person's name, address, telephone number, driver license or state personal identification card number, social security number, place of employment, employee identification number, employer or taxpayer identification number, government passport number, health insurance identification number, mother's maiden name, demand deposit account number, savings account number, financial transaction device account number or the person's account password, stock or other record, or medical records or information."

Id.

" 'Personal information' means the first name or first initial and last name linked to one or more of the following data elements of a resident of this state:

(i) Social Security number.

(ii) Driver license number or state personal identification card number.

(iii) Demand deposit or other financial account number, or credit card or debit card number, in combination with any required security code, access code, or password that would permit access to any of the resident's financial accounts."

Id.

Minnesota

"When not public data is being disposed of, the data must be destroyed in a way that prevents its contents from being determined."

Minn. Stat. § 13.05(5)(b).

Montana

"A business shall take all reasonable steps to destroy or arrange for the destruction of a customer's record within its custody or control containing personal information that is no longer necessary to be retained by the business by shredding, erasing, or otherwise modifying the personal information in those records to make it unreadable or undecipherable."

Mont. Code Anno. §30-14-1703.

" 'Business' means sole proprietorship, partnership, corporation, association, or other group, however organized and whether or not organized to operate at a profit, including a financial institution organized, chartered, or holding a license or authorization certificate under the law of this state, any other state, the United States, or any other country or the parent or subsidiary of a financial institution. The term includes an entity that destroys records. The term also includes industries regulated by the Public Service Commission or under Title 30, chapter 10."

Id. §30-14-1702(1)(a).

" 'Personal information' means an individual's name, signature, address, or telephone number, in combination with one or more additional pieces of information about the individual, consisting of the individual's passport number, driver's license or state identification number, insurance policy number, bank account number, credit card number, debit card number, passwords or personal identification numbers required to obtain access to the individual's finances, or any other financial information as provided by rule. A social security record, in and of itself, constitutes personal information."

Id. §30-14-1702(4).

Nevada

"Sec. 22. 1. A business that maintains records which contain personal information concerning the customers of the business shall take reasonable measures to ensure the destruction of those records when the business decides that it will no longer maintain the records.

2. As used in this section:
(A) 'Business' means a proprietorship, corporation, partnership, association, trust, unincorporated organization or other enterprise doing business in this State.
(B) 'Reasonable measures to ensure the destruction' means any method that modifies the records containing the personal information in such a way as to render the personal information contained in the records unreadable or undecipherable, including, without limitation:
(1) shredding of the record containing the personal information; or
(3) erasing of the personal information from the records."

Nevada 73rd Regular Session, Senate Bill 347; Nev. Rev. Stat. Ann. § 603A.200.

"Sec. 21. 'Personal information' means a natural person's first name or first initial and last name in combination with any one or more of the following data elements, when the name and data elements are not encrypted:

1. Social Security number of employer identification number.
2. Driver's license number or identification card number.
3. Account number, credit card number or debit card number, in combination with any required security code, access code or password that would permit access to the person's financial account.

The term does not include publicly available information that is lawfully made available to the general public."

Id.

New Jersey

"A business or public entity shall destroy, or arrange for the destruction of, a customer's records within its custody or control containing personal information, which is no longer to be retained by the business or public entity, by shredding, erasing, or otherwise modifying the personal information in those records to make it unreadable, undecipherable or nonreconstructable through generally available means."

N.J. Stat. §56:8-162.

" 'Business' means a sole proprietorship, partnership, corporation, association, or other entity, however organized and whether or not organized to operate at a profit, including a financial institution organized, chartered, or holding a license or authorization certificate under the law of this State, any other state, the United States, or of any other country, or the parent or subsidiary of a financial institution."

Id. §56:8-161.

" 'Personal information' means an individual's first name or first initial and last name linked with any one or more of the following data elements: (1) Social Security number; (2) Driver's license number or State identification card number; or (3) account number or credit or debit card number, in combination with any required security code, access code, or password that would permit access to an individual's financial account. Dissociated data that, if linked, would constitute personal information is personal information if the means to link the dissociated data were accessed in connection with access to the dissociated data."

Id.

" 'Public entity' includes the State, and any county, municipality, district, public authority, public agency, and any other political subdivision or public body in the State."

Id.

New York

"A business, firm, partnership, association, corporation, or business person may not dispose of a record containing personal identifying information unless the business, firm, partnership, association, corporation, or business person, or other person under contract with the business, firm, partnership, association, corporation, or any business person does any of the following:

a. shreds the record before the disposal of the records; or
b. destroys the personal identifying information contained in the record; or
c. modifies the record to make the personal identifying information unreadable; or
d. takes actions consistent with commonly accepted industry practices that it reasonably believes will ensure that no unauthorized person will have access to the personal identifying information contained in the record."

NY CLS Gen Bus § 399-h(2).

" 'Record' means any information kept, held, filed, produced or reproduced by, with or for a person or business entity, in any physical form whatsoever including, but not limited to, reports, statements, examinations, memoranda, opinions, folders, files, books, manuals, pamphlets, forms, papers, designs, drawings, maps, photos, letter, microfilms, or computer tapes or disks . . ."

Id. § 399-h(b).

" 'Personal information' shall mean any information concerning a natural person which, because of name, number, personal mark, or other identifier, can be used to identify such person . . ."

Id. § 399-h(c).

" 'Personal identifying information' shall mean personal information consisting of any information in combination with any one or more of the following data elements, when either the personal information or the data element is not encrypted, or encrypted with an encryption key that is included in the same record as the encrypted personal information or data element:

(i) social security number;

(ii) driver's license number or non-driver identification card number; or
(iii) mother's maiden name, financial services account number or code, savings account number or code, checking account number or code, debit card number or code, automated teller machine number or code, electronic serial number or personal identification number . . ."

Id. § 399-h(d).

North Carolina

"Any business that conducts business in North Carolina and any business that maintains or otherwise possesses personal information of a resident of North Carolina must take reasonable measures to protect against unauthorized access to or use of the information in connection with or after its disposal."

N.C. Gen. Stat. §75.64(a).

"The reasonable measures must include:

(1) Implementing and monitoring compliance with policies and procedures that require the burning, pulverizing, or shredding of papers containing personal information so that the information cannot practicably be read or reconstructed.
(2) Implementing and monitoring compliance with policies and procedures that require the destruction or erasure of electronic media and other nonpaper media containing personal information so that the information cannot practicably be read or reconstructed.
(4) Describing procedures relating to the adequate destruction or proper disposal of personal records as official policy in the writings of the business entity."

Id. §75.64(b).

"A business may, after due diligence, enter into a written contract with, and monitor compliance by, another party engaged in the business of record destruction to destroy personal information in a manner consistent with this section. Due diligence should ordinarily include one or more of the following:

(1) Reviewing an independent audit of the disposal business's operations or its compliance with this statute or its equivalent.
(2) Obtaining information about the disposal business from several references or other reliable sources and requiring that the disposal business be certified by a recognized trade association or similar third party with a reputation for high standards of quality review.
(4) Reviewing and evaluating the disposal business's information security policies or procedures or taking other appropriate measures to determine the competency and integrity of the disposal business."

Id. §75-64(c).

"A disposal business that conducts business in North Carolina or disposes of personal information of residents of North Carolina must take all reasonable measures to dispose of records containing personal information by implementing and monitoring compliance with policies and procedures that protect against unauthorized access to or use of personal information during or after the collection and transportation and disposing of such information."

Id. §75-64(d).

"This section does not apply to any of the following:

(1) Any bank or financial institution that is subject to and in compliance with the privacy and security provision of the Gramm Leach Bliley Act, 15 U.S.C. § 6801, et seq., as amended.
(2) Any health insurer or health care facility that is subject to and in compliance with the standards for privacy of individually identifiable health information and the security standards for the protection of electronic health information of the Health Insurance Portability and Accountability Act of 1996.
(4) Any consumer reporting agency that is subject to and in compliance with the Federal [sic] Credit Reporting Act, 15 U.S.C. §1681, et seq., as amended."

Id. §75-64(e).

"The following definitions apply in this Article:

(1) 'Business'.—A sole proprietorship, partnership, corporation, association, or other group, however organized and whether or not organized to operate at a profit. The term includes a financial institution organized, chartered, or holding a license or authorization certificate under the laws of this State, any other state, the United States, or any other country, or the parent or the subsidiary of any such financial institution. Business shall not include any government or governmental subdivision or agency.

Id. §75-61(1).

. . .

(10) 'Personal information'.—A person's first name or first initial and last name in combination with identifying information as defined in G.S. 14-113.20(b). Personal information does not include publicly available directories containing information an individual has voluntarily consented to have publicly disseminated or listed, including name, address, and telephone number, and does not include information made lawfully available to the general public from federal, state, or local government records."

Id. §75-61(10).

Oregon

Note: the following excerpts are from Oregon Senate Bill 583, which passed the Oregon Legislative Assembly on June 26, 2007. At this writing, we cannot confirm that Senate Bill 583 has become law.

OREGON 74TH LEGISLATIVE ASSEMBLY

SENATE BILL 583

SECTION 1. This 2007 Act shall be known as the Oregon Consumer Identity Theft Protection Act.

SECTION 2. As used in this 2007 Act:

(2) 'Consumer' means an individual who is also a resident of this state.
(6) 'Encryption' means the use of an algorithmic process to transform data into a form in which the data is rendered unreadable or unusable without the use of a confidential process or key.
(10) 'Person' means an individual, private or public corporation, partnership, cooperative, association, estate, limited liability company, organization or other entity, whether or not organized to operate at a profit, or a public body as defined in ORS 174.109.
(11) 'Personal Information':
(A) means a consumer's first name or first initial and last name in combination with any one or more of the following data elements, when the data elements are not rendered unusable through encryption, redaction or other methods, or when the data elements are encrypted and the encryption key has also been acquired:
(A) Social Security number;
(B) driver license number or state identification card number issued by the Department of Transportation;
(C) passport number or other United States issued identification number; or
(D) financial account number, credit or debit card number, in combination with any required security code, access code or password that would permit access to a consumer's financial account.
(B) means any of the data elements or any combination of the data elements described in paragraph (A) of this subsection when not combined with the consumer's first name or first initial and last name and when the data elements are not rendered unusable through encryption, redaction or other methods, if the information obtained would be sufficient to permit a person to commit identity theft against the consumer whose information was compromised.
(C) does not include information, other than a Social Security number, in a federal, state or local government record that is lawfully made available to the public.
(12) 'Redacted' means altered or truncated so that no more than the last four digits of a Social Security number, driver license number, state identification card number, account number or credit or debit card number is accessible as part of the data.

SECTION 12. (1) Any person that owns, maintains or otherwise possesses data that includes a consumer's personal information that is used in the course of the person's business, vocation, occupation or volunteer activities must develop, implement and maintain reasonable safeguards to protect the security, confidentiality and integrity of the personal information, including disposal of the data.

(2) The following shall be deemed in compliance with subsection (1) of this section:

(A) a person that complies with a state or federal law providing greater protection to personal information than that provided by this section.
(B) a person that is subject to and complies with regulations promulgated pursuant to Title V of the Gramm-Leach-Bliley Act of 1999 (15 U.S.C. 6801 to 6809) as that Act existed on the effective date of this 2007 Act.
(C) a person that is subject to and complies with regulations implementing the Health Insurance Portability and Accountability Act of 1996 (45 C.F.R. Parts 160 and 164) as the Act existed on the effective date of this 2007 Act.
(D) a person that implements and information security program that includes the following:
(A) administrative safeguards such as the following, in which the person:
(I) designates one or more employees to coordinate the security program;
(II) identifies reasonably foreseeable internal and external risks;
(III) assesses the sufficiency of safeguards in place to control the identified risks;
(IV) trains and manages employees in the security program practices and procedures;
(V) selects service providers capable of maintaining appropriate safeguards, and requires those safeguards by contract; and
(VI) adjusts the security program in light of business changes or new circumstances;
(B) technical safeguards such as the following, in which the person:
(I) assesses risks in network and software design;
(II) assesses risks in information processing, transmission and storage;
(III) detects, prevents and responds to attacks or system failures; and
(IV) regularly tests and monitors the effectiveness of key controls, systems and procedures; and
(C) physical safeguards such as the following in which the person:
(I) assesses risks of information storage and disposal;
(II) detects, prevents and responds to intrusions;
(III) protects against unauthorized access to or use of personal information during or after the collection, transportation and destruction or disposal of the information; and
(IV) disposes of personal information after it is no longer needed for business purposes or as required by local, state or federal law by burning, pulverizing, shredding or modifying a physical record and by destroying or erasing electronic media so that the information cannot be read or reconstructed.
(3) A person complies with subsection (2)(D)(C)(IV) of this section if the person contracts with another person engaged in the business of record destruction to dispose of personal information in a manner consistent with subsection (2)(D)(C)(IV) of this section.
(4) Notwithstanding subsection (2) of this section, a person that is an owner of a small business as defined in ORS 285B.123 (3) complies with subsection (1) of this section if the person's information security and disposal program contains administrative, technical and physical safeguards and disposal measures appropriate to the size and complexity of the small business, the nature and scope of its activities, and the sensitivity of the personal information collected from or about consumers.

Rhode Island

"A business that owns or licenses computerized unencrypted personal information about a Rhode Island resident shall implement and maintain reasonable security procedures and practices appropriate to the nature of the information to protect the personal information from unauthorized access, destruction, use, modification, or disclosure."

Rhode Island 2005-2006 Legislative Session, House Bill 6191, 2005 R.I. Pub. Laws 225.

"For purposes of this section, 'personal information' means an individual's first name or first initial and last name in combination with any one or more of the following data elements, when either the name or the data elements are not encrypted:

(1) Social Security number;
(2) driver's license number or Rhode Island identification card number;
 (2) account number, credit or debit card number, in combination with any required security code, access code, or password that would permit access to an individual's financial account."
 (3) *Id.*

Tennessee

"(g)(1). Notwithstanding any other provision of law to the contrary, if a private entity or business maintains a record that contains any of the personal identifying information set out in subdivision (g)(2) concerning one of its customers, and the entity, by law, practice or policy discards such records after a specified period of time, any such record containing such personal identifying information shall not be discarded unless the business:
(A) shreds or burns the customer's record before discarding the record;
(B) erases the personal identifying information contained in the customer's record before discarding the record;
(C) modifies the customer's record to make the personal identifying information unreadable before discarding the record; or
(C) takes action to destroy the customer's personal identifying information in a manner that it reasonably believes will ensure that no unauthorized persons have access to the personal identifying information contained in the customer's record for the period of time between the record's disposal and the record's destruction."

Tenn. Code. Ann. Sec. 39-14-150(g)(1).

"(g)(2). As used in this subsection (g), 'personal identifying information' means a customer's:
(A) (2) Social Security number;
(B) (2) Driver license identification number;
(C) (2) Savings account number;
(E) PIN (personal identification number) or password;
(F) Complete credit or debit card number;
(G) Demand deposit account number;

(H) Health insurance identification number; or
(I) Unique biometric data."
Id. sec. 39-14-150(g)(2).

Texas

"A business shall implement and maintain reasonable procedures, including taking any appropriate corrective action, to protect and safeguard from unlawful use or disclosure any sensitive personal information collected or maintained by the business in the regular course of business."

Tex. Bus. & Com. Code §48.102(a).

"A business shall destroy or arrange for the destruction of customer records containing sensitive personal information within the business's custody or control that are not to be retained by the business by:

(1) shredding;
(2) erasing; or
(3) otherwise modifying the sensitive personal information in the records to make the information unreadable or undecipherable through any means."

Id. §48.102(b).

"This section does not apply to a financial institution as defined by 15 U.S.C. Section 6809." *Id.* §48.102(c).

" 'Sensitive personal information':

(A) means an individual's first name or first initial and last name in combination with any one or more of the following items, if the name and the items are not encrypted:
(i) social security number;
(ii) driver's license number or government-issued identification number; or
(iii) account number or credit or debit card number in combination with any required security code, access code, or password that would permit access to an individual's financial account; and

(B) does not include publicly available information that is lawfully made available to the general public from the federal government or a state or local government."
Id. §48.002(2).

Utah

"(1) Any person who conducts business in the State and maintains personal information shall implement and maintain reasonable procedures to:
(A) Prevent unlawful use or disclosure of personal information collected or maintained in the regular course of business; and
(B) Destroy, or arrange for the destruction of, records containing personal information that are not retained by the person.
(2) The destruction of records under subsection (1)(B) shall be by:

(A) shredding;
(B) erasing; or
(C) otherwise modifying the personal information to make the information indecipherable.
(3) This section does not apply to a financial institution as defined by 15 U.S.C. section 6809."

Senate Bill 69, Utah 56th Legislature, 2006 General Session, Utah Code Ann. § 13-44-201.

(3)(A) 'Personal information' means a person's first name or first initial and last name, combined with any one or more of the following data elements relating to that person when either the name or data element is unencrypted or not protected by another method that renders the data unreadable or unusable:
(I) Social Security number;
(II)(A) Financial account number, or credit or debit card number; and
(B) Any required security code, access code, or password that would permit access to the person's account; or
(II) Driver license number or state identification number.
(B) 'Personal information' does not include information, regardless of its source, contained in federal, state or local government records or in widely distributed media that are lawfully made available to the general public." *Id.*

Vermont

"A business shall take all reasonable steps to destroy or arrange for the destruction of a customer's records within its custody or control containing personal information which is no longer to be retained by the business by shredding, erasing, or otherwise modifying the personal information in those records to make it unreadable or indecipherable through any means . . ."

9 V.S.A. § 2445(b).

"An entity that is in the business of disposing of personal information that conducts business in Vermont or disposes of personal information of residents of Vermont must take all reasonable measures to dispose of records containing personal information by implementing and monitoring compliance with policies and procedures that protect against unauthorized access to or use of personal information during or after the collection and transportation and disposing of such information."

Id. § 2445(c).

" 'Business' means sole proprietorship, partnership, corporation, association, limited liability company, or other group, however organized and whether or not organized to operate at a profit, including a financial institution organized, chartered, or holding a license or authorization certificate under the laws of this state, any other state, the United States, or any other country, or the parent, affiliate, or subsidiary of a financial institution, but in no case shall it include the state, a state agency, or any political subdivision of the state. The term includes an entity that destroys records."

Id. § 2445(a)(1).

" 'Personal information' means the following information that identifies, relates to, describes, or is capable of being associated with a particular individual: his or her signature, Social Security number, physical characteristics or description, passport number, driver's license or state identification card number, insurance policy number, bank account number, credit card number, or any other financial information."

Id. § 2445(a)(3).

" 'Record' means any material, regardless of the physical form, on which information is recorded or preserved by any means, including in written or spoken words, graphically depicted, printed, or electromagnetically transmitted."

Washington

"An entity must take all reasonable steps to destroy, or arrange for the destruction of, personal financial and health information and personal identification numbers issued by government entities in an individual's records within its custody or control when the entity is disposing of records that it no longer will retain." Rev. Code Wash. §19.215.020(1).

" 'Destroy personal information' means shredding, erasing, or otherwise modifying personal information in records to make the personal information unreadable or undecipherable through any reasonable means." *Id.* §19.215.010(2).

" 'Entity' includes a sole proprietor, partnership, corporation, limited liability company, trust, association, financial institution, governmental entity, other than the federal government, and any other individual or group, engaged in a trade, occupation, enterprise, governmental function, or similar activity in this state, however organized and whether organized to operate at a profit." *Id.* §19.215.010(1).

" 'Personal financial' and 'health information' mean information that is identifiable to an individual and that is commonly used for financial or health care purposes, including account numbers, access codes or passwords, information gathered for account security purposes, credit card numbers, information held for the purpose of account access or transaction initiation, or information that relates to account history or status." *Id.* §19.215.010(4).

" 'Record' includes any material, regardless of the physical form, on which information is recorded or preserved by any means, including in written or spoken words, graphically depicted, printed, or electromagnetically transmitted. 'Record' does not include publicly available directories containing information an individual has voluntarily consented to have publicly disseminated or listed, such as name, address, or telephone number." *Id.* §19.215.010(6).

Wisconsin

"A financial institution, medical business or tax preparation business may not dispose of a record containing personal information unless the financial institution, medical business, tax preparation business or other person under contract with the financial institution, medical business or tax preparation business does any of the following:

(a) Shreds the record before disposal of the record.
(b) Erases the personal information contained in the record before disposal of the records.
(c) Modifies the record to make the personal information unreadable before disposal of the record.
(d) Takes actions that it reasonably believes will ensure that no unauthorized person will have access to the personal information contained in the record for the period between the records disposal and the records destruction." Wis. Stat. §895.505.

" 'Financial institution' means any bank, savings bank, savings and loan association or credit union that is authorized to do business under state or federal laws relating to financial institutions, any issuer of a credit card or any investment company." *Id.* §895.505(b).

" 'Medical business' means any organization or enterprise operated for profit or not for profit, including a sole proprietorship, partnership, firm, business trust, joint venture, syndicate, corporation, limited liability company or association, that possesses information, other than personnel records, relating to a person's physical or mental health, medical history or medical treatment." *Id.* §895.505(d).

" 'Tax preparation business' means any organization or enterprise operated for profit, including a sole proprietorship, partnership, firm, business trust, joint venture, syndicate, corporation, limited liability company or association, that for a fee prepares an individual's federal, state or local tax returns or counsels an individual regarding the individual's federal, state or local tax returns." *Id.* §895.505(h).

" 'Personal information' means any of the following:

1. Personally identifiable data about an individual's medical condition, if the data are not generally considered to be public knowledge.
2. Personally identifiable data that contain an individual's account or customer number, account balance, balance owing, credit balance or credit limit, if the data relate to an individual's account or transaction with a financial institution.
3. Personally identifiable data provided by an individual to a financial institution on opening an account or applying for a loan or credit.
4. Personally identifiable data about an individual's federal, state or local tax returns. *Id.* §895.505(e).

" 'Personally identifiable' means capable of being associated with a particular individual through one or more identifiers or other information or circumstances." *Id.* §895.505(f).

2. State Data Protection Statutes

Several states have enacted statutes that require companies to take reasonable measures to protect personal information, not only when records containing that information are in process of being disposed of or destroyed, but whenever those companies maintain such information.

Arkansas

"A person or business that acquires, owns, or licenses personal information about an Arkansas resident shall implement and maintain reasonable security procedures and practices appropriate to the nature of the information to protect the personal information from unauthorized access, destruction, use, modification, or disclosure." *Id.* §4-110-104(b).

" 'Business' means a sole proprietorship, partnership, corporation, association, or other group, however organized and whether or not organized to operate at a profit, including a financial institution organized, chartered, or holding a license or authorization certificate under the law of this state, any other state, the United States, or of any other country or the parent or subsidiary of a financial institution." *Id.* §4-110-103(2)(A).

" 'Business' includes:

(i) An entity that destroys records; and
(ii) A state agency." *Id.* §4-110-103(2)(B).

" 'Owns or licenses' includes, but is not limited to, personal information that a business retains as part of the internal customer account of the business or for the purpose of using the information in transactions with the person to whom the information relates." *Id.* §4-110-103(6).

" 'Personal information' means an individual's first name or first initial and his or her last name in combination with any one (1) or more of the following data elements when either the name or the data element is not encrypted or redacted:

(A) Social security number;
(B) Driver's license number or Arkansas identification card number;
(C) Account number, credit card number, or debit card number in combination with any required security code, access code, or password that would permit access to an individual's financial account; and
(D) Medical information."

Id. §4-110-103(7).

California

(b) A business that owns or licenses personal information about a California resident shall implement and maintain reasonable security procedures and practices

appropriate to the nature of the information, to protect the personal information from unauthorized access, destruction, use, modification, or disclosure.
(c) A business that discloses personal information about a California resident pursuant to a contract with a nonaffiliated third party shall require by contract that the third party implement and maintain reasonable security procedures and practices appropriate to the nature of the information, to protect the personal information from unauthorized access, destruction, use, modification, or disclosure.
(d) For purposes of this section, the following terms have the following meanings:
(1) "Personal information" means an individual's first name or first initial and his or her last name in combination with any one or more of the following data elements, when either the name or the data elements are not encrypted or redacted:
(A) Social security number.
(B) Driver's license number or California identification card number.
(C) Account number, credit or debit card number, in combination with any required security code, access code, or password that would permit access to an individual's financial account.
(D) Medical information.
(2) "Medical information" means any individually identifiable information, in electronic or physical form, regarding the individual's medical history or medical treatment or diagnosis by a health care professional.
(3) "Personal information" does not include publicly available information that is lawfully made available to the general public from federal, state, or local government records.
(e) The provisions of this section do not apply to any of the following:
(1) A provider of health care, health care service plan, or contractor regulated by the Confidentiality of Medical Information Act (Part 2.6 (commencing with Section 56) of Division 1).
(2) A financial institution as defined in Section 4052 of the Financial Code and subject to the California Financial Information Privacy Act (Division 1.2 (commencing with Section 4050) of the Financial Code).
(3) A covered entity governed by the medical privacy and security rules issued by the federal Department of Health and Human Services, Parts 160 and 164 of Title 45 of the Code of Federal Regulations, established pursuant to the Health Insurance Portability and Availability Act of 1996 (HIPAA).
(4) An entity that obtains information under an agreement pursuant to Article 3 (commencing with Section 1800) of Chapter 1 of Division 2 of the Vehicle Code and is subject to the confidentiality requirements of the Vehicle Code.
(5) A business that is regulated by state or federal law providing greater protection to personal information than that provided by this section in regard to the subjects addressed by this section. Compliance with that state or federal law shall be deemed compliance with this section with regard to those subjects. This paragraph does not relieve a business from a duty to comply with any other requirements of other state and federal law regarding the protection and privacy of personal information.

Cal. Civ. Code § 1798.81.5

Nevada

603A.210. Security measures.

1. A data collector that maintains records which contain personal information of a resident of this State shall implement and maintain reasonable security measures to protect those records from unauthorized access, acquisition, destruction, use, modification or disclosure.
2. A contract for the disclosure of the personal information of a resident of this State which is maintained by a data collector must include a provision requiring the person to whom the information is disclosed to implement and maintain reasonable security measures to protect those records from unauthorized access, acquisition, destruction, use, modification or disclosure.
3. If a state or federal law requires a data collector to provide greater protection to records that contain personal information of a resident of this State which are maintained by the data collector and the data collector is in compliance with the provisions of that state or federal law, the data collector shall be deemed to be in compliance with the provisions of this section.

Nev. Rev. Stat. § 603A.210

Oregon

Note: the following excerpts are from Oregon Senate Bill 583, which passed the Oregon Legislative Assembly on June 26, 2007. At the time of this writing, we cannot confirm that Senate Bill 583 has become law.

OREGON 74TH LEGISLATIVE ASSEMBLY

SENATE BILL 583

SECTION 1. This 2007 Act shall be known as the Oregon Consumer Identity Theft Protection Act.

SECTION 2. As used in this 2007 Act:

(2) 'Consumer' means an individual who is also a resident of this state.
(6) 'Encryption' means the use of an algorithmic process to transform data into a form in which the data is rendered unreadable or unusable without the use of a confidential process or key.
(10) 'Person' means an individual, private or public corporation, partnership, cooperative, association, estate, limited liability company, organization or other entity, whether or not organized to operate at a profit, or a public body as defined in ORS 174.109.
(11) 'Personal Information':
(A) means a consumer's first name or first initial and last name in combination with any one or more of the following data elements, when the data elements are not rendered unusable through encryption, redaction or other methods, or when the data elements are encrypted and the encryption key has also been acquired:
(A) Social Security number;

(B) driver license number or state identification card number issued by the Department of Transportation;
(C) passport number or other United States issued identification number; or
(D) financial account number, credit or debit card number, in combination with any required security code, access code or password that would permit access to a consumer's financial account.
(B) means any of the data elements or any combination of the data elements described in paragraph (A) of this subsection when not combined with the consumer's first name or first initial and last name and when the data elements are not rendered unusable through encryption, redaction or other methods, if the information obtained would be sufficient to permit a person to commit identity theft against the consumer whose information was compromised.
(C) does not include information, other than a Social Security number, in a federal, state or local government record that is lawfully made available to the public.
(12) 'Redacted' means altered or truncated so that no more than the last four digits of a Social Security number, driver license number, state identification card number, account number or credit or debit card number is accessible as part of the data.

SECTION 12. (1) Any person that owns, maintains or otherwise possesses data that includes a consumer's personal information that is used in the course of the person's business, vocation, occupation or volunteer activities must develop, implement and maintain reasonable safeguards to protect the security, confidentiality and integrity of the personal information, including disposal of the data.

(2) The following shall be deemed in compliance with subsection (1) of this section:
(A) a person that complies with a state or federal law providing greater protection to personal information than that provided by this section.
(B) a person that is subject to and complies with regulations promulgated pursuant to Title V of the Gramm-Leach-Bliley Act of 1999 (15 U.S.C. 6801 to 6809) as that Act existed on the effective date of this 2007 Act.
(C) a person that is subject to and complies with regulations implementing the Health Insurance Portability and Accountability Act of 1996 (45 C.F.R. Parts 160 and 164) as the Act existed on the effective date of this 2007 Act.
(D) a person that implements an information security program that includes the following:
(A) administrative safeguards such as the following, in which the person:
(I) designates one or more employees to coordinate the security program;
(II) identifies reasonably foreseeable internal and external risks;
(III) assesses the sufficiency of safeguards in place to control the identified risks;
(IV) trains and manages employees in the security program practices and procedures;
(V) selects service providers capable of maintaining appropriate safeguards, and requires those safeguards by contract; and
(VI) adjusts the security program in light of business changes or new circumstances;
(B) technical safeguards such as the following, in which the person:
(I) assesses risks in network and software design;
(II) assesses risks in information processing, transmission and storage;

(III) detects, prevents and responds to attacks or system failures; and
(IV) regularly tests and monitors the effectiveness of key controls, systems and procedures; and
(C) physical safeguards such as the following in which the person:
(I) assesses risks of information storage and disposal;
(II) detects, prevents and responds to intrusions;
(III) protects against unauthorized access to or use of personal information during or after the collection, transportation and destruction or disposal of the information; and
(IV) disposes of personal information after it is no longer needed for business purposes or as required by local, state or federal law by burning, pulverizing, shredding or modifying a physical record and by destroying or erasing electronic media so that the information cannot be read or reconstructed.
(3) A person complies with subsection (2)(D)(C)(IV) of this section if the person contracts with another person engaged in the business of record destruction to dispose of personal information in a manner consistent with subsection (2)(D)(C)(IV) of this section.
(4) Notwithstanding subsection (2) of this section, a person that is an owner of a small business as defined in ORS 285B.123 (3) complies with subsection (1) of this section if the person's information security and disposal program contains administrative, technical and physical safeguards and disposal measures appropriate to the size and complexity of the small business, the nature and scope of its activities, and the sensitivity of the personal information collected from or about consumers.

Rhode Island

"A business that owns or licenses computerized unencrypted personal information about a Rhode Island resident shall implement and maintain reasonable security procedures and practices appropriate to the nature of the information to protect the personal information from unauthorized access, destruction, use, modification, or disclosure."

Rhode Island 2005-2006 Legislative Session, House Bill 6191, 2005 R.I. Pub. Laws 225.

"For purposes of this section, 'personal information' means an individual's first name or first initial and last name in combination with any one or more of the following data elements, when either the name or the data elements are not encrypted:

(1) Social Security number;
(2) driver's license number or Rhode Island identification card number;
(4) account number, credit or debit card number, in combination with any required security code, access code, or password that would permit access to an individual's financial account."
(5) *Id.*

Texas

§ 48.102. Business Duty to Protect and Safeguard Sensitive Personal Information

(a) A business shall implement and maintain reasonable procedures, including taking any appropriate corrective action, to protect and safeguard from unlawful use or disclosure any sensitive personal information collected or maintained by the business in the regular course of business.

Tex. Bus. & Com. Code § 48.102

Utah

§ 13-44-201. Protection of personal information

(1) Any person who conducts business in the state and maintains personal information shall implement and maintain reasonable procedures to:

(a) prevent unlawful use or disclosure of personal information collected or maintained in the regular course of business; and

(b) destroy, or arrange for the destruction of, records containing personal information that are not to be retained by the person.

(2) The destruction of records under Subsection (1)(b) shall be by:

(a) shredding;

(b) erasing; or

(c) otherwise modifying the personal information to make the information indecipherable.

(3) This section does not apply to a financial institution as defined by 15 U.S.C. Section 6809.

Utah Code Ann. § 13-44-201

3. State Data Security Breach Notification Statutes

A number of states require businesses and other entities that maintain personal information to give notice of incidents that have resulted, or might result, in the compromise of that information. The first such law was enacted by the California General Assembly in 2003. Since that time, more than half of the states in the Union have enacted similar laws, and more of these "breach notification" statutes are pending in several state legislatures.

Arizona

"When a person that conducts business in this State and that owns or licenses unencrypted computerized data that includes personal information becomes aware of an incident of unauthorized acquisition and access to unencrypted or unredacted computerized data that includes an individual's personal information, the person shall conduct a reasonable investigation to promptly determine if there has been a breach of the security system (sic). If the investigation results in a determination that there has been a breach in the security system (sic), the person shall notify the individuals affected. The notice shall be made in the most expedient manner possible and without unreasonable delay subject to the needs of law enforcement as provided in subsection C of this section and any measures necessary to determine the nature and scope of the breach, to identify the individuals affected or to restore the reasonable integrity of the data system."

2006 Arizona Senate Bill 1338, adding chapter 32 to Title 44, Arizona Revised Statutes, codified as A.R.S. sec. 44-7501(A).

"A person that maintains unencrypted computerized data that includes personal information that the person does not own shall notify and cooperate with the owner or licensee of the information of any breach of the security of the system following discovery of the breach without unreasonable delay. Cooperation shall include sharing information relevant to the breach of the security of the system with the owner or licensee. The person that owns or licenses the computerized data shall provide notice to the individual pursuant to this section. The person that maintained the data under an agreement with the owner or licensee is not required to provide notice to the individual pursuant to this section unless the agreement stipulates otherwise." *Id.* sec. 44-7501(B).

"A person who maintains the person's own notification procedures as part of an information security policy for the treatment of personal information and is otherwise consistent with the requirements of this section shall be deemed to be in compliance with the notification requirements of this section if the persons notifies subject individuals in accordance with the person's policies if a breach of the security system occurs." *Id.* sec. 44-7501(E).

"A person that complies with the notification requirements or security breach procedures established pursuant to the rules, regulations, procedures, guidance or guidelines established by the person's primary or functional federal regulator is deemed to be in compliance with this section." *Id.* sec. 44-7501(F).

"This section does not apply to either of the following:

1. A person subject to Title V of the Gramm Leach Bliley Act of 1999 ...
2. Covered entities as defined under regulations implementing the Health Insurance Portability and Accountability Act . . ." *Id.* sec. 44-7501(J).

" 'Breach,' 'breach of the security of the system,' 'breach of the security system,' or 'security breach' means an unauthorized acquisition of and access to unencrypted or unredacted computerized data that materially compromises the security or confidentiality of personal information maintained by a person as part of a database of personal information regarding multiple individuals and that causes or is reasonably likely to cause substantial economic loss to an individual. Good faith acquisition of personal information by an employee or agent of the person for the purposes of the person is not a breach of the security system if the personal information is not used for a purpose unrelated to the person or subject to further willful unauthorized disclosure." *Id.* sec. 44-7501(L)(1).

" 'Encrypted' means use of an algorithmic process to transform data into a form in which the data is rendered unreadable or unusable without use of a confidential process or key." *Id.* sec. 44-7501(L)(3).

" 'Personal information':

(A) means an individual's first name or first initial and last name in combination with any one or more of the following data elements, when the data element is not encrypted, redacted or secured by any other method rendering the element unreadable or unusable:
(I) The individual's Social Security number.
(II) The individual's number on a driver license issued pursuant to section 28-3166 or number on a nonoperating identification license issued pursuant to section 28-3165.
(III) The individual's financial account number or credit or debit card number in combination with any required security code, access code or password that would permit access to the individual's financial account.
(B) Does not include publicly available information that is lawfully made available to the general public from federal, state or local government records or widely distributed media." *Id.* sec. 44-7501(L)(7).

" 'Redact' means alter or truncate data such that no more than the last four digits of a Social Security number, driver license number, nonoperating identification license number, financial account number or credit or debit card number is accessible as part of the personal information." *Id.* sec. 44-7501(L)(9).

(Methods of giving notification are prescribed; delay may be notified for purposes of cooperation with law enforcement.)

Arkansas

"Any person or business that acquires, owns, or licenses computerized data that includes personal information shall disclose any breach of the security of the system following discovery or notification of the breach of the security of the system to any resident of Arkansas whose unencrypted personal information was, or is reasonably believed to have been, acquired by an unauthorized person." A.C.A. § 4-110-105.

"Any person or business that maintains computerized data that includes personal information that the person or business does not own shall notify the owner or licensee of the information of any breach of the security of the system immediately following discovery if personal information was, or is reasonably believed to have been, acquired by an unauthorized person." *Id.* §4-110-105(b).

(Disclosure must be made "in the most expedient time and manner possible," but delayed notification is permitted when required by law enforcement. Notification not required if person or business conducts a reasonable investigation and determines that there is no reasonable likelihood of harm to consumers. Alternative methods of giving notice are prescribed.)

" 'Breach of the security of the system' means unauthorized acquisition of computerized data that compromises the security, confidentiality, or integrity of personal information maintained by a person or business." *Id.* §4-110-103(1)(A).

" 'Personal information' means an individual's first name or first initial and his or her last name in combination with any one (1) or more of the following data elements when either the name or the data element is not encrypted or redacted:

(A) Social security number;
(B) Driver's license number or Arkansas identification card number;
(C) Account number, credit card number, or debit card number in combination with any required security code, access code, or password that would permit access to an individual's financial account; and
(D) Medical information." *Id.* §4-110-103(7).

California

"Any agency that owns or licenses computerized data that includes personal information shall disclose any breach of the security of the system following discovery or notification of the breach in the security of the data to any resident of California whose unencrypted personal information was, or is reasonably believed to have been, acquired by an unauthorized person." Cal. Civ. Code § 1798.29(a).

"Any agency that maintains computerized data that includes personal information that the agency does not own shall notify the owner or licensee of the information of any breach of the security of the data immediately following discovery, if the personal information was, or is reasonably believed to have been, acquired by an unauthorized person." *Id.* §1798.29(b).

(Notification may be delayed for needs of law enforcement; methods of giving notice are prescribed.)

"For purpose of this section, 'breach of the security of the system' means unauthorized acquisition of computerized data that compromises the security, confidentiality, or integrity of personal information maintained by the agency. Good faith acquisition of personal information by an employee or agent of the agency for the purposes of the agency is not a breach of the security of the system, provided that the personal information is not used or subject to further unauthorized disclosure." *Id.* § 1798.29(d).

"For purposes of this section, 'personal information' means an individual's first name or first initial and last name in combination with any one or more of the following data elements, when either the name or the data elements are not encrypted:

(1) Social security number.
(2) Driver's license or California Identification Card number.
(3) Account number, credit or debit card number, in combination with any required security code, access code, or password that would permit access to an individual's financial account. *Id.* § 1798.29(e).

"Any person or business that conducts business in California, and that owns or licenses computerized data that includes personal information, shall disclose any breach of the security of the system following discovery or notification of the breach of the security of the system following discovery or notification of the breach in the security of the data to any resident of California whose unencrypted personal information was, or is reasonably believed to have been, acquired by an unauthorized person." *Id.* § 1798.82(a).

"Any person or business that maintains computerized data that includes personal information that the person or business does not own shall notify the owner or licensee of the information of any breach of the security of the data immediately following discovery, if the personal information was, or is reasonably believed to have been, acquired by an unauthorized person." *Id.* §1798.82(b).

(Notification may be delayed for purposes of law enforcement; methods of notification are prescribed.)

"For purposes of this section, 'breach of the security of the system' means unauthorized acquisition of computerized data that compromises the security, confidentiality, or integrity of personal information maintained by the person or business. Good faith acquisition of personal information by an employee or agent of the person or business for the purposes of the person or business is not a breach of the security of the system, provided that the personal information is not used or subject to further unauthorized disclosure." *Id.* § 1798.82(d).

"For purposes of this section, 'personal information' means an individual's first name or first initial and last name in combination with any one or more of the following data elements, when either the name or the data elements are not encrypted:

(1) Social security number.

(2) Driver's license number or California Identification Card number.

(3) Account number, credit or debit card number, in combination with any required security code, access code, or password that would permit access to an individual's financial account." *Id.* § 1798.82(e).

Colorado

"An individual or a commercial entity that conducts business in Colorado and that owns or licenses computerized data that includes personal information about a resident of Colorado shall, when it becomes aware of a breach of the security of the system, conduct in good faith a prompt investigation to determine the likelihood that personal information has been or will be misused. The individual or the commercial entity shall give notice as soon as possible to the affected Colorado resident unless the investigation determines that the misuse of information about a Colorado resident has not occurred and is not reasonably likely to occur. Notice shall be made in the most expedient time possible and without unreasonable delay, consistent with the legitimate needs of law enforcement and consistent with any measures necessary to determine the scope of the breach and to restore the reasonable integrity of the computerized data system." Colorado 2nd Regular Session of the 65th General Assembly, Colorado House Bill 1119, amending Part 7 of Article 1 of Title 6, Colorado Revised Statues, by the addition of a new C.R.S. sec. 6-1-716, quoting 6 C.R.S. sec. 6-1-716(2)(a).

"An individual or commercial entity that maintains computerized data that includes personal information that the individual or the commercial entity does not own or license shall give notice to and cooperate with the owner or licensee of the information of any breach of the security of the system immediately following discovery of a breach, if misuse of personal information about a Colorado resident occurred or is likely to occur. Cooperation includes sharing with the owner or licensee information relevant to the breach; except that such cooperation shall not be deemed to require the disclosure of confidential business information or trade secrets." *Id.* sec. 6-1-716(2)(b).

"Under this section, an individual or a commercial entity that maintains its own notification procedures as part of an information security policy for the treatment of personal information and whose procedures are otherwise consistent with the timing requirements of this section shall be deemed to be in compliance with the notice requirements of this section if the individual or the commercial entity notifies affected Colorado customers in accordance with its policies in the event of a breach of the security of the system." *Id.* sec. 6-1-716(3)(a).

"An individual or a commercial entity that is regulated by state or federal law and that maintains procedures for a breach of the security of the system pursuant to laws, rules, regulations, guidances, or guidelines established by its primary or functional state or federal regulator is deemed to be in compliance with this section." *Id.* sec. 6-1-716(3)(b).

" 'Breach of the security of the system' means the unauthorized acquisition of unencrypted computerized data that compromises the security, confidentiality, or integrity of personal information maintained by an individual or a commercial entity. Good faith acquisition of personal information by an employee or agent of an individual or commercial entity for the purposes of the individual or commercial entity is not a breach of the security of the system if the personal information is not used for or is not subject to further unauthorized disclosure." *Id.* sec. 6-1-716(a).

" 'Personal information' means a Colorado resident's first name or first initial and last name in combination with any one or more of the following data elements that relate to the resident, when the data elements are not encrypted, redacted, or secured by any other method rendering the name or the data element unreadable or unusable:

(A) Social Security number;
(B) Driver's license number or identification card number;
(C) Account number or credit or debit card number, in combination with any required security code, access code, or password that would permit access to a resident's financial account." *Id.* sec. 6-1-716(d)(I).

" 'Personal information' does not include publicly available information that is lawfully made available to the general public from federal, state, or local government records or widely distributed media." *Id.* sec. 6-1-716(d)(II).

(Methods of giving notice are prescribed; notice may be delayed for purposes of cooperation with law enforcement.)

Connecticut

"Any person who conducts business in this state, and who, in the ordinary course of such person's business, owns, licenses or maintains computerized data that includes personal information, shall disclose any breach of security following discovery of the breach to any resident of this state whose personal information was, or is reasonably believed to have been, accessed by an unauthorized person through such breach of security." Conn. Gen. Stat. § 36a-701.

"Any person that maintains computerized data that includes personalized data that the person does not own shall notify the owner or licensee of the information of any breach of the security of the data immediately following its discovery, if the personal information was, or is reasonably believed to have been, accessed by an unauthorized person." *Id.*

(Notification may be delayed for needs of law enforcement; methods of notification are prescribed.)

"For purposes of this section, 'breach of security' means unauthorized access to or acquisition of electronic files, media, databases or computerized data containing personal information when access to that personal information has not been secured by encryption or by any other method or technology that renders the personal information unreadable or unusable; 'personal information' means an individual's first name or first initial and last name in combination with any one, or more, of the following data:

(1) Social security number;
(2) driver's license number or state identification card number; or
(3) account number, credit or debit card number, in combination with any required security code, access code or password that would permit access to an individual's financial account." *Id.*

Delaware

"An individual or a commercial entity that conducts business in Delaware and that owns or licenses computerized data that includes personal information about a resident of Delaware shall, when it becomes aware of a breach of the security of the system, conduct in good faith a reasonable and prompt investigation to determine the likelihood that personal information has been or will be misused. If the investigation determines that the misuse of information about a Delaware resident has occurred or is reasonably likely to occur, the individual or the commercial entity shall give notice as soon as possible to the affected Delaware resident." 6 Del. C. §102(a).

"An individual or a commercial entity that maintains computerized data that includes personal information that the individual or the commercial entity does not own or license shall give notice to and cooperate with the owner or licensee of the information of any breach of the security of the system immediately following discovery of a breach, if misuse of personal information about a Delaware resident occurred or is reasonably likely to occur. Cooperation includes sharing with the owner or licensee information relevant to the breach." *Id.* §102(b).

(Notification may be delayed for law enforcement purposes; methods of giving notification are prescribed.)

" 'Breach of the security of the system' means the unauthorized acquisition of unencrypted computerized data that compromises the security, confidentiality, or integrity of personal information maintained by an individual or a commercial entity. Good faith acquisition of personal information by an employee or agent of an individual or a commercial entity for the purposes of the individual or the commercial entity is not a breach of the security of the system, provided that the personal information is not used or subject to further unauthorized disclosure." *Id.* §101(1).

" 'Commercial entity' includes corporations, business trusts, estates, trusts, partnerships, limited partnerships, limited liability partnerships, limited liability companies, associations, organizations, joint ventures, governments, governmental subdivisions, agencies, or instrumentalities, or any other legal entity, whether for profit or not-for-profit." *Id.* §101(2).

" 'Personal information' means a Delaware resident's first name or first initial and last name in combination with any 1 or more of the following data elements that relate to the resident, when either the name or the data elements are not encrypted:

a. Social Security number;
b. Driver's license number or Delaware Identification Card number; or
c. Account number, or credit or debit card number, in combination with any required security code, access code, or password that would permit access to a resident's financial account." *Id.* §101(4).

District of Columbia

"Any person or entity who conducts business in the District of Columbia, and who, in the ordinary course of such business, maintains computerized data that includes personal information, and who discovers a breach of the security of the system, shall promptly notify the District of Columbia resident whose personal information was included in the breach. The disclosure shall be made in the most expedient time possible and without unreasonable delay, consistent with the legitimate needs of law enforcement, . . . and with any measures necessary to determine the scope of the breach and restore the reasonable integrity of the system."

District of Columbia Official Code § 28-3852(a).

"Any person who maintains computerized data that includes personal information that the person or business does not own shall notify the owner or licensee of the information of any breach of the security of the data immediately following discovery, if the personal information was, or is reasonably believed to have been, acquired by an unauthorized person."

Id. § 28-3852(b).

" 'Breach of the security of the system' means a likelihood that there has been unauthorized acquisition of computerized data that compromises the security, confidentiality, or integrity of personal information maintained by the person or business. Good faith acquisition of personal information by an employee or agent of the person or business for the purposes of the person or business is not a breach of the security of the system, provided that the personal information is not used improperly or subject to further unauthorized disclosure."

Id. § 28-3851(1).

" 'Personal information' means an individual's first name or initial and last name in combination with any one or more of the following data elements, when either the name or the data elements are not encrypted:

(i) Social security number;
(ii) Driver's license number or District of Columbia Identification Card number;
(iii) Account number, credit card number or debit card number, if circumstances exist wherein such a number could be used without additional identifying information, access codes, or passwords; or
(iv) Account passwords or identity-corroborating personal information, including but not limited to, a mother's maiden name, or personal identification numbers (PINs) or other access codes."

Id. § 28-3851(3)(A).

Florida

"Any person who conducts business in this state and maintains computerized data in a system that includes personal information shall provide notice of any breach of the security of the system, following a determination of the breach, to any resident of the state whose unencrypted personal information was, or is reasonably believed to have been, acquired by an unauthorized person." Fla. Stat. §817.5681(1)(a).

"Any person who maintains computerized data that includes personal information on behalf of another business entity shall disclose to the business entity for which the information is maintained any breach of the security of the system as soon as practicable, but no later than 10 days following the determination, if the personal information was, or is reasonably believed to have been, acquired by an unauthorized person." *Id.* §817.5681(2)(a).

(Notification may be delayed for reasons of law enforcement; methods of giving notice are prescribed.)

"For purposes of this section, the terms 'breach' and 'breach of the security of the system' mean unlawful and unauthorized acquisition of computerized data that materially compromises the security, confidentiality, or integrity of personal information maintained by the person. Good faith acquisition of personal information by an employee or agent of the person is not a breach or breach of the security of the system, provided the information is not used for a purpose unrelated to the business or subject to further unauthorized use." *Id.* §817.5681(4).

"For purposes of this section, the term 'personal information' means an individual's first name, first initial and last name, or any middle name and last name, in combination with any one or more of the following data elements when the data elements are not encrypted:

(a) Social security number.
(b) Driver's license number or Florida Identification Card number.
(c) Account number, credit card number, or debit card number, in combination with any required security code, access code, or password that would permit access to an individual's financial account." *Id.* §817.5681(5).

"For purposes of this section, the term 'person' means a person as defined in s. 1.01(3). [Section 1.01(3) of the Florida Statutes defines "person" to include "individuals, children, firms, association, joint adventures, partnerships, estates, trusts, business trusts, syndicates, fiduciaries, corporations, and all other groups or combinations."] For purposes of this section, the State of Florida, as well as any of its agencies or political subdivisions, and any of the agencies of its political subdivisions, constitutes a person." *Id.* §817.5681(8).

"For purposes of this section, the term 'unauthorized person' means any person who does not have permission from, or a password issued by, the person who stores the computerized data to acquire such data, but does not include any individual to whom the personal information pertains." *Id.* §817.5681(7).

"Notwithstanding subsection (2), notification is not required if, after an appropriate investigation or after consultation with relevant federal, state, and local agencies responsible for law enforcement, the person reasonably determines that the breach has not and will not likely result in harm to the individuals whose personal information has been acquired and accessed. Such a determination must be documented in writing and the documentation must be maintained for 5 years." *Id.* §817.5681(10).

Georgia

"Any information broker that maintains computerized data that includes personal information of individuals shall give notice of any breach of the security of the system following discovery or notification of the breach in the security of the data to any resident of this state whose unencrypted personal information was, or is reasonably believed to have been, acquired by an unauthorized person." O.C.G.A. § 10-1-912(a).

"Any person or business that maintains computerized data on behalf of an information broker that includes personal information of individuals that the person or business does not own shall notify the information broker of any breach of the security of the data immediately following discovery, if the personal information was, or is reasonably believed to have been, acquired by an unauthorized person." *Id.* § 10-1-912(b).

(Notification may be delayed for reasons of law enforcement.)

" 'Information broker' means any person or entity who, for monetary fees or dues, engages in whole or in part in the business of collecting, assembling, evaluating, compiling, reporting, transmitting, transferring, or communicating information concerning individuals for the primary purpose of furnishing personal information to nonaffiliated third parties, but does not include any governmental agency whose records are maintained primarily for traffic safety, law enforcement, or licensing purposes." *Id.* §10-1-911(2).

" 'Person' means any individual, partnership, corporation, limited liability company, trust, estate, cooperative, association, or other entity. The term 'person' as used in this article shall not be construed to require duplicative reporting by any individual, corporation, trust, estate, cooperative, association, or other entity involved in the same transaction." *Id.* §10-1-911(4).

" 'Personal information' means an individual's first name or first initial and last name in combination with any one or more of the following data elements, when either the name or the data elements are not encrypted or redacted:

(A) Social security number;
(B) Driver's license number or state identification card number;
(C) Account number, credit card number, or debit card number, if circumstances exist wherein such a number could be used without additional identifying information, access codes, or passwords;
(D) Account passwords or personal identification numbers or other access codes; or
(E) Any of the items contained in subparagraphs (A) through (D) of this paragraph when not in connection with the individual's first name or first initial and last name, if the information compromised would be sufficient to perform or attempt to perform identity theft against the person whose information was compromised.

The term 'personal information' does not include publicly available information that is lawfully made available to the general public from federal, state, or local government records." *Id.* §10-1-911(5).

(Georgia's data security breach notification statute was amended in May 2007, to extend its research to government agencies, which now must give notice of breach unless they maintain records with personal information "primarily for traffic safety, law enforcement, or licensing purposes or for purposes of providing public access to court records or to real or personal property information." Georgia Senate Bill 236, 2007.)

Hawaii

"Any business that owns or licenses personal information of residents of Hawaii, any business that conducts business in Hawaii that owns or licenses personal information in any form (whether computerized, paper, or otherwise) or any government agency that collects personal information for specific government purposes shall provide notice to the affected person that there has been a security breach following discovery or notification of the breach. The disclosure notification shall be made without unreasonable delay, consistent with the legitimate needs of law enforcement . . . , and consistent with any measures necessary to determine sufficient contact information, determine the scope of the breach, and restore the reasonable integrity, security, and confidentiality of the data system."

HRS § 487N-2(a).

"Any business located in Hawaii or any business that conducts business in Hawaii that maintains or possesses records or data containing personal information of residents of Hawaii that the business does not own or license, or any government agency that maintains or possesses records or data containing personal information of residents shall notify the owner or licensee of the information of any security breach immediately following discovery of the breach, consistent with the legitimate needs of law enforcement . . ."

Id. § 487N-2(b).

" 'Business' means a sole proprietorship, partnership, corporation, association, or other group, however organized, and whether or not organized to operate at a profit. The term includes a financial institution organized, chartered, or holding a license or authorization certificate under the laws of the State, any other state, the United States, or any other country, or the parent or the subsidiary of any such financial institution. The term also includes an entity whose business is records destruction."

Id. § 487N-1.

" 'Personal information' means an individual's first name or first initial and last name in combination with any one or more of the following data elements, when either the name or the data elements are not encrypted:

(1) Social security number;
(2) Driver's license number of Hawaii identification card number; or
(3) Account number, credit or debit card number, access code, or password that would permit access to an individual's financial account.

Id.

" 'Records' means any material on which written, drawn, spoken, visual, or electromagnetic information is recorded or preserved, regardless of physical form or characteristics."

Id.

" 'Security breach' means an incident of unauthorized access to and acquisition of unencrypted or unredacted records or data containing personal information where illegal use of the personal information has occurred, or is reasonably likely to occur and that creates a risk of harm to a person. Any incident of unauthorized access to and acquisition of encrypted records or data containing personal information along with the confidential process or key constitutes a security breach. Good faith acquisition of personal information by an employee or agent of the business for a legitimate purpose is not a security breach; provided that the personal information is not used for a purpose other than a lawful purpose of the business and is not subject to further unauthorized disclosure."

Id.

Idaho

"An agency, individual or a commercial entity that conducts business in Idaho and that owns or licenses computerized data that includes personal information about a resident of Idaho shall, when it becomes aware of a breach of the security of the system, conduct in good faith a reasonable and prompt investigation to determine the likelihood that personal information has been or will be misused. If the investigation determines that the misuse of information about an Idaho resident has occurred or is reasonably likely to occur, the agency, individual or the commercial entity shall give notice as soon as possible to the affected Idaho resident. Notice must be made in the most expedient time possible and without unreasonable delay, consistent with the legitimate needs of law enforcement and consistent with any measures necessary to determine the scope of the breach, to identify the individuals affected, and to restore the reasonable integrity of the computerized data system." 58th Idaho Legislature, Senate Bill No. 1374, Title 28 Idaho Code sec. 28-51-105(1).

"An agency, individual or a commercial entity that maintains computerized data that includes personal information that the agency, individual or the commercial entity does not own or license shall give notice to and cooperate with the owner or licensee of the information of any breach of the security of the system immediately following discovery of a breach, if misuse of personal information about an Idaho resident occurred or is reasonably likely to occur. Cooperation includes sharing with the owner or licensee information relevant to the breach." *Id.* sec. 28-51-105(2).

(Exceptions are provided for entities with their own adequate notification procedures or that are regulated by state or federal law for breach notification purposes.)

" 'Breach of the security of the system' means the illegal acquisition of unencrypted computerized data that materially compromises the security, confidentiality, or integrity of personal information for one (1) or more persons maintained by an agency, individual or a commercial entity. Good faith acquisition of personal information by an employee or agent of an agency, individual or a commercial entity for the purposes of the agency, individual or the commercial entity is not a breach of the security of the system, provided that the personal information is not used or subject to further unauthorized disclosure." *Id.* sec. 28-51-104(2).

" 'Personal information' means an Idaho resident's first name or first initial and last name in combination with any one (1) or more of the following data elements that relate to the resident, when the name or the data elements are not encrypted:

(a) Social Security number;

(b) Driver' s license or Idaho identification card number; or
(c) Account number, or credit or debit card number, in combination with any required security code, access code, or password that would permit access to a resident's financial account.

The term 'personal information' does not include publicly available information that is lawfully made available to the general public from federal, state, or local government records or widely distributed media." *Id.* sec. 28-51-104(5).

(Methods of notification are prescribed; delayed notification is permitted for purposes of cooperation with law enforcement.)

Illinois

"Any data collector that owns or licenses personal information concerning an Illinois resident shall notify the resident that there has been a breach of the security of the system following discovery or notification of the breach." 815 ILCS 530/10(a).

"Any data collector that maintains computerized data that includes personal information that the data collector does not own or license shall notify the owner or licensee of the information of any breach of the security of the data immediately following discovery, if the personal information was, or is reasonably believed to have been, acquired by an unauthorized person." *Id.* § 530/10(b).

(Methods of making notification are prescribed.)

" 'Data collector' may include, but is not limited to, government agencies, public and private universities, privately and publicly held corporations, financial institutions, retail operators, and any other entity that, for any purpose, handles, collects, disseminates, or otherwise deals with nonpublic personal information." H.B. 1633, Public Act 94-36, sec. 5.

" 'Breach of the security of the system data' means unauthorized acquisition of computerized data that compromises the security, confidentiality, or integrity of personal information maintained by the data collector. 'Breach of the security of the system data' does not include good faith acquisition of personal information by an employee or agent of the data collector for a legitimate purpose of the data collector, provided that the personal information is not used for a purpose unrelated to the data collector's business or subject to further unauthorized disclosure." *Id.*

" 'Personal information' means an individual's first name or first initial and last name in combination with any one or more of the following data elements, when either the name or the data elements are not encrypted or redacted:

(1) Social Security number.
(2) Driver's license number or State identification card number.
(3) Account number or credit or debit card number, or an account number or credit card number in combination with any required security code, access code, or password that would permit access to an individual's financial account." *Id.*

Indiana

Indiana Breach Notification Statute Applicable to Private Entities

"Except as provided in section 4(C), 4(D) and 4(E) of this chapter, after discovering or being notified of a breach of the security of a system, the data base owner shall disclose the breach to an Indiana resident whose:

(1) unencrypted personal information was or may have been acquired by an unauthorized person; or
(2) encrypted personal information was or may have been acquired by an unauthorized person with access to the encryption key; if the data base owner knows, should know, or should have known that the unauthorized acquisition constituting the breach has resulted in or could result in identity deception . . . , identity theft, or fraud affecting the Indiana resident." IC Art. 4.9, chapter 3, sec. 1(A).

"A person that maintains computerized data but that is not a data base owner shall notify the data base owner if the person discovers that personal information was or may have been acquired by an unauthorized person." *Id.* sec. 2.

" 'Breach of the security of a system' means unauthorized acquisition of computerized data that compromises the security, confidentiality, or integrity of personal information maintained by a person. The term includes the unauthorized acquisition of computerized data that has been transferred to another medium, including paper, microfilm, or a similar medium, even if the transferred data are no longer in a computerized format.

"The term does not include the following:

(1) Good faith acquisition of personal information by an employee or agent of the person for lawful purposes of the person, if the personal information is not used or subject to further unauthorized disclosure.
(2) Unauthorized acquisition of a personal electronic device on which personal information is stored, if access to the device is protected by a password that has not been disclosed." IC Art. 4.9, chapter 1, sec. 2.

" 'Data base owner' means a person that owns or licenses computerized data that includes personal information." IC Art. 4.9, chapter1, sec. 3.

"Data are encrypted for purposes of this Article if the data:

(1) have been transformed through the use of an algorithmic process into a form in which there is a low probability of assigning meaning without use of a confidential process or key; or
(2) are secured by another method that renders the data unreadable or unusable." *Id.* sec. 5.

" 'Personal information' means:

(1) a Social Security number that is not encrypted or redacted; or
(2) an individual's first and last names, or first initial and last name, and one (1) or more of the following data elements that are not encrypted or redacted:
(A) a driver's license number.

(B) a state identification card number.
(C) a credit card number.
(D) a financial account number or debit card number in combination with a security code, password, or access code that would permit access to the person's account.

The term does not include information that is lawfully obtained from publicly available information or from federal, state, or local government records lawfully made available to the general public." *Id.* sec. 10.

"(A) Data are redacted for purposes of this article if the data have been altered or truncated so that not more than the last four (4) digits of:
(1) a driver's license number;
(2) a state identification number; or
(3) an account number; is accessible as part of personal information.
(B) For purposes of this Article, personal information is 'redacted' if the personal information has been altered or truncated so that not more than five (5) digits of a Social Security number are accessible as part of personal information." *Id.* sec. 11.

(Methods of making notification are prescribed; exemptions are provided for persons with their own adequate notification practices or subject to comparable statutes and regulations; delay is permitted as required to cooperate with law enforcement.)

Indiana Breach Notification Statute Applicable to State Agencies

"Any state agency that owns or licenses computerized data that includes personal information shall disclose a breach of the security of the system following discovery or notification of the breach to any state resident whose unencrypted personal information was or is reasonably believed to have been acquired by an unauthorized person." Burns Ind. Code Ann. § 4-1-11-5(a).

If computerized data maintained by an agency contains personal information that the state agency does not own, and "personal information was or is reasonably believed to have been acquired by an unauthorized person, the state agency shall notify the owner or licensee of the information of a breach of the security of the system immediately following discovery." *Id.*

(Notification may be delayed for purposes of law enforcement.)

"As used in this chapter, 'breach of the security of the system' means unauthorized acquisition of computerized data that compromises the security, confidentiality, or integrity of personal information maintained by a state or local agency." *Id.* §4-1-11-2(a).

"The term does not include the following:

(1) Good faith acquisition of personal information by an agency or employee of the agency for purposes of the agency, if the personal information is not used or subject to further unauthorized disclosure.

(2) Unauthorized acquisition of a portable electronic device on which personal information is stored if access to the device is protected by a password that has not been disclosed." *Id.* §4-1-11-2(b).

"As used in this chapter, 'personal information' means:

(1) An individual's:
(A) first and last name; or
(B) first initial and last name; and
(2) at least one (1) of the following data elements:
(A) Social Security number.
(B) Driver's license number or identification card number.
(C) Account number, credit card number, debit card number, security code, access code, or password of an individual's financial account.
(b) The term does not include the following:
(1) The last four (4) digits of an individual's Social Security number.
(2) Publicly available information that is lawfully made available to the public from records of a federal agency or local agency." *Id.* §4-1-11-3.

Kansas

"A person that conducts business in this state, or a government, governmental subdivision or agency that owns or licenses computerized data that includes personal information shall, when it becomes aware of any breach of the security of the system, conduct in good faith a reasonable and prompt investigation to determine the likelihood that personal information has been or will be misused. If the investigation determines that the misuse of information has occurred or is reasonably likely to occur, the person or government, governmental subdivision or agency shall give notice as soon as possible to the affected Kansas resident. Notice must be made in the most expedient time possible and without unreasonable delay, consistent with the legitimate needs of law enforcement and consistent with any measures necessary to determine the scope of the breach and to restore the reasonable integrity of the computerized data system." Kansas 81st Legislature, Senate Bill 196, sec. 4(a).

"An individual or a commercial entity that maintains computerized data that includes personal information that the individual or the commercial entity does not own or license shall give notice to the owner or licensee of the information of any breach of the security of the data following discovery of a breach, if the personal information was, or is reasonably believed to have been, accessed and acquired by an unauthorized person." *Id.*, sec. 4(b).

" 'Personal information' means a consumer's first name or first initial and last name linked to any one or more of the following data elements that relate to the consumer, when the data elements are neither encrypted nor redacted:

(1) Social Security number;
(2) driver's license number or state identification card number; or
(3) financial account number, or credit or debit card number, alone or in combi-

nation with any required security code, access code or password that would permit access to a consumer's financial account. The term 'personal information' does not include publicly available information that is lawfully made available to the general public from federal, state or local government records." *Id.* sec. 3(g).

" 'Security breach' means the unauthorized access and acquisition of unencrypted or unredacted computerized data that compromises the security, confidentiality or integrity of personal information maintained by an individual or a commercial entity and that causes, or such individual or entity reasonably believes has caused or will cause, identity theft to any consumer. Good faith acquisition of personal information by an employee or agent of an individual or a commercial entity for the purposes of the individual or the commercial entity is not a breach of the security of the system, provided that the personal information is not used for or is not subject to further unauthorized disclosure." *Id.* sec. 3(h).

" 'Encrypted' means transformation of data through the use of an algorithmic process into a form in which there is a low probability of assigning meaning without the use of a confidential process or key, or securing the information by another method that renders the data elements unreadable or unusable." *Id.* sec. 3(b).

" 'Redact' means alteration or truncation of data such that no more than the following are accessible as part of the personal information:

(1) five digits of a Social Security number; or
(2) the last four digits of a driver's license number, state identification card number or account number." *Id.* sec. 3(d).

(Methods of giving notice are prescribed; exceptions are provided for entities with their own adequate notification procedures and for entities subject to comparable statutes and regulations; delays in notification are permitted for cooperation with law enforcement.)

Louisiana

"Any person that conducts business in the state or that owns or licenses computerized data that includes personal information, or any agency that owns or licenses computerized data that includes personal information, shall, following discovery of a breach in the security of the system containing such data, notify any resident of the state whose personal information was, or is reasonably believed to have been, acquired by an unauthorized person." La. R.S. § 51:3074(A).

"Any agency or person that maintains computerized data that includes personal information that the agency or person does not own shall notify the owner or licensee of the information if the personal information was, or is reasonably believed to have been, acquired by an unauthorized person through a breach of security of the system containing such data, following discovery by the agency or person of a breach of security of the system." *Id.* § 51:3074(B).

(Notification may be delayed for purposes of law enforcement; methods of notification are prescribed.)

" 'Agency' means the state, a political subdivision of the state, and any officer, agency, board, commission, department or similar body of the state or any political subdivision of the state." *Id.* § 51:3073(1).

" 'Breach of the security of the system' means the compromise of the security, confidentiality, or integrity of computerized data that results in, or there is a reasonable basis to conclude has resulted in, the unauthorized acquisition of and access to personal information maintained by an agency or person. Good faith acquisition of personal information by an employee or agent of an agency or person for the purposes of the agency or person is not a breach of the security of the system, provided that the personal information is not used for, or is subject to, unauthorized disclosure." *Id.* § 51:3073(2).

" 'Personal information' means an individual's first name or first initial and last name in combination with any one or more of the following data elements, when the name or the data element is not encrypted or redacted:

(i) Social security number.
(ii) Driver's license number.
(iii) Account number, credit or debit card number, in combination with any required security code, access code, or password that would permit access to an individual's financial account." *Id.* § 51:3073(4)(a).

Although the scheduled effective date of Louisiana's breach notification statute was January 1, 2006, the statute provides that it "shall not take effect until rules are promulgated by the attorney general's office." *Id.* § 51:3077.

Maine

"If an information broker that maintains computerized data that includes personal information becomes aware of a breach of the security of the system, the information broker shall conduct in good faith a reasonable and prompt investigation to determine the likelihood that personal information has been or will be misused and shall give notice of a breach of the security of the system following discovery or notification of the security breach to a resident of this state whose personal information has been, or is reasonably believed to have been, acquired by an unauthorized person."

"If any other person who maintains computerized data that includes personal information becomes aware of a breach of the security of the system, the person shall conduct in good faith a reasonable and prompt investigation to determine the likelihood that personal information has been or will be misused and shall give notice of a breach of the security of the system following discovery or notification of the security breach to a resident of this state if misuse of the personal information has occurred or if it is reasonably possible that misuse will occur." Sec. 1.10 MRSA c. 210-B §1348(1).

"A third-party entity that maintains, on behalf of a person, computerized data that includes personal information that the third-party entity does not own shall notify the person maintaining personal information of a breach of the security system immediately following discovery if the personal information was, or is reasonably believed to have been, acquired by an unauthorized person." *Id.* §1348(2).

"If a person discovers a breach of the security of the system that requires notification to more than 1,000 persons at a single time, the person shall also notify, without unreasonable delay, consumer reporting agencies that compile and maintain files on consumers on a nationwide basis . . ." *Id.* §1348(4).

"When notice of a breach of the security of the system is required under subsection 1, the person shall notify the appropriate state regulators within the Department of Professional and Financial Regulation, or if the person is not regulated by the Department, the Attorney General." *Id.* §1348(5).

(Notice may be delayed for law enforcement purposes; methods of giving notice are prescribed.)

" 'Information broker' means a person who, for monetary fees or duties, engages in whole or in part in the business of collecting, assembling, evaluating, compiling, reporting, transmitting, transferring or communicating information concerning individuals for the primary purpose of furnishing personal information to nonaffiliated third parties. 'Information broker' does not include a governmental agency whose records are maintained primarily for traffic safety, law enforcement or licensing purposes." *Id.* §1347(3).

" 'Breach of the security of the system' or 'security breach' means unauthorized acquisition of an individual's computerized data that compromises the security, confidentiality or integrity of personal information of the individual maintained by a person. Good faith acquisition of personal information by an employee or agent of a person on behalf of the person is not a breach of the security of the system if the personal information is not used for or subject to further unauthorized disclosure." *Id.* §1347(1).

" 'Personal information' means an individual's first name, or first initial, and last name in combination with any one or more of the following data elements, when either the name or the data elements are not encrypted or redacted:

A. Social Security number;
B. Driver's license number or state identification card number;
C. Account number, credit card or debit card number, if circumstances exist wherein such a number could be used without additional identify information, access codes or passwords;
D. Account passwords or personal identification numbers or other access codes; or
E. Any of the data elements contained in paragraphs A to D when not in connection with the individual's first name, or first initial, and last name, if the information if compromised would be sufficient to permit a person to fraudulently assume or attempt to assume the identity of the person whose information was compromised." *Id.* §1347(6).

Maryland

MARYLAND 2007 REGULAR SESSION—422ND SESSION
OF THE GENERAL ASSEMBLY
SENATE BILL 194

SUBTITLE 35. MARYLAND PERSONAL INFORMATION PROTECTION ACT.

14-3501.

(A) In this subtitle the following words have the meanings indicated.
(B) (1) "Business" means a sole proprietorship, partnership, corporation, association, or any other business entity, whether or not organized to operate at a profit.
(2) "Business" includes a financial institution organized, chartered, licensed, or otherwise authorized under the laws of this state, any other state, the United States, or any other country, and the parent or subsidiary of a financial institution.
(3) "Business" does not include an entity that has an annual gross income of less than $1,000,000.
(C) "Encrypted" means the transformation of data through the use of an algorithmic process into a form in which there is a low probability of assigning meaning without use of a confidential process or key.
(C) (D) (1) "Personal information" means an individual's first name or first initial and last name in combination with any one or more of the following data elements, when the name or the data elements are not encrypted, redacted, or otherwise protected by another method that renders the information unreadable or unusable:
(I) a Social Security number;
(II) a driver's license number; or
(III) a financial account number, including a credit card number or debit card number, that in combination with any required security code, access code, or password, would permit access to an individual's financial account; or
(IV) an individual taxpayer identification number; or
(V) a consumer report, as defined in Section 14-1201 of this title.
(2) "Personal information" does not include:
(I) publicly available information that is lawfully made available to the general public from federal, state, or local government records;
(II) information that an individual has consented to have publicly disseminated or listed; or
(III) information that is disseminated or listed in accordance with the Federal Health Insurance Portability and Accountability Act.
(D) (E) "Records" means information that is inscribed on a tangible medium or that is stored in an electronic medium and is retrievable in perceivable form.
14-3502.
(A) In this section, "Customer" means an individual residing in the State who provides personal information to a business for the purpose of purchasing or leasing a product or obtaining a service from the business.
14-3504.
(A) In this section:

(1) "Breach of the security of a system" means the unauthorized acquisition of computerized data that compromises the security, confidentiality, or integrity of the personal information maintained by a business and will likely result in a material risk of identity theft; and
(2) "Breach of the security of a system" does not include the good faith acquisition of personal information by an employee or agent of a business for the purposes of the business, provided that:
(I) the personal information is not used or subject to further unauthorized disclosure; and
(II) it is not likely that the acquisition will result in a material risk of identity theft.
(B) (1) A business that owns or licenses computerized data that includes personal information of an individual residing in the state, when it discovers or is notified of a breach of the security of a system, shall conduct in good faith a reasonable and prompt investigation to determine the likelihood that the breach will result in a material risk of identity theft [or that] personal information of the individual has been or will be misused as a result of the breach.
(2) If, after the investigation is concluded, the business reasonably believes [or] determines that the breach of the security of a system has resulted or will result in a material risk of identity theft of personal information of an individual residing in the state [or] misuse of the individual's personal information has occurred or is reasonably likely to occur as a result of the breach of the security of a system, the business shall notify the individual of the breach.

Michigan

Michigan's Senate Bill 309, summarized here, was signed by Governor Granholm on January 3, 2007, and took effect 180 days after that date.

"Unless the person or agency determines that the security has not or is not likely to cause substantial loss or injury to, or result in identity theft with respect to, one or more residents of this state, a person or agency that owns or licenses data that are included in a database that discovers a security breach, or receives notice of a security breach . . ., shall provide a notice of the security breach to each resident of this state who meets one or more of the following:

(A) That resident's unencrypted and unredacted personal information was accessed and acquired by an unauthorized person.
(B) That resident's personal information was accessed and acquired in encrypted form by a person with unauthorized access to the encryption key.
(2) Unless the person or agency determines that the security has not or is not likely to cause substantial loss or injury to, or result in identity theft with respect to, one or more residents of this state, a person or agency that maintains a database that includes data that the person or agency does not own or license that discovers a breach of the security of the database shall provide a notice to the owner or licensor of the information of the security breach.
(3) In determining whether a security breach is not likely to cause substantial loss or injury to, or result in identity theft with respect to, one or more residents of this

state, . . . a person or agency shall act with the care an ordinarily prudent person or agency in like position would exercise under similar circumstances." MCL 445.72.

" 'Breach of the security of a database' or 'security breach' means the unauthorized access and acquisition of data the compromises the security or confidentiality of personal information maintained by a person or agency as part of a database of information regarding multiple individuals."

Id. § 445.63.

" 'Data' means computerized personal information."

Id.

" 'Personal identifying information' means a name, number, or other information that is used for the purpose of identifying a specific person or providing access to a person's financial accounts, including, but not limited to, a person's name, address, telephone number, driver license or state personal identification card number, social security number, place of employment, employee identification number, employer or taxpayer identification number, government passport number, health insurance identification number, mother's maiden name, demand deposit account number, savings account number, financial transaction device account number or the person's account password, stock or other record, or medical records or information."

Id.

" 'Personal information' means the first name or first initial and last name linked to one or more of the following data elements of a resident of this state:

(i) Social Security number.

(ii) Driver license number or state personal identification card number.

(iii) Demand deposit or other financial account number, or credit card or debit card number, in combination with any required security code, access code, or password that would permit access to any of the resident's financial accounts."

Id.

Minnesota

"A state agency that collects, creates, receives, maintains, or disseminates private or confidential data on individuals must disclose any breach of the security of the data following discovery or notification of the breach. Notification must be made to any individual who is the subject of the data and whose private or confidential data was, or is reasonably believed to have been, acquired by an unauthorized person." Minn. Stat. §13.055(2).

" 'Breach of the security of the data' means unauthorized acquisition of data maintained by a state agency that compromises the security and classification of the data. Good faith acquisition of government data by an employee, contractor, or agent of a state agency for the purposes of the state agency is not a breach of the security of the data, if the government data is not provided to an unauthorized person." *Id.* §13.055(1)(a).

"Any person or business that conducts business in this state, and that owns or licenses data that includes personal information, shall disclose any breach of the security of the system following discovery or notification of the breach in the security of the data to any resident of this state whose unencrypted personal information was, or is reasonably believed to have been, acquired by an unauthorized person." Minn. Stat. §325E.61(1)(a).

"Any person that maintains data that includes personal information that the person or business does not own shall notify the owner or licensee of the information of any breach of the security of the data immediately following discovery, if the personal information was, or is reasonably believed to have been, acquired by an unauthorized person." *Id.* §325E.61(1)(b).

(Notice may be delayed for law enforcement purposes; methods of giving notice are prescribed.)

"For purposes of this section, 'breach of the security of the system' means unauthorized acquisition of computerized data that compromises the security, confidentiality, or integrity of personal information maintained by the person or business. Good faith acquisition of information by an employee or agent of the person or business for the purposes of the person or business is not a breach of the security system, provided that the personal information is not used or subject to further unauthorized disclosure." *Id.* §325E.61(1)(d).

"For purposes of this section, 'personal information' means an individual's first name or first initial and last name in combination with any one or more of the following data elements, when either the name or the data elements is not encrypted:

(1) Social Security number;
(2) Driver's license number or Minnesota identification card number; or
(3) account number or credit or debit card number, in combination with any required security code, access code, or password that would permit access to an individual's financial account." *Id.* §325E.61(1)(e).

Montana

"Any person or business that conducts business in Montana and that owns or licenses computerized data that includes personal information shall disclose any breach of the security of the data system following discovery or notification of the breach to any resident of Montana whose unencrypted personal information was or is reasonably believed to have been acquired by an unauthorized person." Mont. Code Anno. §30-14-1704(1).

"Any person or business that maintains computerized data that includes personal information that the person or business does not own shall notify the owner or licensee of the information of any breach of the security of the data system immediately following discovery if the personal information is or was reasonably believed to have been acquired by an unauthorized person." *Id.* §30-14-1704(2).

(Notification may be delayed for law enforcement purposes; methods of giving notice are prescribed.)

" 'Breach of the security of the data system' means unauthorized acquisition of computerized data that materially compromises the security, confidentiality, or integrity of personal information maintained by the person or business and causes or is reasonably believed to cause loss or injury to a Montana resident. Good faith acquisition of personal information by an employee or agent of the person or business for the purposes of the person or business is not a breach of the security of the data system, provided that the personal information is not used or subject to further unauthorized disclosure." *Id.* §30-14-1704(4)(b).

"Any licensee or insurance-support organization that conducts business in Montana and that owns or licenses computerized data that includes personal information shall provide notice of any breach of the security of the system following discovery or notice of the breach of the security of the system to any individual whose unencrypted personal information was or is reasonably believed to have been acquired by an unauthorized person." Mont. Code Anno. §33-19-321(1).

"Any person to whom personal information is disclosed in order for the person to perform an insurance function pursuant to this part that maintains computerized data that includes personal information shall notify the licensee or insurance-support organization of any breach of the security of the system in which the data is maintained immediately following discovery of the breach of the security of the system if the personal information was or is reasonably believed to have been acquired by an unauthorized person." *Id.* §33-19-321(2).

" 'Breach of the security of the system' means unauthorized acquisition of computerized data that compromises the security, confidentiality, or integrity of personal information maintained by a licensee, insurance-support organization, or person to whom information is disclosed pursuant to this part. Acquisition of personal information by a licensee, insurance-support organization, or employee or agent of a person as authorized pursuant to this part is not a breach of the security of the system." *Id.* §33-19-321(5)(a).

" 'Personal information' means an individual's first name or first initial and last name in combination with any one or more of the following data elements, when the name and the data elements are not encrypted:

(A) Social security number;
(B) Driver's license number or state identification number;
(C) Account number or credit or debit card number, in combination with any required security code, access code, or password that would permit access to an individual's financial account." *Id.* §33-19-321(5)(b)(i).

Nebraska

"An individual or a commercial entity that conducts business in Nebraska and that owns or licenses computerized data that includes personal information about a resident of Nebraska shall, when it becomes aware of a breach of the security of the system, conduct in good faith a reasonable and prompt investigation to determine the likelihood that personal information has been or will be used for an unauthorized purpose. If the investigation determines that the use of information about a Nebraska resident for an unauthorized purpose has occurred or is reasonably likely to occur, the individual or commercial entity shall give notice to the affected Nebraska resident. Notice shall be made as soon as possible and without unreasonable delay, consistent with the legitimate needs of law enforcement and consistent with any measures necessary to determine the scope of the breach and to restore the reasonable integrity of the computerized data system." Nebraska 99th Legislature, LB 1986, sec. 3(1).

"An individual or a commercial entity that maintains computerized data that includes personal information that the individual or commercial entity does not own or license shall give notice to and cooperate with the owner or licensee of the information of any breach of the security of the system when it becomes aware of a breach if use of personal information about a Nebraska resident for an unauthorized purpose occurred or is reasonably likely to occur. Cooperation includes, but is not limited to, sharing with the owner or licensee information relevant to the breach, not including information proprietary to the individual or commercial entity." *Id.* sec. 3(2).

"Breach of the security of the system means the unauthorized acquisition of unencrypted computerized data that compromises the security, confidentiality, or integrity of personal information maintained by an individual or a commercial entity. Good faith acquisition of personal information by an employee or agent of an individual or commercial entity for the purposes of the individual or the commercial entity is not a breach of the security of the system if the personal information is not used or subject to further unauthorized disclosure. Acquisition of personal information pursuant to a search warrant, subpoena, or other court order or pursuant to a subpoena or order of a state agency is not a breach of the security of the system." *Id.* sec. 2(1).

"Personal information means a Nebraska resident's first name or first initial and last name in combination with any one or more of the following data elements that relate to the resident if either the name or the data elements are not encrypted, redacted, or otherwise altered by any method or technology in such a manner that the name or data elements are unreadable:

(A) Social Security number;
(B) Motor vehicle operator's license number or state identification card number;
(C) Account number or credit or debit card number, in combination with any required security code, access code, or password that would permit access to a resident's financial account;
(D) Unique electronic identification number or routing code, in combination with any required security code, access code, or password; or
(E) Unique biometric data, such as a fingerprint, voice print, or retina or iris image, or other unique physical representation.

Personal information does not include publicly available information that is lawfully made available to the general public from federal, state or local government records . . ." *Id.* sec. 1(5).

(Methods of giving notice are specified; exceptions are provided for entities with their own adequate notification methods or that are subject to comparable statutes or regulations; notice may be delayed for purposes of cooperation with law enforcement.)

Nevada

"Any data collector that owns or licenses computerized data which includes personal information shall disclose any breach of the security of the system data following discovery or notification of the breach to any resident of this state whose unencrypted personal information was, or is reasonably believed to have been, acquired by an unauthorized person." Amendment to Sec. 17, Title 52 NRS, §24(1).

"Any data collector that maintains computerized data which includes personal information that the data collector does not own shall notify the owner or licensee of the information of any breach of the security of the system data immediately following discovery if the personal information was, or is reasonably believed to have been, acquired by an unauthorized person." *Id.* §24(2).

(Notification may be delayed for law enforcement purposes; methods of notification are prescribed.)

" 'Data collector' means any governmental agency, institution of higher education, corporation, financial institution or retail operator or any other type of business entity or association that, for any purpose, whether by automated collection or otherwise, handles, collects, disseminates or otherwise deals with nonpublic personal information." *Id.* §20.

" 'Breach of the security of the system' means unauthorized acquisition of computerized data that materially compromises the security, confidentiality or integrity of personal information maintained by the data collector. The term does not include good faith acquisition of personal information by an employee or agent of the data collector for a legitimate purpose of the data collector, so long as the personal information is not used for a purpose unrelated to the data collector or subject to further unauthorized disclosure." *Id.* §19.

" 'Personal information' means a natural person's first name or first initial and last name in combination with any one or more of the following data elements, when the name and data elements are not encrypted:

1. Social Security number or employer identification number.
2. Driver's license number or identification card number.
3. Account number, credit card number or debit card number, in combination with any required security code, access code or password that would permit access to the person's financial account. *Id.* §21.

New Hampshire

"Any person doing business in this state who owns or licenses computerized data that includes personal information shall, when it becomes aware of a security breach, promptly determine the likelihood that the information has been or will be misused. If the determination is that misuse of the information has occurred or is reasonably likely to occur, or if a determination cannot be made, the person shall notify the affected individuals as soon as possible . . ."

New Hampshire Revised Statutes Annotated § 359-C:20(I)(a).

"Any person or business that maintains computerized data that includes personal information that the person or business does not own shall notify and cooperate with the owner or licensee of the information of any breach of the security of the data immediately following discovery, if the personal information was acquired by an unauthorized person. Cooperation includes sharing with the owner or licensee information relevant to the breach; except that such cooperation shall not be deemed to require the disclosure of confidential or business information or trade secrets."

Id. § 359-C:20(I)(c).

" 'Personal information' means an individual's first name or initial and last name in combination with any one or more of the following data elements, when the name or the data elements are not encrypted:

(1) Social security number.
(2) Driver's license number or other government identification number.
(3) Account number, credit card number, or debit card number, in combination with any required security code, access code, or password that would permit access to an individual's financial account."

Id. § 359-C:19(IV).

" 'Security breach' means unauthorized acquisition of computerized data that compromises the security or confidentiality of personal information maintained by a person doing business in this state. Good faith acquisition of personal information by an employee or agent of a person for the purposes of the person's business shall not be considered a security breach, provided that the personal information is not used or subject to further unauthorized disclosure."

Id. § 359-C:19(V).

New Jersey

"Any business that conducts business in New Jersey, or any public entity that compiles or maintains computerized records that include personal information, shall disclose any breach of security of those computerized records following discovery or notification of the breach to any customer who is a resident of New Jersey whose personal information was, or is reasonably believed to have been, accessed by an unauthorized person." N.J. Stat. §56:8-163(a).

"Any business or public entity that compiles or maintains computerized records that include personal information on behalf of another business or public entity shall notify that business or public entity, who shall notify its New Jersey customers, as provided in subsection a of this section, of any breach of the computerized records immediately following discovery, if the personal information was, or is reasonably believed to have been, accessed by an unauthorized person. *Id.* §56:8-163(b).

(Notification may be delayed for law enforcement purposes; methods of notification are prescribed.)

" 'Breach of security' means unauthorized access to electronic files, media or data containing personal information that compromises the security, confidentiality or integrity of personal information when access to the personal information has not been secured by encryption or by any other method or technology that renders the personal information unreadable or unusable. Good faith acquisition of personal information by an employee or agent of the business for a legitimate business purpose is not a breach of security, provided that the personal information is not used for a purpose unrelated to the business or subject to further unauthorized disclosure." *Id.* §56:8-161.

" 'Personal information' means an individual's first name or first initial and last name linked with any one or more of the following data elements: (1) Social Security number; (2) driver's license number or State identification card number; or (3) account number or credit or debit card number, in combination with any required security code, access code, or password that would permit access to an individual's financial account. Dissociated data that, if linked, would constitute personal information is personal information if the means to link the dissociated data were accessed in connection with access to the dissociated data." *Id.*

New York

"Any person or business which conducts business in New York state, and which owns or licenses computerized data which includes private information shall disclose any breach of the security of the system following discovery or notification of the breach in the security of the system to any resident of New York state whose private information was, or is reasonably believed to have been, acquired by a person without valid authorization." NY CLS Gen Bus §899-aa(2).

"Any person or business which maintains computerized data which includes private information which such person or business does not own shall notify the owner or licensee of the information of any breach of the security of the system immediately following discovery, if the private information was, or is reasonably believed to have been, acquired by a person without valid authorization." *Id.* §899-aa(3).

(Notification may be delayed for purposes of law enforcement; methods of giving notice are prescribed.)

" 'Personal information' shall mean any information concerning a natural person which, because of name, number, personal mark, or other identifier, can be used to identify such natural person." *Id.* §899-aa(1)(a).

" 'Private information' shall mean personal information consisting of any information in combination with any one or more of the following data elements, when either the personal information or the data element is not encrypted, or encrypted with an encryption key that has also been acquired:

(1) social security number;
(2) driver's license number or non-driver identification card number; or
(3) account number, credit or debit card number, in combination with any required security code, access code, or password that would permit access to an individual's financial account. *Id.* §899-aa(1)(b).

" 'Breach of the security of the system' shall mean unauthorized acquisition or acquisition without valid authorization of computerized data that compromises the security, confidentiality, or integrity of personal information maintained by a business. Good faith acquisition of personal information by an employee or agent of the business for the purposes of the business is not a breach of the security of the system, provided that the private information is not used or subject to unauthorized disclosure." *Id.* §899-aa(c).

"In determining whether information has been acquired, or is reasonably believed to have been acquired, by an unauthorized person or a person without valid authorization, such business may consider the following factors, among others:

(1) indications that the information is in the physical possession and control of an unauthorized person, such as a lost or stolen computer or other device containing information; or
(2) indications that the information has been downloaded or copied; or
(3) indications that the information has been used by an unauthorized person, such as fraudulent accounts opened or instances of identity theft reported." *Id.*

"Any state entity that owns or licenses computerized data that includes private information shall disclose any breach of the security of the system following discovery or notification of the breach in the security of the system to any resident of New York state whose private information was, or is reasonably believed to have been, acquired by a person without valid authorization." NY CLS State Technology Law §208(2).

"Any state entity that maintains computerized data that includes private information which such agency does not own shall notify the owner or licensee of the information of any breach of the security of the system immediately following discovery, if the private information was, or is reasonably believed to have been, acquired by a person without valid authorization." *Id.* §208(3).

(Notification may be delayed for purposes of law enforcement; methods of notification are prescribed.)

" 'Private information' shall mean personal information consisting of any information in combination with any one or more of the following data elements, when either the personal information or the data element is not encrypted, or encrypted with an encryption key that has also been acquired:

(1) social security number;
(2) driver's license number or non-driver identification card number; or
(3) account number, credit or debit card number, in combination with any required security code, access code, or password that would permit access to an individual's financial account." *Id.* §208(1)(a).

" 'Breach of the security of the system' shall mean unauthorized acquisition or acquisition without valid authorization of computerized data that compromises the security, confidentiality, or integrity of personal information maintained by a business. Good faith acquisition of personal information by an employee or agent of a state entity for the purposes of the agency is not a breach of the security of the system, provided that the private information is not used or subject to unauthorized disclosure." *Id.* §208(b).

"In determining whether information has been acquired, or is reasonably believed to have been acquired, by an unauthorized person or a person without valid authorization, such state entity may consider the following factors, among others:

(1) indications that the information is in the physical possession and control of an unauthorized person, such as a lost or stolen computer or other device containing information; or
(2) indications that the information has been downloaded or copied; or
(3) indications that the information has been used by an unauthorized person, such as fraudulent accounts opened or instances of identity theft reported." *Id.*

North Carolina

"Any business that owns or licenses personal information of residents of North Carolina or any business that conducts business in North Carolina that owns or licenses personal information in any form (whether computerized, paper, or otherwise) shall provide notice to the affected person that there has been a security breach following discovery or notification of the breach." N.C. Gen. Stat. §75-65(a).

"Any business that maintains or possesses records or data containing personal information of residents of North Carolina that the business does not own or license, or any business that conducts business in North Carolina that maintains or possesses records or data containing personal information the business does not own or license shall notify the owner or licensee of the information of any security breach immediately following discovery of the breach, consistent with the legitimate needs of law enforcement as provided in subsection (c) of this section." *Id.* §75-65(b).

(Notification may be delayed for law enforcement purposes; methods of notification are prescribed.)

" 'Personal information' [means a] person's first name or first initial and last name in combination with identifying information . . . Personal information does not include publicly available directories containing information an individual has voluntarily consented to have publicly disseminated or listed, including name, address, and telephone number, and does not include information made lawfully available to the general public from federal, state, or local government records." *Id.* §75-61(10).

" 'Security breach' [means an] incident of unauthorized access to and acquisition of unencrypted and unredacted records of data containing personal information where illegal use of the personal information has occurred or is reasonably likely to occur or that creates a material risk of harm to a consumer. Any incident of unauthorized access to and acquisition of encrypted records or data containing personal information along with the confidential process or key shall constitute a security breach. Good faith acquisition of personal information by an employee or agent of the business for a legitimate purpose is not a security breach provided that the personal information is not used for a purpose other than a lawful purpose of the business and is not subject to further unauthorized disclosure." *Id.* §75-61(14).

North Dakota

"Any person that conducts business in this state, and that owns or licenses computerized data that includes personal information, shall disclose any breach of the security of the system following discovery or notification of the breach in the security of the data to any resident of the state whose unencrypted personal information was, or is reasonably believed to have been, acquired by an unauthorized person." N.D. Cent. Code §51-30-02.

"Any person that maintains computerized data that includes personal information that the person does not own shall notify the owner or licensee of the information of the breach of the security of the data immediately following the discovery, if the personal information was, or is reasonably believed to have been, acquired by an unauthorized person." *Id.* §51-30-03.

(Notification may be delayed for law enforcement purposes; methods of notification are prescribed.)

" 'Breach of the security system' means unauthorized acquisition of computerized data when access to personal information has not been secured by encryption or by any other method or technology that renders the electronic files, media, or data bases unreadable or unusable. Good-faith acquisition of personal information by an employee or agent of the person is not a breach of the security of the system, if the personal information is not used or subject to further unauthorized disclosure." *Id.* §51-30-01(1).

" 'Personal information' means an individual's first name or first initial and last name in combination with any of the following data elements, when the name and the data elements are not encrypted:

(1) The individual's social security number;
(2) The operator's license number assigned to an individual by the department of transportation . . .;

(3) A nondriver color photo identification card assigned to the individual by the department of transportation . . .;
(4) The individual's financial institution account number, credit card number, or debit card number in combination with any required security code, access code, or password that would permit access to an individual's financial accounts;
(5) The individual's date of birth;
(6) The maiden name of the individual's mother;
(7) An identification number assigned to the individual by the individual's employer; or
(8) The individual's digitized or other electronic signature." *Id.* §51-30-01(2)(a).

" 'Personal information' does not include publicly available information that is lawfully made available to the general public from federal, state, or local government records." *Id.* §51-30-01(2)(b).

Ohio

"Any state agency or agency of a political subdivision that owns or licenses computerized data that includes personal information shall disclose any breach of the security of the system, following its discovery or notification of the breach of the security of the system, to any resident of this state whose personal information was, or reasonably is believed to have been, accessed and acquired by an unauthorized person if the access and acquisition by the unauthorized person causes or reasonably is believed will cause a material risk of identity theft or other fraud to the resident." ORC Ann. 1347.12(B)(1).

"Any state agency or agency of a political subdivision that, on behalf of or at the discretion of another state agency or agency of a political subdivision, is the custodian of or stores computerized data that includes personal information shall notify other state agency or agency of a political subdivision of any breach of the security of the system in an expeditious manner, if the personal information was, or is reasonably believed to have been, accessed and acquired by an unauthorized person and if the access and acquisition by the unauthorized person causes or is reasonably believed will cause a material risk of identity theft or other fraud to a resident of this state." *Id.* §1347.12(C).

(Notification may be delayed for law enforcement purposes; methods of notification are prescribed.)

" 'Breach of the security of the system' means unauthorized access to and acquisition of computerized data that compromises the security or confidentiality of personal information owned or licensed by a state agency or an agency of a political subdivision and that causes, reasonably is believed to have caused or reasonably is believed will cause a material risk of identity theft or other fraud to the person or property of a resident of this state." *Id.* §1347.12(A)(2)(a).

"For purposes of division (A)(2)(a) of this section:

(i) Good faith acquisition of personal information by an employee or agent of the state agency or agency of the political subdivision for the purposes of the agency is not a breach of the security of the system, provided that the personal information is not used for an unlawful purpose or subject to further unauthorized disclosure. (ii) Acquisition of personal information pursuant to a search warrant, subpoena, or other court order, or pursuant to a subpoena, order, or duty of a regulatory state agency, is not a breach of the security of the system." *Id.* §1347.12(A)(2)(b).

" 'Personal information means . . . an individual's name, consisting of the individual's first name or first initial and last name, in combination with and linked to any one or more of the following data elements, when the data elements are not encrypted, redacted, or altered by any method or technology in such a manner that the data elements are unreadable:

(i) Social security number;
(ii) Driver's license number or state identification card number;
(iii) Account number or credit or debit card number, in combination with and linked to any required security code, access code, or password that would permit access to an individual's financial account." *Id.* §1347.12(A)(6)(a).

" 'Encryption' means the use of an algorithmic process to transform data into a form in which there is a low probability of assigning meaning without use of a confidential process or key." *Id.* §1347.12(A)(4).

" 'Redacted' means altered or truncated so that no more than the last four digits of a social security number, driver's license number, state identification card number, account number, or credit or debit card number is accessible as part of the data." *Id.* §1347.12(A)(9).

Oklahoma

"Any state agency, board, commission or other unit or subdivision of state government that owns or licenses computerized data that includes personal information shall disclose any breach of the security of the system following discovery or notification of the breach in the security of the data to any resident of Oklahoma whose unencrypted personal information was, or is reasonably believed to have been, acquired by an unauthorized person. The disclosure shall be made in the most expedient time possible and without unreasonable delay, consistent with the legitimate needs of law enforcement, . . . or any measures necessary to determine the scope of the breach and restore the reasonable integrity of the data system."

74 Okl. Stat. § 3113.1(A).

" 'Breach of the security of the system' means unauthorized acquisition of computerized data that compromises the security, confidentiality, or integrity of personal information maintained by the state agency, board, commission or other unit or subdivision of state government. Good faith acquisition of personal information by an employee or agent of the state agency, board, commission or other unit or subdivision of state government for the purposes of the entity shall not be a breach of the security of the system, provided that the personal information is not used or subject to further unauthorized disclosure."

Id. § 3113.1(D)(1).

" 'Personal information' means the first name or first initial and last name of an individual in combination with any one or more of the following data elements, when either the name or the data elements are not encrypted:

a. social security number,
b. driver license number, or
c. account number, credit or debit card number, in combination with any required security code, access code, or password that would permit access to the financial account of an individual."

Id. § 3113.1(D)(2).

Oregon

Note: the following excerpts are from Oregon Senate Bill 583, which passed the Oregon Legislative Assembly on June 26, 2007. At the time of this writing, we cannot confirm that Senate Bill 583 has become law.

OREGON 74TH LEGISLATIVE ASSEMBLY

SENATE BILL 583

SECTION 1. This 2007 Act shall be known as the Oregon Consumer Identity Theft Protection Act.

SECTION 2. As used in this 2007 Act:

(1)(A) 'Breach of security' means unauthorized acquisition of computerized data that materially compromises the security, confidentiality or integrity of personal information maintained by the person.
(B) 'Breach of security' does not include good faith acquisition of personal information by a person or that person's employee or agent for a legitimate purpose of that person if the personal information is not used in violation of an applicable law or in a manner that harms or poses an actual threat to the security, confidentiality or integrity of the personal information.
(2) 'Consumer' means an individual who is also a resident of this state.
(3) 'Consumer report' means a consumer report as described in Section 603(D) of the Federal Fair Credit Reporting Act (15 U.S.C. 1681A(D)), as that Act existed on the effective date of this 2007 Act, that is compiled and maintained by a consumer reporting agency.
(6) 'Encryption' means the use of an algorithmic process to transform data into a form in which the data is rendered unreadable or unusable without the use of a confidential process or key.
(10) 'Person' means any individual, private or public corporation, partnership, cooperative, association, estate, limited liability company, organization or other entity, whether or not organized to operate at a profit, or a public body as defined in ORS 174.109.
(11) 'Personal information':
(A) means a consumer's first name or first initial and last name in combination with any one or more of the following elements, when the data elements are not

rendered unusable through encryption, redaction or other methods, or when the data elements are encrypted and the encryption key has also been acquired:
(A) Social Security number;
(B) Driver license number or state identification card number issued by the Department of Transportation;
(C) Passport number or other United States issued identification number; or
(D) Financial account number, credit or debit card number, in combination with any required security code, access code or password that would permit access to a consumer's financial account.
(B) means any of the data elements or any combination of the data elements described in paragraph (A) of this subsection when not combined with the consumer's first name or first initial and last name and when the data elements are not rendered unusable through encryption, redaction, or other methods, if the information obtained would be sufficient to permit a person to commit identity theft against the consumer whose information was compromised.
(C) does not include information, other than a Social Security number, in a federal, state or local government record that is lawfully made available to the public.
(12) 'Redacted' means altered or truncated so that no more than the last four digits of a Social Security number, driver license number, state identification card number, account number or credit or debit card number is accessible as part of the data.

SECTION 3. (1) Any person that owns, maintains or otherwise possesses data that includes a consumer's personal information that is used in the course of the person's business, vocation, occupation, or volunteer activities and was subject to a breach of security shall give notice of the breach of security following discovery of such breach of security, or receipt of notification under subsection (2) of this section, to any consumer whose personal information was included in the information that was breached. The disclosure notification shall be made in the most expeditious time possible and without unreasonable delay, consistent with the legitimate needs of law enforcement as provided in subsection (3) of this section, and consistent with any measures necessary to determine sufficient contact information for the consumers, determine the scope of the breach and restore the reasonable integrity, security and confidentiality of the data.

(2) Any person that maintains or otherwise possesses personal information on behalf of another person shall notify the owner or licensor of the personal information of any breach of security immediately following discovery of such breach of security if a consumer's personal information was included in the information that was breached.
(7) Notwithstanding subsection (1) of this section, notification is not required if, after an appropriate investigation or after consultation with relevant federal, state or local agencies responsible for law enforcement, the person determines that no reasonable likelihood of harm to the consumers whose personal information has been acquired has resulted or will result from the breach. Such determination must be documented in writing and the documentation must be retained for five years.
(8) This section does not apply to:
(A) A person that complies with the notification requirements or breach of security procedures that provide greater protection to personal information and at least as

thorough disclosure requirements pursuant to the rules, regulations, procedures, guidance, or guidelines established by the person's primary or functional federal regulator.
(B) A person that complies with a state or federal law that provides greater protection to personal information and at least as thorough disclosure requirements for breach of security of personal information than that provided by this section.
(C) A person that is subject to and complies with regulations promulgated pursuant to Title V of the Gramm-Leach-Bliley Act of 1999 (15 U.S.C. 6801 to 6809) as that Act existed on the effective date of this 2007 Act.

Pennsylvania

"An entity that maintains, stores or manages computerized data that includes personal information shall provide notice of any breach of the security of the system following discovery of the breach of the security of the system to any resident of the Commonwealth whose unencrypted and unredacted personal information was or is reasonably believed to have been accessed and acquired by an unauthorized person . . ." 73 PS sec. 2303(a).

"An entity must provide notice of the breach of encrypted information if accessed and acquired in an unencrypted form, if the security breach is linked to a breach of the security of the encryption or if the security breach involves a person with access to the encryption key." *Id.* sec. 2303(b).

"A vendor that maintains, stores or manages computerized data on behalf of another entity shall provide notice of any breach of the security system following discovery by the vendor to the entity on whose behalf the vendor maintains, stores or manages the data. The entity shall be responsible for making the determinations and discharging any remaining duties under this act." *Id.* sec. 2303(c).

Definitions.

" 'Breach of the security of the system.' The unauthorized access and acquisition of computerized data that materially compromises the security or confidentiality of personal information maintained by the entity as part of a database of personal information regarding multiple individuals and that causes or the entity reasonably believes has caused or will cause loss or injury to any resident of this Commonwealth. Good faith acquisition of personal information by an employee or agent of the entity for purposes of the entity is not a breach of the security of the system." *Id.* sec. 2302.

" 'Personal information.' An individual's first name or first initial and last name in combination with and linked to any one or more of the following data elements when the data elements are not encrypted or redacted:

(ii) Social Security number.
(iii) Driver's license number or a State identification card number issued in lieu of a driver's license.
(iv) Financial account number, credit or debit card number, in combination with any required security code, access code or password that would permit access to an individual's financial account.

The term does not include publicly available information that is lawfully made available to the general public from Federal, State or local government records." *Id.*

Rhode Island

"Any state agency or person that owns, maintains or licenses computerized data that includes personal information, shall disclose any breach of the security of the system which poses a significant risk of identity theft following discovery or notification of the breach in the security of the data to any resident of Rhode Island whose unencrypted personal information was, or is reasonably believed to have been, acquired by an unauthorized person without authority, to acquire said information." R.I. Gen. Laws §1-49.2-3(a).

"Any state agency or person that maintains computerized unencrypted data that includes personal information that the state agency or person does not own shall notify the owner or licensee of the information of any breach of the security of the data which poses a significant risk of identity theft immediately, following discovery, if the personal information was, or is reasonably believed to have been, acquired by an unauthorized person." *Id.* §1-49.2-3(b).

"Notification of a breach is not required if, after an appropriate investigation or after consultation with relevant federal, state, or local law enforcement agencies, a determination is made that the breach has not and will not likely result in a significant risk of identity theft to the individuals whose personal information has been acquired." *Id.* §11-49.2-4.

"Any state agency or person that maintains its own security breach procedures as part of an information security policy for the treatment of personal information and otherwise complies with the timing requirements of §11-49.2-3, shall be deemed to be in compliance with the security breach notification requirements of §11-49.2-3, provided such person notifies subject persons in accordance with such person's policies in the event of a breach of security. Any person that maintains such a security breach procedure pursuant to the rules, regulations, procedures or guidelines established by the primary functional regulator, as defined in 15 USC 6809(2), shall be deemed to be in compliance with the security breach notification requirements of this section, provided such person notifies subject persons in accordance with the policies or the rules, regulations, procedures or guidelines established by the primary or functional regulator in the event of a breach of the security of the system. A financial institution, trust company, credit union or its affiliates that is subject to and examined for, and found in compliance with the Federal Interagency Guidelines on Response Programs for Unauthorized Access to Customer Information and Customer Notice shall be deemed in compliance with this chapter. A provider of health care, health care service plan, health insurer, or a covered entity governed by the medical privacy and security rules issued by the federal Department of Health and Human Services, Parts 160 and 164 of Title 45 of the Code of Federal Regulations, established pursuant to the Health Insurance Portability and Accountability Act of 1995 (HIPAA) shall be deemed in compliance with this chapter." *Id.* §11-49.2-7.

(Notification may be delayed for law enforcement purposes; methods of notification are prescribed.)

"For purposes of this section, 'breach of the security of the system' means unauthorized acquisition of unencrypted computerized data that compromises the security, confidentiality, or integrity of personal information maintained by the state agency or person. Good faith acquisition of personal information by an employee or agent of the agency is not a breach of the security of the system; provided, that the personal information is not used or subject to further unauthorized disclosure." *Id.* §11-49.2-5(b).

"For purposes of this section, 'personal information' means an individual's first name or first initial and last name in combination with any one or more of the following data elements, when either the name or the data elements are not encrypted:

(1) Social security number;
(2) Driver's license or Rhode Island Identification Card number;
(3) Account number, credit or debit card number, in combination with any required security code, access code, or password that would permit access to an individual's financial account." *Id.* §11-49.2-5(c).

Tennessee

"Any information holder shall disclose any breach of the security of the system following discovery or notification of the breach in the security of the data to any resident of Tennessee whose unencrypted personal information was, or is reasonably believed to have been, acquired by an unauthorized person." 2005 Tenn. Public Acts 473, amending Title 47, Chapter 18, Part 21 of Tennessee Code Annotated.

"Any information holder that maintains computerized data that includes personal information that the information holder does not own shall notify the owner or licensee of the information of any breach of the security of the data immediately following discovery, if the personal information was, or is reasonably believed to have been, acquired by an unauthorized person." *Id.*

(Notification may be delayed for law enforcement purposes; methods of notification are prescribed.)

" 'Breach of the security of the system' means unauthorized acquisition of unencrypted computerized data that materially compromises the security, confidentiality, or integrity of personal information maintained by the information holder. Good faith acquisition of personal information by an employee or agent of the information holder for the purposes of the information holder is not a breach of the security of the system, provided that the personal information is not used or subject to further unauthorized disclosure." *Id.*

" 'Information holder' means any person or business that conducts business in this state, or any agency of the State of Tennessee or any of its political subdivisions, that owns or licenses computerized data that includes personal information." *Id.*

" 'Personal information' means an individual's first name or first initial and last name in conjunction with any one or more of the following data elements, when either the name or the data elements are not encrypted:

(i) Social security number;
(ii) Driver license number; or
(iii) Account number, credit or debit card number, in combination with any required security code, access code, or password that would permit access to an individual's financial account." *Id.*

Texas

"Any person that conducts business in this state and owns or licenses computerized data that includes sensitive personal information shall disclose any breach of system security, after discovering or receiving notification of the breach, to any resident of this state whose sensitive personal information was, or is reasonably believed to have been, acquired by an unauthorized person." Tex. Bus. & Com. Code §48.103(b).

"Any person that maintains computerized data that includes sensitive personal information that the person does not own shall notify the owner or license holder of the information of any breach of system security immediately after discovering the breach, if the sensitive personal information was, or is reasonably believed to have been, acquired by an unauthorized person." *Id.* §48.103(c).

(Notification may be delayed for law enforcement purposes; methods of notification are prescribed.)

"In this section, 'breach of system security' means unauthorized acquisition of computerized data that compromises the security, confidentiality, or integrity of sensitive personal information maintained by a person. Good faith acquisition of sensitive personal information by an employee or agent of the person or business for the purposes of the person is not a breach of system security unless the sensitive personal information is used or disclosed by the person in an unauthorized manner." *Id.* §48.103(a).

" 'Sensitive personal information':

(A) means an individual's first name or first initial and last name in combination with any one or more of the following items, if the name and the items are not encrypted:

(i) social security number;
(ii) driver's license number or government-issued identification number; or
(iii) account number or credit or debit card number in combination with any required security code, access code, or password that would permit access to an individual's financial account; and
(C) does not include publicly available information that is lawfully made available to the general public from the federal government or a state or local government." *Id.* §48.002(2).

Utah

"(1)(A). A person who owns or licenses computerized data that includes personal information concerning a Utah resident shall, when the person becomes aware of a breach of system security, conduct in good faith a reasonable and prompt investigation to determine the likelihood that personal information has been or will be misused for identity theft or fraud purposes.

"(B). If an investigation under subsection (1)(A) reveals that the misuse of personal information for identity theft or fraud purposes has occurred, or is reasonably likely to occur, the person shall provide notification to each affected Utah resident." State of Utah 2006 General Session, Senate Bill 69, chapter 42 of Utah Statutes, sec. 13-42-202(1).

"(3)(A). A person who maintains computerized data that includes personal information that the person does not own or license shall notify and cooperate with the owner or licensee of the information of any breach of system security immediately following the person's discovery of the breach if misuse of the personal information occurs or is reasonably likely to occur." *Id.* sec. 13-42-202(3)(A).

" 'Breach of system security' means an unauthorized acquisition of computerized data maintained by a person that compromises the security, confidentiality, or integrity of persona information." *Id.*, sec. 13-42-102(1)(A).

" 'Personal information' means a person's first name or first initial and last name, combined with any one or more of the following data elements relating to that person when either the name or data element is unencrypted or not protected by another method that renders the data unreadable or unusable:

(II) Social Security number;
(II)(A) financial account number, or credit or debit card number; and
(B) any required security code, access code, or password that would permit access to the person's account; or
(III) driver license number or state identification card number." *Id.*, sec. 13-42-102(3).

(Exceptions are provided for entities that maintain their own adequate notification procedures or that are subject to comparable statutes and regulations; notification may be delayed for purposes of cooperation with law enforcement; methods of notification are prescribed.)

Vermont

"Except as set forth in subsection (d) of this section, any data collector that owns or licenses computerized personal information that includes personal information concerning a consumer shall notify the consumer that there has been a security breach following discovery or notification to the data collector of the breach. Notice of the breach shall be made in the most expedient time possible and without unreasonable delay, consistent with the legitimate needs of the law enforcement agency, . . . or with any measures necessary to determine the scope of the breach and restore the reasonable integrity, security, and confidentiality of the data system."

9 V.S.A. § 2435(b)(1).

"Any data collector that maintains or possesses computerized data containing personal information of a consumer that the business does not own or license or any data collector that conducts business in Vermont maintains or possesses records or data containing personal information that the data collector does not own or license shall notify the owner or licensee of the information of any security breach immediately following discovery of the breach, consistent with the legitimate needs of law enforcement . . ."

Id. § 2435(b)(2).

"Notice of a security breach . . . is not required if the data collector establishes that misuse of personal information is not reasonably possible and the data collector provides notice of the determination that the misuse of the personal information is not reasonably possible pursuant to the requirements of this subsection. If the data collector establishes that misuse of the personal information is not reasonably possible, the data collector shall provide notice of its determination that misuse of the personal information is not reasonably possible and a detailed explanation for said determination to the Vermont attorney general or to the department of banking, insurance, securities and health care administration in the event that the data collector is a person or entity licensed or registered with the department under Title 8 or this title . . ."

Id. § 2435(d)(1).

"If a data collector established that misuse of personal information was not reasonably possible under subdivision (1) of this section, and subsequently obtains facts indicating that misuse of the personal information has occurred or is occurring, the data collector shall provide notice of the security breach . . ."

Id. § 2435(d)(2).

" 'Data collector' may include, but is not limited to, the state, state agencies, political subdivisions of the state, public and private universities, privately and publicly held corporations, limited liability companies, financial institutions, retail operators, and any other entity that, for any purpose, whether by automated collection or otherwise, handles, collects, disseminates, or otherwise deals with nonpublic personal information."

Id. § 2430(3).

" 'Personal information' means an individual's first name or first initial and last name in combination with any one or more of the following data elements, when either the name or the data elements are not encrypted or redacted or protected by another method that renders them unreadable or unusable by unauthorized persons:

(i) Social Security number;
(ii) Motor vehicle operator's license number or nondriver identification card number;

(iii) Financial account number or credit or debit card number, if circumstances exist in which the number could be used without additional identifying information, access codes, or passwords:
(iv) Account passwords or personal identification numbers or other access codes for a financial account."
Id. § 2430(5)(A).

" 'Security breach' means unauthorized acquisition or access of computerized data that compromises the security, confidentiality, or integrity of personal information maintained by the data collector."

Id. § 2430(8)(A).

" 'Security breach' does not include good faith but unauthorized acquisition or access of personal information by an employee or agent of a data collector for a legitimate purpose of the data collector, provided that the personal information is not used for a purpose unrelated to the data collector's business or subject to further unauthorized disclosure."

Id. § 2430(8)(B).

Virgin Islands

"Any person or business that conducts business in the Virgin Islands, and that owns or license computerized data that includes personal information, shall disclose any breach of the security of the system following discovery or notification of the breach in the security of the data to any resident of the Virgin Islands, whose unencrypted personal information was, or is reasonably believed to have been, acquired by an unauthorized person. The disclosure must be made in the most expedient time possible and without unreasonable delay, consistent with the legitimate needs of law enforcement, . . . or any measures necessary to determine the scope of the breach and restore the integrity of the data system."

14 V.I.C. § 2209(a).

"Any person or business that maintains computerized data the includes personal information that the person or business does not own shall notify the owner or licensee of the information of any breach in the security of the data immediately following discovery, if the personal information was, or is reasonably believed to have been, acquired by an unauthorized person."

Id. § 2209(b).

"For purposes of this section, 'breach of the security of the system' means unauthorized acquisition of the computerized data that compromises the security, confidentiality, or integrity of personal information maintained by the person or business. Good faith acquisition of personal information by an employee or agent of the person or business for the purposes of the person or business is not a breach of the security of the system, provided that the personal information is not used or subject to further disclosure."

Id. § 2209(d).

"For purposes of this section, 'personal information' means an individual's first name or first initial and last name in combination with any one or more of the following data elements, when either the name or the data elements are not encrypted:

(1) Social Security number.
(2) Driver's license number.
(3) Account number, credit or debit card number, in combination with any required security code, access code, or password that would permit access to an individual's financial account."

Id. § 2209(e).

Washington

"Any person or business that conducts business in this state that owns or licenses computerized data that includes personal information shall disclose any breach of the security of the system following discovery or notification of the breach in the security of the data to any resident of this state whose unencrypted personal information was, or is reasonably believed to have been, acquired by an unauthorized person." Rev. Code Wash. §19.255.010(1).

"Any person or business that maintains computerized data that includes personal information that the person or business does not own shall notify the owner or licensee of the information of any breach of the security of the data immediately following discovery, if the personal information was, or is reasonably believed to have been, acquired by an unauthorized person." *Id.* §19.255.010(2).

(Notification may be delayed for law enforcement purposes; methods of notification are prescribed.)

"For purposes of this section, 'breach of the security of the system' means unauthorized acquisition of computerized data that compromises the security, confidentiality, or integrity of personal information maintained by the person or business. Good faith acquisition of personal information by an employee or agent of the person or business for the purposes of the person or business is not a breach of the security of the system when the personal information is not used or subject to further unauthorized disclosure." *Id.* §19.255.010(4).

"For purposes of this section, 'personal information' means an individual's first name or first initial and last name in combination with any one or more of the following data elements, when either the name or the data elements are not encrypted:

(a) Social security number;
(b) Driver's license number or Washington identification card number; or
(c) Account number or credit or debit card number, in combination with any required security code, access code, or password that would permit access to an individual's financial account." *Id.* §19.255.010(5).

"Any agency that owns or licenses computerized data that includes personal information shall disclose any breach of the security of the system following discovery or notification of the breach in the security of the data to any resident of this state whose unencrypted personal information was, or is reasonably believed to have been, acquired by an unauthorized person." *Id.* §41.17.31992(1)(a).

"An agency that maintains computerized data that includes personal information that the agency does not own shall notify the owner or licensee of the information of any breach of the security of the data immediately following discovery, if the personal information was, or is reasonably believed to have been, acquired by an unauthorized person." *Id.* §42.17.31922(2).

"For purposes of this section, 'breach of the security of the system' means unauthorized acquisition of computerized data that compromises the security, confidentiality, or integrity of personal information maintained by the agency. Good faith acquisition of personal information by an employee or agent of the agency for the purposes of the agency is not a breach of the security of the system when the personal information is not used or subject to further unauthorized disclosure." *Id.* §42.17.31922(4).

"For purposes of this section, 'personal information' means an individual's first name or first initial and last name in combination with any one or more of the following data elements, when either the name or the data elements are not encrypted:

(a) Social security number;
(b) Driver's license number or Washington identification card number; or
(c) Account number or credit or debit card number, in combination with any required security code, access code, or password that would permit access to an individual's financial account." *Id.* sec. 42.17.31922(5).

Wisconsin

"If an entity whose principal place of business is located in this state or an entity that maintains or licenses personal information in this state knows that personal information in the entity's possession has been acquired by a person whom the entity has not authorized to acquire the personal information, the entity shall make reasonable efforts to notify each subject of the personal information. The notice shall indicate that the entity knows of the unauthorized acquisition of personal information pertaining to the subject of the personal information."

Wis. Stat. § 895.507(2)(a).

(b) If an entity whose principal place of business is not located in this state knows that personal information pertaining to a resident of this state has been acquired by a person whom the entity has not authorized to acquire the personal information, the entity shall make reasonable efforts to notify each resident of this state who is the subject of the personal information. The notice shall indicate that the entity knows of the unauthorized acquisition of personal information pertaining to the resident of this state who is the subject of the personal information.

(bm) If a person, other than an individual, that stores personal information pertaining to a resident of this state, but does not own or license the personal information, knows that the personal information has been acquired by a person whom the person storing the personal information has not authorized to acquire the personal information, and the person storing the personal information has not entered into a contract with the person that owns or licenses the personal information, the person storing the personal information shall notify the person that owns or licenses the personal information of the acquisition as soon as practicable.

(cm) Notwithstanding pars. (a), (b), (bm), and (br), an entity is not required to provide notice of the acquisition of personal information if any of the following applies:

1. The acquisition of personal information does not create a material risk of identity theft or fraud to the subject of the personal information.
2. The personal information was acquired in good faith by an employee or agent of the entity, if the personal information is used for a lawful purpose of the entity.

Id. §§ 895.507(2)(b), (bm), (cm).

(b) "Personal information" means an individual's last name and the individual's first name or first initial, in combination with and linked to any of the following elements, if the element is not publicly available information and is not encrypted, redacted, or altered in a manner that renders the element unreadable:
1. The individual's social security number.
2. The individual's drivers license number or state identification number.
3. The number of the individual's financial account number, including a credit or debit card account number, or any security code, access code, or password that would permit access to the individual's financial account.
4. The individual's deoxyribonucleic acid profile . . .
5. The individual's unique biometric data, including fingerprint, voice print, retina or iris image, or any other unique physical representation.
(c) "Publicly available information" means any information that an entity reasonably believes is one of the following:
1. Lawfully made widely available through any media.
2. Lawfully made available to the general public from federal, state, or local government records or disclosures to the general public that are required to be made by federal, state, or local law.

Id. § 895.507(1)(b).

Wyoming

Wyoming has a data security breach notification statute effective July 1, 2007.
40-12-501. Definitions.

(a) As used in this act:
(i) "Breach of the security of the data system" means unauthorized acquisition of computerized data that materially compromises the security, confidentiality or

integrity of personal identifying information maintained by a person or business and causes or is reasonably believed to cause loss or injury to a resident of this state. Good faith acquisition of personal identifying information by an employee or agent of a person or business for the purposes of the person or business is not a breach of the security of the data system, provided that the personal identifying information is not used or subject to further unauthorized disclosure;

(ii) "Consumer" means any person who is utilizing or seeking credit for personal, family or household purposes;

(iii) "Consumer reporting agency" means any person whose business is the assembling and evaluating of information as to the credit standing and credit worthiness of a consumer, for the purposes of furnishing credit reports, for monetary fees and dues to third parties;

(iv) "Credit report" means any written or oral report, recommendation or representation of a consumer reporting agency as to the credit worthiness, credit standing or credit capacity of any consumer and includes any information which is sought or given for the purpose of serving as the basis for determining eligibility for credit to be used primarily for personal, family or household purposes;

(v) "Creditor" means the lender of money or vendor of goods, services or property, including a lessor under a lease intended as a security, rights or privileges, for which payment is arranged through a credit transaction, or any successor to the right, title or interest of any such lender or vendor, and an affiliate, associate or subsidiary of any of them or any director, officer or employee of any of them or any other person in any way associated with any of them;

(vi) "Financial institution" means any person licensed or chartered under the laws of any state or the United States as a bank holding company, bank, savings and loan association, credit union, trust company or subsidiary thereof doing business in this state;

(vii) "Personal identifying information" means the first name or first initial and last name of a person in combination with one (1) or more of the following data elements when either the name or the data elements are not redacted:

(A) Social security number;

(B) Driver's license number or Wyoming identification card number;

(C) Account number, credit card number or debit card number in combination with any security code, access code or password that would allow access to a financial account of the person;

(D) Tribal identification card; or

(E) Federal or state government issued identification card.

(viii)"Redact" means alteration or truncation of data such that no more than five (5) digits of the data elements provided in subparagraphs (vii)(A) through (D) of this subsection are accessible as part of the personal information;

(ix) "Security freeze" means a notice placed in a consumer's credit report, at the request of the consumer, that prohibits the credit rating agency from releasing the consumer's credit report or any information from it relating to an extension of credit or the opening of a new account, without the express authorization of the consumer . . .

(b) "Personal identifying information" as defined in paragraph (a)(vii) of this section does not include information, regardless of its source, contained in any federal, state or local government records or in widely distributed media that are lawfully made available to the general public.

40-12-502. Computer security breach; notice to affected persons.

(a) An individual or commercial entity that conducts business in Wyoming and that owns or licenses computerized data that includes personal identifying information about a resident of Wyoming shall, when it becomes aware of a breach of the security of the system, conduct in good faith a reasonable and prompt investigation to determine the likelihood that personal identifying information has been or will be misused. If the investigation determines that the misuse of personal identifying information about a Wyoming resident has occurred or is reasonably likely to occur, the individual or the commercial entity shall give notice as soon as possible to the affected Wyoming resident. Notice shall be made in the most expedient time possible and without unreasonable delay, consistent with the legitimate needs of law enforcement and consistent with any measures necessary to determine the scope of the breach and to restore the reasonable integrity of the computerized data system.
(b) The notification required by this section may be delayed if a law enforcement agency determines in writing that the notification may seriously impede a criminal investigation.
(c) Any financial institution as defined in 15 U.S.C. 6809 or federal credit union as defined by 12 U.S.C. 1752 that maintains notification procedures subject to the requirements of 15 U.S.C. 6801(b)(3) and 12 C.F.R. Part 364 Appendix B or Part 748 Appendix B, is deemed to be in compliance with this section if the financial institution notifies affected Wyoming customers in compliance with the requirements of 15 U.S.C. 6801 through 6809 and 12 C.F.R. Part 364 Appendix B or Part 748 Appendix B.
(f) The attorney general may bring an action in law or equity to address any violation of this section and for other relief that may be appropriate to ensure proper compliance with this section, to recover damages, or both. The provisions of this section are not exclusive and do not relieve an individual or a commercial entity subject to this section from compliance with all other applicable provisions of law.
(g) Any person who maintains computerized data that includes personal identifying information on behalf of another business entity shall disclose to the business entity for which the information is maintained any breach of the security of the system as soon as practicable following the determination that personal identifying information was, or is reasonably believed to have been, acquired by an unauthorized person. The person who maintains the data on behalf of another business entity and the business entity on whose behalf the data is maintained may agree which person or entity will provide any required notice as provided in subsection (a) of this section, provided only a single notice for each breach of the security of the system shall be required. If agreement regarding notification cannot be reached, the person who has the direct business relationship with the resident of this state shall provide notice subject to the provisions of subsection (a) of this section.

APPENDIX C

The Jurisdiction and Enforcement Powers of the Federal Trade Commission

A BRIEF OVERVIEW OF THE FEDERAL TRADE COMMISSION'S INVESTIGATIVE AND LAW ENFORCEMENT AUTHORITY [1]

Revised, **September 2002**

I. INVESTIGATIVE AUTHORITY

A. In General

The Commission may "prosecute any inquiry necessary to its duties in any part of the United States" (FTC Act Sec. 3, 15 U.S.C. Sec. 43) and may "gather and compile information concerning, and * * * investigate from time to time the organization, business, conduct, practices, and management of any person, partnership, or corporation engaged in or whose business affects commerce, excepting banks, savings and loan institutions * * * Federal credit unions * * * and common carriers * * *." (FTC Act Sec. 6(a), 15 U.S.C. Sec. 46(a)).[2] Pre-complaint investigations are generally non-public, and thus are not identified on this site. On occasion the existence of an investigation may be identified in a press release.[3]

B. Specific Investigative Powers

The Commission's specific investigative powers are defined in Sections 6, 9, and 20 of the FTC Act, 15 U.S.C. Secs. 46, 49, and 57b-1, which authorize investigations and various forms of compulsory process. In addition, the premerger notification provisions in Section 7A of the Clayton Act, 15 U.S.C. Sec. 18a, prohibit consummation of covered acquisitions until the requested information is provided, thus effectively enabling the Commission to obtain information regarding such acquisitions.

1. *Sections 9 and 20 of the FTC Act*

Section 9 of the FTC Act authorizes the Commission to "require by **subpoena** the attendance and testimony of witnesses and the production of all such documentary evidence relating to any matter under investigation" (15 U.S.C. Sec. 49). Any member of the Commission may sign a subpoena, and both members and "examiners" (employees) of the agency may administer oaths, examine witnesses, and receive evidence.

Under Commission Rule 2.7 (16 C.F.R. Sec. 2.7), a party may raise objections to a subpoena by filing a **petition to quash**. Such petitions are resolved by a designated Commissioner, and the designated Commissioner's ruling may thereafter be appealed to the full Commission.

If a party fails to comply with a subpoena (either without filing a petition to quash, or after a duly filed petition is denied), the Commission may seek enforcement of the subpoena in "[a]ny of the district courts of the United States within the jurisdiction of which such inquiry is carried on" (15 U.S.C. Sec. 49). After the Commission files its petition to enforce a subpoena, and following receipt of any response from the subpoena recipient, the court may enter an order requiring compliance. Refusal to comply with a court enforcement order is subject to penalties for contempt of court.

The subpoena provisions of Section 9 are used routinely by the Bureau of Competition to investigate alleged unfair methods of competition and other antitrust violations. Prior to 1980, the Bureau of Consumer Protection also used subpoenas for investigations. However, as the result of the FTC Improvements Act of 1980, which added a new Section 20 of the FTC Act, 15 U.S.C. Sec. 57b-1, the Bureau of Consumer Protection may now use only "civil investigative demands" ("**CIDs**") to investigate possible "unfair or deceptive acts or practices". By virtue of the FTC Act Amendments of 1994, the Bureau of Competition also may use CIDs (in addition to subpoenas) for investigations of possible antitrust violations.

The scope of a civil investigative demand is different from that of a subpoena. Both subpoenas and CIDs may be used to obtain existing documents or oral testimony. But a CID may also require that the recipient "file written reports or answers to questions" (15.U.S.C. Sec. 57b-1(c)(1)). In addition, Section 20 expressly authorizes the issuance of CIDS requiring the production of tangible things and provides for service of CIDS upon entities not found within the territorial jurisdiction of any court of the United States.

As with subpoenas, the recipient of a civil investigative demand may file a petition to quash. Likewise, the Commission may petition a federal district court to enforce the CID in the event of noncompliance, although permissible venue is narrower in a CID enforcement action than in a subpoena enforcement case.

2. *Section 6(b) of the FTC Act*

Another investigative tool, this one available in both competition and consumer protection matters, appears in Section 6 of the FTC Act, 15 U.S.C. Sec. 46. Section 6(b) empowers the Commission to require the filing of "annual or special * * * reports or answers in writing to specific questions for the purpose of obtaining information about "the organization, business, conduct, practices, management, and relation to other corporations, partnerships, and individuals" of the entities to whom the inquiry is addressed. As with subpoenas and CID's, the recipient of a **6(b) order** may file a petition to quash, and the Commission may seek a court order requiring compliance. In addition, the Commission may commence suit in Federal court under Section 10 of the FTC Act, 15 U.S.C. Sec. 50, against any party who fails to comply with a 6(b) order after receiving a notice of default from the Commission. After expiration of a thirty-day grace period, the defaulting party is liable to a penalty of $110[4] for each day of noncompliance.

The Commission's 6(b) authority enables it to conduct wide-ranging economic studies that do not have a specific law enforcement purpose. (An example is the "Line-of-Business" study conducted in the 1970's, which required corporations to report line of business profitability and other data on a yearly basis.) Section 6(b) also enables the Commission to obtain to specific questions as part of an antitrust law enforcement investigation, where such information would not be available through subpoena because there is no document that contains the desired answers. Section 6 also authorizes the Commission to "make public from time to time" portions of the information that it obtains, where disclosure would serve the public interest (15 U.S.C. Sec. 46(f)).

3. *Premerger Notification*

In merger investigations, the Commission also relies on Section 7A of the Clayton Act, 15 U.S.C. Sec. 18a, which was added by the **Hart-Scott-Rodino** Act of 1976. Under Section 7A, the parties to an acquisition of the requisite size must report the transaction to the government and wait a specified number of days before consummation. Should the Commission or the Department of Justice decide that further examination is warranted, they may seek additional information by issuing to the parties a "second request." When such a request is issued, the waiting period is extended and the subject acquisition may not be consummated until the conclusion of a specified period following the parties' compliance with the request. Although parties are not technically obligated to comply with a second request, as they are with a subpoena, the price of noncompliance is that consummation of the transaction would be illegal. Thus, the premerger notification provisions of the Clayton Act are a powerful incentive for companies to submit information that the government needs to evaluate corporate acquisitions. Should the parties merge without observing the requirements of the Clayton Act, the Commission may seek both injunctive relief and civil penalties, as appropriate, under Section 7A(g) of the Clayton Act. The Commission may also grant an early termination of a waiting period. Notices of early termination are available on this site.

4. *International Antitrust Enforcement*

Under the International Antitrust Enforcement Assistance Act ("IAEAA"), 15 U.S.C. § 6201 *et seq.*, the FTC may invoke all of its investigative tools to obtain materials or information from domestic sources for the use of foreign antitrust authorities, and may seek investigative assistance from those authorities, pursuant to mutual or bilateral assistance agreements established under the IAEAA. New FTC Act Sections 6(i) and 20(a)(8)(C) incorporate the IAEAA investigative authority into the FTC Act.

II. ENFORCEMENT AUTHORITY

Following an investigation, the Commission may initiate an enforcement action if it finds "**reason to believe**" that the law is being violated. The Commission uses certain of its statutory powers to enforce both consumer protection and antitrust laws, but there are also important differences that merit separate discussion of the two missions.

A. Consumer Protection

The basic consumer protection statute enforced by the Commission is Section 5(a) of the FTC Act, which provides that "**unfair or deceptive acts or practices** in or affecting commerce are declared unlawful" (15 U.S.C. Sec. 45(a)(1)).

"Unfair" practices are defined to mean those that "cause[] or [are] likely to cause **substantial injury** to consumers which is **not reasonably avoidable** by consumers themselves and **not outweighed by countervailing benefits** to consumers or to competition" (15 U.S.C. Sec. 45(n)). In addition, the Commission enforces a variety of specific consumer protection statutes (e.g., the Equal Credit Opportunity Act, Truth-in-Lending Act, Fair Credit Reporting Act, the Cigarette Labeling Act) that prohibit specifically-defined trade practices and generally specify that violations are to be treated as if they were "unfair or deceptive" acts or practices under Section 5(a). Summaries of the statutes giving the Commission enforcement powers are available on this site.

The Commission enforces the substantive requirements of consumer protection law through both administrative and judicial processes, as described below.

1. *Administrative Enforcement*

In the administrative process, The Commission makes the initial determination that a practice violates the law, in either an adjudicative or rulemaking proceeding.

(a) Adjudication

Under Section 5(b) of the FTC Act, the Commission may attack "unfair or deceptive practices" (or violations of other consumer protection statutes) through maintenance of an administrative adjudication. When there is "**reason to believe**" that a law violation has occurred, the Commission may issue a complaint setting forth its charges. If the respondent elects to settle the charges, it may sign a consent agreement (without admitting liability) by which it consents to entry of a final order and waives all right to judicial review. If the Commission accepts such a proposed consent, it places the order on the record for thirty days of public comment (or for such other period as the Commission may specify) before determining whether to make the order final.

Administrative Trials

If the respondent elects instead to contest the charges, the complaint is adjudicated before an administrative law judge ("ALJ") in a trial-type proceeding conducted under the Commission's Rules of Practice. The prosecution of a consumer protection matter is conducted by FTC "complaint counsel," who are staff from the Bureau of Consumer Protection or a regional office. Upon conclusion of the hearings, the ALJ issues an "initial decision" setting forth his findings of fact and conclusions of law, and recommending either entry of an order to cease and desist or dismissal of the complaint. Either complaint counsel or respondent, or both, may appeal the initial decision to the full Commission.

Upon appeal of an initial decision, the Commission receives briefs, holds oral argument, and thereafter issues its own final decision and order. The Commission's final decision is appealable by any respondent against which an order is issued. The respondent may file a petition for review with any court of appeals within whose jurisdiction the respondent "resides or carries on business or where the challenged practice was employed." (FTC Act, Section 5(c), 15 U.S.C. Sec. 45(c)). If the court of appeals affirms the Commission's order, the court enters its own order of enforcement. The party losing in the court of appeals may seek review by the Supreme Court. Commission decisions and orders since March 1996 are available.

Enforcing Final Commission Orders

A Commission order (except an order to divest assets) becomes final (*i.e.*, binding on the respondent) 60 days after it is served, unless the order is stayed by the Commission or by a reviewing court. If a respondent violates a final order, it is liable for a civil penalty of up to $11,000 for each violation. The penalty is assessed by a district court in a suit brought to enforce the Commission's order. The court may also issue "mandatory injunctions" and "such other and further equitable relief" as is deemed appropriate. (FTC Act, Section 5(1), 15 U.S.C. Sec. 45(1)). Pending enforcement actions are identified in the Federal Court Litigation Status Report.

Redress After an Administrative Order is Entered

In addition (after all judicial review of its order is complete), the Commission may seek consumer redress from the respondent in district court for consumer jury caused by the conduct that was at issue in the administrative proceeding. In such a suit, which lies under Section 19 of the FTC Act, 15 U.S.C. Sec. 57b, the Commission must demonstrate that the conduct was such as "a reasonable man would have known under the circumstances was dishonest or fraudulent."

Civil Penalty Enforcement against Non-Respondents

Where the Commission has determined in an adjudicatory proceeding that a practice is unfair or deceptive and has issued a final cease and desist order, the Commission may also obtain civil penalties from non-respondents who thereafter violate the standards articulated by the Commission. To accomplish this, the Commission must show that the violator had "actual knowledge that such act or practice is unfair or deceptive and is unlawful" under Section 5(a)(1) of the FTC Act. (FTC Act, Section 5(m)(1)(B); 15 U.S.C. Sec. 45(m)(1)(B)). To prove "actual knowledge," the Commission typically shows that it had provided the violator with a copy of the Commission determination in question, or a "synopsis" of that determination. The virtue of Section 5(m)(1)(B) is that it limits wrongdoers to only a single bite of the apple before they are subject to monetary penalties.

(b) Rulemaking

In lieu of attacking unfair or deceptive practices by administrative adjudications against individual respondents, the Commission may use trade regulation rules to remedy unfair or deceptive practices that occur on an industry-wide basis. Under Section 18 of the FTC Act, 15 U.S.C. Sec. 57a, the Commission is authorized to prescribe "rules which define with specificity acts or practices which are unfair or deceptive acts or practices in or affecting commerce" within the meaning of Section 5(a)(1) of the Act. The statute requires that Commission rulemaking proceedings provide an opportunity for informal hearings at which interested parties are accorded limited rights of cross examination. Before commencing a rulemaking proceeding the Commission must also have reason to believe that the practices to be addressed by the rulemaking are "prevalent" (15 U.S.C. Sec. 57a(b)(3)). Commission rules are published in Title 16 of the Code of Federal Regulations.

Once the Commission has promulgated a trade regulation rule, anyone who violates the rule "with actual knowledge or knowledge fairly implied on the basis of objective circumstances that such act is unfair or deceptive and is prohibited by such rule" is liable for civil penalties of up to $11,000 per violation. The Commission obtains such penalties by filing a suit in district court under Section 5(m)(1)(A) of the FTC Act, 15 U.S.C. Sec. 45(m)(1)(A). In addition, any person who violates a rule (irrespective of the state of knowledge) is liable for injury caused to consumers by the rule violation. The Commission may pursue such recovery in a suit for consumer redress under Section 19 of the FTC Act, 15 U.S.C. Sec. 57b.

2. *Judicial Enforcement*

As the preceding section illustrates, even where the Commission determines through adjudication or rulemaking that a practice is unfair or deceptive, the Commission must still seek the aid of a court to obtain civil penalties or consumer redress for violations of its orders to cease and desist or trade regulation rules. In this section, we discuss the Commission's ability to challenge a practice directly in court, without first making a final agency determination that the challenged conduct is unlawful.

Section 13(b) of the FTC Act, 15 U.S.C. Sec. 53(b), authorizes the Commission to seek **preliminary and permanent injunctions** to remedy "any provision of law enforced by the Federal Trade Commission." Under the first proviso of Section 13(b), whenever the Commission has "reason to believe" that any party "is violating, or is about to violate" a provision of law enforced by the Commission, the Commission may ask the district court to enjoin the allegedly unlawful conduct, pending completion of an FTC administrative proceeding to determine whether the conduct is unlawful. Further, under the second proviso of Section 13(b), "in proper cases," the Commission may seek, and the court may grant, a *permanent* injunction.

Section 13(b) was added to the FTC Act as part of amendments to the Trans-Alaska Pipeline Act of 1973. At the time, the provision was expected to be used principally for obtaining preliminary injunctions against corporate acquisitions, pending completion of FTC administrative hearings. During the 1970's, Section 13(b) was used by the Commission mainly in this way, and the Commission continues to make frequent use of the provision in its merger enforcement program.

However, on occasion in the 1970's, the Commission also used the "preliminary injunction" provision of Section 13(b) to obtain injunctions against ongoing campaigns of deceptive advertising, pending a final FTC adjudication. (Section 13(a) of the Act, passed in 1938, had previously authorized the Commission to seek injunctive relief in cases of false advertisements for "food, drugs, devices, or cosmetics.")

In the early and mid-1980's, the Commission began to make widespread use of the permanent injunction proviso of Section 13(b) in its consumer protection program to challenge cases of basic consumer fraud and deception. Further, the Commission argued that the statutory reference to "permanent injunction" entitled the Commission to obtain an order not only permanently barring deceptive practices, but also imposing various kinds of monetary equitable relief (*i.e.*, restitution and rescission of contracts) to remedy past violations. The Commission also argued that, to preserve the possibility of ultimate monetary equitable relief, it should be able to obtain a freeze of assets and imposition of temporary receivers in appropriate cases.

The courts have uniformly accepted the Commission's construction of Section 13(b), with the result that most consumer protection enforcement is now conducted directly in court under Section 13(b), rather than by means of administrative adjudication. A suit under Section 13(b) is preferable to the adjudicatory process outlined above because, in such a suit, the court may award both prohibitory and monetary equitable relief in one step. In addition, a judicial injunction becomes effective immediately, while a Commission cease and desist order takes effect only 60 days after service. Pending Section 13(b) cases are identified on the Federal Court Litigation Status Report.

Of course, administrative adjudication offers certain advantages over direct judicial enforcement. In particular, in an adjudicatory proceeding, the Commission has the first opportunity to make factual findings and articulate the relevant legal standard. On review, the court is obliged to affirm the Commission's findings of fact if supported by substantial evidence. A reviewing court must also accord substantial deference to constructions of the FTC Act articulated by the Commission in adjudication or rulemaking. In a 13(b) suit, by contrast, the Commission receives no greater deference than would any government plaintiff. Thus, where a case involves novel legal issues or fact patterns, the Commission has tended to prefer administrative adjudication.

B. Antitrust

The Commission enforces various antitrust laws through its Bureau of Competition. The two most significant statutory provisions are Section 5(a) of the FTC Act and the Clayton Act. Section 5(a) of the FTC Act, 15 U.S.C. Sec. 45(a), prohibits, *inter alia*, "unfair methods of competition." **Unfair methods of competition** include any conduct that would violate the Sherman Antitrust Act. The Clayton Act prohibits corporate **acquisitions that may tend substantially to lessen competition** (Section 7, 15 U.S.C. Sec. 18) and also bars certain forms of price discrimination (Section 2 of the Robinson Patman Act, 15 U.S.C. Secs. 13-13b). As with its consumer protection responsibilities, the Commission uses both administrative and judicial remedies to enforce the law.

1. *Administrative Enforcement*

a. Adjudication

The Commission may challenge alleged "unfair methods of competition," as it does "unfair or deceptive acts or practices," by commencing an administrative adjudicatory proceeding under Section 5(b) of the FTC Act. Where a violation of the Clayton Act is alleged, the Commission proceeds under Section 11 of the Clayton Act (15 U.S.C. Sec. 21), which parallels Section 5(b) of the FTC Act in authorizing adjudicatory proceedings. Procedures for judicial review of FTC antitrust orders are the same as those for review of consumer protection orders, except that divestiture orders become final after all judicial review has been completed (or, if no review is sought, after the time for seeking review has elapsed). Violators of antitrust orders are subject to suit for civil penalties under FTC Act Section 5(1) or Clayton Act Section 11(1), as appropriate.

b. Rulemaking

Section 18 of the FTC Act, which authorizes the promulgation of trade regulation rules, applies to "unfair or deceptive acts or practices." Prior to enactment of Section 18, the Commission issued substantive trade regulation rules under Section 6(g), which authorizes the Commission "to make rules and regulations for the purpose of carrying out the provisions of this subchapter." *National Petroleum Refiners Assoc. v. FTC*, 482 F.2d 672 (D.C. Cir. 1973), *cert. denied* 415 U.S. 951 (1974)(Commission has authority to require octane labels on gasoline pumps). Nearly all of the rules that the Commission actually promulgated under Section 6(g) were consumer protection rules. While Section 6(g) authority still exists, in 1975, Section 18 became the exclusive rulemaking method for issuing rules that specify unfair or deceptive acts or practices.

2. *Judicial Enforcement*

As discussed above, **Section 13(b)** empowers the Commission to obtain preliminary and permanent injunctive relief for violations of any provision of law that the Commission enforces. In the competition context, the Commission has used Section 13(b) primarily for the purpose of obtaining preliminary injunctive relief against corporate mergers or acquisitions pending completion of an FTC administrative proceeding. The Commission may also obtain permanent injunctive relief against an antitrust violation in an appropriate case, as well as disgorgement of unjust enrichment, restitution for injury suffered by consumers (e.g., the refund of overcharges attributable to price-fixing) or other appropriate equitable remedies. The Commission has sought a permanent injunction, in two litigated competition cases, and the district court held in both that it had the power to award equitable relief including restitution. *FTC v. Abbott Labs.*, 1992-2 Trade Cas. (CCH) ¶ 69,996 (D.D.C. filed Oct. 13, 1992), dismissed on other grounds, 853 F. Supp. 526 (D.D.C. 1994); *FTC v. Mylan Laboratories, Inc. Cv. 98-3114 (TFH)*(D.D.C. filed July 7, 1999).

III. LITIGATING AUTHORITY

The preceding sections have described a variety of actions that may be pursued in federal court against violators of the laws enforced by the Commission. The Commission has independent authority to litigate some of these cases in its own name, by its own attorneys. The scope of this authority is described below.

Except as otherwise provided by law, the Attorney General is responsible for the conduct of all litigation in which the United States, or one of its agencies, is a party (28 U.S.C. Sec. 516). Section 16 of the FTC Act, 15 U.S.C. Sec. 56, specifically authorizes the Commission to represent itself by its own attorneys in four categories of cases: (1) suits for injunctive relief under Section 13 of the FTC Act, 15 U.S.C. Sec. 53; (2) suits for consumer redress under Section 19 of the FTC Act, 15 U.S.C. Sec. 57b; (3) petitions for judicial review of FTC rules or orders; and (4) suits to enforce compulsory process under Sections 6 and 9 of the FTC Act, 15 U.S.C. Secs. 46 and 49.3[(5)]

In addition to defining four classes of cases in which the Commission may automatically represent itself, Section 16 also provides that with respect to "any civil action involving this subchapter (including an action to collect a civil penalty)," the Commission may represent itself if the Attorney General does not agree to do so after 45-days notice. *See* 15 U.S.C. Sec. 56(a)1. This catchall provision enables the Commission to prosecute and defend by its own attorneys a wide variety of cases that the Department of Justice declines to litigate (particularly civil penalty actions under Sections 5(1) and 5(m) of the FTC Act).

Separate rules govern representation before the Supreme Court. Section 16(a)(3), 15 U.S.C. Sec. 56(a)(3), defines certain circumstances under which the Commission may appear in the Supreme Court "in any civil action in which the Commission represented itself [in the courts below] pursuant to [15 U.S.C. 56(a)(1) or (2)]." Specifically, the Commission may represent itself if it requests authority to do so from the Solicitor General within 10 days of the lower court judgment, and the Solicitor General, within 60 days after entry of the judgment, either authorizes the Commission's appearance, declines to represent the Commission, or fails to respond to the request.[(6)]

In addition to these specific grants of representational authority, there are several situations in which the Department of Justice may appoint Commission attorneys as special United States Attorneys to represent the United States in litigation conducted by the Department of Justice. *See* Telemarketing and Consumer Fraud and Abuse Prevention Act, 15 U.S.C. § 6107, (appointment of Commission attorneys to prosecute criminal contempt); Memorandum of Agreement Between the Department of Justice and the Federal Trade Commission - Premerger Penalties, 4 Trade Reg. Rep. 1 9853 at p. 17,356 (appointment of Commission attorneys to prosecute civil penalty actions under 15 U.S.C. Sec. 18a(g)(1) for violation of premerger reporting requirements); *see also* 28 U.S.C. Secs. 515, 543 appointment of special United States attorneys).

APPENDIX A

SYNOPSIS OF ANTITRUST ENFORCEMENT AUTHORITY

Statute	Federal Trade Commission	Department of Justice	State Enforcement Authorities	Private Parties
Federal Trade Commission Act (15 U.S.C. §41 *et seq.*)	administrative cease and desist authority [§5(b) FTCA]	prosecution [§§ 1 & 2 Sherman Act]		
Injunctive Relief	judicially ordered injunctive relief [§13(b) FTCA; also § 5(l) FTCA (for violations of cease and orders)]			
Redress	judicially ordered redress [§13(b) FTCA]			
Rulemaking	[§6(g) FTCA]			
Civil Penalties	judicially ordered civil penalties for violating cease and desist orders ($11,000 per violation) [§5(l) FTCA]			
Criminal Penalties	referral to U.S. Department of Justice [§16(b) FTCA]			

Statute	Federal Trade Commission	Department of Justice	State Enforcement Authorities	Private Parties
Clayton Act (15 U.S.C. § 12 *et seq.*)	administrative cease and desist authority [§11(b) Clayton Act]			
Injunctive Relief	judicially ordered injunctive relief [§13(b) FTCA; also §7A(g)(2) Clayton Act (for HSR reporting violations) and §11(l) Clayton Act (for violations of cease and desist orders)]	judicially ordered injunctive relief [§15 Clayton Act; also §7A(g)(2) Clayton Act (for HSR reporting violations)]	may apply to the courts as *parens patriae* for injunctive relief [§16 Clayton Act]	may apply to the courts for injunctive relief [§16 Clayton Act]
Damages		may recover for injuries sustained by the United States Government (treble damages) [§4A Clayton Act]	may apply fortreble damages as *parens patriae* [§4C Clayton Act]	may apply for treble damages [§4 Clayton Act]
Civil Penalties	judicially ordered civil penalties for violating cease and desist orders ($5,000 per violation) [§11(l) Clayton Act; also §7A(g)(1) Clayton Act ($11,000 per day for HSR reporting violations)]	judicially ordered civil penalties [§7A(g)(1) Clayton Act ($11,000 per day for HSR reporting violations)]		
Criminal Fines		officer liability for corporate violation of penal provisions [§14Clayton Act]		

Statute	Federal Trade Commission	Department of Justice	State Enforcement Authorities	Private Parties
Sherman Antitrust Act (15 U.S.C. §1 *et seq.*)				
Injunctive Relief		judicially ordered injunctive relief [§4 Sherman Act]	may apply to the courts as *parens patriae* for injunctive relief [§16 Clayton Act]	may apply to the courts for injunctive relief [§16 Clayton Act]
Damages		may recover for injuries sustained by the United States Government (treble damages) [§4A Clayton Act]	may apply for treble damages as *parens patriae* [§4C Clayton Act]	may apply for treble damages [§4 Clayton Act]
Criminal Penalties		combinations [§1 Sherman Act] monopolization [§2 Sherman Act]		
Miscellaneous		forfeiture [§6 Sherman Act]		

APPENDIX B

SYNOPSIS OF CONSUMER PROTECTION ENFORCEMENT AUTHORITY UNDER THE FEDERAL TRADE COMMISSION ACT

Statute	Federal Trade Commission	Departmentl of Justice	State Enforcement Authorities	Private Parties
Federal Trade Commission Act (15 U.S.C. §41 *et seq.*)	administrative cease and desist authority [§5(b) FTCA]	prosecution for violations of §12(a) FTCA [§14 FTCA]		
Injunctive Relief	judicially ordered injunctive relief [§13(b) FTCA; also §13(a) FTCA (for violations of §12(a) FTCA) and §5(l) FTCA (for violations of cease and desist orders)]			
Rulemaking	[§18 FTCA]			
Redress	judicially ordered redress [§13(b) FTCA; also §19(a)(1) FTCA (for rule violations) and §19(a)(2) FTCA (for "fraudulent or dishonest" conduct)]			
Civil Penalties	judicially ordered civil penalties for violating cease and desist orders ($11,000 per violation) [§5(l) FTCA; also §5(m)(1)(A) FTCA (for violations of trade regulation rules) ($11,000 per violation) and §5(m)(1)(B) FTCA (for violations of adjudicatory holdings by non-parties) ($11,000 per violation)]			
Criminal Penalties	referral to U.S. Department of Justice [§16(b) FTCA]			

Endnotes:

1. This memo focuses exclusively on law enforcement by the Federal Trade Commission. Appendices A and B are charts that synopsize the allocation of antitrust and consumer protection powers under the FTC, Clayton, and Sherman Acts to the Commission and to other entities, i.e., the Department of Justice, state enforcers, and private parties. Appendix B covers only the Federal Trade Commission Act. Summaries of Commission enforcement authority under other statutes are available on this site.

2. "Corporation" is defined to include any company, trust or association, incorporated or unincorporated, "which is organized to carry on business for its own profit or that of its members (FTC Act Sec. 4, 15 U.S.C. Sec. 44). 3. Commission policies contemplate the disclosure of certain industry-wide investigations. The Commission will also publicly acknowledge that a particular merger or other transaction is being investigated under Sections 7 and 11 of the Clayton Act in situations where a party to the transaction has disclosed its existence in a press release or other public filing. In addition, the Commission permits limited disclosures about nonmerger investigations where: (1) a target has publicly disclosed the relevant information in either a press release or a filing with a government agency; or (2) the investigation or the practice has received substantial publicity and the disclosure does not identify a target that has not already disclosed its own identity. 4. The original $100 per day penalty has been adjusted to $110 under the Debt Collection Improvement At of 1996, 28 U.S.C. § 2461 note. See Commission Rule 1.98, 16 C.F.R § 1.98. 5. Section 16, added to the FTC Act in 1975, does not specifically mention suits to enforce Civil Investigative Demands, as CID authority was not added to the Commission's investigatory repertoire until 1980. However, Section 20 of the FTC Act, which governs issuance of CID's, provides that a suit to enforce a CID may be prosecuted by the Commission "through such officers or attorneys as it may designate" (15 U.S.C. Sec. 57b-2(e)). The only other statute that expressly vests the Commission with representational authority is the Clayton Act, which provides that injunctive relief for violations of the premerger notification requirements may be granted by a district court "upon application of the Federal Trade Commission or the Attorney General" (15 U.S.C. Sec. 18a(g)(2)).

6. On three of the four occasions in the 1980's in which the Commission was party to a case before the Supreme Court, it was represented by its own attorneys. In two of those cases, the Commission obtained a grant of certiorari after the Solicitor General had declined to file a petition on the Commission's behalf.

APPENDIX D

The Federal Trade Commission Safeguards Rule

Federal Trade Commission Rules Implementing the Information Security Provisions of the Gramm-Leach-Bliley Act

The Gramm-Leach-Bliley Act requires financial institutions to take reasonable measures to safeguard customer information. All regulators of financial institutions, including functional regulators such as the Federal Reserve Board and the Federal Deposit Insurance Corporation, have adopted rules to implement the safeguards requirements. Financial institutions not subject to the jurisdiction of a functional regulator must comply with the "Safeguards Rule" of the Federal Trade Commission, which is set out at Part 314 of Title 16 of the Code of Federal Regulations.

TITLE 16—COMMERCIAL PRACTICES
CHAPTER I—FEDERAL TRADE COMMISSION
SUBCHAPTER C—REGULATIONS UNDER SPECIFIC ACTS OF CONGRESS
PART 314—STANDARDS FOR SAFEGUARDING CUSTOMER INFORMATION

16 CFR 314.1

§ 314.1 Purpose and scope.

(a) Purpose. This part, which implements sections 501 and 505(b)(2) of the Gramm-Leach-Bliley Act, sets forth standards for developing, implementing, and maintaining reasonable administrative, technical, and physical safeguards to protect the security, confidentiality, and integrity of customer information.
(b) Scope. This part applies to the handling of customer information by all financial institutions over which the Federal Trade Commission ("FTC" or "Commission") has jurisdiction. This part refers to such entities as "you." This part applies to all customer information in your possession, regardless of whether such information pertains to individuals with whom you have a customer relationship, or pertains to the customers of other financial institutions that have provided such information to you.

§ 314.2 Definitions.

(a) In general. Except as modified by this part or unless the context otherwise requires, the terms used in this part have the same meaning as set forth in the

Commission's rule governing the Privacy of Consumer Financial Information, 16 CFR part 313.

(b) Customer information means any record containing nonpublic personal information as defined in 16 CFR 313.3(n), about a customer of a financial institution, whether in paper, electronic, or other form, that is handled or maintained by or on behalf of you or your affiliates.
(c) Information security program means the administrative, technical, or physical safeguards you use to access, collect, distribute, process, protect, store, use, transmit, dispose of, or otherwise handle customer information.
(d) Service provider means any person or entity that receives, maintains, processes, or otherwise is permitted access to customer information through its provision of services directly to a financial institution that is subject to this part.

§ 314.3 Standards for safeguarding customer information.

(a) Information security program. You shall develop, implement, and maintain a comprehensive information security program that is written in one or more readily accessible parts and contains administrative, technical, and physical safeguards that are appropriate to your size and complexity, the nature and scope of your activities, and the sensitivity of any customer information at issue. Such safeguards shall include the elements set forth in § 314.4 and shall be reasonably designed to achieve the objectives of this part, as set forth in paragraph (b) of this section.
(b) Objectives. The objectives of section 501(b) of the Act, and of this part, are to:
(1) Insure the security and confidentiality of customer information;
(2) Protect against any anticipated threats or hazards to the security or integrity of such information; and
(3) Protect against unauthorized access to or use of such information that could result in substantial harm or inconvenience to any customer.

§ 314.4 Elements.

In order to develop, implement, and maintain your information security program, you shall:

(a) Designate an employee or employees to coordinate your information security program.
(b) Identify reasonably foreseeable internal and external risks to the security, confidentiality, and integrity of customer information that could result in the unauthorized disclosure, misuse, alteration, destruction or other compromise of such information, and assess the sufficiency of any safeguards in place to control these risks. At a minimum, such a risk assessment should include consideration of risks in each relevant area of your operations, including:
(1) Employee training and management;
(2) Information systems, including network and software design, as well as information processing, storage, transmission and disposal; and
(3) Detecting, preventing and responding to attacks, intrusions, or other systems failures.

(c) Design and implement information safeguards to control the risks you identify through risk assessment, and regularly test or otherwise monitor the effectiveness of the safeguards' key controls, systems, and procedures.
(d) Oversee service providers, by:
(1) Taking reasonable steps to select and retain service providers that are capable of maintaining appropriate safeguards for the customer information at issue; and
(2) Requiring your service providers by contract to implement and maintain such safeguards.
(e) Evaluate and adjust your information security program in light of the results of the testing and monitoring required by paragraph (c) of this section; any material changes to your operations or business arrangements; or any other circumstances that you know or have reason to know may have a material impact on your information security program.

§ 314.5 Effective date.

(a) Each financial institution subject to the Commission's jurisdiction must implement an information security program pursuant to this part no later than May 23, 2003.
(b) Two-year grandfathering of service contracts. Until May 24, 2004, a contract you have entered into with a nonaffiliated third party to perform services for you or functions on your behalf satisfies the provisions of § 314.4(d), even if the contract does not include a requirement that the service provider maintain appropriate safeguards, as long as you entered into the contract not later than June 24.

About the Author

Charles H. Kennedy is an attorney in the Washington, D.C., office of Morrison & Foerster LLP and a member of the adjunct faculty of the Columbus School of Law, Catholic University of America. He is the author or coauthor of five books on communications law, cyberlaw, and privacy, and represents clients in proceedings before the Federal Communications Commission, Federal Trade Commission, and other agencies. Mr. Kennedy is a graduate of The University of Chicago Law School, where he was an associate editor of *The University of Chicago Law Review*. His e-mail address is ckennedy@mofo.com.

About the Author

Index

Recent Titles in the Artech House Telecommunications Series

Vinton G. Cerf, Senior Series Editor

Access Networks: Technology and V5 Interfacing, Alex Gillespie

Achieving Global Information Networking, Eve L. Varma et al.

Advanced High-Frequency Radio Communications, Eric E. Johnson et al.

ATM Interworking in Broadband Wireless Applications, M. Sreetharan and S. Subramaniam

ATM Switches, Edwin R. Coover

ATM Switching Systems, Thomas M. Chen and Stephen S. Liu

Broadband Access Technology, Interfaces, and Management, Alex Gillespie

Broadband Local Loops for High-Speed Internet Access, Maurice Gagnaire

Broadband Networking: ATM, SDH, and SONET, Mike Sexton and Andy Reid

Broadband Telecommunications Technology, Second Edition, Byeong Lee, Minho Kang, and Jonghee Lee

The Business Case for Web-Based Training, Tammy Whalen and David Wright

The Business Privacy Law Handbook, Charles H. Kennedy

Centrex or PBX: The Impact of IP, John R. Abrahams and Mauro Lollo

Chinese Telecommunications Policy, Xu Yan and Douglas Pitt

Communication and Computing for Distributed Multimedia Systems, Guojun Lu

Communications Technology Guide for Business, Richard Downey, Seán Boland, and Phillip Walsh

Community Networks: Lessons from Blacksburg, Virginia, Second Edition, Andrew M. Cohill and Andrea Kavanaugh, editors

Component-Based Network System Engineering, Mark Norris, Rob Davis, and Alan Pengelly

Computer Telephony Integration, Second Edition, Rob Walters

Customer-Centered Telecommunications Services Marketing, Karen G. Strouse

Delay- and Disruption-Tolerant Networking, Stephen Farrell and Vinny Cahill

Deploying and Managing IP over WDM Networks, Joan Serrat and Alex Galis, editors

Desktop Encyclopedia of the Internet, Nathan J. Muller

Digital Clocks for Synchronization and Communications, Masami Kihara, Sadayasu Ono, and Pekka Eskelinen

Digital Modulation Techniques, Second Edition, Fuqin Xiong

E-Commerce Systems Architecture and Applications, Wasim E. Rajput

Engineering Internet QoS, Sanjay Jha and Mahbub Hassan

Error-Control Block Codes for Communications Engineers, L. H. Charles Lee

Essentials of Modern Telecommunications Systems, Nihal Kularatna and Dileeka Dias

FAX: Facsimile Technology and Systems, Third Edition, Kenneth R. McConnell, Dennis Bodson, and Stephen Urban

Fundamentals of Network Security, John E. Canavan

Gigabit Ethernet Technology and Applications, Mark Norris

The Great Telecom Meltdown, Fred R. Goldstein

Guide to ATM Systems and Technology, Mohammad A. Rahman

A Guide to the TCP/IP Protocol Suite, Floyd Wilder

Home Networking Technologies and Standards, Theodore B. Zahariadis

Implementing Value-Added Telecom Services, Johan Zuidweg

Information Superhighways Revisited: The Economics of Multimedia, Bruce Egan

Installation and Maintenance of SDH/SONET, ATM, xDSL, and Synchronization Networks, José M. Caballero et al.

Integrated Broadband Networks: TCP/IP, ATM, SDH/SONET, and WDM/Optics, Byeong Gi Lee and Woojune Kim

Internet E-mail: Protocols, Standards, and Implementation, Lawrence Hughes

Introduction to Telecommunications Network Engineering, Second Edition, Tarmo Anttalainen

Introduction to Telephones and Telephone Systems, Third Edition, A. Michael Noll

An Introduction to U.S. Telecommunications Law, Second Edition, Charles H. Kennedy

IP Convergence: The Next Revolution in Telecommunications, Nathan J. Muller

LANs to WANs: The Complete Management Guide, Nathan J. Muller

The Law and Regulation of Telecommunications Carriers, Henk Brands and Evan T. Leo

Litigating with Electronically Stored Information, Marian K. Riedy, Susman Beros and Kim Sperduto

Managing Internet-Driven Change in International Telecommunications, Rob Frieden

Marketing Telecommunications Services: New Approaches for a Changing Environment, Karen G. Strouse

Mission-Critical Network Planning, Matthew Liotine

Multimedia Communications Networks: Technologies and Services, Mallikarjun Tatipamula and Bhumip Khashnabish, editors

Next Generation Intelligent Networks, Johan Zuidweg

Open Source Software Law, Rod Dixon

Performance Evaluation of Communication Networks, Gary N. Higginbottom

Performance of TCP/IP over ATM Networks, Mahbub Hassan and Mohammed Atiquzzaman

The Physical Layer of Communications Systems, Richard A. Thompson, David Tipper, Prashant Krishnamurthy, and Joseph Kabara

Practical Guide for Implementing Secure Intranets and Extranets, Kaustubh M. Phaltankar

Practical Internet Law for Business, Kurt M. Saunders

Practical Multiservice LANs: ATM and RF Broadband, Ernest O. Tunmann

Principles of Modern Communications Technology, A. Michael Noll

A Professional's Guide to Data Communication in a TCP/IP World, E. Bryan Carne

Programmable Networks for IP Service Deployment, Alex Galis et al., editors

Protocol Management in Computer Networking, Philippe Byrnes

Pulse Code Modulation Systems Design, William N. Waggener

Reorganizing Data and Voice Networks: Communications Resourcing for Corporate Networks, Thomas R. Koehler

Security, Rights, and Liabilities in E-Commerce, Jeffrey H. Matsuura

Service Assurance for Voice over WiFi and 3G Networks, Richard Lau, Ram Khare, and William Y. Chang

Service Level Management for Enterprise Networks, Lundy Lewis

SIP: Understanding the Session Initiation Protocol, Second Edition, Alan B. Johnston

Smart Card Security and Applications, Second Edition, Mike Hendry

SNMP-Based ATM Network Management, Heng Pan

Spectrum Wars: The Policy and Technology Debate, Jennifer A. Manner

Strategic Management in Telecommunications, James K. Shaw

Strategies for Success in the New Telecommunications Marketplace, Karen G. Strouse

Successful Business Strategies Using Telecommunications Services, Martin F. Bartholomew

Telecommunications Cost Management, S. C. Strother

Telecommunications Department Management, Robert A. Gable

Telecommunications Deregulation and the Information Economy, Second Edition, James K. Shaw

Telecommunications Technology Handbook, Second Edition, Daniel Minoli

Telemetry Systems Engineering, Frank Carden, Russell Jedlicka, and Robert Henry

Telephone Switching Systems, Richard A. Thompson

Understanding Modern Telecommunications and the Information Superhighway, John G. Nellist and Elliott M. Gilbert

Understanding Networking Technology: Concepts, Terms, and Trends, Second Edition, Mark Norris

Understanding Voice over IP Security, Alan B. Johnston and David M. Piscitello

Videoconferencing and Videotelephony: Technology and Standards, Second Edition, Richard Schaphorst

Visual Telephony, Edward A. Daly and Kathleen J. Hansell

Wide-Area Data Network Performance Engineering, Robert G. Cole and Ravi Ramaswamy

Winning Telco Customers Using Marketing Databases, Rob Mattison

WLANs and WPANs towards 4G Wireless, Ramjee Prasad and Luis Muñoz

World-Class Telecommunications Service Development, Ellen P. Ward

For further information on these and other Artech House titles,
including previously considered out-of-print books now available through our In-Print-Forever® (IPF®) program, contact:

Artech House
685 Canton Street
Norwood, MA 02062
Phone: 781-769-9750
Fax: 781-769-6334
e-mail: artech@artechhouse.com

Artech House
46 Gillingham Street
London SW1V 1AH UK
Phone: +44 (0)20 7596-8750
Fax: +44 (0)20 7630-0166
e-mail: artech-uk@artechhouse.com

Find us on the World Wide Web at: www.artechhouse.com